Marx and Modernity

MODERNITY AND SOCIETY

General Editor: *Ira J. Cohen*

Modernity and Society is a series of readers edited by the most eminent scholars working in social theory today. The series makes a distinctive and important contribution to the field of sociology by offering one-volume overviews that explore the founding visions of modernity originating in the classic texts. In addition, the volumes look at how ideas have been reconstructed and carried in new directions by social theorists throughout the twentieth century. Each reader builds a bridge from classical selections to modern texts to make sense of the fundamental social forces and historical dynamics of the twentieth century and beyond.

1 *Marx and Modernity: Key Readings and Commentary*, edited by Robert J. Antonio
2 *Emile Durkheim: Sociologist of Modernity*, edited by Mustafa Emirbayer

Marx and Modernity

KEY READINGS AND COMMENTARY

Edited by
Robert J. Antonio

Series Editor
Ira J. Cohen

Blackwell
Publishing

© 2003 by Blackwell Publishers Ltd
a Blackwell Publishing company

350 Main Street, Malden, MA 02148-5018, USA
108 Cowley Road, Oxford OX4 1JF, UK
550 Swanston Street, Victoria 3053, Australia
Kurfürstendamm 57, 10707 Berlin, Germany

The right of Robert J. Antonio to be identified as the Author of the Editorial
Material in this Work has been asserted in accordance with the UK Copyright,
Designs and Patents Act 1988.

First published 2003 by Blackwell Publishers Ltd

Library of Congress Cataloging-in-Publication Data

Marx and modernity : key readings and commentary / edited by
Robert Antonio.
     p. cm. — (Modernity and society ; 1)
    Includes bibliographical references and index.
    ISBN 0-631-22549-8 (alk. paper) — ISBN 0-631-22550-1 (pb. : alk. paper)
    1. Marxian economics. 2. Capitalism. 3. Marx, Karl, 1818–1883.   I. Antonio,
    Robert.   II. Series.

    HB 97.5 .M334196 2002 2013
    335.4—dc21   2001043227

A catalogue record for this title is available from the British Library.

Set in 10/12 pt Book Antique
by Graphicraft Limited, Hong Kong
Printed and bound in Great Britain
by MPG Books, Bodmin, Cornwall

For further information on
Blackwell Publishing, visit our website:
http://www.blackwellpublishing.com

Contents

Contents   vii

Notes on Contributors

Ronald Aronson is Professor in the Interdisciplinary Studies Program at Wayne State University in Detroit, where he teaches philosophy and social theory. Among his works are *Sartre's Second Critique* (1987) and *Stay out of Politics: A Philosopher Views South Africa* (1990).

John Cassidy is economics correspondent of the *New Yorker*.

Mike Davis has taught Urban Theory at Southern California Institute of Architecture. Recently, he received a prestigious MacArthur Fellowship, and he serves on the Editorial Committee of *New Left Review*. Among his publications are *Prisoners of the American Dream* (1986) and *The Ecology of Fear* (1999).

Jeff Faux is an economist who has worked for the US Office of Economic Opportunity and the US Departments of State, Commerce, and Labor. He is President of the Economic Policy Institute, which collects and disseminates data and proposes policy on US economic affairs and, especially, the economic condition of low- and middle-income Americans. Among his publications are *Fast Track, Fast Shuffle* (1991) and, edited with Todd Schafer and Lester C. Thurow, *Reclaiming Prosperity: A Blueprint for Progressive Economic Reform* (1996).

Thomas Frank has a PhD in American History from the University of Chicago, and is a founding editor of *The Baffler*, a magazine of cultural criticism. He is also the author of *The Conquest of Cool* (1997).

Nancy Fraser is Professor of Political Science and Philosophy at the New School for Social Research. A leading feminist theorist and critical theorist, she analyzes the intersection of class inequality and cultural exclusion. Among her books are *Unruly Practices* (1989) and, with Axel Honneth, *Redistribution or Recognition? A Philosophical Exchange* (2001).

John Gray is Professor of European Thought at the London School of Economics and a regular contributor to the *Guardian* and the *Times Literary Supplement*. An expert on classical liberalism, he earlier helped revitalize free-market ideas and advance "Thatcherism," or British neoliberalism. Currently, he is a very prominent critic of the neoliberal agenda. Among his works are *Enlightenment's Wake* (1993) and *Two Faces of Liberalism* (2000).

William Greider has been a national correspondent, editor, and columnist for the *Washington Post* and an on-air correspondent for TV documentaries. He is National Editor for *Rolling Stone*. Among his publications are *Secrets of the Temple: How the Federal Reserve Runs the Country* (1987) and *Who Will Tell the People?: The Betrayal of American Democracy* (1992).

David Harvey is Professor of Geography at Johns Hopkins University. His *Limits to Capital* (1982) and *Condition of Postmodernity* (1989) are among the most important Marxist works of the later twentieth century. Recently, he published *Justice, Nature and the Geography of Difference* (1996).

Jeremy Rifkin is President of the Foundation on Economic Trends and has published widely on the impact of scientific and technological innovation on the economy, workers, society, and the environment. Among his recent works is *The Biotech Century* (1998).

Saskia Sassen is Ralph Lewis Professor of Sociology at the University of Chicago. Among her recent publications are *Losing Control? Sovereignty in an Age of Globalization* (1996) and *Guests and Aliens* (1999).

Bruce Shapiro is a political journalist who serves as a contributing editor to *The Nation* and as a national correspondent for the internet magazine *Salon.com*. He also teaches investigative journalism at Yale. Recently, he has published *One Violent Crime: A Testimony* (2001) and, with Reverend Jesse Jackson and Congressman Jesse Jackson Jr., *Legal Lynching: The Death Penalty and America's Future* (forthcoming).

Jeffrey St. Clair is a contributing editor to *In These Times* and a co-editor with Alexander Cockburn of the muckraking newsletter, *CounterPunch*. He has published, with Alexander Cockburn, *Whiteout: The CIA, Drugs, and the Press* (1998) and *Al Gore: A User's Manual* (2000).

William Julius Wilson is Lewis P. and Linda L. Geyser Professor and Director of the Joblessness and Urban Poverty Program in the Kennedy School of Government at Harvard University and a past President of the American Sociological Association. Among his works are *The Truly Disadvantaged* (1987) and *Bridge over the Racial Divide* (1999).

Erik Olin Wright is Professor of Sociology at the University of Wisconsin at Madison. He is one of the most prominent Marxist scholars, who has done major theoretical and empirical work on class and social inequality. Among his books are *Classes* (1985) and *Class Counts* (1997).

General Editor's Foreword

Robert J. Antonio's volume on Marx and modernity is the first of four volumes in the *Modernity and Society* series to be published by Blackwell Publishers. When I asked Bob to undertake this volume, I had a specific vision of the purposes that the series in general would serve. Let me say a few words about the purposes of the series as a contextual frame within which to introduce some of the special virtues of Bob's work.

The larger community of social scientists, including sociologists, political scientists, anthropologists, and social historians and philosophers as well, draw upon a select group of early modern theorists for intellectual inspiration. Notable examples are Karl Marx, Max Weber, and Émile Durkheim. Why do we read these theorists from the past? Why do we insist that our students read them as well? After all, the last of these theorists left the intellectual scene at the close of the First World War. It understates matters considerably to say that a good deal has changed since then. Yet the reason we still read the early modern classics is that some very basic features of modernity have operated continuously for over two centuries, and show no signs of weakening any time soon. The classical social theorists understood many of these basic features in a more profound manner than any of their successors.

Karl Marx, Max Weber, and Émile Durkheim worked in a unique intellectual moment when metaphysics and theology had lost their persuasive powers, but sociological and political analyses retained the historical scale and moral depth and passionate spirit of the general philosophies of the past. The early modern classical theorists believed that they grasped the fundamental forces that shaped and organized social relations and directed the course of history and social change. They didn't just believe they understood *facts* about these forces, intuitively they felt they understood the *realities* beneath the facts. But the classical theorists wrote at a unique moment in a second respect as well. In their era, the basic forces of modernity overtook tradition-bound forms of social organization with a raw, unrestrained momentum that transformed reality more extensively and more rapidly than anyone had imagined prior to that time. The challenge confronting the classical social theorists was to reach beneath the chaotic surfaces of historical events and determine the fountainheads from which modernity derived its unstoppable force.

Of course, as we now know, each of these theorists overlooked some basic forces as well. History has revealed great intellectual blunders in their works. Enormous intellectual ambition not only fuels great accomplishments, but also great mistakes. Nonetheless, when the classical theorists got things right, they laid the intellectual cornerstones for the ways in which we understand modernity today. In saying this, I have no intention to diminish the insights of *contemporary* theorists. The best theorists today must come to grips with a new stage in modernity in which the forces identified by classical social thinkers have operated together, pulled against one another, and twisted the course of historical events for a century or more. The best contemporary theorists are continually challenged to rewrite the classics in order to grasp the fundamental realities of our times.

Given this way of framing the nature of classical and contemporary theory, the *Modernity and Society* series pursues a different agenda than many texts and readers that have been published over the years. From the first days when I sat down with the Blackwell editors, the series has been designed as a bridge to carry the insights, and the wisdom about modernity that endure in the classical texts, to new generations of students and faculty in the twenty-first century. Neither the extensive editor's essay with which each volume begins nor the carefully selected original texts necessarily include all the leading points of emphasis that the classical theorists themselves made in their works. *Instead, the commentaries and selected texts are designed to preserve and sustain the portions of the classics that are truly relevant today.*

One vitally important component of each volume is a broad selection of readings from leading *contemporary* authors, who demonstrate the ways in which the deepest and truest insights into modernity that we have inherited from the classics retain their ability to inspire new insights about modernity as we know it now. These are books for students and faculty to carry with them from classical courses in early modern social and political theory, to courses in contemporary theories of modernity.

Both in his extensive introductory essay on Marx and modernity, and in his careful selection and introduction of specific readings, Bob Antonio makes just the kind of contribution for which the *Modernity and Society* series was designed.

Every autumn in university classrooms around the world, professors revisit Marx's theories. But it sometimes seems that the rationale for these excursions into the difficult prose of a nineteenth-century thinker has been overtaken by contemporary events. If the Soviet Union adapted some of Marx's ideas as a legitimating ideology, didn't the collapse of the Soviet empire and the Soviet Union eliminate any further reason to study Marx?

Does even one true believer still accept Marx's tragically mistaken theory of history, with its denouement in a proletarian revolution followed by a form of communist society that can never be? Bob doesn't deny that Marx made fundamental errors and he never asks readers to accept that Marx might have been right in some vague, ever-receding "final analysis" that will never see the light of day. Instead, he draws our attention to the core of Marx's writings, which were always more about the inner workings and powerful consequences of capitalism than they were about history at large, or class revolution, or communist society, or anything else. Here, it may be best to let Bob speak in his own words from his essay in this volume:

> Even in the most complex premodern civilizations, productive forces usually have developed incrementally over many hundreds or even thousands of years, and major innovations have tended to diffuse very slowly, if at all, between different regions. By contrast, as Marx and Engels argued in the (Communist) *Manifesto*, modern capitalism generated with lightning speed, a nascent world market, global division of labor, and greater variety of productive forces than all preceding civilizations put together . . . (Marx's) approach is best understood as an effort to come to terms with this unique, new capitalist world.

Who would deny that capitalism still matters to the course of modern history, or the forms of social organization that constrain and channel our lives? Who would deny that Marx saw as deeply as anyone ever has into the fundamental truth that we must live with the consequences of capitalism until modernity itself comes to an end? And who would deny that, whatever his mistakes, Marx identified, in their most oppressive forms, many of the most troubling characteristics of the consequences of capitalism? Bob Antonio shows us that Marx's theories of capitalist society continue to matter today. And he shows us as well how Marx still matters to how contemporary theorists think about capitalism in modern times.

Bob Antonio is the ideal choice as the editor for this volume. Even now, the intellectual echoes of ideologically driven arguments prevent a good number of commentators from hearing what Marx actually had to say. To do justice to Marx's relevance to modernity in a context which is so charged with political zeal and intellectual controversy, one must be able to maintain a delicate sense of theoretical balance. For over two decades, Bob has brought his fine sense of balance to a remarkably challenging set of topics. His early essay in *The American Sociological Review* (1979) uses the decline of the Roman empire as an occasion to develop a subtle, but vital distinction between production and domination in Max Weber's ideal type of bureaucracy. His essays on critical theory during the 1980s in the *British Journal of Sociology* (1981) and *Sociological Quarterly* (1983) synthesize the normative virtues of a body of social thought that too often veered into flights of optimism or the waves of despair. *A Weber–Marx Dialogue*, which Bob co-edited in the mid-1980s, broke down partisan barriers that had segregated commentary on these two classical masters. More recently in two essays, the first in *What Is Social Theory?*, edited by Alan Sica (1998), the second in the *American Journal of Sociology* (2000), Bob brings that same sense of balanced insight to bear on postmodern theory, a body of normative theory that is just as prone to hyperbole as critical theories of the past. Most remarkable, at least to me, Bob has performed a feat I would have thought no one could ever achieve: separating the sociological value from the philosophical exaggerations in the thought of Friedrich Nietzsche (*American Journal of Sociology*, 1995). Bob has also found ways to bring John Dewey into the center of normative social theory (*American Journal of Sociology*, 1989) and backed all of this with many additional works on the political economy and sociology of our times, sociological metatheory, and more.

But publications tell only part of the story. Bob's students know him as a dedicated, gifted, and caring teacher. To his good friends Bob is all of this and a good deal more besides. He is also modest enough that I probably will have to exercise my prerogative as General Editor of this series to get these words into print. But I have ample justification.

Readers are entitled to know why they should trust someone who offers to retrieve the best and most relevant insights from a theorist as complex and controversial as Marx. In this volume, readers have very good reasons to trust the wisdom and judgment Bob brings to his work.

Ira J. Cohen

Acknowledgments

The publishers thank the publishers and copyright holders for permission to reproduce the following material, listed here by author. Every effort has been made to trace copyright holders but if there are any errors or omissions in this list the publishers would be glad to be notified and to make the necessary corrections at the first opportunity.

Marx, Karl, and Frederick Engels: unless otherwise indicated, the works listed below are reprinted in full, or taken as extracts, from *Karl Marx, Frederick Engels, Collected Works*, 48 vols., London: Lawrence and Wishart, 1975–.

Marx, Karl, "Historical Tendency of Capitalist Accumulation" (1845).
——, *The Eighteenth Brumaire of Louis Bonaparte* (1852).
——, "The Economic Crisis in Europe" (1856).
——, "The Crisis in England" (1857).
——, "The Indian Revolt" (1857).
——, "Fixed Capital and the Development of the Productive Forces of Society" (1857–8).
——, "The Increase of Lunacy in Great Britain," *Daily Tribune*, New York (1858).
——, Preface to *A Contribution to the Critique of Political Economy* (1859).
——, *Value, Price and Profit* (1865).
——, "Co-operation" (1867).
——, "Division of Labour and Manufacture" (1867).
——, "The General Law of Capitalist Accumulation" (1867).
——, "Machinery and Modern Industry (1867).
——, "Modern Industry and Agriculture" (1867).
——, "Progressive Production of a Relative Surplus Population or Industrial Reserve Army" (1867).
——, "Repulsion and Attraction of Workpeople" (1867).
——, "The Factory Acts" (1867).
——, "The Fetishism of Commodities and the Secret Thereof" (1867).
——, "The General Formula for Capital" (1867).
——, "The Secret of Primitive Accumulation" (1867).
——, "The Two Factors of a Commodity" (1867).

——, *The Civil War in France* (1871).
——, *Critique of the Gotha Programme* (1875).
——, "British Incomes in India" (1887).
——, "Cardinal Facts of Capitalist Production" (1894).
——, "Foreign Trade" (1894).
——, "Labour Rent" (1894).
——, "The Role of Credit in Capitalist Production" (1894).
——, "The Tendency of the Rate of Profit to Fall" (1894).

Marx, Karl, and Frederick Engels, "Primary Historical Relations, or the Basic Aspects of Social Activity" (1845–6).
—— and ——, "Development of the Division of Labour" (1845–6).
—— and ——, "The Formation of Classes" (1845–6).
—— and ——, "The Ruling Class and the Ruling Ideas" (1845–6).
—— and ——, "Bourgeois and Proletarians" (1848).
—— and ——, "Proletarians and Communists" (1848).
—— and ——, "The Rise of the Revolutionary Proletariat" (1848).

Engels, Frederick, "Karl Marx" (1878).
——, "Letter to Joseph Bloch," from Karl Marx and Frederick Engels, *Basic Writings on Politics and Philosophy*, ed. Lewis S. Feuer et al., New York: Anchor Books, 1959.

Aronson, Ronald, "Mourning Marxism," from *After Marxism*, New York and London: Guilford Press, 1995.
Cassidy, John, "The Return of Karl Marx," *The New Yorker*, 20 and 27 October 1997, reprinted by permission of *The New Yorker* and the author.
Davis, Mike, "Fortress L.A.," from *City of Quartz: Evacuating the Future in Los Angeles*, London: Verso, 1990.
Faux, Jeff, "Slouching toward Seattle," reprinted with permission from *The American Prospect*, 11/2 (December 6, 1999). *The American Prospect*, 5 Broad Street, Boston, MA 02109. All rights reserved.
Frank, Thomas, "Getting to Yes: The Architecture of a New Consensus," from *One Market Under God: Extreme Capitalism, Market Populism, and the End of the Economic Democracy*, by Thomas Frank, copyright © 2000 by Tom Frank. Used by permission of Doubleday, a division of Random House, Inc. and The Spieler Agency, New York.
Fraser, Nancy, "From Redistribution to Recognition?," from *Justice Interruptus*. Copyright 1997 from *Justice Interruptus* by Nancy Fraser. Reproduced by permission of Routledge, Inc., part of The Taylor & Francis Group.
Gray, John, "From the Great Transformation to the Global Free Market." Copyright © 1998 from *False Dawn: The Delusions of Global Capitalism* by John Gray. Reprinted by permission of The New Press.

Greider, William, "These Dark Satanic Mills," from *One World, Ready or Not*, New York: Touchstone Books, 1998.

Harvey, David, "Marx Redux," from *Spaces of Hope*, Berkeley: University of California Press, 2000. © 2000 David Harvey.

Rifkin, Jeremy, "The Connected and the Disconnected," from *The Age of Access* by Jeremy Rifkin, copyright © 2000 by Jeremy Rifkin. Used by permission of Jeremy P. Tarcher, a division of Penguin Putnam Inc., New York.

St. Clair, Jeffrey, "Seattle Diary: It's a Gas, Gas, Gas," *New Left Review* November/December 1999.

Sassen, Saskia, "America's Immigration 'Problem'," from *Globalization and Its Discontents*, New York: The New Press, 1998.

Shapiro, Bruce, "Not just a Seattle Sequel", website article 15.4.2000, reprinted by permission of www.salon.com.

Wilson, William Julius, "Societal Changes and Vulnerable Neighborhoods," from *When Work Disappears* by William Julius Wilson, copyright © 1996 by William Julius Wilson. Used by permission of Alfred A. Knopf, a division of Random House, Inc. and Carol Mann Agency, New York.

Wright, Erik Olin, "Class Analysis, History and Emancipation," *New Left Review* November/December 1993.

Editor's Acknowledgments

I thank my colleague David Smith for a careful read and astute criticism that contributed substantially to the introductory essay, for help with several of the part introductions, and various constructive ideas along the way. I wish I could have taken up more thoroughly his many excellent suggestions. Eric Hanley and Cotten Seiler also deserve thanks for helpful criticism. I would also like to thank Ira Cohen for our many discussions about Marx, modern social theory, and this project. His points and suggestions helped determine the direction of this work. I am also grateful for the generous assistance from Ken Provencher, the Blackwell commissioning editor, and from Mary Dortch, the desk editor who oversaw the process of getting the typescript ready for production. Finally, thanks to Geraldine Beare for doing a fine job on the index, Virginia Stroud-Lewis for taking care of the difficult task of securing permissions, and to Jean van Altena for excellent copy-editing.

The Introduction is a very extensive revision of my earlier "Karl Marx," which appeared in George Ritzer (ed.), *The Blackwell Companion to the Major Social Theorists* (2000).

Introduction: Marx and Modernity

Robert J. Antonio

Karl Marx is a central figure in a broader theoretical tradition: *modern social theory*. In post-Second World War US sociology he has been constructed, along with Émile Durkheim and Max Weber, as the founder of one of the three major sociological traditions. Many thinkers, who attack this canon for being too narrow and too Eurocentric, still concede Marx's enormous importance across disciplinary, national, and cultural borders. His advocates and critics alike contend that he personifies, for better or worse, modern social theory. The roots of this tradition go back to the Enlightenment and, perhaps, before, and are a contested terrain. However, Marx is arguably the first of a group of mostly later nineteenth- and early twentieth-century theorists who called for an empirical social science, and who theorized about the rise of modernity and the erosion of traditional societies. Before the emergence of specialized social science and readily available data, they developed theories of society that engaged systematically empirical-historical facts and that addressed the sociocultural rupture caused by the Second Industrial Revolution (i.e., the rise of mechanized production, corporate firms, the interventionist state, mass politics, culture, and warfare).

Marx preceded most of the other first-generation modern theorists by about 20 to 30 years. He wrote his masterwork after moving to England, the starting place of the Second Industrial Revolution, and spending years gathering economic and social data in the British Museum. In the emergent cultural crisis, he and other modern theorists created new ways to grasp, orient to, and control increasingly secular societies composed of diverse types of people. They stressed new types of complex cooperation and communicative capacities that advance individual autonomy and social participation. They argued that the development of a more differentiated, calculable, and systematically organized society, regardless of its repressive features, provides vital resources for overcoming the material and cultural limitations of earlier societies, coping with modern pathologies, and creating a more liberated or pacified future (Antonio and Kellner 1992a, 1992b; Antonio 2000). Modern social theory continues today, albeit in more diverse geographic locations and in more culturally and intellectually diverse forms. Marx is a core figure for this tradition, who continues to be engaged.

Perhaps no other modern social theorist has generated more intense feelings among more widely dispersed audiences than Karl Marx. His name is identified with some of the twentieth century's major emancipatory struggles and worst forms of repression. As capitalism spread throughout the world from its original centers in Europe and North America, his ideas were appropriated in nearly every corner of the globe, revised, blended with local traditions, and applied in heterodox ways. Different Marxisms bear the imprints of highly divergent cultures, times, and sociopolitical aims. The importance of Marx's thought for labor movements and other forms of resistance and insurgency, as well as for various Socialist and Communist movements, parties, and regimes, has made it a topic of intense debate on the Left and the Right. However, his work is as analytical and sociological as it is political. For this reason, his ideas have generated diverse lines of social research and social theory. However, divergent thinkers have more often criticized or dismissed his fundamental challenges. Marx has been an oppositional reference point for very different types of theory. Debates over his thought have been intense even on the Left. In recent years, "post-Marxist" approaches (e.g., postmodernism, feminism, environmentalism) have often portrayed Marx and Marxism as quintessential, fundamentally flawed modernism. Although pronounced dead many times, Marx always seems to rise again from the ashes. At the millennium, his thought has increased in force, free of the weight of communism, in a world where "neoliberal," or deregulated, free-market capitalism has triumphed over competing post-Second World War social democratic and state-centered forms of capitalism. Moreover, the twentieth century's closing decades were characterized by a major expansion of a hyper-exploited, feminized, globally dispersed working class that often toils under nineteenth century-like conditions. Because the issues of class, property, exploitation, ideology, and capitalism are as important as ever, Marx remains one of the greatest social theorists and social critics.

Note that original dates are used in citations of works by Marx and Engels and other earlier theorists; these refer to the time of publication, or to the time the work was written. The aim is to inform the reader about the sequence in which the works were developed and their historical context. Nevertheless, page numbers are those in the *Collected Works*. Original spelling and punctuation have been retained, but footnotes have been omitted.

Marx's Life and Contexts

Young Marx: Hegelian historicism and critical theory

In 1815, three years before Karl Marx was born, his Rhineland birth-place of Trier was ceded back to Prussia. Previously, the town had been annexed by Napoleon Bonaparte, and the French regime had begun to dismantle the region's semi-feudal institutions and to extend individual and constitutional rights. Because many townspeople supported the French Revolution's progressive reforms, reimposition of conservative Prussian rule generated political tensions. A weakened economy and increased poverty made matters worse. Especially during the revolutionary years of 1830 and 1848, bourgeois and left-leaning political opposition grew in the region. Even the utopian socialists Saint-Simon and Fourier had followers there (McLellan 1973: 1–2; Seigel 1993: 38–41).

Marx was born into a comfortable middle-class household, the oldest male of six surviving children. His mother, Henrietta, was of Dutch ancestry, and his father, Heinrich, was a successful lawyer who embraced Enlightenment ideals and liberal democratic politics. Both sides of Marx's family had Jewish origins and rabbis as recent ancestors. Facing prejudicial restrictions, his parents converted to Protestantism. Jewish ancestry, however, still made the Marx family outsiders, and was a major impediment to Karl's entry into German academe. Marx received a mostly liberal humanist or Enlightenment-oriented high school education. The liberal headmaster and two other teachers were threatened by police authorities for their progressive political views. Although several teachers were excellent, the students were mediocre. Even among this group, Marx was hardly an exceptional student, graduating eighth in a class of 32. Ironically, he did poorly in history. Although Marx was a playful and energetic child, well liked by many of his fellow students, he was also feared and held in disregard by the targets of his sarcastic wit. His talent for cleverly and humorously skewering opponents earned him enemies throughout his life. Young Marx embraced Enlightenment ideals and reformist social views, which were nurtured by his friendly relations with the progressive Baron von Westphalen, his future father-in-law. Taking a liking to Marx, the baron helped to stir his interests in romanticism and socialism (McLellan 1973: 3–16; Seigel 1993: 41–4).

In 1835, Marx became a student at the University of Bonn. Although formally studying law, he spent much of his time "drinking and dueling," overspending, and writing poetry. Unhappy with Karl's behavior, his father forced him to transfer to the University of Berlin the following year. In a much more serious intellectual environment, he worked hard and became a committed scholar. His very intense study habits probably contributed to his contracting a respiratory disorder so serious that he was released from military obligations. Maintaining extremely strenuous work habits as an adult, he suffered recurrent bouts of illness throughout his life. Young Marx joined the "Berlin Doctors Club," an informal group of Left-Hegelian, radical intellectuals. Hegel's philosophy exerted enormous influence on many younger German intellectuals at this time. Its emphasis on humanity making itself historically was an attractive position to those wanting to put philosophy on more thoroughly secular grounds. Conservative thinkers embraced Hegel's theory of the state, which seemed to justify the Prussian regime, while the Left was attracted to his secular philosophical emphasis on human creativity and labor. Marx's Left-Hegelian ties exposed him to ideas and people that helped shape his later intellectual and political path. He completed a doctoral dissertation on the philosophies of Epicurus and Democritus, submitting it successfully at Jena in 1841. Marx gave up work on the second thesis required for entry into German academe, when Bruno Bauer, his associate and leading Left-Hegelian, lost his academic position for political reasons (McLellan 1973: 16–40; Seigel 1993: 65–75). Engels (1842: 336) portrayed, in rhyme, young Marx:

> A swarthy chap of Trier, a marked monstrosity,
> He neither hops nor skips, but moves in leaps and bounds,
> Raving aloud. As if to seize and then pull down
> To Earth the spacious tent of heaven up on high,
> He opens wide his arms and reaches for the sky.
> He shakes his wicked fist, raves with a frantic air,
> As if ten thousand devils had him by the hair.

Marx became a journalist, and soon editor, at the progressive *Rheinische Zeitung* in Cologne. A sharp social critic, he attacked the remains of the aristocratic regime and socially unjust facets of the emergent capitalist order, especially the arbitrary imposition of political power and new forms of socioeconomic inequality. Criticizing new laws that forbade peasants from gathering wood, Marx decried the monopolization of property by the rich and declared the poor to be "the elemental class of human society" (1842: 234–5). Also, he criticized Hegelian political theory, which portrayed the state as a neutral mediator and rational manifestation of the general will (a position that divided Right- and Left-Hegelians). Comparing Hegel's rosy *idea* of the state to the grim *reality* of Prussian bureaucracy, Marx attacked officialdom's crass pursuit of material self-interest and slavish service to aristocratic and nascent bourgeois elites. He also lambasted state censorship and authoritarianism, defending the free press and emergent democratic public sphere and inveighing against the chilling effect of the police state's detainment and trial of vocal citizens for alleged "excesses" or "insolence" to officials. Favoring a free society that encourages open discussion and democratic procedures, he held that citizens often know more about the scope of sociopolitical problems and how to solve them than officials, and that they should be allowed to criticize state functionaries publicly, especially their corruption. More generally, he attacked the authoritarian bureaucracy for producing "passive uninformed citizens," who quietly accede to "administration" (Marx 1843b: 343–51). Marx's early views on bureaucratic power, free speech, local knowledge, and active citizens anticipated twentieth-century Critical Theory critiques of "total administration" and ideas of "radical" or "discursive" democracy (e.g., by John Dewey, Jürgen Habermas, Anthony Giddens). The circulation of *Rheinische Zeitung* grew substantially under Marx's editorship. A skilled editor and writer, he continued journalistic endeavors, on a part-time basis, throughout much of his life (several of his newspaper articles are included in this volume). However, in 1843, the Prussian government shut down his newspaper, largely because of its attacks on the monarchy and bureaucracy. That same year he married Jenny von Westphalen, and took another editorial position in Paris, where he experienced more directly the growing working-class and emerging Socialist and Communist ideas and movements (McLellan 1973: 62–6; Seigel 1993: 65–75).

In *On the Jewish Question* (1843d), Marx attacked Bruno Bauer's plea to deny Jewish people political rights. However, Marx's ambiguous and sometimes negative comments about Jews indicate that he had not come to terms with his own roots and identity. It is possible that he did not resolve this tension in his later life. However, young Marx moved in a more radical anti-capitalist direction, away from his earlier progressive liberalism. He opposed capitalism's "abstract" individualism, which stressed the egoistic pursuit of "self-interest" by "isolated monads." He held that this liberal, or bourgeois, "freedom" dissolves feudal ties and extends formal, or negative, rights, which eliminate certain legal blockages to participation. But he argued that such freedom – "liberty" – ignores the crucial matter that activation of individual rights depends on access to material resources. For example, in Marx's view, former slaves are not genuinely free if they lack the opportunity to support themselves, and a right to education means little if one is denied the means to attain it. He contended that, except for the old landholding elites and new business stratum, the vast majority of people, propertyless peasants and poor artisans and wageworkers, lacked the social and material means to participate in emergent bourgeois, or capitalist, society and to share its benefits. For Marx, liberty is *not* "human emancipation." He thought that it obscured the unfreedom of the majority. Desiring a sweeping sociopolitical transformation that goes far beyond the establishment of negative rights and liberal reform, Marx now called for "ruthless criticism of all that exists," "practical struggles," and "communism." Revolutionary rhetoric aside, he argued that emergent capitalism's exclusive emphasis on negative rights generates intense conflicts and cannot sustain community. He held that substantive, or true, freedom means that people have access to the means of participation, which requires socioeconomic equality as well as legal and political equality (1843c: 141–5; 1843d: 162–74). This fundamental issue of genuine inclusion remained crucial in Marx's later thought, and is still a major problem in contemporary liberal democracies (e.g., neoliberal policymakers see capitalist free markets and legal rights as the primary measure of a nation's freedom and democracy, regardless of levels of poverty, misery, and nonparticipation).

In *Contribution to the Critique of Hegel's Philosophy of Law* Marx attacked Hegel's equation of the actuality of the Prussian state with its democratic constitution, arguing that the work justified the oppressive monarchy by attributing a more abstract logic to an already abstract document that concealed political reality. In his view, Hegel sanctified the regime as "Rational" (Marx 1843a). In the *Economic and Philosophical Manuscripts of 1844*, Marx accused the Hegelians of not starting with real "corporeal" people in their actual social relations, but with "abstract nature" and "thought entities." He held that their "idealism" confuses legitimations with reality, and thereby encourages passive acceptance of existing social and political conditions. Marx implied that all bourgeois thought is prone to this fatal error. He objected to Hegel's effort to explain human development and history in the idiom of "spirit" and as an evolution of consciousness. By contrast, Marx and other Left-Hegelians followed Ludwig Feuerbach's "inversion" of Hegel, or shift to materialist explanations of theology and philosophy (i.e., religion is seen to be a human creation). This reversal of the primacy of spirit was aimed to avert the alienation from, and concealment of, human agency that Hegel himself decried. However, Marx broke with Feuerbach, arguing that his "materialism" was too philosophical, dwelled too much on the critique of religion, viewed the material realm too inertly, and focused too exclusively on generic "Man" or the human "essence" (Marx 1845). Marx believed that Hegelians lacked the explicitly historical, *social* focus needed to address pressing human problems.

Marx said, in an earlier letter to his father, announcing his conversion to Hegelianism: "I arrived at the point of seeking the idea in reality itself. If previously the gods had dwelt above the earth, now they became its center" (1837: 18). This statement expresses a Hegelian methodological theme that Marx retained long after his "break" with the Hegelians. He saw Hegel's "historicism" as a bridge between "is" and "ought," which were split by Western religion and philosophy. For Hegel, the values that guide and give meaning to action originate entirely within historical experience. Rejecting transcendental views of such values and the consequent epistemological dualism between "subject" and "object," Hegel argued that we are the authors of our world – as historical beings, we negate existing conditions, create new ones, and make ourselves in the process.

However, he held that our self-creation is "estranged," because we see our own "objectifications," or ideas and creations, as alien, external objects, and thus lose our agency. Yet, in the long run, he argued, we gradually overcome this alienation by coming to terms with the contradictory facets of experience through heightened self-consciousness, struggle, and labor. Hegel's argument about "masters and slaves" was especially important for Marx. Hegel held that masters seek self-recognition by dominating slaves, but languish in the contradiction that coerced recognition from an unfree person is worthless. By contrast to the master's falsity and inactivity, Hegel contended, slaves grow wiser and stronger through their struggles and labor, and ultimately triumph over the master. Through such striving, he believed, humanity will discover its authorship of the world, creating eventually an emancipated condition of "Absolute Spirit," a state of total freedom and rationality, in which we make ourselves and our world according to our will and in a manner that each person's particularity and worth are recognized actively by all others (Hegel 1807).

Marx substituted social productive practices, capitalists and wage-workers, and exploited labor for Hegel's Spirit, metaphorical masters and slaves, and highly generalized alienated objectification. However, Hegel's idea of self-constitutive labor remained at the center of Marx's thought. At the very moment of his break with Hegelianism, he argued that Socialist humanity and world history are "nothing but the creation of man through human labor" (Marx 1844: 305, 332–3). Marx also called for a Hegelian-like "determinate negation" that preserves capitalism's progressive facets (i.e., capacities to produce real wealth and a freer, more just society) and employs them to achieve a new Socialist world of genuine freedom and rationality. He wanted to turn capitalist legitimations, or modern democratic claims about freedom and rationality, against the reality of bourgeois inequality and exploitation, and to pit what he saw as progressive facets of capitalist production against its backward features. In this way, he aimed to justify his critical standpoint toward capitalism on contestable historical grounds, rather than on the basis of dogmatic, irrefutable "Truths" of tradition, religion, and philosophy. Reframing Hegel's method of "immanent critique," Marx sought to anchor his theory in specific historical conditions rather than in mere philosophical claims about humanity's historicist nature. This move began the broader tradition of "Critical Theory," which aims to root critique in actual historical contradictions, social movements, and developmental directions of society. Although shifting from speculative philosophy to sociological materialism, Marx retained a strong Hegelian residue that is visible in his emancipatory argument, effort to link theory and practice, and most fruitful empirical questions. But this core aspect of his thought and of later Marxist approaches also is the source of distinct, often strong tensions between the tradition's sociological and political sides.

Partnership with Engels: the materialist move

In the middle and late 1840s, Marx framed the analytical basis of his later theoretical program. Responding to early capitalist industrialization and the creation of a heavily exploited, impoverished working class, young-Hegelians Moses Hess and Friedrich Engels became Communists and shifted their focus from philosophical issues to economic inequality. Engels's study of the English working class (1845) was an especially important work. Marx shifted his focus to a more empirical approach to inequality, and Engels became his lifelong collaborator. Although Engels understated his role in the partnership, he contributed substantially to their project through his theoretical and empirical work and through the analytical and editorial assistance that he gave to Marx. Also, he contributed to the financial support of the spendthrift Marx and his family. With the help of Engels, Marx broke with Hegelian philosophy and developed a materialist approach to history and sociology. Although political upheavals were an immediate stimulus to Marx during this period, accelerating capitalist development became more and more his chief concern.

In the *Economic and Philosophical Manuscripts of 1844*, Marx shifted from Hegel's philosophical historicism to a materialist theory of social development and a critique of the capitalist "mode of production." This unfinished work is famous for transforming Hegel's sweeping idea of estranged objectification, which applies to all past and existing human settings, into a historically specific concept of capitalist "alienated labor." Moreover, Marx began to formulate his views on class struggle, proletarian revolution, and the abolition of private productive property. He saw the capitalist division of labor's fusion of repressive class hierarchy with progressive productive forces to be a fundamental contradiction. In his view, capitalist development and property relations "fetter," or sharply limit, social progress in the same stroke that they advance it. Marx held that we are social beings, and that modernity's "economic" transformation and problems have a "social character" (i.e., however distorted, even liberal individualism and private property arise from capitalism's social matrix). He argued that overcoming capitalism's limitations and injustices calls for a social transformation (1844: 298–9, 317–22).

After expulsion from turbulent Paris in 1845, Marx made his decisive break from philosophy in an unfinished, collaborative effort with Engels, *The German Ideology*. They claimed to turn the Hegelian primacy of ideas and passive view of the material domain "right-side up." This text articulated much more explicitly the bases for their later views of capitalism and proletarian revolution. This collaboration consolidated the partnership between Marx and Engels, and their ties to Moses Hess faded. Marx considered this work to be the start of their mature program. He also became engaged with Communist organizations at this time (Marx and Engels 1845–6; Seigel 1993: 177, 181). Marx and Engels established "mode of production" and "class" as the fundamental analytical categories of their materialist method and as the conceptual keys to understanding capitalism. They argued that ruling-class extraction of surpluses from direct producers is decisive in shaping a society as a whole, and their materialist method focuses especially on analysis of the extractive relations between different historical forms of ruling and producing classes. They also held that "large-scale industry" was enlisting the aid of "natural science" in production, and was overturning rapidly the pre-modern world and creating a new global, capitalist order. They saw capitalist factories, markets, and class relations supplanting traditional forms of production, social ties, and hierarchies and replacing local autonomy and particularity with centralized interdependence and homogeneity. In their view, the emergent form of industry was creating "world history for the first time, insofar as it made all civilized nations and every individual member of them dependent for their satisfaction of their wants on the whole world, thus destroying the former natural exclusiveness of separate nations" (Marx and Engels 1845–6: 73). The themes of large-scale industry, scientific production, and globalization were core aspects of Marx's much later *Capital*. Engaging political economy even more directly, Marx's *The Poverty of Philosophy* (1847) provided an early published version of this new materialist point of view and critique of capitalism.

Marx's and Engels's famous political pamphlet *Manifesto of the Communist Party* (1848) probed similar modernizing themes dramatically and eloquently. Originally the party platform of the "Communist League," the essay became a political catechism for later communism. Circulated throughout the world by Communist parties, revolutionary insurgencies, and labor movements, the *Manifesto* is probably the most widely read of Marx's and Engels's works, and the one with the most political and social impact. Writing when the 1848 revolutions were sweeping across Europe (i.e., struggles for bourgeois democracy and rights), Marx and Engels hoped that the capitalist class would soon smash the remains of the old order and old elites, attain political power, and create global capitalism and worldwide liberal democracy, which they saw as the stage for proletarian revolution. Marx and Engels expressed their materialism lucidly and succinctly, applied it to capitalism, and located it vis-à-vis competing Socialist and anti-capitalist positions. Their immanent critique pointed to capitalism's nascent crises and revolutionary tendencies, and outlined steps of a future Communist transition. They held that capitalism's new "massive" and "colossal" productive forces were greater than those of all previous humanity, and that exceptionally extensive social cooperation, or "universal interdependence," was a major facet of this transformation. Speaking as if their critique and political proposals were merely giving

voice to intensifying historical contradictions and mounting opposition
to capitalism, they argued that cutthroat economic competition drives the
bourgeoisie to constantly revolutionize the productive forces, radically and
untiringly transform society and culture, and create a proletariat that is
destined to overthrow them and capitalism. Marx and Engels asserted that
the entirety of traditional society's "fixed, fast-frozen relations, with their
train of ancient and venerable prejudices" were being "swept away," and
"all new-formed ones" were becoming "antiquated before they can ossify."
Regardless of unparalleled material progress, they saw capitalism as "like
the sorcerer, who is no longer able to control the powers of the nether
world . . . called up by his spells." They were optimistic, however, that
after "all that is solid melts into air," people will come to their "sober
senses." Seeing things clearly, they argued, proletarians, especially their
Communist leadership, will distinguish the progressive from the reactionary
facets of capitalism, assert their self-conscious collective agency and capacity to plan socially, and, consequently, provide history with a rational,
emancipatory direction (Marx and Engels 1848: 487–9).

The most decisive context for Marx's future work was the Second
Industrial Revolution, or the rise of mechanized production, large firms,
mass labor unions, the interventionist state, modern urbanism, and the
world market. Although these changes were barely getting under way
in the late 1840s, he already detected an emergent profound alteration of
everyday life caused by "large-scale capitalism," which he inscribed later
under the sign of "modern industry." Marx was the first modern social
theorist to address social change so radical and so extensive that it overturned nearly all accustomed modes of experience, identity, association,
and organization. The first section of the *Manifesto* is still perhaps the most
powerful representation of this sensibility by a social theorist. The consequent crisis of representation subverted the old ways of thinking and
acting, and called forth new secular approaches to the social world.
Modern social theory was a key part of the fabric of a nascent world
view. Later in the century, other modern theorists addressed the epochal
rupture with the past by pitting the "modern" against the "traditional."
They wrote their major works when the Second Industrial Revolution
spread beyond Great Britain and reached its height. Operating in Marx's
wake, they often criticized, tacitly or overtly, his argument about capitalism
and modernity.

Marx's mature project: the critique of capitalism

Expelled from Belgium in 1848, Marx was invited back to France, and then
went to Germany as editor of the radical *Neue Rheinische Zeitung*. When
politics shifted rightward in 1849 after the defeat of the democratic forces,

he was expelled from Germany with a passport good only for Paris. Because the new, reactionary French regime restricted him to Brittany, he fled to London. Living the rest of his life in the belly of the beast, the great critic of capitalism experienced directly the modern rupture in the first nation to undergo the Second Industrial Revolution and the birthplace of liberal individualism. The leading capitalist country, Great Britain, was already experiencing sweeping changes that came late in the nineteenth century or in the early twentieth century to other parts of Europe and North America. Marx was active in working-class movements when the opportunity arose, and he led the First International, 1864–72. However, at times, when prospects for change looked dim, he withdrew from a direct role in politics. Although he continued his journalism, he and his family depended on generous financial support from Engels. Marx fathered eight children, of whom four died before reaching adolescence. He and the family maid had a son, who was given to foster parents and kept secret. But Marx was generally an attentive, loving father, very supportive of his three daughters' intellectual and cultural development. The Marx family apparently was closely knit and warm. Residing first in a poor neighborhood of London, they later moved to a middle-class area and life-style. But Marx suffered from his children's deaths, and from recurrent, painful, probably work-related health problems (i.e., vision, stomach, liver, lungs, inflammations, headaches, and boils). Although he left an enormous corpus of works, he was tormented by his inability to finish projects, especially his magnum opus, *Capital*. Also, he regretted his trouble with creditors, financial dependency, and the privation and humiliation that these problems caused his family. In a letter to Engels, he lamented, at 50 years old, that he was "still a pauper," recalling his mother's earlier admonition that he should have "made capital" instead of merely writing about it (Marx 1868: 25; McLellan 1973: 189–225; Seigel 1993: 195–9, 253–89, 375–87).

Although reactionary forces held sway in Europe by mid-century, Marx at first remained optimistic that the bourgeois revolution would succeed on the Continent, and that England's liberal democracy and powerful bourgeoisie and highly developed working class would soon sweep away all the pre-capitalist remains and barriers to proletarian revolution. In 1850, Marx and Engels declared that a "new revolution can no longer be very far away." But Marx's *Class Struggles in France* (1850) reported counterrevolutionary paralysis and internecine class and subclass conflict, and a pessimistic tone replaced his earlier revolutionary hopefulness (Marx and Engels 1850b: 377; Marx 1850: 71–145). Marx's *Eighteenth Brumaire of Louis Bonaparte* (1852a) was even more pessimistic. At the start of this scalding report on the rise of the second Napoleonic dictatorship, Marx recalled Hegel's point that major historical "facts and personages" happen twice, stating that he "forgot to add: the first time as tragedy, the second time as farce." Marx's opening paragraphs, among the most beautifully written and circumspect in all of his corpus, declared that we do not make our history of our own accord, or "just as we please." Rather:

> The tradition of all the dead generations weighs like a nightmare on the brain of the living. And just when they seemed engaged in revolutionizing themselves and things, in creating something that never yet existed, precisely in such periods of revolutionary crisis they anxiously conjure up the spirits of the past to their service and borrow from them names, battle-cries and costumes in order to present the new scene of world history in this time-honored disguise and this borrowed language.

After the "revolution," Marx held, the French state returned "to its oldest form" based on "the shamelessly simple domination of the sabre and the cowl" (1852a: 103–4, 106).

In the *Eighteenth Brumaire*, Marx reported how Louis Bonaparte became dictator, aided by the Parisian *lumpenproletariat*, or underclass mob of easily bribed riffraff. In his view, the new regime echoed previous absolutism, but concentrated power much more totally and effectively, sweeping both bourgeoisie and proletariat from center stage. Anticipating facets of Max Weber's famous argument about bureaucratization, Marx held that the earlier parliamentary democracy's efficient, modernized, centralized, and rationalized bureaucracy was an ideal means for carrying out a *coup d'état* and usurping total power. He blamed the bourgeoisie for creating the conditions of their own demise; their manifestly selfish, one-sided pursuit of short-term, material interest had opened the way for creation of a Frankenstein's monster, or total state, that appeared to be "completely independent" of the material base and bourgeois "ruling class." Arguing that "state power" could not really be "suspended in mid air," Marx stated that "the dictatorship represented the class interests of small-holding peasantry" (who voted heavily for Louis Napoleon before he ended the democracy). Marx considered the peasantry to be the most backward stratum in French society, living in what he saw as "stupefied seclusion," isolated by their feudal productive forces and backward culture. Although still claiming that proletarianization and commodification of rural life would eventually undermine the new regime, the *Brumaire* reversed the *Manifesto*'s characteristic, modernist vision of progress, and illustrated dramatically that capitalism's supposed modernizing and rationalizing locomotive could lead to unexpected, dangerous fusions of modernity and tradition rather than to socialism's promised land of freedom and rationality. Marx portrayed the French dictatorship as modernity breaking down into a new nightmare barbarism that lacks a visible escape route (1852a: 147–51, 181–97). The Frankfurt School, which carried on the Marxian tradition of Critical Theory, made a similar pessimistic move a century later, reeling from the Holocaust and the Fascist, Nazi, and Stalinist dictatorships, which the *Brumaire* scenario portended.

Engels also provided a highly pessimistic report about the complete failure of the bourgeois revolution in Germany, which he attributed to the nation's backward class structure. He argued that the bourgeoisie were defeated more decisively in Germany than anywhere else in Europe, and that the dissolution of the provincial and national assemblies and the restoration of aristocratic power constituted the death of political liberalism in that nation. Rather than decisive bourgeois hegemony and liberal democracy on the Continent, he argued, the revolutions of 1848 had stirred counterrevolution and new configurations of aristocratic and capitalist power. Engels held that the staging conditions for a class-conscious, revolutionary proletariat were absent in Germany. Moreover, Marx observed that Britain's prosperity was creating "political indifference," neutralizing progressive possibilities of its highly developed bourgeois institutions and advanced working class, and generating a conservative drift away from progressive democracy (Engels 1851–2: 5–13, 91–6; Marx 1852b, 1852c). This depoliticizing impact of affluence has been a major factor in the decline of Socialist parties and labor-centered, Left politics in the rich European social democracies of the later twentieth century.

Although Marx stuck to his materialist agenda, he was no longer optimistic about capitalist modernization bringing us to our senses and making capitalism transparent, or open to straightforward empirical observation. In the *Brumaire*, he spoke about the Napoleonic regime's "superficial appearance," or state autonomy, as a veil covering the underlying reality of continued capitalist domination in everyday affairs. This idea of the blinding and fettering effects of ideological illusion can be found in his earlier work, but now he held that immanent critique must dig much more deeply and theoretically to grasp the factors that shape capitalism's highly distorted sociopolitical surface (1852a: 127–8). As Seigel argues, the 1850s reversals caused Marx to doubt his former belief that "empirical experience" provides direct access to the "real truth" (Seigel 1993: 362; see also 193–216).

In the early 1850s, Marx carried out intense economic study, but it was not until 1857, spurred by an international economic crisis and rekindled revolutionary hopes, that he started to formulate his later theory of capitalism in the *Grundrisse* (*Outlines of the Critique of Political Economy*, 1857–8a, 1857–8b), or his unpublished outline for his later masterwork, and in *Contribution to the Critique of Political Economy* (1859a). Stressing culture's distorted ideological surface obscuring social relations, he declared that the "semblance of simplicity disappears in more advanced relations of production" (1859a: 275). He held that everyday experiences of the "economy" and "money" are hidden by a fundamental "mystification"; commodity exchange is treated as an independent realm of "things" rather than "a social relation of production." Although "monetary crises" draw out "immanent" contradictions of capitalism, Marx argued, the money form's illusory independence from social life "shrouds" these tensions, or manifests them in an indirect, distorted way. He said that "in the process of exchange, as it appears on the surface of bourgeois society, each gives only while taking, and takes only while giving." However, he asserted that such exchange depends on "having," or ownership. He claimed that the reigning concept of exchange leaves out the question of how entrepreneurs attain the products of labor that they trade and earn a profit in capitalist markets. In his view, the role of capitalist property and class inequalities and consequent bourgeois methods of appropriation are hidden by the ideological view of capital circulation as "free" and "equal" exchange. Marx contended that the systematically unequal exchange between capitalists and workers (i.e., wages for labor power) is the most profoundly mystified social relation and most pivotal to capitalist accumulation. His critique of everyday economic categories and bourgeois political economy aimed to demystify capitalism and to make its modes of appropriation, or exploitation, visible. Marx's "labor theory of value" held that the apparent relations between things (i.e., commodity prices) are shaped by expropriated labor time and an unequal relation between persons. He argued that capitalists' profits originate from their not paying workers the full value of their labor, and that this "exchange" gives capitalist society a distinctive shape (1859a: 275–6, 289; 1859b: 433, 462). In his view, wage labor is the distinct capitalist form of the exploitative, extractive relation between ruling classes and direct producers that he stressed in his materialist theory of history and that he argued exerts decisive influence on overall sociocultural development in all class societies.

The first volume of *Capital* (1867a) appeared about a decade after Marx began his major effort to theorize capitalist political economy. He planned originally to complete six books (several of these were to include multiple volumes) of his magnum opus. Although writing thousands of pages of text and filling many notebooks for the broader study, he never finished it. After Marx's death in 1883, Engels edited and assembled the two unfinished core volumes (Marx 1885, 1894). Karl Kautsky later edited the three volumes of *Theories of Surplus Value* (1905–10), Marx's critical history of economic theory. Various thinkers have speculated about the reasons why Marx did not complete his masterwork. Engels held that his various bouts of ill health and political activism slowed the project. He also thought that Marx's tendency to leave theoretical work to the late night and dim candlelight limited his output (his daytime hours were often occupied with journalistic, polemical, and letter writing and with family activities) (Engels 1885: 1–5). Seigel speculates that Marx was slowed by unresolved tensions between his Hegelian residue and his materialism, reservations about core aspects of his theory, and psychological problems originating in his childhood (Seigel 1993: 329–92).

An obvious complicating factor was Marx's dogged pursuit of an enormously complex project. Engels described how his "incessant study" and "unparalleled conscientiousness and strict self-criticism" led to constant broadening of the scope of issues and searching for ever more historical support (1885: 6). Marx's effort to develop his theory fully, or to find the elusive, hidden "truth" of capitalist development, was far more important to him than publication. Certain other first-generation modern theorists (e.g., Max Weber and George Herbert Mead) also demonstrated this intense commitment to the development of theory and tendency to leave major bodies of unfinished work to be published posthumously. Aiming to provide an empirical-historical alternative to religion's received truths and the intuitive truths of philosophy, these theorists saw the establishment of their new method of knowledge creation as a rocky and uncertain road that required enormous effort to attain the desired results. Although their new social or cultural "science" was in its infancy, they believed that their efforts could yield major "discoveries" and exert decisive impact on public life. Thus, they dedicated their lives to their theoretical practices. The material and cultural climate of today's professionally specialized, academic theory circles is very different. "Doing theory" is now often equated with writing, and unpublished work is considered to be stillborn, or a dead letter. Few theorists believe that they will "discover" ideas that will alter public life. Although earlier modern theorists' sunny ideas of "science" and "truth" are often seen as passé or misguided, their theoretical practices should be read in the context of their very different institutional settings and ethical and social meanings. Reflection on these matters might provide insight into some of the weaknesses as well as the strengths of contemporary social theory.

Marx's Social Theory

Beyond liberal individualism: Marx's sociological realism and the power of social cooperation

Adam Smith's thought is one of the most important roots of the liberal individualism criticized by Marx. Smith wrote before the Second Industrial Revolution and large-scale industry; his emphases on individualism and markets were pitched against the powerful state of the mercantile era. Opening the *Wealth of Nations* (1776), he illustrated his core concept of the "division of labor" with his famous pinmaker example: a single worker, carrying out all the steps of production alone, would be hard pressed to make 20 pins, or possibly even one pin, a day, while ten specialized producers, working together, could produce 48,000 a day, or about 4,800 each. He suggested that the division of labor increases productivity geometrically. Smith implied that capitalist specialization generates qualitatively enhanced productive capacities, but he did not dwell on complex social cooperation in production. Rather, he emphasized changes in the realm of exchange, or the market, as the source of productive advances and overall modern social progress. He held that the division of labor arises in an unplanned, unintentional manner, animated by individualistic human nature, or the universal "propensity to truck, barter, and exchange one thing for another" and the "natural" inclination of the individual to pursue his or her "interest." In his view, the competitive facets of capitalist markets unleash the individual's heretofore repressed self-interest, generating an ever more dynamic, efficient, abundant division of labor and a freer, more rational society. Smith claimed that competitive individualism generates spontaneous association, and that capitalist markets produce, unintendedly, social harmony. He warned that this "invisible hand" depends on free markets, and must avoid sociopolitical regulation (Smith 1776: 3–5, 13–17, 420–5).

Paralleling Smith, Marx held that 12 cooperating masons accomplish much more than one mason working alone for the same number of hours. But he argued that this difference derives from "the creation of a new power, namely, the collective power of the masses." Describing the cooperating masons as "omnipresent" and having "hands and eyes before and behind," Marx implied that cooperative activity gives rise to new capacities that do not exist at the individual level *per se*. He stated that:

> Just as the offensive power of a squadron of cavalry . . . is essentially different from the sum of the offensive . . . powers of the individual cavalry . . . taken separately, so the sum total of the mechanical forces exerted by isolated workmen differs from the social force that is developed, when many hands take part simultaneously by one and the same undivided operation, such as raising a heavy weight, turning a winch, or removing an obstacle.
>
> (Marx 1867a: 330–1)

Although Marx agreed that market growth stimulates expansion of the division of labor, his view of the process differs sharply from that of Smith. Marx saw modern industry's spectacular productive advances as deriving from its quantitative extension and qualitative transformation of *sui generis* social powers, which transcend the individual level. As suggested above, a cavalry formation or organized group of masons has distinct *social* features, which do not derive from, and cannot be reduced to, the individual traits of the participants. Marx contended that these emergent social properties and social capacities existed already in the "simple cooperation" of early humanity, or at the dawn of society (e.g., joint hunting and gathering), many millennia before the rise of markets.

By contrast to Smith's claims about the primacy of the individual, Marx believed that social cooperation is the most fundamental facet of human nature. He held that even "mere social contact" and consequent "emulation" and "stimulation" enhance individual powers, while active cooperation overcomes the "fetters of . . . individuality" and harnesses the "capabilities of the species." Marx argued that capitalism's great productive advances derive from its wider, more complex forms of social cooperation, rather than from market competition. In his view, capitalists created a new ultra-powerful "combined organism" based on highly organized cooperation. By contrast to markets, he saw the factory as depending on deliberate planning, which he believed ought to be extended to other institutions and to the societal division of labor. He rejected the idea that modern specialized activity can exist only under capitalism, or even that it could be developed fully on that basis. Marx portrayed capitalists as separating the individual producer from his or her means of production, concentrating the appropriated productive forces in their own hands, and, overall, overthrowing the traditional forms of independent production and imposing the new type of complex, social cooperation by coercive, exploitative methods. Rather than the spontaneous harmony predicted by Smith, Marx claimed that the unrestrained pursuit of self-interest in unregulated capitalist markets generates a profound tension between the individual and the community, incurs great social costs, and leads to intense social conflicts. As Engels said, this "contradiction" appears as the fundamental "antagonism" between bourgeoisie and proletariat (Engels 1892: 311; Marx 1867a: 326–41, 359–6).

Reversing Smith's individualistic conception of human nature, Marx held that the human being is "at all events a social animal," an "ensemble of social relations," or product of "definite" social relationships. He argued that "sheep-like or tribal consciousness" dominated all early human groupings, and that individualism is a much later *social product*, arising with more advanced forms of production and their complex patterns of association, cooperation, and linguistic interchange (Marx 1845: 4; 1867a: 331; Marx and Engels 1845–6: 43–5). Marx saw modern claims about an "inherent" split between the individual and society as manifesting capitalism's primary contradiction between private productive property, monopolized by the rich, and complex social cooperation, imposed on the working classes. He held that the liberal vision of individualism, naturalized and universalized as unchangeable human nature, is an ideological concept, and implies that nothing can be done about capitalism's highly unequal division of wealth and burdens. By contrast to Smith, Marx believed that social regulation inheres in the very facets of capitalism that have increased productivity and material wealth and could be employed to eliminate the misery and injustice that have heretofore accompanied capitalist development. In his view, capitalist production's cooperative facets

are the matrix for a richer, freer social individuality attuned to social ties
and responsibilities to others and to the mutual benefits of deliberately
planned, socially just cooperation. Marx implied that such individuality
was already emergent among proletarians, and that their consequent, future
collective agency would forge an emancipated, post-capitalist order.

Marx's theory of history: sociological materialism

"Just as Darwin discovered the law of development of organic nature, so
Marx discovered the law of development of human history," Engels
declared after Marx's funeral (1883: 467). He was speaking of Marx's
"historical materialism," which for reasons explained in the last section
I prefer to call *sociological materialism*. This approach focused explicitly on
collective practices that give shape to specific peoples' social institutions
and cultures. Engels helped Marx frame this approach in the early years
of their collaboration. For simplicity's sake, I will refer mostly to Marx
alone, but the reader should keep in mind that Engels contributed substantially to this project. Following Darwin, Marx wanted to specify, qual-
ify, and surpass earlier Enlightenment ideas of social science and social
knowledge, which he believed spoke too generally about "man" and paid
insufficient attention to the actual activities and variations of historical
peoples. He aimed to formulate general principles parallel to Darwinian
theory, which address the specific conditions of differentiated forms
of life as well as overall development. With varying success, other early
modern social theorists made similar moves toward historical specificity. They aimed to go beyond the early modern, philosophical idea of a
"science of man," which made grand gestures about "Reason" and tran-
scendence of superstition, but failed to generate much empirical-historical
inquiry or add much to knowledge about actual sociocultural development. Marx embraced the Hegelian argument about the historical nature
of culture, but rejected its "abstract" emphasis on stages of the Spirit, which
he contended retained taints of religion and metaphysics and thus
stopped short of a "scientific" method. Although crediting classical
economists' emphasis on the importance of material conditions, Marx
attacked their "abstract," individualistic idea of human nature and inatten-
tion to historical peoples' actual cooperative practices. He wanted to
transcend dialectically Hegelianism and bourgeois political economy,
retaining some of their key features, yet breaking with many other of their
core points and creating a new materialism that takes account of specific
forms of *social* life.

Marx and Engels (1845–6: 37) asserted that "it is not consciousness that
determines life, but life that determines consciousness." Like Darwin, they
stressed the fundamental centrality of material activities and struggles.

In particular, they held that a genuine social science would take account of the uniquely creative and diverse ways in which human groups produce for their basic animal needs and, in the process, give rise to new, exclusively human needs and capacities and distinct patterns of social development, or history. However, friends and foes alike have often interpreted Marx's and Engels's materialism to imply reductionist determination of social life by narrowly conceived technical and economic conditions. Responding to critics and vulgar interpreters, Engels asserted, after Marx's death, that "the *ultimately* determining element in history is the production and reproduction of real life. More than this neither Marx nor I ever asserted" (Engels 1890b: 397–8). Marx's and Engels's materialism focuses on "human society" or "social humanity." But they considered the "historical life-process" to be "twofold," or "natural" as well as "social"; our physical needs link us to nature, but the ways and means by which we meet them are mediated and structured socially (e.g., by cooperation, organization, language, ideas, customs). By contrast to other animal species' material practices, they argued, human production is mindful, and thus progresses in the long run; our intelligent, deliberate labor frees us from our original, total subservience to nature, and makes possible liberation from our "second nature," or domination of person by person (Marx and Engels 1845–6: 31–2, 36–75, 41–5; Marx 1845: 5).

Marx did not elevate material practices above cultural practices, as many critics argue. Rather, he implied that human groupings attain a relative autonomy from nature as their productive progress reduces the proportion of their labor time devoted to direct subsistence activity and increases that expended in sociocultural production. He held that it is precisely our productive practices' sociocultural nature and consequent historical development and variation that distinguish human societies from other animal groupings. However, he objected to the ideological separation of culture from the material realm and the consequent concealment of the importance of material practices. Marx hoped that, in the long run, people could be freed from drudgery and nurture higher, more distinctively human cultural wants and practices. He dreamed of a time when ordinary people could focus on art and science and develop their "individualities" culturally (Marx 1857–8b: 91).

Marx stressed "real," "active," or "definite individuals," entering "definite social and political relations," producing themselves in specific ways, and thus acting as agents of their own history. As stated above, however, he argued that we do not create ourselves of our own accord. Rather, people operate "under definite material limits, presuppositions, and conditions independent of their will" (Marx and Engels 1845–6: 35–6; Marx 1852a: 103). Like other modern social theorists, Marx stressed that we are born into ready-made, hierarchical sociocultural worlds, which fix our ideas and actions in innumerable ways. However, he saw *class* to be the most pervasive source of this systematic social constraint. In his view, a class is an aggregate of people who share the same social location in a society's system of property relations and, consequently, experience common material limits and possibilities for their individual development. Marx and Engels contended that class has an "independent existence as against individuals" – it frames the conditions under which we make ourselves, regardless of our conscious identity, will, or effort (Marx and Engels 1845–6: 77–9). For example, under feudalism, peasant producers were tied by law to their plots and to endless toil, while lords ruled by military means and appropriated peasant surpluses. The class relation between lord and peasant reproduced, generation after generation, distinct types of superordinate and subordinate social beings. The vast majority of these individuals were born into these class positions, and could not imagine alternatives or choose roles freely, especially those that were different from their parents' roles (i.e., without costs and hardships). Such relations did not preclude individual differences or unexpected individual moves (e.g., peasants who fled to towns or squires who joined the clergy). Notwithstanding, Marx thought that class location establishes definite, unavoidable sociocultural limits and opportunities for individuals, and imposes substantial costs for deviation from expected roles. The distinct "structural" thrust of his *sui generis* idea of class stresses pervasive socio-material conditioning of individual lives.

Marx held that as soon as a society's productive powers are advanced to a level where surpluses are large enough to free a significant portion of the adult populace from labor, a fundamental class split arises between "ruling classes," who govern politically and culturally, and "direct producers," whose labor activates the productive forces. He argued that ruling classes exert effective control over productive forces, subordinate direct producers, and appropriate their surpluses. Marx stressed that ruling classes and direct producers vary historically, especially between societies with fundamentally different productive forces. For example, under capitalist manufacture, capitalists and wageworkers replaced the feudal manor's lords and serfs and the medieval guild's masters and journeymen. Seeing these two types of class location to be all-important and nearly universal sites of structural constraint, Marx believed that inquiry into their social patterning in different cultural and historical settings would reveal decisive facts about overall sociocultural development. He saw relations between ruling classes and direct producers to be dynamic. In his view, major sociocultural transformations are usually rooted in changes in the productive forces, but he argued that "class struggle" is the effective mobilizing force in such shifts. He contended that "class-conscious," politically organized, class struggle sometimes forges new class structures, reshapes social life *in toto*, and can even, as in the case of capitalism, ignite epochal ruptures. However, he was aware that class struggle is much more often haphazard, sporadic, local, and disconnected from overt class identity and conscious collective agency (e.g., individual serfs hiding surplus or stealing from lords). Thus, rather than basic transformation, he saw it to be, in most cases, the source of microscopic changes and variations that prevent clockwork regimentation in a productive system. Marx thought that the development of advanced productive forces frees more and more people from subsistence labor, and thus gives rise to larger, more diverse intermediate classes and fluid, multi-sided class relations. His point that, in advanced capitalist societies, "middle and intermediate strata . . . obliterate lines of demarcation everywhere" and deflect class consciousness dimmed his hopes for working-class solidarity and a final political showdown between the proletariat and the bourgeoisie (Marx 1894: 870). He understood that the diverse classes and subclasses engage in internecine conflicts and complicated alliances. These relations are made even more complex by cross-cutting, status-based, cultural splits and ties (i.e., ethnic, racial, gender, religious, and other sociocultural factors), which segment and fragment classes and subclasses internally. Marx's and Engels's declaration that the "history of all hitherto existing society is the history of class struggles" does not mean that these battles are always readily visible, organized politically, or socially transforming (Marx and Engels 1848: 482). By contrast to the *Manifesto*'s linear, predictable scenario, capitalist class relations are usually complex and variable, and lack transparency. This was a prime reason why Marx and Engels called for a materialist social science.

Marx understood that change in productive forces had been very slow or static for long periods of time before capitalism, and had been characterized by local frequent setbacks and much unevenness. However, he still argued that, in the very long run, incremental productive advances accumulate, are diffused regionally and globally, and thus progress. Consequently, he held that "surplus product" (i.e., that exceeding minimal subsistence) increases relative to "necessary product" (i.e., that required for minimal subsistence). He implied that the employment of higher and higher levels of "surplus labor" in sociocultural production generates ever more technically enhanced powers of production for physical needs, higher standards of subsistence, more differentiated sociocultural orders, and more varied, distinctively human, or cultural, wants and needs. As explained above, however, he held that this materially driven civilizing process has been class-based, and thus has operated nearly everywhere in a highly unequal way. Ruling classes, with the assistance of allied intermediate classes, have appropriated the labor and product of direct producers, and employed these resources for the development of productive forces, built environments, and symbolic culture. For example, the spectacular and highly complex cultures of "great civilizations" were based on huge divides between "mental" and "physical" labor and tyrannical ruling classes' relentless extraction of surplus labor and surplus product from impoverished, brutally oppressed slaves and serfs. Marx wanted to address facts that were "overlooked" by historians and philosophers – that even in Athenian "democracy," free citizens were a ruling minority who relied on thorough domination and regular extraction from unfree masses. In Marx's view, material and cultural progress has been, and continues to be, thoroughly entwined with class domination.

According to Marx's materialist "guiding principle," knowledge about production and extraction is necessary to understand the fates of individuals as well as the development of social orders (Marx 1859a: 262–4). In particular, he stressed the need to study the most important and most veiled social process: how ruling classes appropriate labor and product and ideologically obscure the process. Marx saw the historically specific way "in which unpaid surplus labor is pumped out of direct-producers" to be the "hidden basis of the entire social structure" (Marx 1894: 777–8). He argued that ruling classes and their allied intermediate strata (e.g., priests, intellectuals, politicians) create ideologies that mystify this class exploitation, presenting it as a reflection of God, nature, or inherent right, and making it moral, inevitable, and legal. For Marx, ideology originates from unintentional class-blinders, or people defining reality passively in accord with the limits of their unquestioned, parochial class situations, as well as from political and cultural elites' conscious, strategic efforts to distort reality and dominate. Marx saw materialism as a tool to resist this ideological mystification; used properly, it lays bare the systematically suppressed "real bases" of society and their agents, structures, dynamics, and forms of reproduction.

Marx spoke of societies, or "social formations," as being characterized by systematic interdependence and internal relations between their sociocultural parts. He held that the *mode of production* is their primary, albeit not exclusive, structuring factor. Marx argued that a mode of production is composed of an ensemble of "productive forces" (i.e., natural resources, tools, labor power, technology/science, modes of cooperation), or factors that contribute directly to the creation of necessary and surplus product, and "property relations," or class-based social relationships that determine who has effective control over the productive forces and the disposition of product and who must engage in productive labor. He considered the mode of production as the "base," or ultimate determinant, of sociocultural life. However, as explained above, he conceived of the "material factor" as largely a sociocultural construct, which includes physical materials. Even the simplest productive forces, such as prehistorical stone tools, require application of rudimentary technical ideas, communication, and social cooperation. Arguably, Marx's materialist analyses stress most centrally class struggles over the forms of productive property. In this regard, his materialism focuses more on social relationships oriented to material factors than on material conditions *per se*.

Marx held that social formations are also composed of *superstructure*, which entails "modes of intercourse" and "ideology," which do not contribute directly to the creation of necessary product or surplus product, but reproduce the conditions needed to perpetuate the mode of production. For example, Marx saw the state's military, police, legal, and administrative arms to be primary means of perpetuating class power and the existent productive forces and property relations. But he also argued that other types of organization and association (e.g., families or voluntary groups) control, socialize, indoctrinate, or otherwise fashion people to fit the existing mode of production. Marx sometimes spoke too sweepingly about the scope of this reproduction, and other times left it vague, but he did not imply that all organizations, associations, and culture beyond the mode of production play an equally important role in the process. For example, Marx knew that, in liberal societies, counter-hegemonic labor organizations and political parties, like his own, found their way into public life. Also, he recognized that "ruling ideas" refer to the delimited areas of culture that justify the mode of production in a reasonably direct manner (e.g., today's leading public ideas about the economy and state). For example, his claims to distinguish depth "realities" from surface "illusions" implied that he distinguished his materialist point of view from ideology. More generally, he often had high praise for literature, art, and science, and did not reduce them to a mere reflux of class society. Marx saw certain facets of society and culture as playing a very direct role in reproduction of the mode of production and others as having little to do with the process, and thus having a relative autonomy from class structure. But he still thought that all parts of the social world bear some imprint of the underlying mode of production. The boundaries of superstructure are much more complex and problematic than Marx could have imagined in contemporary capitalism's highly segmented class structures, differentiated organizations and associations, variegated popular culture, and niche markets. However, the facets of state organization and of political economic thought that Marx pointed to as key aspects of superstructure are still easy to identify and perform similar functions today.

Marx spoke of relations of "correspondence," which facilitate the reproduction of a mode of production, and relations of "contradiction," which undermine this process. For example, he held that feudal laws and customs that bound serfs to lords and journeymen to masters and that forbade the free movement of peasants, unrestricted sale of property, and market competition "corresponded" to, or reproduced, the productive forces and property relations of the manor and the guild. But he argued that new capitalist forms of labor organization and technology were fettered by the feudal mode of production and its complex of laws and customs.

These technical and sociocultural "contradictions" intensified class conflicts, and led eventually to political conflict between the bourgeoisie and
the feudal aristocracy and guild masters. The victorious bourgeoisie captured the state, and created political, legal, and sociocultural forms that
"corresponded" to, and fostered development of, the emergent capitalist
mode of production.

Marx saw class struggle as an immediate "motor" of change, but he
argued that major shifts of productive forces are the "ultimate causal agent"
of fundamental transformations of modes of production and overall
social formations. For example, Marx stated:

> The mode of production of material life conditions the general process of
> social, political and intellectual life. . . . At a certain stage of development,
> the material productive forces of society come into conflict with the exist-
> ing relations of production or . . . with the property relations. . . . From
> forms of development of the productive forces these relations turn into
> their fetters. Then begins an era of social revolution. The changes in the eco-
> nomic foundation lead sooner or later to the transformation of the whole
> immense superstructure.   (1859a: 263)

The issue of the "primacy" of the material factor, or its status as the "ultimate determining" force, has been one of the most enduring and intense
topics of Marxist debate and of anti-Marxist criticism. However, Marx was
somewhat ambiguous about the topic. Like Adam Smith and other early
economists, his "moderate" materialist position implied that overall
sociocultural development depends on the level of material production
and types of appropriation. For example, from this standpoint, today's
popular culture cannot be grasped adequately without reference to
advanced capitalism's vast productive powers, global division of labor,
new communications technologies, and highly differentiated and polarized class structure. Today, Marx's argument that epochal transitions are
rooted in qualitative transformations of production is a relatively uncon-
troversial position, embraced by many non-Marxist anthropologists and
comparative sociologists (who stress major changes in the methods of production in their discussions of the shifts between hunting and gathering,
horticultural, agricultural, and industrial societies). Moreover, Marx did
not argue consistently that all substantial social change must originate
in a shift in productive forces. His view of the relation of culture to physical nature is complex, because he saw the "material" realm as *social* as
well as natural. For example, he considered science/technology and
forms of cooperation to be part of the "determining" productive forces,
and these sociocultural elements also depend on, and are embedded in,
a social formation's overall culture system. Thus, causality is a complicated matter in Marx's moderate materialism. The claim that capitalism

"determines" culture's overall complexity and the quality, quantity, and diversity of its goods does not deny that these goods have relative autonomy from the economy, or that they are shaped by a multiplicity of causes. Marx's moderate materialism treats the mode of production as a matrix that sets material limits and exerts a general influence, but it does not reduce politics and culture to epiphenomena.

However, Marx also suggested at times a "totalizing" material determination. For example, he asserted that "social relations are very closely bound to productive forces" (e.g., "The hand-mill gives you society with the feudal lord; the steam-mill, society with the industrial capitalist"), and that technological transformations change all our social relations. He also held that a social formation is never "destroyed before all the productive forces for which it is sufficient have been developed and new superior relations of production never replace older ones before the material conditions for their existence have matured within the framework of the old society" (Marx 1847: 166; 1859a: 263). This totalizing approach also appears in his claims about the "inevitability" of certain tendencies of capitalist development and of proletarian victory and socialism. Such points imply that politics and culture are mere "reflections" of material dynamics. "Scientific," "mechanical," or "orthodox" Marxists have often emphasized the more totalizing position, while "critical," "Western," or "cultural" Marxists have usually stressed the moderate approach. Emphasizing a sweeping, or even total, autonomy of politics and culture, recent "post-Marxist" critics usually see Marx exclusively as a totalizer, and, on that basis, reject his ideas *in toto*.

Although rigidly determinist passages exist in his texts, Marx suggested much more often a complex, historically contingent materialism, which is not reducible to the totalizing position's "technological determinism" (i.e., social change arises only from technical change) or to "reflection theory" (i.e., ideas are mere emanations of physical reality). He frequently pointed to changes arising from diverse sources (e.g., cultural and political, as well as material), which can either heighten or deflect class struggles. After Marx's death, Engels criticized the totalizing materialism of younger Marxists. Although admitting that heated debates with opponents led Marx and him to sometimes overstate rhetorically "the economic side," he insisted that they intended to create "above all a guide to study, not a lever for construction after the manner of the Hegelian." Embracing a moderate view of material primacy, he held that the various facets of culture and society exert their own effects. He insisted that he and Marx always believed that "history must be studied afresh," different societies must be "examined individually," and the relations between the various conditions are contingent and cannot be deduced in advance (Engels 1890a: 396; 1890b). Later Marxist splits over determinism have been primarily between positions that provide warrants about "inevitable" change or indubitable historical truths and approaches that employ it as a heuristic principle pointing to likely sources of tension, conflict, and change and to distinctive types of questions about contingent historical processes. However, as Engels implied, Marx treated materialism primarily as a heuristic device that poses foci, problems, and issues for a distinctly Marxian sociology.

Even in the most complex pre-modern civilizations, productive forces have usually developed incrementally over many hundreds or even thousands of years, and major innovations have tended to diffuse very slowly, if at all, between different regions. By contrast, as Marx and Engels argued in the *Manifesto*, modern capitalism generated, with lightning speed, a nascent world market, global division of labor, and greater variety of powerful productive forces than all preceding civilizations put together. His materialism bears the marks of this peculiar time, and his approach is perhaps best understood as an effort to come to terms with this unique, new capitalist world, rather than with history as a whole. The primacy that he gave to material factors arose from his experience of the radical changes wrought by the revolution in productive forces, which, as at no previous time, advanced sweepingly and altered everyday life profoundly. Max Weber (1904–5: 181) later held that capitalist productive conditions "determine the lives of all the individuals born into this mechanism . . . with irresistible force," and will probably continue to do so "until the last ton of fossilized coal is burned." Marx's materialism has relevance today, because we still live in the wake of the world-historical transformation that he analyzed – the capitalist mode of production, its dominant classes, and revolution of productive forces are still going on. Today's neoliberal capitalism makes capital accumulation the measure of nearly everything, vastly increases the pace and diversity of material and sociocultural change, and gives rise to a more narrowly economic, exactly calculated, global form of material determination than even Marx could have imagined.

Marx's theory of capitalism: labor, value, and extraction

Along with his sociological materialism, Marx's theory of capitalism is a major contribution to social theory. He held that the core materialist dynamic of all previous class societies is still operative – capitalist development is animated by the appropriation of unpaid labor and product and by class struggle over this extractive process. By contrast with the view of today's economists that market competition, supply and demand, entrepreneurship, and consumer choice are decisive, Marx stressed capitalism's complex fusion of powerful, new productive forces with top-down, precisely planned, complex social cooperation and systematic, exactly calculable methods of extraction. But he emphasized most strongly the relationship between the historically specific ruling class and the class of direct producers – *capitalists* and *wageworkers* (or bourgeoisie and proletariat). He saw the consequent extractive process to be the secret of capitalism's unparalleled economic growth and the ultimate source of the epochal modern rupture.

Marx's conception of capitalism as a "social formation" opposed liberal individualism's dissolution of the social world into an aggregate of competing, calculating, trading monads. He believed that bourgeois ideology's emphases on competitive market relations, individual interest, and individual economic success conceal the cooperative relations between workers and the exploitative social relations between capitalists and workers. Marx contended that "the specific social character of each producer's labor does not show itself except in the act of exchange" and that, even there, it appears in the distorted form of monetary relations between commodities or as "a relation between things." Consequently, capitalism's unique, exceptionally extensive, highly impersonal forms of cooperation and extraction are invisible to average people (Marx 1867a: 83–4). Marx employed the word "social" repeatedly, stressing emphatically that the economy is a product of culturally mediated, collective practices that can be reshaped by class-conscious collective agency. He rejected the bourgeois view that capital is a "mysterious and self-creating source of interest" and of other forms of monied wealth (1894: 388–90). He thought that this mystified understanding of capital as *the* self-contained motor of economic growth typifies the reigning, gravely distorted commonsense view of capitalism's commercial surface. Marx referred to this mystified state as the "fetishism of commodities" – markets, products, and prices appear to be "independent beings," with their own extra-human motions and interrelations, and to be detached from socially organized production and extraction. In his view, workers and labor processes vanish from sight, and the products of our own creation dominate us. This idea of fetishism has roots in Marx's youthful, Left-Hegelian critique of religiously based alienation, but in his later work he referred specifically to capitalist mystification (i.e., the collective hallucination that capitalism runs on its own accord and is impervious to social intervention). He compared this fetishism to medieval historians' equation of "the middle-ages with spirituality," which hides the "secret history . . . of its landed property." In *Capital*, Marx declared that under capitalism the "appearance of simplicity vanishes" and that immediately given experience of the economy is a gravely distorted refraction of material forces. Every commodity, he asserted, is transformed into a "social hieroglyphic," or "secret" for us to "decipher." Marx wanted to bring to light these ideologically shrouded, social "conditions and relations of a definite, historically determined mode-of-production" (1867a: 83–5, 90–4).

Marx formulated the conceptual core of his general theory of capitalist development – the "labor theory of value" – to illuminate capitalism's central class, or extractive, relation, which he argued drives overall capitalist accumulation. He held that the structure and dynamics of capitalism can be brought into view only by analyzing it as a system, or "organic whole." Just as with early Copernican and Galilean science, Marx implied, his approach needed the counterintuitive "force of abstraction" to overcome a mystified everyday reality backed by the most powerful classes. He also argued that fetishistic beliefs about the character of money have origins that pre-date capitalism, carrying baggage of more than "2000 years" of misunderstanding. Although his theory of value is stated abstractly, he did not claim to capture timeless economic truths. Rather, he contended that he employed rational argument to isolate the decisive facets (i.e., from secondary and accidental conditions) of an emergent capitalism that was, at the time, substantially developed only in England. He theorized historical "laws," or the animating principles, of a social formation still in the process of development. Marx acknowledged, however, that those awash in capitalism's fetishistic reality would find the theory of value hard to grasp (1867b; 1873).

Marx stated that capitalist wealth appears as an "immense accumulation of commodities." Thus, he began *Capital* by analyzing the *commodity*. Commodities are products that meet some need or want and that are produced for exchange, rather than for direct consumption by the producer. They are traded either directly or by money. Commodities exist wherever market exchanges occur, but capitalism is the only mode of production in which commodity exchange dominates material provision of daily life (i.e., almost everyone fulfills material needs through purchases on the market, rather than through independent production). Marx stated that commodities have "use value," or qualitative properties that satisfy human wants and needs, and "exchange value," or a quantitative side expressed in the rates by which they trade against each other. Under capitalism, Marx said, the study of use values produces "commercial knowledge" (e.g., information about commodities' highly variable, intrinsic qualities is needed to estimate consumer demand). Rather than inform business practices, however, he wanted to explore capitalism's hidden structures and dynamics. Arguing that capitalism subordinates use value to exchange value, Marx held that his inquiry must start with the question of what factors regulate exchange values.

Marx rejected the commonsense notion that the proportions in which commodities trade against each other are determined by their use values' highly divergent, intrinsic qualities and by consumers' aggregated, subjective valuations of their worth. He argued that these exchange values must have a more systematic cause that derives from some common attribute. Revising earlier arguments by Adam Smith and David Ricardo,

Marx saw the only relevant commonality of commodities to be that they are all products of "social labor." Consequently, he declared that exchange values are surface manifestations of *value*, or the "crystallized social labor" contained in commodities. Marx argued that this common "social substance" is the time that it takes to find, mine, refine, fashion, assemble, or otherwise make the object. He held that the exchange value of a commodity is determined by the "labor time" that it takes to produce it (i.e., from the acquisition of raw material to the delivery of the finished product). Marx's reference to the twofold nature of the commodity refers to the fundamental polarity between use value and value (i.e., exchange value is merely a phenomenal form of value). From this vantage point, the proportional rates by which gold watches trade, in kind or in monetary units, against jade rings, linen sheets, or paper boxes are determined by their respective differences in value, or crystallized labor time. Marx stated that exchange value is "simply the form under which certain social relations manifest themselves" or "the material envelope of the human labor spent upon it." He saw appropriated labor time to be the hidden social determinant that gives shape to the market's apparent animistic, or self-governed, surface of market exchanges, prices, and products (1867a: 45–81, 101; 1865: 120–4).

Marx qualified his theory of value in a number of ways. Rather than concrete producers' labor time *per se*, he stipulated that value is set by "socially-necessary labor time," or the average intensity of labor characteristic of a society's and an industry's overall level of development. This means that the value of commodities is set by producers who operate with average efficiency, rather than by slower, inefficient producers or by the fastest ones. Marx held that, other factors being equal, overall values tend to fall as capitalist competition eliminates slower, backward producers and replaces them with more efficient producers (i.e., commodities take less time to produce, and prices fall). However, he also stated that supply and demand have substantial conditioning effects on prices and cause them to deviate from their values. For example, when a commodity is in great oversupply or is not in demand (e.g., out-of-style clothing), it may be priced at far less than its value or even be worthless. The converse is true when a highly desired or essential commodity is in short supply. Marx stressed that "competition" is an important facet of capitalism, which interacts with and influences value relations in a variety of ways, but he believed that it was a complex matter that required a separate study. He acknowledged that myriad, particular historical circumstances and subjective factors (which effect supply and demand) play an important role in setting prices of individual commodities. However, he argued that these happenstance variations equilibrate, or cancel each other out, over time, and thus do not explain the central tendencies of prices. Marx conceded that knowledge of supply and demand is important for business management, and that bourgeois economists provide reasonably effective approaches for analysis of such issues. However, he argued that their theories fail to grasp the causes of overall price patterns, and thus cannot explain the bases of exchange value or the factors that drive overall capitalist accumulation. Recall his point that the logic of capitalism is visible only when we analyze it as an organic whole. Marx's theory of value also presumed market competition, or conditions that approximate the free market. He held that prices set by monopolies or states manifest organizational power or politics, rather than pure value relations. Depending on the situation, such managed prices may be set far below, or far above, the values of the commodities being traded. In Marx's view, the more monopolies or state organizations set prices, the less his theory of value applies. As will be seen below, he implied that monopoly capitalism and the interventionist state depart from capitalism *per se*, or from the unregulated English capitalism that his theory of value modeled. These conditions aside, Marx argued that aggregate prices of commodities in a capitalist industry or overall capitalist economy gravitate toward averages set by their socially necessary labor times, or values (1865: 126–7; 1867a: 45–81, 276; 1885: 292; 1894: 189–98, 234, 434–6).

Marx saw the commodification of "labor power," or the growth of the numbers of wage laborers, to be the most important factor in capitalist accumulation. He contended that it was a unique commodity that holds the secret to the entire capitalist system. Like all other commodities, he held, the value of labor power is set by the labor time needed to produce it, which is, in this case, the time needed to produce "the means of subsistence necessary for the maintenance of the laborer." He stressed that subsistence standards vary with a society's level of development and culture, and with different social groups and occupations. However, Marx argued that capitalists organize the hours and intensity of wage labor to insure that workers produce much more product than is returned to them in wages. Therefore, the wage pays for only part of the labor time that a worker transfers to the product during a normal workday. Marx held that the capitalist keeps the unpaid portion, and that this "surplus labor time" is realized in the form of money when capitalists sell the items. In contrast to all other commodities, Marx asserted, labor power produces regularly and systematically more value than it commands in exchange. As stated above, he recognized that a wide variety of variable conditions can impact on individual commodity prices, and therefore affect profits. But he contended that such circumstances result in losses as often as profits, and thus cannot explain overall profits and the capitalist class's great accumulated wealth. Marx contended that the unequal, wage–labor exchange and consequent appropriation of surplus labor time, or *surplus value*, is the basis of general capitalist profitability (1867a: 177–86; 1865: 127–33). However, he did not treat capitalist accumulation as an automatic process.

For example, he argued that the class struggle between capitalists and workers and the respective power of capital and labor, which vary historically, determine how closely wages approximate subsistence, and thus have a major impact on the rate of surplus value and profitability. Also, Darwinian economic competition between capitalists requires them to employ a multiplicity of strategies to maximize the rate of surplus value, such as increasing labor discipline, reducing real wages, extending work hours without added compensation, finding new pools of workers accustomed to lower levels of subsistence, and engineering the work process and overall factory regime to maximize the speed and intensity of labor per time unit. In this fashion, Marx theorized capitalism's specific form of unpaid labor and core site of class conflict.

Marx argued that serfs could not help observing that their surplus was being appropriated when they had to perform corvée labor in the lord's fields or when they were forced to give him a portion of their crop. He also contended that slaves feel that even the paid portion of their labor is unpaid. Marx knew that feudal and ancient ruling classes made no pretense about the inequality and lack of freedom of their direct producers; ruling class extraction of unpaid labor was an unadorned facet of personal dependency relations, and thus was transparent to feudal and ancient direct producers. By contrast, Marx argued, capitalist wageworkers' unpaid labor appears to be paid (1867a: 88–9, 177–86). He explained that the ideological portrayal of wage labor as a voluntary contract and commensurable exchange between equals veils extraction. Marx saw the wage exchange to be compelled by the force of hunger; early capitalist workers lacked productive forces to support themselves, were forbidden to organize collectively, "chose" from among equally poorly paid and unstable jobs, and had little or no welfare compensation or pensions. He believed that capitalism's political, legal, and popular culture views of individual freedom and free labor operate along with commodity fetishism to cloak the unequal wage–labor relation and exploitation with legitimacy.

Marx saw this ideological estrangement as manifested in the commodity's contradictory sides. He distinguished the "concrete labor" that produces use values from the "abstract labor" that is crystallized in commodities. He argued that these opposed types of labor amplify a more fundamental polarity between *real wealth*, the use values that meet basic wants and needs, and *abstract wealth*, the monetary profits and accumulated capital that derive from unpaid labor and devolve to the ruling class and the intermediate strata that serve it. Marx held that bourgeois ideology conflates, or confuses, these two fundamentally different types of wealth. For example, political economists claimed that modern production and continued sociocultural progress can be perpetuated *only* by means of capitalist accumulation, and that investors and entrepreneurs "create wealth" *per se*. These points still tend to be treated as verities by today's capitalists and their political leaders. Marx rejected this equation of private fortune with overall social wealth. He held that the two types of wealth need to be decoupled analytically and socially, to liberate people from capitalism's unnecessary drudgery and misery. Marx wanted to create a post-capitalist society in which use value is the exclusive goal of production and surplus labor is appropriated only communally for humane purposes, rather than for private enrichment.

From manufacture to modern industry

Marx criticized sharply Adam Smith's portrayal of the origin of capitalist property relations, in which the emergent capitalist class supposedly gained control of the productive forces peacefully through their "diligent," "intelligent," "frugal" ways and their ability to organize "lazy rascals," or the proletariat, into a disciplined work force. Marx pointed out that Smith and other political economists omitted the most important part of the story – the "conquest of social power" that began before the rise of capitalism and that continued under its dominion. For capitalism to arise, feudal and guild relations had to be dissolved. The expropriation of serfs, the vast majority of the feudal populace, was the most important event. Marx asserted that peasants were "robbed of all their means of production" and "hurled as free and unattached proletarians on the labor market." This removal of the peasantry from the land, he argued, was "written . . . in the letters of blood and fire." Marx stressed that capitalism presupposes a "complete separation" of direct producers from their productive property; peasants and craftsmen had to be forced by material necessity to sell their labor power and to become wageworkers (1867a: 704–7). Destruction of the feudal manor and medieval guilds and forced proletarianization of their independent producers opened the way for capitalist development, which Marx saw in two broad phases.

According to Marx, the dominant type of production in the early phase of capitalism, *manufacture*, arose gradually from the mid-sixteenth century through the late eighteenth century in more developed, or market-oriented parts of Europe, especially England. The labor force of mostly propertyless peasants and displaced craftsmen worked in small factories, owned by capitalists. The primary innovations were the institution of capitalist property relations and sweeping transformation of the social organization of the work process. Separating labor from the household and family, and employing it within a regime of impersonal authority, capitalists forged a distinct, specialized, social space for wagework. The clear demarcation of work from family and community activities, development of a strictly "economic" relationship between capital and labor, and monetary compensation for labor time provided capitalists with the calculable, purely workaday environment needed for precisely organizing the intense extraction of surplus labor time. Marx held that capitalists created a "deliberate plan," exercised careful oversight, and, overall, forged a heretofore unparalleled systematic organization of labor. He also stressed that Darwinian competition between capitalists pressed them to continually improve the efficiency and coordination of production and appropriation. Marx explained that capitalism "as a pumper-out of surplus labor and exploiter of labor power . . . surpasses in energy, disregard for bounds, recklessness and efficiency, all earlier systems of production based on directly compulsory labor." However, he stated also that, "At first, capital subordinates labor on the basis of the technical conditions in which it historically finds it" (1867a: 314). Technical transformation was modest in the phase of manufacture.

Marx explained that manufacture combined separate handicrafts into a single, multiphase process, and decomposed generalized craft production into specialized detail operations. He argued that the new regime simplified work routines (e.g., closed temporal gaps between steps in the labor process and reduced the number of steps), focused and intensified labor, and thus reduced the socially necessary labor time of commodities and increased the rate of surplus value. Hailing the start of a new era of cooperative production, Marx conceived of the move from "isolated," independent production to more centralized, differentiated manufacture to be a fundamental progressive material advance. Recall his glowing points about the *sui generis*, social powers of cooperation. Marx asserted that manufacture transfers intelligence and agency from the individual worker to the "workshop as a whole," or to the (more powerful and rich in productive capacities) "collective laborer." In his view, manufacture's enhanced production of use values derives from its "cooperative character." Stressing that the cooperation is coercive and oppressive, however, Marx described the de-skilled wageworker as an "automatic motor" and "crippled monstrosity." Under manufacture, average workers were tied to a single detail operation of their old handicraft. Repeating the same motions over and over, they were reduced to cogs in the cooperative process. Marx also held that manufacture multiplies cooperative linkages between more numerous producers, and gives rise to a societal division of labor. But he saw increased interdependence to be neutralized by capitalism's unplanned competitive ways. He concluded that manufacture creates "despotism" in the workshop and "anarchy" in the wider society. Overall, Marx contended that manufacture was "fettered" by its incomplete break with handicraft and by a work process that was still mostly by hand. He argued that manufacture created an uneven, unscientific specialization, leaving substantial numbers of partially skilled workers and pockets of highly skilled ones. If workers quit or were fired, owners had to find others with similar skills, and sometimes train them. These workers' leverage in the labor markets provided them with resources to resist workplace control and discipline (1967a: 349–50, 359–60, 364–74).

Marx argued that *modern industry* began a new phase of capitalism that cut the ties to handicraft production and that overcame the fetters of manufacture. He stated that, "In manufacture the revolution in the mode of production begins with the labor power, in modern industry it begins with the instruments of labor" (1867a: 374). Here he is referring to the mechanization of production that began in England during the late eighteenth century. As early as *The German Ideology* and the *Manifesto*, Marx and Engels already implied the importance of this technical shift in their points about the great modernizing rupture caused by "large-scale industry's" revolutionary, new productive forces. However, Marx did not address modern industry closely until the 1850s, after his move to England. When he wrote *Capital*, modern industry was relatively advanced only in England, and was not diffused widely in Western Europe and North America until late in the century, after his death. Marx stressed that mechanization brings "science" into production, employing it to execute a much more systematic, calculated, and thorough type of specialization than that of manufacture, and to substitute "natural forces" for labor power (1867a: 389). Marx argued that modern industry's labor process is planned meticulously and is governed by "objective" criteria (by contrast with manufacture's limited rationalization and traditionalist roots in handicraft). He contended that modern industry makes cooperation "a technical necessity dictated by the instrument of labor itself" and increases greatly its scale, complexity, and reflexivity (i.e., it is more consciously planned) (1867a: 383, 389). Marx's hopes regarding the emancipatory potentialities of modern industry flow, in large part, from his belief that its technical basis is creative social intelligence (i.e., "science"), and that this resource is both the product and the agent of extremely advanced material development, based on extensive, reflexive cooperation. However, he criticized science's linkage to exchange value. For example, he explained that political economists advocated the industrial application of science to undercut unions and bring militant workers under control. In his view, mechanization was driven as much by the desire to discipline labor as by the desire to improve the technical efficiency of production. Marx still believed that modern technology's stunning capacity to produce use values could be employed to serve all of humanity and to generate equally amazing progress in the socio-cultural and political realms. But he insisted that, as long as science and modern industry remain subordinated to capitalist property relations and extraction, their technological powers will be used to extend and radicalize the separation of workers from their means of production and products of their labor (1867a: 439–40).

According to Marx, the mechanized labor process is broken down into microscopic steps, which eliminate all thought and decision from the worker. He contended that the vast majority of modern industrial workers are reduced to factory operatives, performing exceptionally simple, robotic routines and becoming "mere appendages" to a "collective machine." Hyperspecialization and extreme de-skilling sped up production, overcame bottlenecks, and minimized worker training and turnover costs. The consequent radical split of manual labor from mental labor manifests a much more top-down regime than manufacture (in which owners often came from the old handicrafts and operated on the shop floor with the workers). By contrast, in modern industry, managers and technical personnel, distant from the actual workplace, planned and organized the entire operation more systematically for the effective pursuit of surplus value. In the "automatic factory," Marx argued, workers were increasingly controlled technically by the machinery's design, operation, and pace; the consequent continuous, simplified motions greatly increased the intensity of their labor (1867a: 420–30). Most importantly, he held that mechanization reduced sharply the socially necessary labor time. Producing much more per time unit, modern industrial workers, under normal conditions, receive back in wages a much smaller proportion of their product than manufacturing workers, operating by hand. Marx also argued that modern industry reduces the costs of reproducing workers; productive efficiency causes the prices of necessary goods for workers' subsistence to drop, and de-skilling greatly increases the supply of potential workers. Thus, wage costs fall. Marx understood that mechanized industries were huge, rich operations, exerting enormous political and social power and increasing capital's leverage over labor. He explained that traditional restraints on the exploitation of labor were eroded; for example, workdays were extended, extremely unsafe and unhealthy work conditions became the norm, women and children were recruited into the labor force, and a "reserve army" of poor and often desperate underemployed and unemployed workers multiplied (1867a: 397–462, 607–42). Marx acknowledged that modern industry produces an enormous array of new use values, or real wealth. But he argued that its main role, under capitalism, is to pump out surplus value from workers with historically unparalleled speed and intensity. Marx held that unnecessary misery and drudgery were increasing as rapidly as capital and products. He asserted that "official pauperism" grows with the "lazarus-layers" of the working class and the reserve army, and that this trend is "*the absolute general law of capitalist accumulation*" (1867a: 638).

Marx saw machinery as a form of "crystallized labor" that speeds up the transfer of value from labor to commodities and contributes even more directly to the creation of use value, or real wealth. However, he contended that machines cannot create value or be the motor of accumulation. He argued that the commonsense idea, voiced by political economists, that "profit" derives from technology *per se* obscures the "secret of capitalist

production" (1885: 201). He insisted that the only systematic source of capitalist profit is the unequal wage relation and, explicitly, the unpaid portion of labor time. Because of modern industry's huge scale, Marx held,
it initially increases the overall mass of unpaid labor and surplus value.
Also, he argued that mechanization provides windfall profits to the first
capitalist to mechanize an industry or develop new types of machinery
that produce faster than the overall industry's socially necessary labor time.
This producer is able to sell his or her commodity far above its value,
and make windfall profits. But profits equalize and values fall when other
competitors adopt similar technologies. Marx held that competition
drives modern industrial producers to seek continually new technological
advantages and surplus profits, stimulating an upward spiral of labor-
saving technology and a trend toward automated production. He also
acknowledged that cutthroat competition and high barriers to entry (i.e.,
massive costs of very complex machinery) reduce the number of producers
in an industry, and lead to monopoly or oligopoly markets. These firms
boost their profits by bureaucratic pricing, but the break with value
relations generates contradictions and problems in the capitalist system
as a whole. Overall, Marx held that modern industry alters the "organic
composition of capital" – the proportion of "constant capital" (i.e., machinery, tools, land, and raw materials) increases relative to "variable capital"
(i.e., "living labor") (1867a: 607–23). He thought that the trend toward
automated production causes a relative decrease in the active portion of
the working class, and thus will increase unemployment and poverty. But
recall his point that capitalist accumulation depends on "increase of
the proletariat" (1867a: 609). Thus, Marx contended that widely spread
automation would cut the very wellspring of value, and thus must lead
eventually to an accumulation crisis.

Marx formulated his "law" of the "tendency of the rate of profit to
fall" to address this expected crisis tendency (1894: 209–30). He contended
that gains made by the increase in the absolute numbers of factory workers
would, in the long run, be neutralized by the proportional shrinkage of
living labor and of unpaid labor time. He asserted that the rate of surplus
value and profits must fall. However, Marx pointed out "counteracting
influences," or capitalist strategies that avert or slow this tendency –
namely, intensifying labor, sinking wages below subsistence, lowering
the costs of machinery and raw materials, increasing the size of the
reserve army, and raising stock-market capital. Especially important,
Marx held that modern industrial capitalists seek surplus profits by foreign trade with less developed regions of the world, which have much
higher rates of socially necessary labor time for many commodities and
lack the technological means to produce others. According to Marx, selling goods far above their value in these places generates huge windfall
profits. Capitalists take advantage of the cheap labor power of "backward"

regions, which have lower living standards and lower costs of subsistence. The consequent wage savings can offset the advantage of more efficient, costly types of automated production in the home country. Marx saw profitability crises at home and the search for surplus profits abroad to be a major impetus of uneven capitalist globalization; he thought that intensifying efforts to stave off falling profits would generate a backward, dependent type of development in other parts of the world (1894: 230–9). He warned of a "new and international division of labor" refashioning the globe according "to the requirements of the chief centers of modern industry" and instituting one-sided development and backwardness in peripheral regions (1867a: 454–5).

The law of falling profits was an important part of Marx's overall theory of capitalism, and he considered it a keystone of his crisis theory. However, he knew that verifying empirically system-wide falling profit would be extremely difficult or impossible because of the limited, unreliable data on profits and myriad technical problems in computation of overall profit. He also understood that the various counteracting forces, mentioned above, might slow the process interminably. Moreover, Engels had more serious doubts about the theory than Marx. In a section that Engels added to the third volume of *Capital*, he held that new technologies do not necessarily cause modern industry's profit rates to fall. He also thought that such innovations do not even have to increase the ratio of constant capital costs to variable capital (Engels 1894; Seigel 1993: 336–47). Marx's own uncertainty about his theory of falling profits is manifested by his reference to it as a "tendency" as well as a "law." The debate about falling profits continues today in some Marxist circles, and problems of measurement remain daunting. However, Marx's related points about the future of modern industry and of capitalism have more theoretical and cultural significance today than his problematic theory of the falling rate of profit. For example, it is much easier to gather evidence in support of his arguments about scientific production, centralized capital, monopoly, poverty and unemployment, the "disposable" underclass, financial speculation, cyclical economic crises, and globalization (Marx 1867a: 607–42).

Marx implied that the tendency of the automatic factory to "equalize and reduce" all work below the emergent, salaried elite of technicians, engineers, and managers to machine tending has divergent consequences (1867a: 423). On the one hand, he held that homogenization of labor smashed manufacture's skill hierarchy and facilitated a top-down rationalization; on the other, he claimed that it stirred proletarian class consciousness and politically organized, proletarian class struggles. He thought that workers would develop increased solidarity and militancy in the face of crises arising from the intensifying economic cycle, growing workplace despotism, increasing unemployment, and polarizing wealth.

Marx held that working-class unity is "organized by the very mechanism of the process of capitalist production itself" (1867a: 455–7, 748–51). He thought that proletarians' experience of the combined effects of participating in a cooperative productive process and of being leveled downward together in degraded workplaces and impoverished home lives was an objective basis for shared class interests and revolutionary class consciousness. However, in *Capital*, Marx did not dwell on the victorious proletarian scenario that he and Engels articulated in the *Manifesto*. Also, he acknowledged that modern industry's complex class structure was blunting proletarian solidarity. He gave more systematic attention to structural bases for emancipatory change, rather than political revolution *per se*. He stressed especially capitalism's contradiction between much increased technical capacities for the production of use value, or real wealth, and the ever more frenzied capitalist drive for expanded value.

Marx argued that a progressive sociopolitical transformation was already under way in the most advanced type of capitalism. He pointed to the English Factory Acts as the "first conscious and methodical reaction of society" against unregulated capitalism, and argued that state intervention was a "necessary" facet of modern industry. Although Marx railed against the paltry nature of the Factory Acts (which did more to justify than to eliminate extreme exploitation), he treated them as a precursory sign of more profound changes (e.g., justice and participation for women and children, safer and less monotonous workplaces, and a nondestructive relation to nature), which he believed were called forth by advanced capitalism's "socialized," interdependent nature (1867a: 483–508). He contended that modern industry's concentrated and centralized features, in addition to their various deleterious consequences, forge "cooperation on a large scale" (1867a: 616–23). He equated the trend toward monopolistic collusion, managerial control, and state interference with "the abolition of the capitalist mode of production within the capitalist mode of production itself . . . which *prima facie* represents a mere phase of transition to a new form of production" (1894: 436). He argued that the corporate operations reduce owners to "mere money capitalists," who receive stock dividends, but relinquish effective control of the firm to managers. According to Marx, these huge firms generate "associated production" on a societal-wide scale; the entire populace comes to depend on the continuous coordinated activity of the various corporate operations and, consequently, demands "state interference" to insure that interdependence is maintained. Marx argued that these big stock companies were transforming capitalist productive property into "social capital" and creating the condition for the elimination of private property. In his view, even monopoly or oligopoly producers' efforts to control markets manifest, albeit in a distorted form, "socialization." Marx anticipated Adolf A. Berle's and Gardiner C. Means's Depression Era argument about corporate capitalism's collectivist tendencies and necessary break with unregulated free markets. Marx held that emergent corporate planning, separation of management from ownership, employment of knowledge-based technologies, interfirm cooperation, and increased state regulation were "transitional forms" to an emergent post-capitalist order. His vision of advanced capitalism as "a self-dissolving contradiction" implies the possibility of a peaceful Communist transition that opens the way for proletarian takeover. But he was still well aware that the emergent form of monopoly capitalism allowed the "financial aristocracy" that owned the stock companies to determine how "social labor" was utilized, to appropriate its surpluses, and to "gamble" on the stock markets, and thus cause intense speculative crises and increased instability (Marx 1894: 265, 432–9; Berle and Means 1932).

The relations Marx portrayed in his value theory were rooted in labor-intensive manufacture and competitive markets. Systematically appropriating unpaid labor, he contended, capitalism replays human "prehistory." Following the dialectical method, however, Marx held that basic structural contradictions intensify with mechanization and initiate eventually a determinate negation of capitalism. He thought that modern industry's deeply contradictory fusion of systematic exploitation and employment of collective intelligence contained seeds of an entirely new historical dynamic. From his standpoint, the vastly increased importance of technical knowledge in the production of use value made applied science an increasingly autonomous social force opening new horizons beyond capitalism and value relations and, ultimately, undermining the class and property relations that originally conjured it up. He implied that modern industry refines and suffuses, more widely than ever before, the tacit knowledge of associated producers, and that its application of science rationalizes this knowledge, making it more reflective, deliberate, and ever more social (1857–8b: 92). He stressed emphatically, however, that only a complete severing of the ties between technical knowledge and capitalism could control applied science's destructive tendencies and, finally, decouple production from extraction, coercion, and devastation.

In *Capital*, Marx declared that "modern industry . . . makes science a productive force distinct from labor and presses it into the service of capital" (1867a: 366). As suggested above, his core argument about modern industry states that as automation advances, production of use values depends more and more on accumulated technical knowledge. Depending on appropriation of surplus value, however, Marx argued that industrial capitalists must intensify wage labor and hold back a greater proportion of its product to survive. In the notebooks for *Capital*, Marx spoke of highly automated capitalism, in which "the creation of real wealth becomes less dependent on labor time and the quantity of labor employed," and "depends, rather, upon the general development of science and the progress of technology or application of science in production." He stated that the worker becomes "overseer and regulator," rather than the "main agent" of the productive process, and that the "general intellect" controls production and social life. Marx believed that the combined powers of "general scientific work" and related intricate, system-wide cooperation would dissolve capitalism (1857–8b: 86, 90–2). In a regime characterized by scientifically orchestrated continuous-process production, Marx thought, capitalist accumulation would be based on a profoundly contradictory, vestigial property relation and perpetuation of unnecessary, repressive forms of labor, while use value, or real wealth, would depend on the "objectified power of knowledge." Under this end-game capitalism, Marx declared, "production based upon exchange value collapses, and . . . material production . . . is stripped of its form of indigence and antagonism." Referring to the final decoupling of real wealth from abstract wealth, he said, "Free development of individualities, and hence not the reduction of necessary labor time in order to posit surplus labor, but in general the reduction of necessary labor of society to a minimum, to which corresponds the artistic, scientific, etc., development of individuals made possible by the time thus set free and the means produced for all of them" (1857–8b: 91). According to Marx, science domesticated by communal democratic ends would be deployed to help guide an epochal, emancipatory rupture with all preexisting modes of production. Society and culture based on ruling classes appropriating the surplus product of direct producers would end. Marx dreamed of the moment when his modes of production and value theories would have merely historical relevance.

After capitalism: dictatorship or democracy?

In my view, Marx's materialist method and theory of capitalism constitute his core legacy in social theory. His enormous public significance, however, has derived mainly from his impact on politics and social movements. He has been an inspirational figure for Communist, Socialist, and Social Democratic movements, parties, and regimes, Left-leaning labor movements, anti-colonial insurgencies, liberation struggles, radical student movements, radical Left terrorism, revolutionary regimes, and even certain "post-Marxist" movements. Yet their identification with him has probably derived as much, or even more, from what they perceive him to stand for (e.g., social justice, revolution) than from the explicit content of his social theory or of his critique of capitalism. Marx advocated the unity of theory and praxis, but his political thought about democracy has contradictory facets. He did not elaborate a detailed theory of post-capitalism, even though he embraced communism as a normative ideal and participated in the early Communist movement. According to his historicist method of immanent critique, the prospects for fundamental change depend on the specific historical situation and particular level of development. In Marx's view, divergent social contexts require different types of agency, and forbid a comprehensive, general blueprint of post-capitalism in advance. His emphasis on local knowledge and local conditions has been ignored by the later twentieth-century critics who treat him as the prototypical "totalizer." Even in Marx's and Engels's most famous programmatic statement about communism – the *Manifesto*'s ten-point program on the "transitional" proletarian dictatorship – they stated that the "measures will of course be different in different countries" (Marx and Engels 1848: 505). In a new preface, nearly 25 years later, they repeated the qualification emphatically, saying that "practical application" of their principles depends "everywhere and at all times, on the obtaining historical conditions." They added that times had indeed changed, and that their ten-point program needed to be revised and should no longer be stressed (Marx and Engels 1872). They said that they left the work unrevised to preserve it as a "historical document." It is ironic that no other facet of their work has been embraced more avidly by Communist regimes and movements than these two pages.

Images of post-capitalism can be gleaned from mostly brief statements and asides in various parts of Marx's and Engels's writings. Generally, they held that capitalist ownership, investment, and profits would be eliminated, and that public administration would perform functions provided formerly by capitalist markets, firms, and states. They argued that a substantial amount of surplus would be held back for social purposes, and that the rest would be apportioned according to a person's contribution and need. They also suggested that a full Communist regime would be a "community" or "association"; people would be conscious of their interdependence, act in concert, and even sacrifice to sustain it, but they would cultivate individuality as well. Marx and Engels identified fully developed, collective agency with effective social planning. In *Capital*, Marx said that "a community of free individuals" would operate their productive forces "in common," and that each person's labor would be "*consciously* applied" (my emphasis) as part of the community's "combined labor power" (i.e., "a definite social plan" would coordinate work with wants). Although qualifying that programs and methods would vary according to a community's "productive organization" and "historical development," he stressed that, in any setting, freely associated people would treat labor and product as part of a social process and as shared wealth, rather than as individual activity and private property (Marx 1867a: 89–90). His point is that a social plan devolving from such views would have a transparency, efficiency, and justice lacking under capitalist commodity fetishism. Similarly, Engels held that "systematic, definite organization" would end the anarchy of production and war of all against all, raising society above "mere animal conditions of existence into really human ones."

He said that people would make their history "more and more consciously"; their social interventions would be more intelligent and directive, and, consequently, the "social causes" they unleash would increasingly have their intended consequences (Engels 1892: 321–4). Marx held that the "settled plan" of a highly developed, fully socialized regime would evaporate all traces of capitalism's "mystical veil." But such a regime, he asserted, requires "a certain material groundwork" arising from a "long and painful process of development." He did not suggest that this condition, or emancipatory moment, was near at hand (Marx 1867a: 90–1).

In the ten-point program of the *Manifesto*, Marx and Engels argued that a Communist revolution must first seize control of the state from the bourgeoisie and allow the proletariat to organize itself as the ruling class. This strategy would provide the proletarian leadership with the political and administrative apparatus to end capitalist property relations, suppress counterrevolutionary opposition, and initiate a transition to communism. Marx and Engels held that the leadership would centralize the primary means of production and infrastructure (e.g., banking, communication, transportation), "increase the total productive forces as rapidly as possible," and create "industrial armies." Although suggesting other reforms (e.g., free education, progressive income tax), they called for a near total centralization of power in a much enlarged state, which they acknowledged would have to employ "despotic" force to expropriate the capitalists and modernize society. They held that, at the end of the transition, "class distinctions" would be eradicated totally, society would be a "vast association," and "public power will lose its political character." They imply that the huge public apparatus would have sweeping legitimacy; debates would focus on policy implementation, rather than on the system's very existence (i.e., the entire publicly owned productive system and huge social welfare operation would be accepted like public roads are today). Marx and Engels suggested that the state would be transformed from a means to enforce class domination to a benign system of administration. They conclude that communism would be "an association, in which the free development of each is the condition for the free development of all." In the revolutionary times, when the *Manifesto* was written, young Marx and Engels were not inclined to warn their readers that this emancipatory moment might be a very hard road or a long way off (Marx and Engels 1848: 503–6).

In the much later *Critique of the Gotha Programme*, Marx spoke of the Communist transition in a coldly realistic, even gloomy tone. He said that the transitional regime, or "first phase of communism," would be "in every respect, economically, morally, and intellectually, still stamped with the birthmarks of the old society from whose womb it emerges." He also spoke very briefly of a "higher phase of communist society" in which productive force development will have freed people from the division of labor, and a consequent cultural renaissance will have nurtured "all-round development of the individual" and prepared people for participatory, self-managed association. Marx thought that full communism requires a radical rupture with capitalism and an epochal transformation of institutions, culture, and selves. All this presumes a much higher level of material and sociocultural development, requiring a very long period of gestation (1875: 85, 87). He explained that communism has to be built initially on capitalist foundations. For example, sweeping planning capacities cannot be created *de novo*, but must draw on resources of the former capitalist regime. Planners would have to borrow methods employed by capitalist firms and states, especially their uses of science and technology in production, distribution, and administration. Marx thought that these partially socialized facets of capitalism would be enhanced greatly after capitalists were expropriated and productive property socialized. However, he knew that planners would still face the very hard task of remaking science and technology incrementally and experimentally to fit the new regime's emergent conditions. Marx scolded Socialist radicals who promised full communism and copious benefits to workers as soon as their party comes to power. He argued that their promises will be deflated quickly and will result in certain political failure (1875: 81–8). By contrast, he held that a major portion of each worker's surplus product would have to be held back to pay for expanded public administration, schools, welfare, and other public services, as well as to cope with crises. Marx also contended that the new regime would have to reinvest huge amounts of surplus in scientific-technical development and expanded production to create a material base for full emancipation. He argued that the labor process could not be revolutionized immediately, and that people would still be paid unequally. He believed that a new transitional regime would eliminate some terrible bourgeois abuses, but he stressed that it would retain many capitalist "defects." He also thought that it would face opposition and would not easily achieve the popular legitimacy that he and Engels referred to passingly in the *Manifesto*. Three years after the aforementioned qualification about the *Manifesto*'s program of transition, Marx reasserted the need for a transition to communism "in which the state can be nothing but *the revolutionary dictatorship of the proletariat*" (1875: 95). And now he stressed emphatically that full emancipation was definitely not on the near horizon.

Explaining the need for the "strictest centralization" a few years after the *Manifesto*, Marx and Engels argued that Communists should not "be misguided by the democratic talk of freedom for the communities, of self-government etc." (1850a: 285). They were responding to the counter-revolutionary climate that followed the 1848 revolutions and the ideological use of democratic rhetoric to derail radical labor movements and justify top-down bourgeois rule. More generally, however, they believed that capitalism's representative, or parliamentary, political structures and civil society (i.e., private organizations, associations, and media) were distorted totally by bourgeois money, power, and culture, and thus were devoid of resources for sociopolitical and cultural reconstruction. As early as *On the Jewish Question* (1843d), Marx held that capitalism's perverted, possessive individualism ruled in state and civil society. He saw bourgeois democracy and the remains of traditional associations (e.g., Judaism) as barriers to proletarian solidarity and emancipation, which needed to be swept away. In the *Gotha Programme* essay, Marx spoke in a totally disparaging way about the "democratic republic" and bourgeois "freedom of conscience." His idea of "capitalist *society*" (my emphasis) implied that bourgeois property relations and mystification suffused the entirety of its primary political associations and political culture (1875: 94–8). But he did not reject democracy *per se*. Stressing that full communism would be free of top-down rule, he implied that it would be self-managed by associated producers. The problem is that Marx saw liberal democracy as so bankrupt that mediating institutions to build participatory habits and values would be absent at the start of proletarian rule. Then what prepares the way for radical democracy? Neither Marx's view of revolutionary proletarian politics transforming into transitional Communist dictatorship nor his idea of accentuating late capitalist economic rationalization to build a material foundation for full communism articulates historical bases for nurturing democratic association and culture. Marx did not explain how the demos could possibly constrain the proposed dictatorship, how the party leadership could avert seduction by *carte blanche* power, or how they could even visualize and plan for democracy. How could such a centrally administered regime forge the types of citizenship, groups, values, selves, and imagination needed for Marx's ultimate goal of a self-regulating, emancipated society of "associated producers"? In this light, his "higher stage" of communism would, at some point, have to be created *de novo*.

A sharply opposing scenario to nearly everything said above appears in Marx's impassioned report on the Paris Commune, *The Civil War in France* (Marx 1871: 328–43). In this essay, he embraced enthusiastically the two-month insurgency, celebrating its "positive form of the Republic," its decentralized, participatory features, which his comments about the need for a transitional dictatorship seemed to rule out. Marx said that the Commune reduced officials' pay to the level of workers' wages and began to abolish private productive property and establish full "cooperative production." However, he did not dwell on economic matters or stress the material bases and material limits of the new regime. Rather, his ebullient portrayal emphasized the new regime's self-managed political and social relations. He held that the Commune working class did not expect "miracles," and that their greatest achievement was the regime's "working existence," which was forged pragmatically by average people employing participatory means, rather than by a political vanguard and scientific planning elite asserting total power in the name of a hoped-for Communist utopia. Marx described how the Commune reduced social inequality, dismantled capitalist and clerical power, instituted short terms of office, extended suffrage, established governance by a participatory assembly, exercised public openness about its problems and defects, and even created "cheap government" by disbanding the army and debureaucratizing administration. Contradicting his idea that radical democracy requires a long gestation, he portrayed "plain" working people, who lacked experience in politics and administration, rising to the occasion immediately, harmonizing prudence with radical democratic ideals and undergoing personal transformation in the process. He implied that they were committed to their duties and motivated by social ends, rather than private interests. Marx reported similar tendencies among "all the healthy" elements of other classes, including some functionaries of the old regime. Finally, he spoke graphically of the "self-sacrificing heroism of men, women, and children," defending their new democracy against the national army and paying with "heaps of corpses" (Marx 1871: 348–55; Marx and Engels 1971).

Leaving aside questions of historical accuracy, Marx's Paris Commune essay expresses a side of his later political thought, appearing in scattered places throughout his work as well as in this essay, that clashes with his passages on dictatorship and expands the democratic ideas of his youthful, pre-Communist days. Here, he converges with radical democrats (e.g., John Dewey), who argue that emancipatory goals can be reached only through active employment of democratic means and through direct, local democratic participation, which cultivate the type of human being capable of building democracy on a wider scale. However, Marx's essay leaves problematic questions. Was the Commune initiating an immediate leap to the "higher stage" of communism, or was it a transitory moment of revolutionary solidarity? Could radical democracy have been sustained? Regrettably, the Commune was too short-lived to address these questions, being crushed brutally by the national army. Moreover, how can this essay be harmonized with Marx's advocacy of the transitional dictatorship? Overall, Marx's political writings manifest the inherent complexity and ambiguities of instituting revolutionary change and radical democracy together. Are these two goals compatible? Are they possible? No political theorist has yet resolved these problems. Marx and other radicals may well be right that we can find out the answer only through practice and experimentation. And critics are right to ask, at what costs?

Neoclassical economists and other neoliberal critics claim that social planning is doomed to bureaucratic inefficiency, and that only competitive markets could effectively process vastly complicated information about production and consumption and harmonize supply and demand. They

also contend that political control of the economy leads inevitably to authoritarianism; the expansion of the state and the abrogation of productive
property rights undermine other political and cultural rights. These critics
were prescient about Soviet-style, total-planning regimes, but they failed
to anticipate the successes of twentieth-century mixed regimes; thus,
post-Second World War social democracies placed substantial limits on
private productive property, nationalized some industries, redistributed
income, and established large social welfare systems, and have been usually considered, outside of neoliberal circles, global leaders in human rights,
political rights, and democratic inclusion. Their decommodified public
goods, at least for a time, attained broad legitimacy, and debates over them
shifted to instrumental matters of cost, efficiency, and technique. However,
post-Second World War advances in social rights, substantive equality,
and living standards, ironically, weakened the impetus of labor's struggle
for full socialism. Similar taming of labor's political goals occurred in other
postwar, advanced capitalist societies (Przeworski 1985). Nevertheless,
postwar social democracy demonstrated that partly socialized regimes can
work efficiently and democratically. Finally, neoliberal critics do not confront the failure of market-centered institutions to provide for the needs
of the poor, cope with economic inequality, or foster social solidarity.

Marx referred to proletarian dictatorship infrequently in his overall
corpus of work. Moreover, his comments on the topic were brief. Some
thinkers argue that these points were a sidetrack, and that his overall work
was fundamentally democratic (Draper 1987). However, Marx's affirmative
view of technical and organizational facets of capitalist rationalization, his
enthusiasm for modernization and socialization, and his argument that
early communism must build on the structure of late capitalist firms
and states have an affinity for centralized authority. Twentieth-century
"Communists" deployed these themes to justify forced modernization,
top-down planning, bureaucratic domination, and general oppression.
Moreover, Marx did not address the very complex technical issues
involved in creating a substitute for markets. His optimistic comments
about the future of applied science and planning under communism
manifested a somewhat uncritical faith in "science" and in the emergent
strata of technicians and planners. His critics argue that these comments favor technocracy. Marx left vague the political processes by
which "associated producers" would create and implement the plan. Who
would plan? How would the planners be selected? By what political means
would they be regulated? How would the demos be represented?
Radical democrats argue that upholding democratic goals by undemo-
cratic means ultimately deflates the original principles, and ends in
despotism of some sort. Marx did not focus on this profound problem of
how to mesh democratic means with his ultimate democratic principles
and thereby to avert the problem of democratic formalism, which he

dissected so brilliantly and sharply in his youthful critique of Hegel's theory of the state. But there is a deeply democratic side to Marx's work. He stressed repeatedly and emphatically the need for universal provision of the means of participation and of substantive freedom; he urged the elimination of unnecessary suffering, and reminded us that there can be no peace without justice. More than any of his analytical tools, these values, which suffuse his texts and are inscribed in his very name, have animated interest in his ideas across the globe. Global neoliberalism's silence and disregard concerning such matters of social justice open the way for Marx to be rediscovered.

Marx after Communism

In 1989, the collapse of Eastern European communism and the Chinese state's repression of the reform movement in Tiananmen Square were benchmark events in the erosion of global communism. Its legitimacy had been long been under challenge, because of its politically repressive and economically inefficient aspects. However, by the late 1980s, Communist regimes were either on the verge of collapse or forced to adopt more market-oriented economic policies. Communist national liberation movements faltered in the Third World, and in highly developed capitalist democracies, Socialist and Social Democratic parties lost political ground or shifted to more market-oriented policies. Amplifying the politics of 1989, American neoconservative Francis Fukuyama posed his very well-publicized "end of history" argument, holding that Hegel's vision of the "liberal state" as the highest possible realization of "rationality and freedom" has been vindicated by "the monumental failure of Marxism as a basis for real-world societies." Fukuyama implied that Western capitalist society, especially the United States, is the absolute pinnacle of human sociopolitical development. He suggested that we may now be "at a point where we cannot imagine a world substantially different than our own," or where it does not seem possible that, in the future, we could ever make a "fundamental improvement over our current order." He was speaking of the "neoliberal" regimes that were recently brought into being by the Thatcher–Reagan revolution, which returned liberal democracy to free-market, free-trade, and lower tax policies (i.e., scaling back post-Second World War regulation, redistribution, and welfare). Fukuyama's reference to the "end of history" meant that there are no plausible alternatives to the stripped-down liberal state, and that no ideological competitor could claim convincingly that it could be more effective and just. He contended that neoliberalism was spreading over the globe and would soon exist wherever people choose modernity over backwardness. He attributed to the liberal state and society the type of sweeping legitimacy that Marx claimed for second-phase, or full, communism. Fukuyama concluded that history had stood Marx, rather than Hegel, "right-side up" (Fukuyama 1989; 1992: 51, 62–7).

A decade later, Thomas L. Friedman's bestseller, *The Lexus and the Olive Tree*, confirms the arrival of the global capitalism that Fukuyama predicted. Friedman portrays neoliberal globalization as a "golden straightjacket" – its wealth-producing benefits are so great that any country wishing to avoid poverty has no choice but to join the process. He contends that there is no middle ground between state control and markets, and that the postwar type of regulatory, redistributive, welfare regime cannot be revived once neoliberal policies are in place (Friedman 2000). He sees the neoliberal program of deregulated markets, free trade, and, especially, enhanced investor access to the business information, financial instruments, and technologies needed for on-line trading as the economic and social equivalent to tearing down the Berlin Wall. In this regard, he treats the neoliberal revival in the United States as a beacon to the entire world. Embracing effusively the US stock-market boom of the middle and late 1990s, he argues that markets have defeated – even routed – politics. Political choices being reduced to "Pepsi or Coke," he claims, the "Electronic Herd" of on-line investors now make the important decisions that make the economy grow and that determine the overall development of sociocultural life. The state becomes their servant. Friedman celebrates rule by investors as a "democratic revolution." He is not bothered by the fact that the majority of Americans, who own little or no stock, are excluded from the decision-making process, or that a tiny number of rich stockholders, empowered by their huge stock portfolios, dominate the overall process (whether they are citizens or not). Outside the United States, stockholders of any type are a small or tiny minority. Friedman sees the staggering power of the mostly American "Electronic Herd" in international markets as ultimately serving human progress.

Friedman states that the neoliberal United States is a "winner take all society"; already large class divisions grow substantially wider. He also acknowledges that deregulated capitalism increases the huge class divides in poor countries and causes enormous social disruptions there. For Friedman, investor empowerment is the real measure of "democracy" (rather than participation or representation of the overall populace). In his view, the fruits of investor decisions will, at some point, improve the condition of the whole populace. Friedman argues that neoliberal globalization offers the only workable model for development. A Clinton Democrat, he agrees with Fukuyama's view that the postwar era's big social programs (e.g., the American war on poverty) are no longer feasible, and that free markets are the only hope for the poor. On the back cover of the book, Fukuyama states that Friedman penetrates "the real character of the new world order." The convergence between Friedman and

Fukuyama reflects a broader consensus, at the millennium, between the two leading US political parties over deregulation, free trade, and neoliberal globalization. As Friedman states, neoliberalism, the so-called "Washington consensus," has attained almost worldwide hegemony. His vision of a stockholders' republic, in which wealthy investors reap the benefits of an international division of labor and dominate with a minimum of political regulation, implies that the global capitalism that Marx predicted has finally become a reality.

Marx's view of the capitalist locomotive flattening traditional structures is a troublesome and, perhaps, naive idea to some thinkers. Marx himself had doubts about the scenario near the end of his life, suggesting that it might be limited to Western Europe (Marx 1881). Yet a case could be made that later twentieth-century, neoliberal globalization has realized his fears about capitalist leveling. The more capitalism triumphs globally, especially in its current highly unregulated and unequal neoliberal form, the more likely Marx's theory will have renewed critical value. His theory poses basic questions about loosening restrictions on property rights, reducing regulation, and recommodifying public goods. Treated as a heuristic tool, his materialist approach need not diminish the importance of culture or the importance of other critical theories that focus on matters other than class. And perhaps the movements of 1989 have decoupled Marx from association with authoritarian, Soviet-style Communist regimes. After communism, Marx's emphasis on the tension between "abstract wealth" and "real wealth" has renewed pertinence in the current climate of global capitalism's economic polarization and substantial expansion of the power and privilege of propertied wealth. His core argument, that the benefits of real wealth generated by capitalism's scientifically mediated production should be extended in a much wider, more just fashion, poses sharp critical questions about the current tendency to treat as tolerable, and even as inevitable, the increasing misery, drudgery, and insecurity of less advantaged people, while private wealth and privileged life-styles grow explosively for the fewer fortunate ones. One does not have to accept Marx's overall theoretical position or his communism to appreciate the heuristic value of his social theory. At the millennium, some thinkers and activists have begun to question whether the trend toward a global "shareholders' society" that gives primacy to property rights ought to be shifted in the direction of a "stakeholders' society" that favors rights of participation. In this context, Marx's specter is visible again; his social theory is still a vital point of departure for an alternative way of seeing, thinking, and inquiring.

The intent of this volume is to draw together portions of Marx's thought that will provide the reader with a clear idea of his overall project and that shed light on neoliberal capitalism. This volume will provide (1) integrated Marx readings that cover core facets of his overall analytical approach and his theory of capitalist modernity; (2) contemporary (post-1990) readings that address neoliberal capitalism and globalization and that illustrate the pertinence of Marx's thought; (3) part introductions that clarify main points of the readings, explain the contexts, and link each piece to Marx's overall work. The Marx readings are organized analytically, in order to bring the key features of his thought to the fore and help readers learn the framework of this thought. All chapters in Section I are by Marx unless specified otherwise.

The contemporary selections, in Section II, address pressing social issues that relate to major themes in the Marx readings. Although some of the contributors have been influenced by Marx, most of them use non-Marxist approaches. Rather than illustrate recent Marxist scholarship, my intention is to provide materials that provoke critical thought about how key facets of Marx's thought converge with and diverge from today's lived realities. Below, David Harvey writes about requiring undergraduate students, in his course on *Capital*, to complete a final paper on the relevance of Marx's ideas to issues reported in recent *New York Times* articles. He implies that this project helps his students learn and appreciate Marx, regardless of their political values. Harvey asserts that, after the return to dominance of unrestricted or "free-market" capitalism, it is not hard to connect Marx's thought to contemporary life. One simply has to be introduced to Marx, and have his or her attention turned to the relevant materials. The contemporary readings below are drawn from social science as well as from popular sources; but the logic of selection parallels Harvey's strategy, aiming to facilitate learning about Marx by encouraging readers to think critically about the fit of his ideas to current conditions. Most of the readings pertain to the leading role of the United States in the revival of free-market capitalism, or neoliberalism, and the process of globalization. They also address the impact of this form of global capitalism on other parts of the world.

SECTION I: MARX READINGS

part 1

Marx's Vision of History: "Historical Materialism"

This part focuses on the broader conceptual framework, or overall view of history and human nature, that informed Marx's analysis of capitalism. With the help of Engels, Marx formulated this metatheory in his early writings before moving to England and beginning serious work on economic issues. The first three selections are drawn from Marx's and Engels's "Feuerbach" essay, or the first comprehensive statement of their materialist vision of history. Appearing in *The German Ideology* (written in late 1845 and 1846, but not published in full until 1932), this essay states emphatically the central premises of Marx's work: that people "must be in a position to live in order to be able to 'make history'," and that consciousness is "a social product." Marx and Engels deployed these simple presuppositions against German philosophy and historiography, which gave primacy to "ideas" or "consciousness" and ignored or understated the role of material factors in political and cultural affairs. Marx's and Engels's counter-argument about the primacy of biological needs (e.g., for food and shelter) does not diminish the importance of sociocultural practices. By contrast, they considered language and other complex social institutions as defining attributes of humanity's distinct "historical being." In their view, sociocultural and historical variations, largely absent among other animals, manifest humanity's unique capacity for linguistically or culturally mediated, and thus highly complex, cooperative productive activities. Most important, Marx's materialism is a *social conception*; its presuppositions oppose the individualistic premises of Adam Smith and other free-market liberals, and provide a basis for a vision of the economy as a socio-cultural complex.

The Feuerbach essay establishes *mode of production* and *class* as central analytical concepts; members of a class share a common location in a mode of production's characteristic types of division of labor and forms of property. Marx and Engels assert that class has an "independent existence as against individuals," influencing substantially a person's "position in life" and "personal development," regardless of his or her will. Although acknowledging individuality, they hold that individual actions, capacities, and differences are conditioned powerfully by a person's sociocultural contexts. In particular, they imply that class location is the source of fundamental constraints and opportunities that have nearly unavoidable, and even life-defining, consequences for every individual sharing a common position in the class hierarchy. Marx and Engels hold that class exerts a similarly broad determining influence on the rest of sociocultural life. For example, they contend that the *ruling class*, which controls the means of production and its surplus product, dominates intellectually as well as economically and politically. In their view, regulation of the cultural domain by the ruling class may not always be direct or all-encompassing, but it usually exerts substantial influence over the dominant modes of expression (especially in vital political and economic matters) and obscures the role of its own material and class interest. Overall, Marx and Engels considered classes to be the main agents of historical development, shaping sociocultural life through their collective actions and struggles.

Marx's famous preface to *A Contribution to the Critique of Political Economy* (1859) summarized briefly the historical materialist concepts that informed his mature analysis of capitalism, and stressed, most centrally, that a society's mode of production determines its *superstructure*, or its ensemble of legal and political institutions and closely related forms of *social consciousness*. Marx also contended that superstructure justifies and perpetuates the material base, but that this functional relationship is eventually upset by technical progress. In his view, class conflicts arise in response to outmoded legal and political institutions and ideologies, which cannot justify or support effectively the emergent productive forces, and thus stunt or "fetter" their development. However, he held that, in the long run, materially based social progress was inevitable, arising from the refinement of productive forces, revolutionary responses to consequent societal contradictions, and emergence of new ruling classes that support the rise of nascent, more advanced modes of production. Marx asserted that capitalism's powerful productive forces and new class dynamics constitute the "last antagonistic" mode of production, and will bring into being an entirely new social formation that will end the human "prehistory" of class domination and extraction. He implies, here, technologically determined, evolutionary progress, which guarantees an emancipatory political outcome. This facet of Marx's historical materialism contradicts its more qualified, historically contingent, sociological side. Some Marxists later fashioned the deterministic aspect of his approach into an orthodox ideology of Communist movements, parties, and regimes (i.e., "dialectical materialism"). This orthodoxy became a focal point of critiques by twentieth-century "critical Marxists" and non-Marxists. In the selection below from the third volume of *Capital*, Marx restates very succinctly and clearly the core idea of his historical materialism and central analytical theme of his magnum opus: the social mechanisms or institutions whereby "surplus labor is pumped out of direct producers" is the "hidden basis of the entire social structure." But he argued that this fundamental, and almost always ideologically distorted, matter is manifested in "innumerable different historical circumstances." This version of his materialism is still sweeping, but does not offer a warranty for sociopolitical progress. Rather, it suggests a conceptual tool, or heuristic device, to orient empirical inquiry about variable social forms and contingent consequences of extractive relations between dominant classes and direct producers.

The two selections from Engels manifest the contradictory sides of historical materialism. The first portrays Marx's metatheory as a major scientific discovery that returns history to its "real basis" (later Engels claimed that it paralleled the Darwinian revolution in biology). By contrast, the second, Engels's letter to Joseph Bloch, confessed that he and Marx sometimes overstated their approach in heated polemical battles with opponents, and thus were partly to blame for the ahistorical, economistic determinism that had arisen among younger "Marxists." Engels argued emphatically that the qualified, sociological version of historical materialism was Marx's real or intended position. However, this tension did not disappear in twentieth-century Marxism, perhaps because it is entwined with Marxist efforts to unify theory and practice, or science and politics. Yet, a similar tension between historically contingent approaches and mechanistic evolutionary progressivism has often appeared in other modern social theories, manifesting broader tensions between social-scientific methods and optimistic hopes about the potentialities of modernity and, especially, of modern science.

chapter 1

Primary Historical Relations, or The Basic Aspects of Social Activity (with Engels) (1845–6)

... the first premise of all human existence and, therefore, of all history, the premise, namely, that men must be in a position to live in order to be able to "make history". But life involves before everything else eating and drinking, housing, clothing and various other things. The first historical act is thus the production of the means to satisfy these needs, the production of material life itself. And indeed this is an historical act, a fundamental condition of all history, which today, as thousands of years ago, must daily and hourly be fulfilled merely in order to sustain human life. Even when the sensuous world is reduced to a minimum, to a stick as with Saint Bruno, it presupposes the action of producing this stick. Therefore in any conception of history one has first of all to observe this fundamental fact in all its significance and all its implications and to accord it its due importance. It is well known that the Germans have never done this, and they have never, therefore, had an *earthly* basis for history and consequently never a historian. ...

The second point is that the satisfaction of the first need, the action of satisfying and the instrument of satisfaction which has been acquired, leads to new needs; and this creation of new needs is the first historical act. ...

The third circumstance which, from the very outset, enters into historical development, is that men, who daily re-create their own life, begin to make other men, to propagate their kind: the relation between man and woman, parents and children, the *family*. The family, which to begin with is the only social relation, becomes later, when increased needs create new social relations and the increased population new needs, a subordinate one ... and must then be treated and analysed according to the existing empirical data, not according to "the concept of the family" ...

These three aspects of social activity are not of course to be taken as three different stages, but just as three aspects or ... three "moments", which have existed simultaneously since the dawn of history and the first men, and which still assert themselves in history today.

The production of life, both of one's own in labour and of fresh life in procreation, now appears as a twofold relation: on the one hand as a natural, on the other as a social relation – social in the sense that it denotes the co-operation of several individuals, no matter under what conditions, in what manner and to what end. It follows from this that a certain mode of production, or industrial stage, is always combined with a certain mode of co-operation, or social stage, and this mode of co-operation is itself a "productive force". Further, that the aggregate of productive forces accessible to men determines the condition of society, hence, the "history of humanity" must always be studied and treated in relation to the history of industry and exchange. . . . Thus it is quite obvious from the start that there exists a materialist connection of men with one another, which is determined by their needs and their mode of production, and which is as old as men themselves. This connection is ever taking on new forms, and thus presents a "history" irrespective of the existence of any political or religious nonsense which would especially hold men together.

Only now, after having considered four moments, four aspects of primary historical relations, do we find that man also possesses "consciousness". But even from the outset this is not "pure" consciousness. The "mind" is from the outset afflicted with the curse of being "burdened" with matter, which here makes its appearance in the form of agitated layers of air, sounds, in short, of language. Language is as old as consciousness, language *is* practical, real consciousness that exists for other men as well, and only therefore does it also exist for me; language, like consciousness, only arises from the need, the necessity, of intercourse with other men. Where there exists a relationship, it exists for me: the animal does not "*relate*" itself to anything, it does not "*relate*" itself at all. For the animal its relation to others does not exist as a relation. Consciousness is, therefore, from the very beginning a social product, and remains so as long as men exist at all. Consciousness is at first, of course, merely consciousness concerning the *immediate* sensuous environment and consciousness of the limited connection with other persons and things outside the individual who is growing self-conscious. At the same time it is consciousness of nature, which first confronts men as a completely alien, all-powerful and unassailable force, with which men's relations are purely animal and by which they are overawed like beasts; it is thus a purely animal consciousness of nature (natural religion) precisely because nature is as yet hardly altered by history – on the other hand, it is man's consciousness of the necessity of associating with the individuals around him, the beginning of the consciousness that he is living in society at all. This beginning is as animal as social life itself at this stage. It is mere herd-consciousness, and at this point man is distinguished from sheep only by the fact that with him consciousness takes the place of instinct or that his instinct is a conscious one. This sheep-like or tribal consciousness receives its further development and extension through increased productivity, the increase of needs, and, what is fundamental to both of these, the increase of population. With these there develops the division of labour, which was originally nothing but the division of labour in the sexual act, then the division of labour which develops spontaneously or "naturally" by virtue of natural predisposition (e.g., physical strength), needs, accidents, etc., etc. Division of labour only becomes truly such from the moment when a division of material and mental labour appears. From this moment onwards consciousness *can* really flatter itself that it is something other than consciousness of existing practice, that it *really* represents something without representing something real; from now on consciousness is in a position to emancipate itself from the world and to proceed to the formation of "pure" theory, theology, philosophy, morality, etc. But even if this theory, theology, philosophy, morality, etc., come into contradiction with the existing relations, this can only occur because existing social relations have come into contradiction with existing productive forces; moreover, in a particular national sphere of relations this can also occur through the contradiction, arising not within the national orbit, but between this national consciousness and the practice of other nations. . . .

Incidentally, it is quite immaterial what consciousness starts to do on its own: out of all this trash we get only the one inference that these three moments, the productive forces, the state of society and consciousness, can and must come into contradiction with one another, because the *division of labour* implies the possibility, nay the fact, that intellectual and material activity, that enjoyment and labour, production and consumption, devolve on different individuals, and that the only possibility of their not coming into contradiction lies in negating in its turn the division of labour. It is self-evident, moreover, that "spectres", "bonds", "the higher being", "concept", "scruple", are merely idealist, speculative, mental expressions, the concepts apparently of the isolated individual, the mere images of very empirical fetters and limitations, within which move the mode of production of life, and the form of intercourse coupled with it. . . .

chapter 2

The Ruling Class and the Ruling Ideas ... (with Engels) (1845–6)

The ideas of the ruling class are in every epoch the ruling ideas: i.e., the class which is the ruling *material* force of society is at the same time its ruling *intellectual* force. The class which has the means of material production at its disposal, consequently also controls the means of mental production, so that the ideas of those who lack the means of mental production are on the whole subject to it. The ruling ideas are nothing more than the ideal expression of the dominant material relations, the dominant material relations grasped as ideas; hence of the relations which make the one class the ruling one, therefore, the ideas of its dominance. The individuals composing the ruling class possess among other things consciousness, and therefore think. Insofar, therefore, as they rule as a class and determine the extent and compass of an historical epoch, it is self-evident that they do this in its whole range, hence among other things rule also as thinkers, as producers of ideas, and regulate the production and distribution of the ideas of their age: thus their ideas are the ruling ideas of the epoch. For instance, in an age and in a country where royal power, aristocracy and bourgeoisie are contending for domination and where, therefore, domination is shared, the doctrine of the separation of powers proves to be the dominant idea and is expressed as an "eternal law".

The division of labour, ... one of the chief forces of history up till now, manifests itself also in the ruling class as the division of mental and material labour, so that inside this class one part appears as the thinkers of the class (its active, conceptive ideologists, who make the formation of the illusions of the class about itself their chief source of livelihood), while the others' attitude to these ideas and illusions is more passive and receptive, because they are in reality the active members of this class and have less time to make up illusions and ideas about themselves. Within this class this cleavage can even develop into a certain opposition and hostility between the two parts, but whenever a practical collision occurs in which the class itself is endangered they automatically vanish, in which case there also vanishes the appearance of the ruling ideas being not the ideas of the ruling class and having a power distinct from the power of this class. The existence of revolutionary ideas in a particular period presupposes the existence of a revolutionary class. . . .

If now in considering the course of history we detach the ideas of the ruling class from the ruling class itself and attribute to them an independent existence, if we confine ourselves to saying that these or those ideas were dominant at a given time, without bothering ourselves about the conditions of production and the producers of these ideas, if we thus ignore the individuals and world conditions which are the source of the ideas, then we can say, for instance, that during the time the aristocracy was dominant, the concepts honour, loyalty, etc., were dominant, during the dominance of the bourgeoisie the concepts freedom, equality, etc. The ruling class itself on the whole imagines this to be so. This conception of history, which is common to all historians, particularly since the eighteenth century, will necessarily come up against the phenomenon that ever more abstract ideas hold sway, i.e., ideas which increasingly take on the form of universality. For each new class which puts itself in the place of one ruling before it is compelled, merely in order to carry through its aim, to present its interest as the common interest of all the members of society, that is, expressed in ideal form: it has to give its ideas the form of universality, and present them as the only rational, universally valid ones. The class making a revolution comes forward from the very start, if only because it is opposed to a *class*, not as a class but as the representative of the whole of society, as the whole mass of society confronting the one ruling class. It can do this because initially its interest really is as yet mostly connected with the common interest of all other non-ruling classes, because under the pressure of hitherto existing conditions its interest has not yet been able to develop as the particular interest of a particular class. Its victory, therefore, benefits also many individuals of other classes which are not winning a dominant position, but only insofar as it now enables these individuals to raise themselves into the ruling class. . . .

Once the ruling ideas have been separated from the ruling individuals and, above all, from the relations which result from a given stage of the mode of production, and in this way the conclusion has been reached that history is always under the sway of ideas, it is very easy to abstract from these various ideas "the Idea", the thought, etc., as the dominant force in history, and thus to consider all these separate ideas and concepts as "forms of self-determination" of the Concept developing in history. It follows then naturally, too, that all the relations of men can be derived from the concept of man, man as conceived, the essence of man, Man. This has been done by speculative philosophy. Hegel himself confesses . . . that he "has considered the progress of *the concept* only" and has represented in history the "true *theodicy*". Now one can go back again to the producers of "the concept", to the theorists, ideologists and philosophers, and one comes then to the conclusion that the philosophers, the thinkers as such, have at all times been dominant in history: a conclusion, as we see, already expressed by Hegel. . . .

This historical method which reigned in Germany, and especially the reason why, must be explained from its connection with the illusion of ideologists in general, e.g., the illusions of the jurists, politicians (including the practical statesmen), from the dogmatic dreamings and distortions of these fellows; this is explained perfectly easily from their practical position in life, their job, and the division of labour.

Whilst in ordinary life every shopkeeper is very well able to distinguish between what somebody professes to be and what he really is, our historiography has not yet won this trivial insight. It takes every epoch at its word and believes that everything it says and imagines about itself is true.

chapter 3

The Formation of Classes . . . (with Engels) (1845–6)

. . . In the Middle Ages the citizens in each town were compelled to unite against the landed nobility to defend themselves. The extension of trade, the establishment of communications, led separate towns to establish contacts with other towns, which had asserted the same interests in the struggle with the same antagonist. Out of the many local communities of citizens in the various towns there arose only gradually the middle *class*. The conditions of life of the individual citizens became – on account of their contradiction to the existing relations and of the mode of labour determined by this – conditions which were common to them all and independent of each individual. The citizens created these conditions insofar as they had torn themselves free from feudal ties, and were in their turn created by them insofar as they were determined by their antagonism to the feudal system which they found in existence. With the setting up of intercommunications between the individual towns, these common conditions developed into class conditions. The same conditions, the same contradiction, the same interests were bound to call forth on the whole similar customs everywhere. The bourgeoisie itself develops only gradually together with its conditions, splits according to the division of labour into various sections and finally absorbs all propertied classes it finds in existence (while it develops the majority of the earlier propertyless and a part of the hitherto propertied classes into a new class, the proletariat) in the measure to which all property found in existence is transformed into industrial or commercial capital.

The separate individuals form a class only insofar as they have to carry on a common battle against another class; in other respects they are on hostile terms with each other as competitors. On the other hand, the class in its turn assumes an independent existence as against the individuals, so that the latter find their conditions of life predetermined, and have their position in life and hence their personal development assigned to them by their class, thus becoming subsumed under it. This is the same phenomenon as the subjection of the separate individuals to the division of labour and can only be removed by the abolition of private property and of labour itself. We have already indicated several times that this subsuming of individuals under the class brings with it their subjection to all kinds of ideas, etc.

If this development of individuals, which proceeds within the common conditions of existence of estates and classes, historically following one another, and the general conceptions thereby forced upon them – if this development is considered from a *philosophical* point of view, it is certainly very easy to imagine that in these individuals the species, or man, has evolved, or that they evolved man – and in this way one can give history some hard clouts on the ear. One can then conceive these various estates and classes to be specific terms of the general expression, subordinate varieties of the species, or evolutionary phases of man.

This subsuming of individuals under definite classes cannot be abolished until a class has evolved which has no longer any particular class interest to assert against a ruling class.

The transformation, through the division of labour, of personal powers (relations) into material powers, cannot be dispelled by dismissing the general idea of it from one's mind, but can only be abolished by the individuals again subjecting these material powers to themselves and abolishing the division of labour. This is not possible without the community. Only within the community has each individual the means of cultivating his gifts in all directions; hence personal freedom becomes possible only within the community. In the previous substitutes for the community, in the state, etc., personal freedom has existed only for the individuals who developed under the conditions of the ruling class, and only insofar as they were individuals of this class. The illusory community in which individuals have up till now combined always took on an independent existence in relation to them, and since it was the combination of one class over against another, it was at the same time for the oppressed class not only a completely illusory community, but a new fetter as well. In the real community the individuals obtain their freedom in and through their association.

Individuals have always proceeded from themselves, but of course from themselves within their given historical conditions and relations, not from the "pure" individual in the sense of the ideologists. But in the course of historical development, and precisely through the fact that within the division of labour social relations inevitably take on an independent existence, there appears a cleavage in the life of each individual, insofar as it is personal and insofar as it is determined by some branch of labour and the conditions pertaining to it. (We do not mean it to be understood from this that, for example, the rentier, the capitalist, etc., cease to be persons; but their personality is conditioned and determined by quite definite class relations, and the cleavage appears only in their opposition to another class and, for themselves, only when they go bankrupt.) . . .

chapter 4

Preface to *A Contribution to the Critique of Political Economy (1859)*

... The first work which I undertook to dispel the doubts assailing me was a critical re-examination of the Hegelian philosophy of law; the introduction to this work being published in the *Deutsch-Französische Jahrbücher* issued in Paris in 1844. My inquiry led me to the conclusion that neither legal relations nor political forms could be comprehended whether by themselves or on the basis of a so-called general development of the human mind, but that on the contrary they originate in the material conditions of life, the totality of which Hegel, following the example of English and French thinkers of the eighteenth century, embraces within the term "civil society"; that the anatomy of this civil society, however, has to be sought in political economy. The study of this, which I began in Paris, I continued in Brussels, where I moved owing to an expulsion order issued by M. Guizot. The general conclusion at which I arrived and which, once reached, became the guiding principle of my studies can be summarised as follows. In the social production of their existence, men inevitably enter into definite relations, which are independent of their will, namely relations of production appropriate to a given stage in the development of their material forces of production. The totality of these relations of production constitutes the economic structure of society, the real foundation, on which arises a legal and political superstructure and to which correspond definite forms of social consciousness. The mode of production of material life conditions the general process of social, political and intellectual life. It is not the consciousness of men that determines their existence, but their social existence that determines their consciousness. At a certain stage of development, the material productive forces of society come into conflict with the existing relations of production or – this merely expresses the same thing in legal terms – with the property relations within the framework of which they have operated hitherto. From forms of development of the productive forces these relations turn into their fetters. Then begins an era of social revolution. The changes in the economic foundation lead sooner or later to the transformation of the whole immense superstructure. In studying such transformations it is always necessary to distinguish between the material transformation of the economic conditions of production, which can be determined with the precision of natural science, and the legal, political, religious, artistic or philosophic – in short, ideological forms in which men become conscious of this conflict and fight it out. Just as one does not judge an individual by what he thinks about himself, so one cannot judge such a period of transformation by its consciousness, but, on the contrary, this consciousness must be explained from the contradictions of material life, from the conflict existing between the social forces of production and the relations of production. No social formation is ever destroyed before all the productive forces for which it is sufficient have been developed, and new superior relations of production never replace older ones before the material conditions for their existence have matured within the framework of the old society. Mankind thus inevitably sets itself only such tasks as it is able to solve, since closer examination will always show that the problem itself arises only when the material conditions for its solution are already present or at least in the course of formation. In broad outline, the Asiatic, ancient, feudal and modern bourgeois modes of production may be designated as epochs marking progress in the economic development of society. The bourgeois relations of production are the last antagonistic form of the social process of production – antagonistic not in the sense of individual antagonism but of an antagonism that emanates from the individuals' social conditions of existence – but the productive forces developing within bourgeois society create also the material conditions for a solution of this antagonism. The prehistory of human society accordingly closes with this social formation. . . .

chapter 5

Labour Rent (1894)

If we consider ground rent in its simplest form, that of *labour rent*, where the direct producer, using instruments of labour (plough, cattle, etc.) which actually or legally belong to him, cultivates soil actually owned by him during part of the week, and works during the remaining days upon the estate of the feudal lord without any compensation from the feudal lord, the situation here is still quite clear, for in this case rent and surplus value are identical. Rent, not profit, is the form here through which unpaid surplus labour expresses itself. To what extent the labourer (A SELF-SUSTAINING SERF) can secure in this case an excess above his indispensable necessities of life, i.e., an excess above that which we would call wages under the capitalist mode of production, depends, other circumstances remaining unchanged, upon the proportion in which his labour time is divided into labour time for himself and enforced labour time for his feudal lord. This excess above the indispensable requirements of life, the germ of what appears as profit under the capitalist mode of production, is therefore wholly determined by the amount of ground rent, which in this case is not only directly unpaid surplus labour, but also appears as such. It is unpaid surplus labour for the "owner" of the means of production, which here coincide with the land, and so far as they differ from it, are mere accessories to it. That the product of the serf must here suffice to reproduce his conditions of labour, in addition to his subsistence, is a circumstance which remains the same under all modes of production. For it is not the result of their specific form, but a natural requisite of all continuous and reproductive labour in general, of any continuing production, which is always simultaneously reproduction, i.e., including reproduction of its own operating conditions. It is furthermore evident that in all forms in which the direct labourer remains the "possessor" of the means of production and labour conditions necessary for the production of his own means of subsistence, the property relationship must simultaneously appear as a direct relation of lordship and servitude, so that the direct producer is not free; a lack of freedom which may be reduced from serfdom with enforced labour to a mere tributary relationship. The direct producer, according to our assumption, is to be found here in possession of his own means of production, the necessary material labour conditions required for the realisation of his labour and the production of his means of subsistence. He conducts his agricultural activity and the rural home industries connected with it independently. This independence is not undermined by the circumstance that the small peasants may form among themselves a more or less natural production community, as they do in India, since it is here merely a question of independence from the nominal lord of the manor. Under such conditions the surplus labour for the nominal owner of the land can only be extorted from them by other than economic pressure, whatever the form assumed may be. This differs from slave or plantation economy in that the slave works under alien conditions of production and not independently. Thus, conditions of personal dependence are requisite, a lack of personal freedom, no matter to what extent, and being tied to the soil as its accessory, bondage in the true sense of the word. Should the direct producers not be confronted by a private landowner, but rather, as in Asia, under direct subordination to a state which stands over them as their landlord and simultaneously as sovereign, then rent and taxes coincide, or rather, there exists no tax which differs from this form of ground rent. Under such circumstances, there need exist no stronger political or economic pressure than that common to all subjects to that state. The state is then the supreme lord. Sovereignty here consists in the ownership of land concentrated on a national scale. But, on the other hand, no private ownership of land exists, although there is both private and common possession and use of land.

The specific economic form, in which unpaid surplus labour is pumped out of direct producers, determines the relationship of rulers and ruled, as it grows directly out of production itself and, in turn, reacts upon it as a determining element. Upon this, however, is founded the entire formation of the economic community which grows up out of the production relations themselves, thereby simultaneously its specific political form. It is always the direct relationship of the owners of the conditions of production to the direct producers – a relation always naturally corresponding to a definite stage in the development of the methods of labour and thereby its social productivity – which reveals the innermost secret, the hidden basis of the entire social structure, and with it the political form of the relation of sovereignty and dependence, in short, the corresponding specific form of the state. This does not prevent the same economic basis – the same from the standpoint of its main conditions – due to innumerable different empirical circumstances, natural environment, racial relations, external historical influences, etc., from showing infinite variations and gradations in appearance, which can be ascertained only by analysis of the empirically given circumstances. . . .

chapter 6

Karl Marx (Engels) (1878)

... Of the many important discoveries through which Marx has inscribed his name in the annals of science, we can here dwell on only two.

The first is the revolution brought about by him in the whole conception of world history. The entire view of history hitherto was based on the conception that the ultimate causes of all historical changes are to be sought in the changing ideas of human beings, and that of all historical changes political changes are the most important and dominate the whole of history. But the question was not asked as to whence the ideas come into men's minds and what the driving causes of the political changes are. Only upon the newer school of French, and partly also of English, historians had the conviction forced itself that, since the Middle Ages at least, the driving force in European history had been the struggle of the developing bourgeoisie with the feudal aristocracy for social and political domination. Now Marx has proved that the whole of history hitherto is a history of class struggles, that in all the manifold and complicated political struggles the only thing at issue has been the social and political rule of classes of society, the maintenance of domination by older classes and the conquest of domination by newly arising classes. To what, however, do these classes owe their origin and their continued existence? They owe it to the particular material, physically sensible conditions in which society in a given period produces and exchanges its means of subsistence. The feudal rule of the Middle Ages rested on the self-sufficient economy of small peasant communities, which themselves produced almost all their requirements, in which there was almost no exchange and which received from the arms-bearing nobility protection from without and national or at least political cohesion. When the towns arose and with them separate handicraft industry and trade, at first internal and later international, the urban bourgeoisie developed, and already during the Middle Ages achieved, in struggle with the nobility, its inclusion in the feudal order as a likewise privileged estate. But with the discovery of the extra-European lands, from the middle of the fifteenth century onwards, this bourgeoisie acquired a far more extensive sphere of trade and therewith a new spur for its industry; in the most important branches handicrafts were supplanted by manufacture, now on a factory scale, and this again was supplanted by large-scale industry, which became possible owing to the discoveries of the previous century, especially that of the steam engine. Large-scale industry, in its turn, had an effect on trade, driving out the old manual labour in backward countries and creating the present-day new means of communication: steam engines, railways, electric telegraphy, in the more developed ones. Thus the bourgeoisie came more and more to combine social wealth and social power in its hands, while it still for a long period remained excluded from political power which was in the hands of the nobility and the monarchy supported by the nobility. But at a certain stage – in France since the Great Revolution – it also conquered political power, and now in turn became the ruling class over the proletariat and small peasants. From this point of view all the historical phenomena are explicable in the simplest possible way – with sufficient knowledge of the particular economic condition of society, which it is true is totally lacking in our professional historians – and in the same way the conceptions and ideas of each historical period are most simply to be explained from the economic conditions of life and from the social and political relations of the period, which are in turn determined by these economic conditions. History was for the first time placed on its real basis; the palpable but previously totally overlooked fact that men must first of all eat, drink, have shelter and clothing, therefore must *work*, before they can fight for domination, pursue politics, religion, philosophy, etc. – this palpable fact at last came into its historical right.

This new conception of history, however, was of supreme significance for the socialist outlook. It showed that all history hitherto revolved around class antagonisms and class struggles, that there have always existed ruling and ruled, exploiting and exploited classes, and that the great majority of mankind has always been condemned to arduous labour and little enjoyment. Why is this? Simply because in all earlier stages of development of mankind production was so little developed that historical development could proceed only in this antagonistic form, that historical progress on the whole was assigned to the activity of a small privileged minority, while the great mass remained condemned to producing by their labour their own meagre means of subsistence and also the increasingly rich means of the privileged. But the same investigation of history, which in this way provides a natural and reasonable explanation of class rule hitherto, otherwise only explicable from the wickedness of man, also leads to the realisation that, in consequence of the so tremendously increased productive forces of the present time, even the last pretext has vanished, at least in the most advanced countries, for a division of mankind into rulers and ruled, exploiters and exploited . . .

The second important discovery of Marx is the final elucidation of the relation between capital and labour, in other words, the demonstration

how, within present society and under the existing capitalist mode of production, the exploitation of the worker by the capitalist takes place. Ever
since political economy had put forward the proposition that labour is
the source of all wealth and of all value, the question became inevitable:
How is this then to be reconciled with the fact that the wage labourer
does not receive the whole sum of value created by his labour but has to
surrender a part of it to the capitalist? Both the bourgeois economists and
the socialists exerted themselves to give a scientifically valid answer to
this question, but in vain, until at last Marx came forward with the solution. This solution is as follows: The present-day capitalist mode of production presupposes the existence of two social classes – on the one hand,
that of the capitalists, who are in possession of the means of production
and subsistence, and, on the other hand, that of the proletarians, who,
being excluded from this possession, have only a single commodity for
sale, their labour power, and who therefore have to sell this labour
power of theirs in order to obtain possession of means of subsistence. . . .
the worker in the service of the capitalist not only reproduces the value
of his labour power, for which he receives pay, but over and above that
he also produces a *surplus value* which, appropriated in the first place by
the capitalist, is subsequently divided according to definite economic laws
among the whole capitalist class and forms the basic stock from which
arise ground rent, profit, accumulation of capital, in short, all the wealth
consumed or accumulated by the non-labouring classes. But this proved
that the acquisition of riches by the present-day capitalists consists just
as much in the appropriation of the unpaid labour of others as that of
the slaveowner or the feudal lord exploiting serf labour, and that all these
forms of exploitation are only to be distinguished by the difference in manner and method by which the unpaid labour is appropriated. This, however, also removed the last justification for all the hypocritical phrases of
the possessing classes to the effect that in the present social order right
and justice, equality of rights and duties and a universal harmony of interests prevail, and present-day bourgeois society, no less than its predecessors,
was exposed as a grandiose institution for the exploitation of the huge
majority of the people by a small, ever-diminishing minority. . . .

chapter 7

Letter to Joseph Bloch
(Engels) (1890)

London, September 21–22, 1890

... According to the materialist conception of history, the *ultimately* determining element in history is the production and reproduction of real life. More than this neither Marx nor I has ever asserted. Hence if somebody twists this into saying that the economic element is the *only* determining one he transforms that proposition into a meaningless, abstract, senseless phrase. The economic situation is the basis, but the various elements of the superstructure – political forms of the class struggle and its results, to wit: constitutions established by the victorious class after a successful battle, etc., juridical forms, and even the reflexes of all these actual struggles in the brains of the participants, political, juristic, philosophical theories, religious views, and their further development into systems of dogmas – also exercise their influence upon the course of the historical struggles and in many cases preponderate in determining their *form*. There is an interaction of all these elements in which, amidst all the endless host of accidents (that is, of things and events whose inner interconnection is so remote or so impossible of proof that we can regard it as non-existent, as negligible), the economic movement finally asserts itself as necessary. Otherwise the application of the theory to any period of history would be easier than the solution of a simple equation of the first degree.

We make our history ourselves, but, in the first place, under very definite assumptions and conditions. Among these the economic ones are ultimately decisive. But the political ones, etc., and indeed even the traditions which haunt human minds also play a part, although not the decisive one. The Prussian state also arose and developed from historical, ultimately economic, causes. But it could scarcely be maintained without pedantry that among the many small states of north Germany, Brandenburg was specifically determined by economic necessity to become the great power embodying the economic, linguistic, and, after the Reformation, also the religious difference between North and South, and not by other elements

as well (above all, by its entanglement with Poland, owing to the possession of Prussia, and hence with international political relations – which
were indeed also decisive in the formation of the Austrian dynastic power).
Without making oneself ridiculous it would be a difficult thing to explain
in terms of economics the existence of every small state in Germany, past
and present, or the origin of the High German consonant permutations,
which widened the geographic partition wall formed by the mountains
from the Sudetic range to the Taunus to form a regular fissure across
all Germany.

In the second place, however, history is made in such a way that the
final result always arises from conflicts between many individual wills,
of which each in turn has been made what it is by a host of particular
conditions of life. Thus there are innumerable intersecting forces, an
infinite series of parallelograms of forces which give rise to one resultant
– the historical event. This may again itself be viewed as the product of
a power which works as a whole *unconsciously* and without volition. For
what each individual wills is obstructed by everyone else, and what emerges
is something that no one willed. Thus history has proceeded hitherto in
the manner of a natural process and is essentially subject to the same laws
of motion. But from the fact that the wills of individuals – each of whom
desires what he is impelled to by his physical constitution and external,
in the last resort economic, circumstances (either his own personal circumstances or those of society in general) – do not attain what they want,
but are merged into an aggregate mean, a common resultant, it must not
be concluded that they are equal to zero. On the contrary, each contributes
to the resultant and is to this extent included in it. . . .

Marx and I are ourselves partly to blame for the fact that the younger
people sometimes lay more stress on the economic side than is due to it.
We had to emphasize the main principle vis-à-vis our adversaries, who
denied it, and we had not always the time, the place, or the opportunity
to give their due to the other elements involved in the interaction. But
when it came to presenting a section of history, that is, to making a practical application, it was a different matter and there no error was per-
missible. Unfortunately, however, it happens only too often that people
think they have fully understood a new theory and can apply it without
more ado from the moment they have assimilated its main principles, and
even those not always correctly. And I cannot exempt many of the more
recent "Marxists" from this reproach, for the most amazing rubbish has
been produced in this quarter, too. . . .

part 2

The Juggernaut of Capitalist Modernity: The Revolutionary Bourgeoisie, the End of Tradition, and New Social Powers

Although posed as a general approach for interpreting history, historical materialism bore the clear imprint of the time at which it was formulated – during the dawning of a modern era of heretofore unimaginably sudden and profound technical and social change. In the *Manifesto of the Communist Party*, Marx and Engels asserted that the bourgeoisie, or the emergent capitalist ruling class, stimulated the development, in a single century, of a greater array of powerful productive forces than all the previous civilizations together, and that the fundamental material shift generated equally sweeping sociocultural and political change. Declaring famously that "all that is solid melts into air, all that is holy is profaned" (1848: 487), Marx and Engels saw capitalism as a kind of runaway train or wrecker's ball demolishing traditional society and culture. However, they also held that capitalism was forging simultaneously, among the ruins and tumult, highly complex, globally extensive social "connections," which they considered to be among the most vital resources of modernity, yet poorly understood and underutilized. They intended their historical materialist point of view to illuminate and tap them.

In the selection from the first volume of *Capital* on "primitive accumulation," Marx contended that expropriation of the means of production from peasant and crafts producers was a decisive moment in the rise of capitalism and modernity, creating a propertyless class that could no longer support themselves by independent production and had to become wageworkers for their expropriators. He attacked political economists' claims that the bourgeoisie arose purely by means of their diligent work and prudent habits, and that the working class originated from individuals too lazy and profligate to maintain productive property. Marx held that such views ignored the brutal and forceful nature of the expropriation, and constituted a new ideology that affirmed the emergent ruling class's control of productive property. From his vantage point, economists concealed a most important facet of the shift – that the new relationship between capitalist and worker pumped surplus out of producers much more effectively than the feudal mode had done.

The second piece in this part, drawn from the earlier Feuerbach essay, demonstrates that Marx and Engels formulated their historical materialist position in light of capitalist modernization. They traced the roots of capitalism to medieval towns and their leading strata of craft producers and merchants, who fought for and won independence from feudal lords. Marx and Engels explained how these forerunners of the bourgeoisie expanded trade, created larger markets, fashioned a more complex division of labor, and, overall, built an infrastructure for capitalist development. Marx and Engels held that the patriarchal relations in guilds, which paralleled the traditional family's personal ties and hierarchies, bound journeymen and apprentices to their masters. The shift to an impersonal monetary or wage relationship shattered this bond (e.g., workers could be fired, and could no longer ascend to the top of the firm), and was a fundamental facet of the broader transformation from independent crafts production to capitalist manufacture. Marx and Engels explained how the expropriation of peasants, colonial expansion, increased trade, and protection of home markets made manufacture the dominant form of production in important regions of Europe by the early nineteenth century. They argued that England, the most industrially advanced nation at the time they wrote, was developing "large-scale industry," and that its mechanized "automatic system" was revolutionizing production. Marx and Engels held that its owners, the leading sector of the capitalist class, were creating a world market and a global capitalist system dominated by urban centers and highly industrialized nations.

The *Manifesto of the Communist Party* (1848) was composed at a time when democratic revolutions were sweeping across Europe and creating political institutions that empowered the bourgeoisie. Portraying them as a revolutionary class, Marx and Engels described vividly how they demolished the authority of feudal institutions (e.g., the traditional family and traditional religion) and forged the most powerful productive forces and most extensive division of labor in history. According to Marx and Engels, capitalist modernity initiated an epochal rupture that exacted immense costs and opened entirely new possibilities. They saw the bourgeoisie, driven by ceaseless competition amongst themselves, as the historical agent of modernization. The selection presented in chapter 10 expresses eloquently a cultural sensibility that characterizes modernity – that of the ending of a traditional order, in which technical and socio-cultural change was slow and incremental, and the dawning of a new world of restless innovation. Modernity's "tradition of the new" became a central focus of later generations of modern social theorists. However, Marx's and Engels's unique contribution to this discourse is the view that capitalist manufacture and large-scale industry were successive, pro-gressive steps animating modernization. Their points about emerging global markets and eroding national borders and cultures foreshadowed strik-ingly today's globalization.

The selections from *Capital* on accumulation and cooperation express Marx's mature views about capitalist modernity, which built on the earlier ones. Marx held that feudalism's small-scale peasant plots and tiny craft shops ("pygmy property") blocked the rise of more advanced productive forces. Although portraying capitalist expropriation of this property as "fearful and painful," he nevertheless treated the seizure as a progressive step. In his view, this move "dissolved" patriarchal exploita-tion and the decentralized mode of production, and thus made way for the concentrated resources and extensive scale of cooperation that he believed were needed to ignite technical innovation and social progress. However, Marx qualified his enthusiasm for capitalist modernization, saying that it also increases "the mass of misery, oppression, slavery, degradation, exploitation."

Marx asserted that "cooperation ever constitutes the fundamental form of the capitalist mode of production" (1867a: 340). He argued that large-scale industry's complex division of labor, or "combined organism," exceeds greatly the powers of independent production by "isolated" individual peasants and craftsmen in the same way that the force of a "regiment of infantry" towers over that of an equal number of unorgan-ized individual soldiers. Similarly, he contended that twelve masons working collectively produce much more in a specified time than the same number of workers operating alone. Marx thought that large-scale cap-italism's highly extensive webs of cooperation increase geometrically and qualitatively the ability to produce, organize, think, and plan. He implied that complex cooperation generates *sui generis*, or emergent, social capa-cities and social structures, which do not exist on the individual level or even in simple forms of social cooperation. He held that manufacture and large-scale industry advance "socialization" or "interdependence." As later readings will elaborate, he believed that the vital resources for creating a future emancipated society were already "immanent" in the embryonic "collective capitalist" of his day.

In the brief selection from the third volume of *Capital*, Marx summar-ized the "cardinal facts" of this nascent order: concentrated means of production, highly organized "social labour," and global markets. But he stressed that the new system generates "crises" as well as "stupendous productive powers." In his view, the most advanced capitalism was still a class society, and thus the epochal rupture and promise of modernity would not be complete until the new social powers were decoupled from the bourgeoisie and capitalism.

Marx's views about capitalism and modernity were prescient as regards the rise of the world market and the global division of labor, and about the fact that they would bring increased inequality and misery along with productive and social advances. A valuable aspect of his approach is that it poses entirely different questions about globalization than neoliberalism, or the free-market approach that reemerged worldwide in the later twentieth century and was hegemonic among American policy-makers. Marx's emphases on cooperation and interdependence manifest a competing sociological optic that points to the limits of neoliberalism's individualist, anti-regulatory, and free-trade policies and challenges its assumptions about property rights and social justice. However, Marx's claims about the virtues of concentrated resources and centralized organization and about the leveling of traditional culture have deeply problematic facets. The recent resurgence of free-market capitalism and decline of Marxist regimes and politics were, in part, responses to abuses and inefficiencies of centralized forms of state power (e.g., in Communist regimes, fascism, and even welfare state capitalism). Moreover, critics, addressing mounting environmental problems and consumer culture, question the very worth of modernity and its related ideas of progress. Finally, capitalism has not eliminated regional and national differences as completely as Marx sometimes suggested. Although recent globalization has manifested, in certain key respects, almost exactly the type of leveling, or sociocultural homogenization, that Marx predicted, the process has also demonstrated that local cultures can be surprisingly resilient and can mount intense resistance (e.g., today's anti-corporate social movements, reawakened nationalism, and ethnic identity politics). Regardless of problematic facets, Marx's views about capitalism and modernity framed core problems and questions that have exerted substantial influence (direct and indirect) on recent debates about modernity, postmodernity, and glob-alization and that offer analytical resources for addressing critically today's conditions and trends of thought.

chapter 8

The Secret of Primitive Accumulation (1867)

... This primitive accumulation plays in political economy about the same part as original sin in theology. Adam bit the apple, and thereupon sin fell on the human race. Its origin is supposed to be explained when it is told as an anecdote of the past. In times long gone by there were two sorts of people; one, the diligent, intelligent, and, above all, frugal élite; the other, lazy rascals, spending their substance, and more, in riotous living. The legend of theological original sin tells us certainly how man came to be condemned to eat his bread in the sweat of his brow; but the history of economic original sin reveals to us that there are people to whom this is by no means essential. Never mind! Thus it came to pass that the former sort accumulated wealth, and the latter sort had at last nothing to sell except their own skins. And from this original sin dates the poverty of the great majority that, despite all its labour, has up to now nothing to sell but itself, and the wealth of the few that increases constantly although they have long ceased to work. Such insipid childishness is every day preached to us in the defence of property.... But as soon as the question of property crops up, it becomes a sacred duty to proclaim the intellectual food of the infant as the one thing fit for all ages and for all stages of development. In actual history it is notorious that conquest, enslavement, robbery, murder, briefly, force, play the great part. In the tender annals of political economy, the idyllic reigns from time immemorial. Right and "labour" were from all time the sole means of enrichment, the present year of course always excepted. As a matter of fact, the methods of primitive accumulation are anything but idyllic.

In themselves money and commodities are no more capital than are the means of production and of subsistence. They want transforming into capital. But this transformation itself can only take place under certain circumstances that centre in this, viz., that two very different kinds of commodity possessors must come face to face and into contact; on the one hand, the owners of money, means of production, means of subsistence, who are eager to increase the sum of values they possess, by buying other people's labour power; on the other hand, free labourers, the sellers of their own labour power, and therefore the sellers of labour. Free labourers, in the double sense that neither they themselves form part and parcel of the means of production, as in the case of slaves, bondsmen, &c., nor do the means of production belong to them, as in the case of peasant proprietors; they are, therefore, free from, unencumbered by, any means of production of their own. With this polarisation of the market for commodities, the fundamental conditions of capitalist production are given. The capitalist system presupposes the complete separation of the labourers from all property in the means by which they can realise their labour. As soon as capitalist production is once on its own legs, it not only maintains this separation, but reproduces it on a continually extending scale. The process, therefore, that clears the way for the capitalist system, can be none other than the process which takes away from the labourer the possession of his means of production; a process that transforms, on the one hand, the social means of subsistence and of production into capital, on the other, the immediate producers into wage labourers. The so-called primitive accumulation, therefore, is nothing else than the historical process of divorcing the producer from the means of production. It appears as primitive, because it forms the pre-historic stage of capital and of the mode of production corresponding with it.

The economic structure of capitalistic society has grown out of the economic structure of feudal society. The dissolution of the latter set free the elements of the former.

The immediate producer, the labourer, could only dispose of his own person after he had ceased to be attached to the soil and ceased to be the slave, serf, or bondman of another. To become a free seller of labour power, who carries his commodity wherever he finds a market, he must further have escaped from the regime of the guilds, their rules for apprentices and journeymen, and the impediments of their labour regulations. Hence, the historical movement which changes the producers into wage workers, appears, on the one hand, as their emancipation from serfdom and from the fetters of the guilds, and this side alone exists for our bourgeois historians. But, on the other hand, these new freedmen became sellers of themselves only after they had been robbed of all their own means of production, and of all the guarantees of existence afforded by the old feudal arrangements. And the history of this, their expropriation, is written in the annals of mankind in letters of blood and fire.

The industrial capitalists, these new potentates, had on their part not only to displace the guild masters of handicrafts, but also the feudal lords, the possessors of the sources of wealth. In this respect their conquest of social power appears as the fruit of a victorious struggle both against feudal lordship and its revolting prerogatives, and against the guilds and the fetters they laid on the free development of production and the free exploitation of man by man. The chevaliers d'industrie, however, only succeeded in supplanting the chevaliers of the sword by making use of events of which they themselves were wholly innocent. They have risen by means as vile as those by which the Roman freedman once on a time made himself the master of his *patronus*.

The starting point of the development that gave rise to the wage labourer as well as to the capitalist, was the servitude of the labourer. The advance consisted in a change of form of this servitude, in the transformation of feudal exploitation into capitalist exploitation. To understand its march, we need not go back very far. Although we come across the first beginnings of capitalist production as early as the 14th or 15th century, sporadically, in certain towns of the Mediterranean, the capitalistic era dates from the 16th century. Wherever it appears, the abolition of serfdom has been long effected, and the highest development of the Middle Ages, the existence of sovereign towns, has been long on the wane.

In the history of primitive accumulation, all revolutions are epoch-making that act as levers for the capitalist class in course of formation; but, above all, those moments when great masses of men are suddenly and forcibly torn from their means of subsistence, and hurled as free and "unattached" proletarians on the labour market. The expropriation of the agricultural producer, of the peasant, from the soil, is the basis of the whole process. The history of this expropriation, in different countries, assumes different aspects, and runs through its various phases in different orders of succession, and at different periods. In England alone, which we take as our example, has it the classic form.

chapter 9

Development of the Division of Labour (with Engels) (1845–6)

Separation of Town and Country

. . . The advent of the town implies, at the same time, the necessity of administration, police, taxes, etc., in short, of the municipality . . . , and thus of politics in general. Here first became manifest the division of the population into two great classes, which is directly based on the division of labour and on the instruments of production. The town is in actual fact already the concentration of the population, of the instruments of production, of capital, of pleasures, of needs, while the country demonstrates just the opposite fact, isolation and separation. The contradiction between town and country can only exist within the framework of private property. It is the most crass expression of the subjection of the individual under the division of labour, under a definite activity forced upon him – a subjection which makes one man into a restricted town-animal, another into a restricted country-animal, and daily creates anew the conflict between their interests. Labour is here again the chief thing, power *over* individuals, and as long as this power exists, private property must exist. . . . The separation of town and country can also be understood as the separation of capital and landed property, as the beginning of the existence and development of capital independent of landed property – the beginning of property having its basis only in labour and exchange.

In the towns which, in the Middle Ages, did not derive ready-made from an earlier period but were formed anew by the serfs who had become free, the particular labour of each man was his only property apart from the small capital he brought with him, consisting almost solely of the most necessary tools of his craft. The competition of serfs constantly escaping into the town, the constant war of the country against the towns and thus the necessity of an organised municipal military force, the bond of common ownership in a particular kind of labour, the necessity of common buildings for the sale of their wares at a time when craftsmen were also traders, and the consequent exclusion of the unauthorised from these buildings, the conflict among the interests of the various crafts, the necessity of protecting their laboriously acquired skill, and the feudal organisation of the whole of the country: these were the causes of the union of the workers of each craft in guilds. In this context we do not have to go further into the manifold modifications of the guild-system, which arise through later historical developments. The flight of the serfs into the towns went on without interruption right through the Middle Ages. These serfs, persecuted by their lords in the country, came separately into the towns, where they found an organised community, against which they were powerless and in which they had to subject themselves to the station assigned to them by the demand for their labour and the interest of their organised urban competitors. These workers, entering separately, were never able to attain to any power, since, if their labour was of the guild type which had to be learned, the guildmasters bent them to their will and organised them according to their interest; or if their labour was not such as had to be learned, and therefore not of the guild type, they were day-labourers, never managed to organise, but remained an unorganised rabble. The need for day-labourers in the towns created the rabble.

These towns were true "unions", called forth by the direct need of providing for the protection of property, and of multiplying the means of production and defence of the separate members. The rabble of these towns was devoid of any power, composed as it was of individuals strange to one another who had entered separately, and who stood unorganised over against an organised power, armed for war, and jealously watching over them. The journeymen and apprentices were organised in each craft as it best suited the interest of the masters. The patriarchal relations existing between them and their masters gave the latter a double power – on the one hand because of the direct influence they exerted on the whole life of the journeymen, and on the other because, for the journeymen who worked with the same master, it was a real bond which held them together against the journeymen of other masters and separated them from these. And finally, the journeymen were bound to the existing order even by their interest in becoming masters themselves. While, therefore, the rabble at least carried out revolts against the whole municipal order, revolts which remained completely ineffective because of its powerlessness, the journeymen never got further than small acts of insubordination within separate guilds, such as belong to the very nature of the guild-system. . . .

Capital in these towns was a naturally evolved capital, consisting of a house, the tools of the craft, and the natural, hereditary customers; and not being realisable, on account of the backwardness of intercourse and the lack of circulation, it had to be handed down from father to son. Unlike modern capital, which can be assessed in money and which may be indifferently invested in this thing or that, this capital was directly connected with the particular work of the owner, inseparable from it and to this extent *estate* capital. –

In the towns, the division of labour between the individual guilds was as yet very little developed and, in the guilds themselves, it did not exist at all between the individual workers. Every workman had to be versed in a whole round of tasks, had to be able to make everything that was to be made with his tools. The limited intercourse and the weak ties between the individual towns, the lack of population and the narrow needs did not allow of a more advanced division of labour, and therefore every man who wished to become a master had to be proficient in the whole of his craft. Medieval craftsmen therefore had an interest in their special work and in proficiency in it, which was capable of rising to a limited artistic sense. For this very reason, however, every medieval craftsman was completely absorbed in his work, to which he had a complacent servile relationship, and in which he was involved to a far greater extent than the modern worker, whose work is a matter of indifference to him. –

Further Division of Labour

The next extension of the division of labour was the separation of production and intercourse, the formation of a special class of merchants; a separation which, in the towns bequeathed by a former period, had been handed down. . . . With this there was given the possibility of commercial communications transcending the immediate neighbourhood, a possibility the realisation of which depended on the existing means of communication, the state of public safety in the countryside, which was determined by political conditions (during the whole of the Middle Ages, as is well known, the merchants travelled in armed caravans), and on the cruder or more advanced needs (determined by the stage of culture attained) of the region accessible to intercourse.

With intercourse vested in a particular class, with the extension of trade through the merchants beyond the immediate surroundings of the town, there immediately appears a reciprocal action between production and intercourse. The towns enter into relations *with one another*, new tools are brought from one town into the other, and the separation between production and intercourse soon calls forth a new division of production between the individual towns, each of which is soon exploiting a predominant branch of industry. The local restrictions of earlier times begin gradually to be broken down. –

It depends purely on the extension of intercourse whether the productive forces evolved in a locality, especially inventions, are lost for later development or not. As long as there exists no intercourse transcending the immediate neighbourhood, every invention must be made separately in each locality, and mere chances such as irruptions of barbaric peoples, even ordinary wars, are sufficient to cause a country with advanced productive forces and needs to have to start right over again from the beginning. . . . Only when intercourse has become world intercourse and has as its basis large-scale industry, when all nations are drawn into the competitive struggle, is the permanence of the acquired productive forces assured. –

The immediate consequence of the division of labour between the various towns was the rise of manufactures, branches of production which had outgrown the guild-system. Intercourse with foreign nations was the historical premise for the first flourishing of manufactures, in Italy and later in Flanders. In other countries, England and France for example, manufactures were at first confined to the home market. Besides the premises already mentioned manufactures presuppose an already advanced concentration of population, particularly in the countryside, and of capital, which began to accumulate in the hands of individuals, partly in the guilds in spite of the guild regulations, partly among the merchants.

. . . Weaving, earlier carried on in the country by the peasants as a secondary occupation to procure their clothing, was the first labour to receive an impetus and a further development through the extension of intercourse. Weaving was the first and remained the principal manufacture. The rising demand for clothing materials, consequent on the growth of population, the growing accumulation and mobilisation of natural capital through accelerated circulation, and the demand for luxuries called forth by this and favoured generally by the gradual extension of intercourse, gave weaving a quantitative and qualitative stimulus, which wrenched it out of the form of production hitherto existing. Alongside the peasants weaving for their own use, who continued, and still continue, with this sort of work, there emerged a new class of weavers in the towns, whose fabrics were destined for the whole home market and usually for foreign markets too.

Weaving, an occupation demanding in most cases little skill and soon splitting up into countless branches, by its whole nature resisted the trammels of the guild. Weaving was, therefore, carried on mostly in villages and market centres, without guild organisation, which gradually became towns, and indeed the most flourishing towns in each land.

With guild-free manufacture, property relations also quickly changed. The first advance beyond naturally derived estate capital was provided by the rise of merchants, whose capital was from the beginning movable, capital in the modern sense as far as one can speak of it, given the circumstances of those times. The second advance came with manufacture, which again mobilised a mass of natural capital, and altogether increased the mass of movable capital as against that of natural capital.

At the same time, manufacture became a refuge of the peasants from the guilds which excluded them or paid them badly, just as earlier the guild-towns had served the peasants as a refuge from the landlords. –

Simultaneously with the beginning of manufactures there was a period of vagabondage caused by the abolition of the feudal bodies of retainers, the disbanding of the armies consisting of a motley crowd that served the kings against their vassals, the improvement of agriculture, and the transformation of large strips of tillage into pasture land. From this alone it is clear that this vagabondage is strictly connected with the disintegration of the feudal system. As early as the thirteenth century we find isolated epochs of this kind, but only at the end of the fifteenth and beginning of the sixteenth does this vagabondage make a general and permanent appearance. These vagabonds, who were so numerous that, for instance, Henry VIII of England had 72,000 of them hanged, were only prevailed upon to work with the greatest difficulty and through the most extreme necessity, and then only after long resistance. The rapid rise of manufactures, particularly in England, absorbed them gradually. –

With the advent of manufacture the various nations entered into competitive relations, a commercial struggle, which was fought out in wars, protective duties and prohibitions, whereas earlier the nations, insofar as they were connected at all, had carried on an inoffensive exchange with each other. Trade had from now on a political significance.

With the advent of manufacture the relations between worker and employer changed. In the guilds the patriarchal relations between journeyman and master continued to exist; in manufacture their place was taken by the monetary relations between worker and capitalist – relations which in the countryside and in small towns retained a patriarchal tinge, but in the larger, the real manufacturing towns, quite early lost almost all patriarchal complexion.

Manufacture and the movement of production in general received an enormous impetus through the extension of intercourse which came with the discovery of America and the sea-route to the East Indies. The new products imported thence, particularly the masses of gold and silver which came into circulation, had totally changed the position of the classes towards one another, dealing a hard blow to feudal landed property and to the workers; the expeditions of adventurers, colonisation, and above all the extension of markets into a world market, which had now become possible and was daily becoming more and more a fact, called forth a new phase of historical development. . . . Through the colonisation of the newly discovered countries the commercial struggle of the nations against one another was given new fuel and accordingly greater extension and animosity.

The expansion of commerce and manufacture accelerated the accumulation of movable capital, while in the guilds, which were not stimulated to extend their production, natural capital remained stationary or even declined. Commerce and manufacture created the big bourgeoisie; in the guilds was concentrated the petty bourgeoisie, which no longer was dominant in the towns as formerly, but had to bow to the might of the great merchants and manufacturers. Hence the decline of the guilds, as soon as they came into contact with manufacture.

The relations between nations in their intercourse took on two different forms in the epoch of which we have been speaking. At first the small quantity of gold and silver in circulation occasioned the ban on the export of these metals; and industry, made necessary by the need for employing the growing urban population and for the most part imported from abroad, could not do without privileges which could be granted not only, of course, against home competition, but chiefly against foreign. The local guild privilege was in these original prohibitions extended over the whole nation. Customs duties originated from the tributes which the feudal lords exacted from merchants passing through their territories as protection money against robbery, tributes later imposed likewise by the towns, and which, with the rise of the modern states, were the Treasury's most obvious means of raising money.

The appearance of American gold and silver on the European markets, the gradual development of industry, the rapid expansion of trade and the consequent rise of the non-guild bourgeoisie and the increasing importance of money, gave these measures another significance. The state, which was daily less and less able to do without money, now retained the ban on the export of gold and silver out of fiscal considerations. . . .

The second period began in the middle of the seventeenth century and lasted almost to the end of the eighteenth. Commerce and navigation had expanded more rapidly than manufacture, which played a secondary role; the colonies were becoming considerable consumers; and after long struggles the various nations shared out the opening world market among themselves. This period begins with the Navigation Laws and colonial monopolies. The competition of the nations among themselves was excluded as far as possible by tariffs, prohibitions and treaties; and in the last resort the competitive struggle was carried on and decided by wars (especially naval wars). The mightiest maritime nation, the English, retained preponderance in commerce and manufacture. Here, already, we find concentration in one country.

Manufacture was all the time sheltered by protective duties in the home market, by monopolies in the colonial market, and abroad as much as possible by differential duties. The working-up of home-produced material was encouraged (wool and linen in England, silk in France), the export of home-produced raw material forbidden (wool in England), and the [working-up] of imported raw material neglected or suppressed (cotton in England). The nation dominant in maritime trade and colonial power naturally secured for itself also the greatest quantitative and qualitative expansion of manufacture. Manufacture could not be carried on without protection, since, if the slightest change takes place in other countries, it can lose its market and be ruined; under reasonably favourable conditions it may easily be introduced into a country, but for this very reason can easily be destroyed. At the same time through the mode in which it is carried on, particularly in the eighteenth century in the countryside, it is to such an extent interwoven with the conditions of life of a great mass of individuals, that no country dare jeopardise their existence by permitting free competition. Consequently, insofar as manufacture manages to export, it depends entirely on the extension or restriction of commerce, and exercises a relatively very small reaction [on the latter]. Hence its secondary [role] and the influence of [the merchants] in the eighteenth century. It was the merchants and especially the shipowners who more than anybody else pressed for state protection and monopolies; the manufacturers also demanded and indeed received protection, but all the time were inferior in political importance to the merchants. The commercial towns, particularly the maritime towns, became to some extent civilised and acquired the outlook of the big bourgeoisie, but in the factory towns an extreme petty-bourgeois outlook persisted.... The eighteenth century was the century of trade....

The movement of capital, although considerably accelerated, still remained, however, relatively slow. The splitting-up of the world market into separate parts, each of which was exploited by a particular nation, the prevention of competition between the different nations, the clumsiness of production and the fact that finance was only evolving from its early stages, greatly impeded circulation. The consequence of this was a haggling, mean and niggardly spirit which still clung to all merchants and to the whole mode of carrying on trade. Compared with the manufacturers, and above all with the craftsmen, they were certainly big bourgeois; compared with the merchants and industrialists of the next period they remain petty bourgeois....

This period is also characterised by the cessation of the bans on the export of gold and silver and the beginning of money trade, banks, national debts, paper money, speculation in stocks and shares, stockjobbing in all articles and the development of finance in general. Again capital lost a great part of the natural character which had still clung to it.

Most Extensive Division of Labour: Large-Scale Industry

The concentration of trade and manufacture in one country, England, developing irresistibly in the seventeenth century, gradually created for this country a relative world market, and thus a demand for the manufactured products of this country which could no longer be met by the industrial productive forces hitherto existing. This demand, outgrowing the productive forces, was the motive power which, by producing large-scale industry – the application of elemental forces to industrial ends, machinery and the most extensive division of labour – called into existence the third period of private property since the Middle Ages. There already existed in England the other preconditions of this new phase: freedom of competition inside the nation, the development of theoretical mechanics, etc. . . .

Competition soon compelled every country that wished to retain its historical role to protect its manufactures by renewed customs regulations (the old duties were no longer any good against large-scale industry) and soon after to introduce large-scale industry under protective duties. In spite of these protective measures large-scale industry universalised competition (it is practical free trade; the protective duty is only a palliative, a measure of defence *within* free trade), established means of communication and the modern world market, subordinated trade to itself, transformed all capital into industrial capital, and thus produced the rapid circulation (development of the financial system) and the centralisation of capital. By universal competition it forced all individuals to strain their energy to the utmost. It destroyed as far as possible ideology, religion, morality, etc., and, where it could not do this, made them into a palpable lie. It produced world history for the first time, insofar as it made all civilised nations and every individual member of them dependent for the satisfaction of their wants on the whole world, thus destroying the former natural exclusiveness of separate nations. It made natural science subservient to capital and took from the division of labour the last semblance of its natural character. It altogether destroyed the natural character, as far as this is possible with regard to labour, and resolved all natural relations into money relations. In the place of naturally grown towns it created the modern, large industrial cities which have sprung up overnight. It destroyed the crafts and all earlier stages of industry wherever it gained mastery. It completed the victory of the town over the country. Its [basis] is the automatic system. . . . Generally speaking, large-scale industry created everywhere the same relations between the classes of society, and thus destroyed the peculiar features of the various nationalities. . . .

It is evident that large-scale industry does not reach the same level of development in all districts of a country. . . . The countries in which large-scale industry is developed act in a similar manner upon the more or less non-industrial countries, insofar as the latter are swept by world intercourse into the universal competitive struggle.

chapter 10

Bourgeois and Proletarians (with Engels) (1845)

. . . Each step in the development of the bourgeoisie was accompanied by a corresponding political advance of that class. An oppressed class under the sway of the feudal nobility, an armed and self-governing association in the medieval commune; here independent urban republic (as in Italy and Germany), there taxable "third estate" of the monarchy (as in France), afterwards, in the period of manufacture proper, serving either the semi-feudal or the absolute monarchy as a counterpoise against the nobility, and, in fact, cornerstone of the great monarchies in general, the bourgeoisie has at last, since the establishment of Modern Industry and of the world market, conquered for itself, in the modern representative State, exclus-ive political sway. The executive of the modern State is but a committee for managing the common affairs of the whole bourgeoisie.

The bourgeoisie, historically, has played a most revolutionary part.

The bourgeoisie, wherever it has got the upper hand, has put an end to all feudal, patriarchal, idyllic relations. It has pitilessly torn asunder the motley feudal ties that bound man to his "natural superiors", and has left remaining no other nexus between man and man than naked self-interest, than callous "cash payment". It has drowned the most heavenly ecstasies of religious fervour, of chivalrous enthusiasm, of philistine sentimentalism, in the icy water of egotistical calculation. It has resolved personal worth into exchange value, and in place of the numberless indefeasible chartered freedoms, has set up that single, unconscionable freedom – Free Trade. In one word, for exploitation, veiled by religious and political illusions, it has substituted naked, shameless, direct, brutal exploitation.

The bourgeoisie has stripped of its halo every occupation hitherto honoured and looked up to with reverent awe. It has converted the physician, the lawyer, the priest, the poet, the man of science, into its paid wage-labourers.

The bourgeoisie has torn away from the family its sentimental veil, and has reduced the family relation to a mere money relation.

The bourgeoisie has disclosed how it came to pass that the brutal display of vigour in the Middle Ages, which Reactionists so much admire, found its fitting complement in the most slothful indolence. It has been the first to show what man's activity can bring about. It has accomplished wonders far surpassing Egyptian pyramids, Roman aqueducts, and Gothic cathedrals; it has conducted expeditions that put in the shade all former Exoduses of nations and crusades.

The bourgeoisie cannot exist without constantly revolutionising the instruments of production, and thereby the relations of production, and with them the whole relations of society. Conservation of the old modes of production in unaltered form, was, on the contrary, the first condition of existence for all earlier industrial classes. Constant revolutionising of production, uninterrupted disturbance of all social conditions, everlasting uncertainty and agitation distinguish the bourgeois epoch from all earlier ones. All fixed, fast-frozen relations, with their train of ancient and venerable prejudices and opinions, are swept away, all new-formed ones become antiquated before they can ossify. All that is solid melts into air, all that is holy is profaned, and man is at last compelled to face with sober senses, his real conditions of life, and his relations with his kind.

The need of a constantly expanding market for its products chases the bourgeoisie over the whole surface of the globe. It must nestle everywhere, settle everywhere, establish connexions everywhere.

The bourgeoisie has through its exploitation of the world market given a cosmopolitan character to production and consumption in every country. To the great chagrin of Reactionists, it has drawn from under the feet of industry the national ground on which it stood. All old-established national industries have been destroyed or are daily being destroyed. They are dislodged by new industries, whose introduction becomes a life and death question for all civilised nations, by industries that no longer work up indigenous raw material, but raw material drawn from the remotest zones; industries whose products are consumed, not only at home, but in every quarter of the globe. In place of the old wants, satisfied by the productions of the country, we find new wants, requiring for their satisfaction the products of distant lands and climes. In place of the old local and national seclusion and self-sufficiency, we have intercourse in every direction, universal inter-dependence of nations. And as in material, so also in intellectual production. The intellectual creations of individual nations become common property. National one-sidedness and narrow-mindedness become more and more impossible, and from the numerous national and local literatures, there arises a world literature.

The bourgeoisie, by the rapid improvement of all instruments of production, by the immensely facilitated means of communication, draws all, even the most barbarian, nations into civilisation. The cheap prices of its commodities are the heavy artillery with which it batters down all

Chinese walls, with which it forces the barbarians' intensely obstinate hatred of foreigners to capitulate. It compels all nations, on pain of extinction, to adopt the bourgeois mode of production; it compels them to introduce what it calls civilisation into their midst, i.e., to become bourgeois themselves. In one word, it creates a world after its own image.

The bourgeoisie has subjected the country to the rule of the towns. It has created enormous cities, has greatly increased the urban population as compared with the rural, and has thus rescued a considerable part of the population from the idiocy of rural life. Just as it has made the country dependent on the towns, so it has made barbarian and semi-barbarian countries dependent on the civilised ones, nations of peasants on nations of bourgeois, the East on the West.

The bourgeoisie keeps more and more doing away with the scattered state of the population, of the means of production, and of property. It has agglomerated population, centralised means of production, and has concentrated property in a few hands. The necessary consequence of this was political centralisation. Independent, or but loosely connected provinces with separate interests, laws, governments and systems of taxation, became lumped together into one nation, with one government, one code of laws, one national class-interest, one frontier and one customs-tariff.

The bourgeoisie, during its rule of scarce one hundred years, has created more massive and more colossal productive forces than have all preceding generations together. Subjection of Nature's forces to man, machinery, application of chemistry to industry and agriculture, steam-navigation, railways, electric telegraphs, clearing of whole continents for cultivation, canalisation of rivers, whole populations conjured out of the ground – what earlier century had even a presentiment that such productive forces slumbered in the lap of social labour? . . .

chapter 11

Historical Tendency of Capitalist Accumulation (1845)

What does the primitive accumulation of capital, i.e., its historical genesis, resolve itself into? In so far as it is not immediate transformation of slaves and serfs into wage labourers, and therefore a mere change of form, it only means the expropriation of the immediate producers, i.e., the dissolution of private property based on the labour of its owner. Private property, as the antithesis to social, collective property, exists only where the means of labour and the external conditions of labour belong to private individuals. But according as these private individuals are labourers or not labourers, private property has a different character. The numberless shades, that it at first sight presents, correspond to the intermediate stages lying between these two extremes. The private property of the labourer in his means of production is the foundation of petty industry, whether agricultural, manufacturing, or both; petty industry, again, is an essential condition for the development of social production and of the free individuality of the labourer himself. Of course, this petty mode of production exists also under slavery, serfdom, and other states of dependence. But it flourishes, it lets loose its whole energy, it attains its adequate classical form, only where the labourer is the private owner of his own means of labour set in action by himself: the peasant of the land which he cultivates, the artisan of the tool which he handles as a virtuoso. This mode of production presupposes parcelling of the soil, and scattering of the other means of production. As it excludes the concentration of these means of production, so also it excludes co-operation, division of labour within each separate process of production, the control over, and the productive application of the forces of Nature by society, and the free development of the social productive powers. It is compatible only with a system of production, and a society, moving within narrow and more or less primitive bounds. . . . At a certain stage of development it brings forth the material agencies for its own dissolution. From that moment new forces and new passions spring up in the bosom of society; but the old social organisation fetters them and keeps them down. It must be annihilated;

it is annihilated. Its annihilation, the transformation of the individualised and scattered means of production into socially concentrated ones, of the pigmy property of the many into the huge property of the few, the expropriation of the great mass of the people from the soil, from the means of subsistence, and from the means of labour, this fearful and painful expropriation of the mass of the people forms the prelude to the history of capital. It comprises a series of forcible methods, of which we have passed in review only those that have been epoch-making as methods of the primitive accumulation of capital. The expropriation of the immediate producers was accomplished with merciless Vandalism, and under the stimulus of passions the most infamous, the most sordid, the pettiest, the most meanly odious. Self-earned private property, that is based, so to say, on the fusing together of the isolated, independent labouring individual with the conditions of his labour, is supplanted by capitalistic private property, which rests on exploitation of the nominally free labour of others, i.e., on wage labour.

As soon as this process of transformation has sufficiently decomposed the old society from top to bottom, as soon as the labourers are turned into proletarians, their means of labour into capital, as soon as the capitalist mode of production stands on its own feet, then the further socialisation of labour and further transformation of the land and other means of production into socially exploited and, therefore, common means of production, as well as the further expropriation of private proprietors, takes a new form. That which is now to be expropriated is no longer the labourer working for himself, but the capitalist exploiting many labourers. This expropriation is accomplished by the action of the immanent laws of capitalistic production itself, by the centralisation of capital. One capitalist always kills many. Hand in hand with this centralisation, or this expropriation of many capitalists by few, develop, on an ever-extending scale, the co-operative form of the labour process, the conscious technical application of science, the methodical cultivation of the soil, the transformation of the instruments of labour into instruments of labour only usable in common, the economising of all means of production by their use as the means of production of combined, socialised labour, the entanglement of all peoples in the net of the world market, and with this, the international character of the capitalistic régime. Along with the constantly diminishing number of the magnates of capital, who usurp and monopolise all advantages of this process of transformation, grows the mass of misery, oppression, slavery, degradation, exploitation; but with this too grows the revolt of the working class. . . .

chapter 12

Co-operation (1867)

Capitalist production only then really begins . . . when each individual capital employs simultaneously a comparatively large number of labourers; when consequently the labour process is carried on on an extensive scale and yields, relatively, large quantities of products. A greater number of labourers working together, at the same time, in one place (or, if you will, in the same field of labour), in order to produce the same sort of commodity under the mastership of one capitalist, constitutes, both historically and logically, the starting point of capitalist production. . . .

When numerous labourers work together side by side, whether in one and the same process, or in different but connected processes, they are said to co-operate, or to work in co-operation.

Just as the offensive power of a squadron of cavalry, or the defensive power of a regiment of infantry, is essentially different from the sum of the offensive or defensive powers of the individual cavalry or infantry soldiers taken separately, so the sum total of the mechanical forces exerted by isolated workmen differs from the social force that is developed, when many hands take part simultaneously in one and the same undivided operation, such as raising a heavy weight, turning a winch, or removing an obstacle. In such cases the effect of the combined labour could either not be produced at all by isolated individual labour, or it could only be produced by a great expenditure of time, or on a very dwarfed scale. Not only have we here an increase in the productive power of the individual, by means of co-operation, but the creation of a new power, namely, the collective power of masses.

Apart from the new power that arises from the fusion of many forces into one single force, mere social contact begets in most industries an emulation and a stimulation of the animal spirits that heighten the efficiency of each individual workman. Hence it is that a dozen persons working together will, in their collective working day of 144 hours, produce far more than twelve isolated men each working 12 hours, or than one man who works twelve days in succession. The reason of this is that man is . . . at all events a social animal.

Although a number of men may be occupied together at the same time on the same, or the same kind of work, yet the labour of each, as a part of the collective labour, may correspond to a distinct phase of the labour process, through all whose phases, in consequence of co-operation, the subject of their labour passes with greater speed. For instance, if a dozen masons place themselves in a row, so as to pass stones from the foot of a ladder to its summit, each of them does the same thing; nevertheless, their separate acts form connected parts of one total operation; they are particular phases, which must be gone through by each stone; and the stones are thus carried up quicker by the 24 hands of the row of men than they could be if each man went separately up and down the ladder with his burden. The object is carried over the same distance in a shorter time. Again, a combination of labour occurs whenever a building, for instance, is taken in hand on different sides simultaneously; although here also the co-operating masons are doing the same, or the same kind of work. The 12 masons, in their collective working day of 144 hours, make much more progress with the building than one mason could make working for 12 days, or 144 hours. The reason is, that a body of men working in concert has hands and eyes both before and behind, and is, to a certain degree, omnipresent. The various parts of the work progress simultaneously.

In the above instances we have laid stress upon the point that the men do the same, or the same kind of work, because this, the most simple form of labour in common, plays a great part in co-operation, even in its most fully developed stage. If the work be complicated, then the mere number of the men who co-operate allows of the various operations being apportioned to different hands, and, consequently, of being carried on simultaneously. The time necessary for the completion of the whole work is thereby shortened.

In many industries, there are critical periods, determined by the nature of the process, during which certain definite results must be obtained. For instance, if a flock of sheep has to be shorn, or a field of wheat to be cut and harvested, the quantity and quality of the product depends on the work being begun and ended within a certain time. In these cases, the time that ought to be taken by the process is prescribed, just as it is in herring fishing. A single person cannot carve a working day of more than, say 12 hours, out of the natural day, but 100 men co-operating extend the working day to 1,200 hours. The shortness of the time allowed for the work is compensated for by the large mass of labour thrown upon the field of production at the decisive moment. The completion of the task within the proper time depends on the simultaneous application of numerous combined working days; the amount of useful effect depends on the number of labourers; this number, however, is always smaller than the number of isolated labourers required to do the same amount of work in the same period. . . .

On the one hand, co-operation allows of the work being carried on over an extended space; it is consequently imperatively called for in certain undertakings, such as draining, constructing dykes, irrigation works, and the making of canals, roads and railways. On the other hand, while extending the scale of production, it renders possible a relative contraction of the arena. This contraction of arena simultaneous with, and arising from, extension of scale, whereby a number of useless expenses are cut down, is owing to the conglomeration of labourers, to the aggregation of various processes, and to the concentration of the means of production.

The combined working day produces, relatively to an equal sum of isolated working days, a greater quantity of use values, and, consequently, diminishes the labour time necessary for the production of a given useful effect. Whether the combined working day, in a given case, acquires this increased productive power, because it heightens the mechanical force of labour, or extends its sphere of action over a greater space, or contracts the field of production relatively to the scale of production, or at the critical moment sets large masses of labour to work, or excites emulation between individuals and raises their animal spirits, or impresses on the similar operations carried on by a number of men the stamp of continuity and many-sidedness, or performs simultaneously different operations, or economises the means of production by use in common, or lends to individual labour the character of average social labour – whichever of these be the cause of the increase, the special productive power of the combined working day is, under all circumstances, the social productive power of labour, or the productive power of social labour. This power is due to co-operation itself. When the labourer co-operates systematically with others, he strips off the fetters of his individuality, and develops the capabilities of his species.

As a general rule, labourers cannot co-operate without being brought together: their assemblage in one place is a necessary condition of their co-operation. Hence wage labourers cannot co-operate, unless they are employed simultaneously by the same capital, the same capitalist, and unless therefore their labour powers are bought simultaneously by him. . . .

All combined labour on a large scale requires, more or less, a directing authority, in order to secure the harmonious working of the individual activities, and to perform the general functions that have their origin in the action of the combined organism, as distinguished from the action of its separate organs. A single violin player is his own conductor; an orchestra requires a separate one. The work of directing, superintending, and adjusting, becomes one of the functions of capital, from the moment that the labour under the control of capital, becomes co-operative. Once a function of capital, it acquires special characteristics.

. . . As the number of the co-operating labourers increases, so too does their resistance to the domination of capital, and with it, the necessity for capital to overcome this resistance by counterpressure. The control exercised by the capitalist is not only a special function, due to the nature of the social labour process, and peculiar to that process, but it is, at the same time a function of the exploitation of a social labour process, and is consequently rooted in the unavoidable antagonism between the exploiter and the living and labouring raw material he exploits.

... [I]n proportion to the increasing mass of the means of production, now no longer the property of the labourer, but of the capitalist, the necessity increases for some effective control over the proper application of those means. Moreover, the co-operation of wage labourers is entirely brought about by the capital that employs them. Their union into one single productive body and the establishment of a connexion between their individual functions, are matters foreign and external to them, are not their own act, but the act of the capital that brings and keeps them together. Hence the connexion existing between their various labours appears to them, ideally, in the shape of a preconceived plan of the capitalist, and practically in the shape of the authority of the same capitalist, in the shape of the powerful will of another, who subjects their activity to his aims. If, then, the control of the capitalist is in substance twofold by reason of the twofold nature of the process of production itself, – which, on the one hand, is a social process for producing use values, on the other, a process for creating surplus value in form that control is despotic. As co-operation extends its scale, this despotism takes forms peculiar to itself. Just as at first the capitalist is relieved from actual labour so soon as his capital has reached that minimum amount with which capitalist production, as such, begins, so now, he hands over the work of direct and constant supervision of the individual workmen, and groups of workmen, to a special kind of wage labourer. An industrial army of workmen, under the command of a capitalist, requires, like a real army, officers (managers), and sergeants (foremen, overlookers), who, while the work is being done, command in the name of the capitalist. The work of supervision becomes their established and exclusive function. . . . It is not because he is a leader of industry that a man is a capitalist; on the contrary, he is a leader of industry because he is a capitalist. The leadership of industry is an attribute of capital, just as in feudal times the functions of general and judge, were attributes of landed property.

... Being independent of each other, the labourers are isolated persons, who enter into relations with the capitalist, but not with one another. This co-operation begins only with the labour process, but they have then ceased to belong to themselves. On entering that process, they become incorporated with capital. As co-operators, as members of a working organism, they are but special modes of existence of capital. Hence, the productive power developed by the labourer when working in co-operation, is the productive power of capital. This power is developed gratuitously, whenever the workmen are placed under given conditions, and it is capital that places them under such conditions. Because this power costs capital nothing, and because, on the other hand, the labourer himself does not develop it before his labour belongs to capital, it appears as a power with which capital is endowed by Nature – a productive power that is immanent in capital.

The colossal effects of simple co-operation are to be seen in the gigantic structures of the ancient Asiatics, Egyptians, Etruscans, &c. . . .

This power of Asiatic and Egyptian kings, Etruscan theocrats, &c., has in modern society been transferred to the capitalist, whether he be an isolated, or as in joint-stock companies, a collective capitalist.

Co-operation, such as we find it at the dawn of human development, among races who live by the chase, or, say, in the agriculture of Indian communities, is based, on the one hand, on ownership in common of the means of production, and on the other hand, on the fact, that in those cases, each individual has no more torn himself off from the navel-string of his tribe or community, than each bee has freed itself from connexion with the hive. Such co-operation is distinguished from capitalistic co-operation by both of the above characteristics. The sporadic application of co-operation on a large scale in ancient times, in the Middle Ages, and in modern colonies, reposes on relations of dominion and servitude, principally on slavery. The capitalistic form, on the contrary, pre-supposes from first to last, the free wage labourer, who sells his labour power to capital. Historically, however, this form is developed in opposition to peasant agriculture and to the carrying on of independent handicrafts whether in guilds or not. From the standpoint of these, capitalistic co-operation does not manifest itself as a particular historical form of co-operation, but co-operation itself appears to be a historical form peculiar to, and specifically distinguishing, the capitalist process of production. . . .

Co-operation ever constitutes the fundamental form of the capitalist mode of production, nevertheless the elementary form of co-operation continues to subsist as a particular form of capitalist production side by side with the more developed forms of that mode of production.

chapter 13

Cardinal Facts of Capitalist Production (1894)

Three cardinal facts of capitalist production:

1) Concentration of means of production in few hands, whereby they cease to appear as the property of the immediate labourers and turn into social production capacities. Even if initially they are the private property of capitalists. These are the trustees of bourgeois society, but they pocket all the proceeds of this trusteeship.

2) Organisation of labour itself into social labour: through co-operation, division of labour, and the uniting of labour with the natural sciences.

In these two senses, the capitalist mode of production abolishes private property and private labour, even though in contradictory forms.

3) Creation of the world market.

The stupendous productive power developing under the capitalist mode of production relative to population, and the increase, if not in the same proportion, of capital values (not just of their material substance), which grow much more rapidly than the population, contradict the basis, which constantly narrows in relation to the expanding wealth, and for which all this immense productive power works. They also contradict the conditions under which this swelling capital augments its value. Hence the crises.

part 3

Marx's Labor Theory of Value: The Hidden Social Relationship beneath Capitalism's Distorted "Economic" Surface

Marx argued that extractive relations between pre-capitalist ruling classes and direct producers were transparent; abject dependency and lack of freedom made slaves and serfs aware that their master or lord expropriated their labor time and product. By contrast, Marx held, capitalist extraction is obscured by wage labor's "false appearance" as a voluntary contract between equals and fair or commensurate exchange. In his view, political economists' portrayals of capitalist freedom and choice hide exploitation – that workers are not paid for the full value of their labor and product. Marx claimed that new concepts are needed to overcome this ideological distortion. In his view, genuine understanding of capitalism requires a move parallel to that of modern physics, which defied everyday experience and seemed paradoxical (e.g., "the earth moves round the sun"). Marx aimed to create a social theory that would upset taken-for-granted economic views and bring to light matters they conceal.

This section addresses *Capital*'s core analytical framework – the "labor theory of value." Although departing from broader historical materialist principles (stressing the centrality of labor and surplus extraction), Marx formulated the theory to illuminate the capitalist mode of production's historically specific types of class relations, expropriation, and ideology. He designed the theory to counter commonsense categories, and thus it may seem abstract or be hard to grasp the first time through. Marx developed his concepts by engaging concrete social issues and moving back and forth between history and theory. Thus, a good way to assimilate his theory of value as well as the broad theoretical issues discussed in the previous two parts is to return to them while you read the more descriptive sociological and historical commentaries in later parts.

Drawn from the start of the first volume of *Capital*, the first selection addresses "commodities," products traded in capitalist markets, and the basis of capitalism's accumulated wealth. Marx held that commodities have a twofold nature: qualitative properties that satisfy human needs and wants – "use value" – and a quantitative side manifested in proportional rates by which they trade against each other – "exchange value." He asserted that the study of use values yields "commercial knowledge of commodities" (thus informing entrepreneurs about the types of products that stimulate or meet consumer demand). Having different purposes, however, Marx focused on exchange value. He contended that prices are regulated ultimately by "value," or the "labor time" that it takes to produce commodities (e.g., to locate and refine raw materials, build or repair worn tools, fashion parts, construct products). Thus, their value on the market is proportional to the amount of labor time that goes into them. Marx opposed his theory of value to commonsense economic categories, which saw market prices of commodities as deriving from intrinsic qualities, or use values, and implied that proportional exchange rates are accidental or arbitrary. He intended to expose the underlying "social substance" that shapes the most important events on this ideologically distorted economic surface.

The selection from "Value, Price and Profit" presents, in very condensed form, broader facets of Marx's theory of value, which appear in greater detail in the first volume of *Capital*. He elaborated and qualified his idea that value is "crystallized social labor." He stressed that concrete conditions of production and labor times vary with each producer, and that prices fluctuate above and below their value. Marx even acknowledged the role of supply and demand. For example, it takes much labor time to make a nuclear reactor, and thus, on average, its price is high. However, if the public, in some regions, deem nuclear energy to be dangerous and shift to another form of power, reactors may be sold far below their value, or even be worthless. For Marx, value exerts its force in central tendencies of aggregate prices. He explained that it manifests *socially necessary* labor time, or average productive conditions for an overall economy and industry. Thus, although specific producers and prices may vary widely, efficient producers set overall value and shape the central tendencies. Most important, Marx saw "labor power" as containing the secret of capitalist exchange. In his view, it is fundamentally different from any other commodity, because it is the only one to produce more value than the costs of its production. Recall Marx's point that workers do not own productive property, and therefore must sell their labor power to capitalists. Like other commodities, he contended, its price is the average labor time to produce it – in this case that needed for worker subsistence. However, Marx explained that labor power, under capitalism, produces surpluses beyond a worker's subsistence costs, and that wages do *not* pay the full value of his or her product and labor time. Overall, Marx saw this "unpaid labor," or "surplus value," to be the ultimate source of profit. He stipulated that other factors (e.g., good management) may impact and even have fateful consequences in particular cases, but that the expropriated surplus of wage labor is *the* systematic basis of overall capitalist accumulation. In this way, Marx identified capitalism's unique form of surplus extraction and distinct type of ruling class and direct producer.

The selection on commodity fetishism, from the first volume of *Capital*, compares everyday views about value inhering in useful properties of commodities to totemic religious beliefs. Marx described how this commonsense economic standpoint conceals the vital social processes operating below capitalism's distorted surface. He declared that the social relationship between capitalist and worker appears in "the fantastic form of a relation between things." Arguing that value does not "stalk about" with a self-explanatory label, Marx held that expropriated labor time constitutes a secret hidden in the economic surface's "social hieroglyphic." In his view, capitalism generates a profound mystification that makes productive life appear as a natural event outside human control and that allows objects of our own creation to dominate us. Marx insisted that a genuinely free culture would restore our grip on social life, and that production and its fruits would be subjected to a plan oriented to individual and community wants and capacities.

Commenting on the "general formula for capital," Marx held that distinctively capitalist circulation is based on buying in order to sell for an increased price and reinvesting the money in more purchases to seek more and more profit, *ad infinitum* (i.e., rather than buying for personal consumption). In his view, the capitalist is a "rational miser" who aims at ceaseless accumulation of "wealth in the abstract." Although holding that capitalists revolutionized production and created a heretofore unparalleled quantity and array of products, Marx argued that use values proliferate only because they inhere in commodities that are produced to increase exchange value and that depend on value, or appropriated labor time. His insistence on the dominance of value does not merely split analytical hairs. Rather, Marx framed his view to address a new capitalist world in which global poverty grew along with expanded wealth and in which economic crisis and social misery could result from production of too many products as well as too few. In his view, employing the same productive forces under a different regime or mode of production oriented primarily to use value would bring fundamental change and reduce sharply unnecessary suffering. For Marx, capitalist circulation, above all, is designed to realize surplus value, or unpaid labor, which is crystallized in the commodity and is reappropriated by capitalists in the money-form through market exchange or sale.

Critics of Marx's theory of value, including neo-Marxists, have argued that it is exceptionally difficult to subject the approach to decisive empirical test, and that this problem is growing in today's "high-tech," "information economy." Also, Marxists and interpreters of Marx have frequently ignored, with mixed results, his theory of value, treating his historical and sociological analyses independently. Others have dismissed the theory on various grounds, often holding that its failure bankrupts all of Marx's thought. Putting aside the debate over the theory's validity as an overall explanation of capitalist prices and profits, it still has heuristic value insofar as it raises important questions, which can be subjected to inquiry. Most important, it counters the all too frequent claim that investors create the wealth in the so-called new economy, and that consumer preferences rule. Such views ignore the later twentieth century's dramatic increases in the global working class and their contribution to the values at Wal-Mart and on Wall Street. Economic expansion in rich nations was accompanied by increased global economic inequality, poverty, and profound immiseration in certain groups and regions (e.g., sub-Saharan Africa). Marx's theory challenges us to ask if the increased leverage of capital over labor (deriving from global production and deregulation) and consequent longer work week, intensified labor regimes, and reduced benefits for many workers might have contributed to the high corporate profits, soaring stock market, and low inflation in the late 1990s in the United States.

Overall, Marx's argument about the two-sided commodity manifests a broader dualism that he felt suffused capitalism – a fundamental tension between "real wealth," products that meet human needs and satisfy wants and enrich us individually and culturally, and "abstract wealth," monetary or investment capital accumulated by capitalists and shared today by privileged portions of the middle class. Marx attacked the arguments by economic elites and bourgeois economists that naturalize and put a halo around this split (e.g., that accumulation by capitalists is the motor of all wealth creation, and that its benefits trickle down to everyone). Emphasizing contradictions between the two forms of wealth, Marx challenges us to ask whether the already extreme and growing gap in the global economy between masses of people who lead lives of poverty and drudgery and the chief beneficiaries of capitalist accumulation is a product of capitalism and is necessary.

chapter 14

The Two Factors of a Commodity: Use Value and Value (1867)

The wealth of those societies in which the capitalist mode of production prevails, presents itself as "an immense accumulation of commodities".... Our investigation must therefore begin with the analysis of a commodity.

A commodity is, in the first place, an object outside us, a thing that by its properties satisfies human wants of some sort or another. The nature of such wants, whether, for instance, they spring from the stomach or from fancy, makes no difference. Neither are we here concerned to know how the object satisfies these wants, whether directly as means of subsistence, or indirectly as means of production.

Every useful thing, as iron, paper, &c., may be looked at from the two points of view of quality and quantity. It is an assemblage of many properties, and may therefore be of use in various ways. To discover the various uses of things is the work of history. So also is the establishment of socially-recognised standards of measure for the quantities of these useful objects. The diversity of these measures has its origin partly in the diverse nature of the objects to be measured, partly in convention.

The utility of a thing makes it a use value. But this utility is not a thing of air. Being limited by the physical properties of the commodity, it has no existence apart from that commodity. A commodity, such as iron, corn, or a diamond, is therefore, so far as it is a material thing, a use value, something useful. This property of a commodity is independent of the amount of labour required to appropriate its useful qualities. When treating of use value, we always assume to be dealing with definite quantities, such as dozens of watches, yards of linen, or tons of iron. The use values of commodities furnish the material for a special study, that of the commercial knowledge of commodities. Use values become a reality only by use or consumption: they also constitute the substance of all wealth, whatever may be the social form of that wealth. In the form of society we are about to consider, they are, in addition, the material depositories of exchange value.

Exchange value, at first sight, presents itself as a quantitative relation, as the proportion in which values in use of one sort are exchanged for those of another sort, a relation constantly changing with time and place. Hence exchange value appears to be something accidental and purely relative, and consequently an intrinsic value, i.e., an exchange value that is inseparably connected with, inherent in commodities, seems a contradiction in terms. . . .

Let us take two commodities, e.g., corn and iron. The proportions in which they are exchangeable, whatever those proportions may be, can always be represented by an equation in which a given quantity of corn is equated to some quantity of iron: e.g., 1 quarter corn = x cwt. iron. What does this equation tell us? It tells us that in two different things – in 1 quarter of corn and x cwt. of iron, there exists in equal quantities something common to both. The two things must therefore be equal to a third, which in itself is neither the one nor the other. Each of them, so far as it is exchange value, must therefore be reducible to this third.

A simple geometrical illustration will make this clear. In order to calculate and compare the areas of rectilinear figures, we decompose them into triangles. But the area of the triangle itself is expressed by something totally different from its visible figure, namely, by half the product of the base multiplied by the altitude. In the same way the exchange values of commodities must be capable of being expressed in terms of something common to them all, of which thing they represent a greater or less quantity.

This common "something" cannot be either a geometrical, a chemical, or any other natural property of commodities. Such properties claim our attention only in so far as they affect the utility of those commodities, make them use values. But the exchange of commodities is evidently an act characterised by a total abstraction from use value. Then one use value is just as good as another, provided only it be present in sufficient quantity. . . .

As use values, commodities are, above all, of different qualities, but as exchange values they are merely different quantities, and consequently do not contain an atom of use value.

If then we leave out of consideration the use value of commodities, they have only one common property left, that of being products of labour. But even the product of labour itself has undergone a change in our hands. If we make abstraction from its use value, we make abstraction at the same time from the material elements and shapes that make the product a use value; we see in it no longer a table, a house, yarn, or any other useful thing. Its existence as a material thing is put out of sight. Neither can it any longer be regarded as the product of the labour of the joiner, the mason, the spinner, or of any other definite kind of productive labour. Along with the useful qualities of the products themselves, we put out of sight both the useful character of the various kinds of labour embodied in them, and the concrete forms of that labour; there is nothing left but what is common to them all; all are reduced to one and the same sort of labour, human labour in the abstract.

Let us now consider the residue of each of these products; it consists of the same unsubstantial reality in each, a mere congelation of homogeneous human labour, of labour power expended without regard to the mode of its expenditure. All that these things now tell us is, that human labour power has been expended in their production, that human labour is embodied in them. When looked at as crystals of this social substance, common to them all, they are – Values.

We have seen that when commodities are exchanged, their exchange value manifests itself as something totally independent of their use value. But if we abstract from their use value, there remains their Value as defined above. Therefore, the common substance that manifests itself in the exchange value of commodities, whenever they are exchanged, is their value. The progress of our investigation will show that exchange value is the only form in which the value of commodities can manifest itself or be expressed. . . .

chapter 15

From Value, Price and Profit *(1898)*

Value and Labour

... The first question we have to put is: What is the *value* of a commodity? How is it determined?

At first sight it would seem that the value of a commodity is a thing quite *relative*, and not to be settled without considering one commodity in its relations to all other commodities. In fact, in speaking of the value, the value in exchange of a commodity, we mean the proportional quantities in which it exchanges with all other commodities. But then arises the question: How are the proportions in which commodities exchange with each other regulated?

We know from experience that these proportions vary infinitely. Taking one single commodity, wheat, for instance, we shall find that a quarter of wheat exchanges in almost countless variations of proportion with different commodities. Yet, *its value remaining always the same*, whether expressed in silk, gold, or any other commodity, it must be something distinct from, and independent of, these *different rates of exchange* with different articles. It must be possible to express, in a very different form, these various equations with various commodities. . . .

As the *exchangeable values* of commodities are only *social functions* of those things, and have nothing at all to do with their *natural* qualities, we must first ask, What is the common *social substance* of all commodities? It is *Labour*. To produce a commodity a certain amount of labour must be bestowed upon it, or worked up in it. And I say not only *Labour*, but *social Labour*. A man who produces an article for his own immediate use, to consume it himself, creates a *product*, but not a *commodity*. As a self-sustaining producer he has nothing to do with society. But to produce a *commodity*, a man must not only produce an article satisfying some *social* want, but his labour itself must form part and parcel of the total sum of labour expended by society. It must be subordinate to the *Division of Labour within*

Society. It is nothing without the other divisions of labour, and on its part is required to *integrate* them.

If we consider *commodities as values*, we consider them exclusively under the single aspect of *realised, fixed*, or, if you like, *crystallised social labour*. In this respect they can *differ* only by representing greater or smaller quantities of labour, as, for example, a greater amount of labour may be worked up in a silken handkerchief than in a brick. But how does one measure *quantities of labour*? By the *time the labour lasts*, in measuring the labour by the hour, the day, etc. Of course, to apply this measure, all sorts of labour are reduced to average or simple labour as their unit.

We arrive, therefore, at this conclusion. A commodity has *a value*, because it is a *crystallisation of social labour*. The *greatness* of its value, or its *relative* value, depends upon the greater or less amount of that social substance contained in it; that is to say, on the relative mass of labour necessary for its production. The *relative values of commodities* are, therefore, determined by the *respective quantities* or *amounts of labour, worked up, realised, fixed in them*. The *correlative* quantities of commodities which can be produced in the *same time of labour* are *equal*. Or the value of one commodity is to the value of another commodity as the quantity of labour fixed in the one is to the quantity of labour fixed in the other.

I suspect that many of you will ask, Does then, indeed, there exist such a vast, or any difference whatever, between determining the values of commodities by *wages*, and determining them by the *relative quantities of labour* necessary for their production? You must, however, be aware that the *reward* for labour, and *quantity* of labour, are quite disparate things. Suppose, for example, *equal quantities of labour* to be fixed in one quarter of wheat and one ounce of gold. . . . We suppose, then, that one quarter of wheat and one ounce of gold are *equal values* or *equivalents*, because they are *crystallisations of equal amounts of average labour*, of so many days' or so many weeks' labour respectively fixed in them. In thus determining the relative values of gold and corn, do we refer in any way whatever to the *wages* of the agricultural labourer and the miner? Not a bit. We leave it quite *indeterminate how* their day's or week's labour was paid, or even whether wages labour was employed at all. If it was, wages may have been very unequal. The labourer whose labour is realised in the quarter of wheat may receive two bushels only, and the labourer employed in mining may receive one-half of the ounce of gold. Or, supposing their wages to be equal, they may deviate in all possible proportions from the values of the commodities produced by them. They may amount to one-half, one-third, one-fourth, one-fifth, or any other proportional part of the one quarter of corn or the one ounce of gold. Their *wages* can, of course, not *exceed*, not be *more* than the values of the commodities they produced, but they can be *less* in every possible degree. Their *wages* will be *limited* by the *values* of the products, but the *values of their products* will not be limited by the wages. And above all, the values, the relative values of corn and gold, for example, will have been settled without any regard whatever to the value of the labour employed, that is to say, to *wages*. To determine the values of commodities by the *relative quantities of labour fixed in them*, is, therefore, a thing quite different from the tautological method of determining the values of commodities by the value of labour, or by *wages*. This point, however, will be further elucidated in the progress of our inquiry.

In calculating the exchangeable value of a commodity we must add to the quantity of labour *last* employed the quantity of labour *previously* worked up in the raw material of the commodity, and the labour bestowed on the implements, tools, machinery, and buildings, with which such labour is assisted. For example, the value of a certain amount of cotton-yarn is the crystallisation of the quantity of labour added to the cotton during the spinning process, the quantity of labour previously realised in the cotton itself, the quantity of labour realised in the coal, oil and other auxiliary substances used, the quantity of labour fixed in the steam engine, the spindles, the factory building, and so forth. Instruments of production properly so-called, such as tools, machinery, buildings, serve again and again for a longer or shorter period during repeated processes of production. If they were used up at once, like the raw material, their whole value would at once be transferred to the commodities they assist in producing. But as a spindle, for example, is but gradually used up, an average calculation is made, based upon the average time it lasts, and its average waste or wear and tear during a certain period, say a day. In this way we calculate how much of the value of the spindle is transferred to the yarn daily spun, and how much, therefore, of the total amount of labour realised in a pound of yarn, for example, is due to the quantity of labour previously realised in the spindle. For our present purpose it is not necessary to dwell any longer upon this point.

It might seem that if the value of a commodity is determined by the *quantity of labour bestowed upon its production*, the lazier a man, or the clumsier a man, the more valuable his commodity, because the greater the time of labour required for finishing the commodity. This, however, would be a sad mistake. You will recollect that I used the word "*Social* labour", and many points are involved in this qualification of "*Social*". In saying that the value of a commodity is determined by the *quantity of labour* worked up or crystallised in it, we mean *the quantity of labour necessary* for its production in a given state of society, under certain social average conditions of production, with a given social average intensity, and average skill of the labour employed. When, in England, the power-loom came to compete with the hand-loom, only one half of the former time of labour was wanted to convert a given amount of yarn into a yard of cotton or cloth. The poor hand-loom weaver now worked seventeen or eighteen hours daily, instead of the nine or ten hours he had worked before. Still the product of twenty hours of his labour represented now only ten social hours of labour, or ten hours of labour socially necessary for the conversion of a certain amount of yarn into textile stuffs. His product of twenty hours had, therefore, no more value than his former product of ten hours.

If then the quantity of socially necessary labour realised in commodities regulates their exchangeable values, every increase in the quantity of labour wanted for the production of a commodity must augment its value, as every diminution must lower it.

If the respective quantities of labour necessary for the production of the respective commodities remained constant, their relative values also would be constant. But such is not the case. The quantity of labour necessary for the production of a commodity changes continuously with the changes in the productive powers of the labour employed. The greater the productive powers of labour, the more produce is finished in a given time of labour, and the smaller the productive powers of labour, the less produce is finished in the same time. If, for example, in the progress of population it should become necessary to cultivate less fertile soils, the same amount of produce would be only attainable by a greater amount of labour spent, and the value of agricultural produce would consequently rise. On the other hand, if with the modern means of production, a single spinner converts into yarn, during one working day, many thousand times the amount of cotton which he could have spun during the same time with the spinning wheel, it is evident that every single pound of cotton will absorb many thousand times less of spinning labour than it did before, and, consequently, the value added by spinning to every single pound of cotton will be a thousand times less than before. The value of yarn will sink accordingly.

Apart from the different natural energies and acquired working abilities of different peoples, the productive powers of labour must principally depend:

Firstly. Upon the *natural* conditions of labour, such as fertility of soil, mines, and so forth;

Secondly. Upon the progressive improvement of the *Social Powers of Labour*, such as are derived from production on a grand scale, concentration of capital and combination of labour, subdivision of labour, machinery, improved methods, appliance of chemical and other natural agencies, shortening of time and space by means of communication and transport, and every other contrivance by which science presses natural agencies into the service of labour, and by which the social or co-operative character of labour is developed. The greater the productive powers of labour, the less labour is bestowed upon a given amount of produce; hence the smaller the value of this produce. The smaller the productive powers of labour, the more labour is bestowed upon the same amount

of produce; hence the greater its value. As a general law we may, therefore, set it down that: –

*The values of commodities are directly as the times of labour employed in their
production, and are inversely as the productive powers of the labour employed.*

Having till now only spoken of *Value*, I shall add a few words about
Price, which is a peculiar form assumed by value.

Price, taken by itself, is nothing but the *monetary expression of value*. The
values of all commodities of this country, for example, are expressed in
gold prices, while on the Continent they are mainly expressed in silver
prices. The value of gold or silver, like that of all other commodities,
is regulated by the quantity of labour necessary for getting them. You
exchange a certain amount of your national products, in which a certain
amount of your national labour is crystallised, for the produce of the gold
and silver producing countries, in which a certain quantity of *their* labour
is crystallised. It is in this way, in fact by barter, that you learn to express
in gold and silver the values of all commodities, that is, the respective
quantities of labour bestowed upon them. Looking somewhat closer into
the *monetary expression of value*, or what comes to the same, the *conversion
of value into price*, you will find that it is a process by which you give to
the *values* of all commodities an *independent* and *homogeneous form*, or by
which you express them as quantities of *equal* social labour. So far as it
is but the monetary expression of value, price has been called *natural price*
by Adam Smith, "*prix nécessaire*" by the French physiocrats.

What then is the relation between *value* and *market prices*, or between
natural prices and *market prices*? You all know that the *market price* is the
same for all commodities of the same kind, however the conditions of
production may differ for the individual producers. The market price
expresses only the *average amount of social labour* necessary, under the average conditions of production, to supply the market with a certain mass
of a certain article. It is calculated upon the whole lot of a commodity of
a certain description.

So far the *market price* of a commodity coincides with its *value*. On the
other hand, the oscillations of market prices, rising now over, sinking now
under the value or natural price, depend upon the fluctuations of supply
and demand. . . .

I cannot now sift this matter. It suffices to say that *if* supply and
demand equilibrate each other, the market prices of commodities will
correspond to their natural prices, that is to say, to their values, as determined by the respective quantities of labour required for their production. But supply and demand *must* constantly tend to equilibrate each other,
although they do so only by compensating one fluctuation by another, a
rise by a fall, and vice versa. If instead of considering only the daily fluctuations you analyse the movement of market prices for longer periods . . .
you will find that the fluctuations of market prices, their deviations from

values, their ups and downs, paralyse and compensate each other; so that, apart from the effect of monopolies and some other modifications I must now pass by, all descriptions of commodities are, on the average, sold at their respective *values* or natural prices. The average periods during which the fluctuations of market prices compensate each other are different for different kinds of commodities, because with one kind it is easier to adapt supply to demand than with the other.

If then, speaking broadly, and embracing somewhat longer periods, all descriptions of commodities sell at their respective values, it is nonsense to suppose that profit, not in individual cases, but that the constant and usual profits of different trades, spring from *surcharging* the prices of commodities, or selling them at a price over and above their *value*. The absurdity of this notion becomes evident if it is generalised. What a man would constantly win as a seller he would as constantly lose as a purchaser. It would not do to say that there are men who are buyers without being sellers, or consumers without being producers. What these people pay to the producers, they must first get from them for nothing. If a man first takes your money and afterwards returns that money in buying your commodities, you will never enrich yourselves by selling your commodities too dear to that same man. This sort of transaction might diminish a loss, but would never help in realising a profit.

To explain, therefore, the *general nature of profits*, you must start from the theorem that, on an average, commodities are *sold at their real value*, and that *profits are derived from selling them at their values*, that is, in proportion to the quantity of labour realised in them. If you cannot explain profit upon this supposition, you cannot explain it at all. This seems paradox and contrary to everyday observation. It is also paradox that the earth moves round the sun, and that water consists of two highly inflammable gases. Scientific truth is always paradox, if judged by everyday experience, which catches only the delusive appearance of things.

Labouring Power

Having now, as far as it could be done in such a cursory manner, analysed the nature of *Value*, of the *Value of any commodity whatever*, we must turn our attention to the specific *Value of Labour*. And here, again, I must startle you by a seeming paradox. All of you feel sure that what they daily sell is their Labour; that, therefore, Labour has a Price, and that, the price of a commodity being only the monetary expression of its value, there must certainly exist such a thing as the *Value of Labour*. However, there exists no such thing as the *Value of Labour* in the common acceptance of the word. We have seen that the amount of necessary labour crystallised in a commodity constitutes its value. Now, applying this notion of value, how could we define, say, the value of a ten hours' working day? How much labour is contained in that day? Ten hours' labour. To say that the value of a ten hours' working day is equal to ten hours' labour, or the quantity of labour contained in it, would be a tautological and, moreover, a nonsensical expression. Of course, having once found out the true but hidden sense of the expression "*Value of Labour*", we shall be able to interpret this irrational, and seemingly impossible application of value, in the same way that, having once made sure of the real movement of the celestial bodies, we shall be able to explain their apparent or merely phenomenal movements.

What the working man sells is not directly his *Labour*, but his *Labouring Power*, the temporary disposal of which he makes over to the capitalist. This is so much the case that I do not know whether by the English Laws, but certainly by some Continental Laws, the *maximum time* is fixed for which a man is allowed to sell his labouring power. If allowed to do so for any indefinite period whatever, slavery would be immediately restored. Such a sale, if it comprised his lifetime, for example, would make him at once the lifelong slave of his employer. . . .

Proceeding from this basis, we shall be able to determine the *Value of Labour* as that of all other commodities.

But before doing so, we might ask, how does this strange phenomenon arise, that we find on the market a set of buyers, possessed of land, machinery, raw material, and the means of subsistence, all of them, save land in its crude state, the *products of labour*, and on the other hand, a set of sellers who have nothing to sell except their labouring power, their working arms and brains? That the one set buys continually in order to make a profit and enrich themselves, while the other set continually sells in order to earn their livelihood? The inquiry into this question would be an inquiry into what the economists call "*Previous, or Original Accumulation*", but which ought to be called *Original Expropriation*. We should find that this so-called *Original Accumulation* means nothing but a series of historical processes, resulting in a *Decomposition of the Original Union* existing between the Labouring Man and his Instruments of Labour. Such an inquiry, however, lies beyond the pale of my present subject. The *Separation* between the Man of Labour and the Instruments of Labour once established, such a state of things will maintain itself and reproduce itself upon a constantly increasing scale. . . .

What, then, is the *Value of Labouring Power*?

Like that of every other commodity, its value is determined by the quantity of labour necessary to produce it. The labouring power of a man exists only in his living individuality. A certain mass of necessaries must be consumed by a man to grow up and maintain his life. But the man, like the machine, will wear out, and must be replaced by another man. Beside the mass of necessaries required for *his own* maintenance, he wants another amount of necessaries to bring up a certain quota of children that are to replace him on the labour market and to perpetuate the race of labourers. Moreover, to develop his labouring power, and acquire a given skill, another amount of values must be spent. For our purpose it suffices to consider only *average* labour, the costs of whose education and development are vanishing magnitudes. Still I must seize upon this occasion to state that, as the costs of producing labouring powers of different quality differ, so must differ the values of the labouring powers employed in different trades. The cry for an *equality of wages* rests, therefore, upon a mistake, is an *insane* wish never to be fulfilled. It is an offspring of that false and superficial radicalism that accepts premises and tries to evade conclusions. Upon the basis of the wages system the value of labouring power is settled like that of every other commodity; and as different kinds of labouring power have different values, or require different quantities of labour for their production, they *must* fetch different prices in the labour market. To clamour for *equal or even equitable retribution* on the basis of the wages system is the same as to clamour for *freedom* on the basis of the slavery system. What you think just or equitable is out of the question. The question is: What is necessary and unavoidable with a given system of production?

After what has been said, it will be seen that the *value of labouring power* is determined by the *value of the necessaries* required to produce, develop, maintain, and perpetuate the labouring power.

Production of Surplus-Value

Now suppose that the average amount of the daily necessaries of a labouring man require *six hours of average labour* for their production. Suppose, moreover, six hours of average labour to be also realised in a quantity of gold equal to 3s. Then 3s. would be the *Price*, or the monetary expression of the *Daily Value* of that man's *Labouring Power*. If he worked daily six hours he would daily produce a value sufficient to buy the average amount of his daily necessaries, or to maintain himself as a labouring man.

But our man is a wages labourer. He must, therefore, sell his labouring power to a capitalist. If he sells it at 3s. daily, or 18s. weekly, he sells it at its value. Suppose him to be a spinner. If he works six hours daily he will add to the cotton a value of 3s. daily. This value, daily added by him, would be an exact equivalent for the wages, or the price of his labouring power, received daily. But in that case *no surplus-value* or *surplus-produce* whatever would go to the capitalist. Here, then, we come to the rub.

In buying the labouring power of the workman, and paying its value, the capitalist, like every other purchaser, has acquired the right to consume or use the commodity bought. You consume or use the labouring power of a man by making him work as you consume or use a machine by making it run. By paying the daily or weekly value of the labouring power of the workman, the capitalist has, therefore, acquired the right to use or make that labouring power work during the *whole day or week*. The working day or the working week has, of course, certain limits, but those we shall afterwards look more closely at.

For the present I want to turn your attention to one decisive point.

The *value* of the labouring power is determined by the quantity of labour necessary to maintain or reproduce it, but the *use* of that labouring power is only limited by the active energies and physical strength of the labourer. The daily or weekly *value* of the labouring power is quite distinct from the daily or weekly *exercise* of that power, the same as the food a horse wants and the time it can carry the horseman are quite distinct. The quantity of labour by which the *value* of the workman's labouring power is limited forms by no means a limit to the quantity of labour which his labouring power is apt to perform. Take the example of our spinner. We have seen that, to daily reproduce his labouring power, he must daily reproduce a value of three shillings, which he will do by working six hours daily. But this does not disable him from working ten or twelve or more hours a day. But by paying the daily or weekly *value* of the spinner's labouring power, the capitalist has acquired the right of using that labouring power during the *whole day or week*. He will, therefore, make him work daily, say, *twelve* hours. *Over and above* the six hours required to replace his wages, or the value of his labouring power, he will, therefore, have to work *six other hours*, which I shall call hours of *surplus-labour*, which surplus labour will realise itself in a *surplus-value* and a *surplus-produce*. If our spinner, for example, by his daily labour of six hours, added three shillings' value to the cotton, a value forming an exact equivalent to his wages, he will, in twelve hours, add six shillings' worth to the cotton, and produce *a proportional surplus of yarn*. As he has sold his labouring power to the capitalist, the whole value or produce created by him belongs to the capitalist, the owner *pro tempore* of his labouring power. By advancing three shillings, the capitalist will, therefore, realise a value of six shillings, because, advancing a value in which six hours of labour are crystallised, he will receive in return a value in which twelve hours of labour are crystallised. By repeating this same process daily, the capitalist will daily advance three shillings and daily pocket six shillings, one-half of which will go to pay wages anew, and the other half of which will form *surplus-value*, for which the capitalist pays no equivalent. It is *this sort of exchange between capital and labour* upon which capitalistic production, or the wages system, is founded, and which must constantly result in reproducing the working man as a working man, and the capitalist as a capitalist.

The rate of surplus-value, all other circumstances remaining the same, will depend on the proportion between that part of the working day necessary to reproduce the value of the labouring power and the *surplus-time* or *surplus-labour* performed for the capitalist. It will, therefore, depend on the *ratio in which the working day is prolonged over and above that extent*, by working which the working man would only reproduce the value of his labouring power, or replace his wages.

Value of Labour

We must now return to the expression, *"Value, or Price of Labour"*.

We have seen that, in fact, it is only the value of the labouring power, measured by the values of commodities necessary for its maintenance. But since the workman receives his wages *after* his labour is performed, and knows, moreover, that what he actually gives to the capitalist is his labour, the value or price of his labouring power necessarily appears to him as the *price* or *value of his labour itself*. If the price of his labouring power is three shillings, in which six hours of labour are realised, and if he works twelve hours, he necessarily considers these three shillings as the value or price of twelve hours of labour, although these twelve hours of labour realise themselves in a value of six shillings. A double consequence flows from this.

Firstly. The value or price of the labouring power takes the semblance of the *price or value of labour itself*, although, strictly speaking, value and price of labour are senseless terms.

Secondly. Although one part only of the workman's daily labour is *paid,* while the other part is *unpaid,* and while that unpaid or surplus-labour constitutes exactly the fund out of which *surplus-value* or *profit* is formed, it seems as if the aggregate labour was paid labour.

This false appearance distinguishes *wages labour* from other *historical* forms of labour. On the basis of the wages system even the *unpaid* labour seems to be *paid* labour. With the *slave,* on the contrary, even that part of his labour which is paid appears to be unpaid. Of course, in order to work the slave must live, and one part of his working day goes to replace the value of his own maintenance. But since no bargain is struck between him and his master, and no acts of selling and buying are going on between the two parties, all his labour seems to be given away for nothing.

Take, on the other hand, the peasant serf, such as he, I might say, until yesterday existed in the whole East of Europe. This peasant worked, for example, three days for himself on his own field or the field allotted to him, and the three subsequent days he performed compulsory and gratuitous labour on the estate of his lord. Here, then, the paid and unpaid parts of labour were visibly separated, separated in time and space; and our Liberals overflowed with moral indignation at the preposterous notion of making a man work for nothing.

In point of fact, however, whether a man works three days of the week for himself on his own field and three days for nothing on the estate of his lord, or whether he works in the factory or the workshop six hours daily for himself and six for his employer, comes to the same, although in the latter case the paid and unpaid portions of labour are inseparably mixed up with each other, and the nature of the whole transaction is completely masked by the *intervention of a contract* and the *pay* received at the end of the week. The gratuitous labour appears to be voluntarily given in the one instance, and to be compulsory in the other. That makes all the difference.

In using the expression *"value of labour"*, I shall only use it as a popular slang term for *"value of labouring power"*.

Profit is Made by Selling a Commodity *at* its Value

Suppose an average hour of labour to be realised in a value equal to sixpence, or twelve average hours of labour to be realised in six shillings. Suppose, further, the value of labour to be three shillings or the produce of six hours' labour. If, then, in the raw material, machinery, and so forth, used up in a commodity, twenty-four hours of average labour were realised, its value would amount to twelve shillings. If, moreover, the workman employed by the capitalist added twelve hours of labour to those means of production, these twelve hours would be realised in an additional value of six shillings. The *total value of the product* would, therefore, amount to thirty-six hours of realised labour, and be equal to eighteen shillings. But as the value of labour, or the wages paid to the workman, would be three shillings only, no equivalent would have been paid by the capitalist for the six hours of surplus-labour worked by the workman, and realised in the value of the commodity. By selling this commodity at its value for eighteen shillings, the capitalist would, therefore, realise a value of three shillings, for which he had paid no equivalent. These three shillings would constitute the surplus-value or profit pocketed by him. The capitalist would consequently realise the profit of three shillings, not by selling his commodity at a price *over and above* its value, but by selling it *at its real value*.

The value of a commodity is determined by the *total quantity of labour* contained in it. But part of that quantity of labour is realised in a value for which an equivalent has been paid in the form of wages; part of it is realised in a value for which *no* equivalent has been paid. Part of the labour contained in the commodity is *paid* labour; part is *unpaid* labour. By selling, therefore, the commodity *at its value*, that is, as the crystallisation of the *total quantity of labour* bestowed upon it, the capitalist must necessarily sell it at a profit. He sells not only what has cost him an equivalent, but he sells also what has cost him nothing, although it has cost his workman labour. The cost of the commodity to the capitalist and its real cost are different things. I repeat, therefore, that normal and average profits are made by selling commodities not *above* but *at their real values*. . . .

chapter 16

The Fetishism of Commodities and the Secret Thereof (1867)

A commodity appears, at first sight, a very trivial thing, and easily understood. Its analysis shows that it is, in reality, a very queer thing, abounding in metaphysical subtleties and theological niceties. So far as it is a value in use, there is nothing mysterious about it, whether we consider it from the point of view that by its properties it is capable of satisfying human wants, or from the point that those properties are the product of human labour. It is as clear as noon-day, that man, by his industry, changes the forms of the materials furnished by Nature, in such a way as to make them useful to him. The form of wood, for instance, is altered, by making a table out of it. Yet, for all that, the table continues to be that common, every-day thing, wood. But, so soon as it steps forth as a commodity, it is changed into something transcendent. . . .

A commodity is therefore a mysterious thing, simply because in it the social character of men's labour appears to them as an objective character stamped upon the product of that labour; because the relation of the producers to the sum total of their own labour is presented to them as a social relation, existing not between themselves, but between the products of their labour. This is the reason why the products of labour become commodities, social things whose qualities are at the same time perceptible and imperceptible by the senses. In the same way the light from an object is perceived by us not as the subjective excitation of our optic nerve, but as the objective form of something outside the eye itself. But, in the act of seeing, there is at all events, an actual passage of light from one thing to another, from the external object to the eye. There is a physical relation between physical things. But it is different with commodities. There, the existence of the things *quâ* commodities, and the value relation between the products of labour which stamps them as commodities, have absolutely no connection with their physical properties and with the material relations arising therefrom. There it is a definite social relation between men, that assumes, in their eyes, the fantastic form of a relation between things. In order, therefore, to find an analogy, we must have recourse to the mist-enveloped regions of the religious world. In that world the productions of the human brain appear as independent beings endowed with life, and entering into relation both with one another and the human race. So it is in the world of commodities with the products of men's hands. This I call the Fetishism which attaches itself to the products of labour, so soon as they are produced as commodities, and which is therefore inseparable from the production of commodities.

This Fetishism of commodities has its origin . . . in the peculiar social character of the labour that produces them.

As a general rule, articles of utility become commodities, only because they are products of the labour of private individuals or groups of individuals who carry on their work independently of each other. The sum total of the labour of all these private individuals forms the aggregate labour of society. Since the producers do not come into social contact with each other until they exchange their products, the specific social character of each producer's labour does not show itself except in the act of exchange. In other words, the labour of the individual asserts itself as a part of the labour of society, only by means of the relations which the act of exchange establishes directly between the products, and indirectly, through them, between the producers. To the latter, therefore, the relations connecting the labour of one individual with that of the rest appear, not as direct social relations between individuals at work, but as what they really are, material relations between persons and social relations between things. It is only by being exchanged that the products of labour acquire, as values, one uniform social status, distinct from their varied forms of existence as objects of utility. This division of a product into a useful thing and a value becomes practically important, only when exchange has acquired such an extension that useful articles are produced for the purpose of being exchanged, and their character as values has therefore to be taken into account, beforehand, during production. From this moment the labour of the individual producer acquires socially a twofold character. On the one hand, it must, as a definite useful kind of labour, satisfy a definite social want, and thus hold its place as part and parcel of the collective labour of all, as a branch of a social division of labour that has sprung up spontaneously. On the other hand, it can satisfy the manifold wants of the individual producer himself, only in so far as the mutual exchangeability of all kinds of useful private labour is an established social fact, and therefore the private useful labour of each producer ranks on an equality with that of all others. The equalisation of the most different kinds of labour can be the result only of an abstraction from their inequalities, or of reducing them to their common denominator, viz., expenditure of human labour power or human labour in the abstract. The twofold social character of the labour of the individual appears to him, when reflected in his brain, only under those forms which are impressed upon that labour in everyday practice by the exchange of products. In this way, the character that his own labour possesses of being socially useful takes the form of the condition, that the product must be not only useful, but useful for others, and the social character that his particular labour has of being the equal of all other particular kinds of labour, takes the form that all the physically different articles that are the products of labour, have one common quality, viz., that of having value.

Hence, when we bring the products of our labour into relation with each other as values, it is not because we see in these articles the material receptacles of homogeneous human labour. Quite the contrary: whenever, by an exchange, we equate as values our different products, by that very act, we also equate, as human labour, the different kinds of labour expended upon them. We are not aware of this, nevertheless we do it. Value, therefore, does not stalk about with a label describing what it is. It is value, rather, that converts every product into a social hieroglyphic. Later on, we try to decipher the hieroglyphic, to get behind the secret of our own social products; for to stamp an object of utility as a value, is just as much a social product as language. The recent scientific discovery, that the products of labour, so far as they are values, are but material expressions of the human labour spent in their production, marks, indeed, an epoch in the history of the development of the human race, but, by no means, dissipates the mist through which the social character of labour appears to us to be an objective character of the products themselves. . . .

What, first of all, practically concerns producers when they make an exchange, is the question, how much of some other product they get for their own? in what proportions the products are exchangeable? When these proportions have, by custom, attained a certain stability, they appear to result from the nature of the products, so that, for instance, one ton of iron and two ounces of gold appear as naturally to be of equal value as a pound of gold and a pound of iron in spite of their different physical and chemical qualities appear to be of equal weight. The character of having value, when once impressed upon products, obtains fixity only by reason of their acting and reacting upon each other as quantities of value. These quantities vary continually, independently of the will, foresight and action of the producers. To them, their own social action takes the form of the action of objects, which rule the producers instead of being ruled by them. It requires a fully developed production of commodities before, from accumulated experience alone, the scientific conviction springs up, that all the different kinds of private labour, which are carried on independently of each other, and yet as spontaneously developed branches of the social division of labour, are continually being reduced to the quantitative proportions in which society requires them. And why? Because, in the midst of all the accidental and ever fluctuating exchange relations between the products, the labour time socially necessary for their production forcibly asserts itself like an overriding law of Nature. The law of gravity thus asserts itself when a house falls about our ears. The determination of the magnitude of value by labour time is therefore a secret, hidden under the apparent fluctuations in the relative values of commodities. Its discovery, while removing all appearance of mere accidentality from the determination of the magnitude of the values of products, yet in no way alters the mode in which that determination takes place.

Man's reflections on the forms of social life, and consequently, also, his scientific analysis of those forms, take a course directly opposite to that of their actual historical development. He begins . . . with the results of the process of development ready to hand before him. The characters that stamp products as commodities, and whose establishment is a necessary preliminary to the circulation of commodities, have already acquired the stability of natural, self-understood forms of social life, before man seeks to decipher, not their historical character, for in his eyes they are immutable, but their meaning. Consequently it was the analysis of the prices of commodities that alone led to the determination of the magnitude of value, and it was the common expression of all commodities in money that alone led to the establishment of their characters as values. It is, however, just this ultimate money form of the world of commodities that actually conceals, instead of disclosing, the social character of private labour, and the social relations between the individual producers. When I state that coats or boots stand in a relation to linen, because it is the universal incarnation of abstract human labour, the absurdity of the statement is self-evident. Nevertheless, when the producers of coats and boots compare those articles with linen, or, what is the same thing, with gold or silver, as the universal equivalent, they express the relation between their own private labour and the collective labour of society in the same absurd form.

The categories of bourgeois economy consist of such like forms. They are forms of thought expressing with social validity the conditions and relations of a definite, historically determined mode of production, viz., the production of commodities. The whole mystery of commodities, all the magic and necromancy that surrounds the products of labour as long as they take the form of commodities, vanishes therefore, so soon as we come to other forms of production.

Since Robinson Crusoe's experiences are a favourite theme with political economists, let us take a look at him on his island. Moderate though he be, yet some few wants he has to satisfy, and must therefore do a little useful work of various sorts, such as making tools and furniture, taming goats, fishing and hunting. Of his prayers and the like we take no account, since they are a source of pleasure to him, and he looks upon them as so much recreation. In spite of the variety of his work, he knows that his labour, whatever its form, is but the activity of one and the same

Robinson, and consequently, that it consists of nothing but different modes of human labour. Necessity itself compels him to apportion his time accurately between his different kinds of work. Whether one kind occupies a greater space in his general activity than another, depends on the difficulties, greater or less as the case may be, to be overcome in attaining the useful effect aimed at. This our friend Robinson soon learns by experience, and having rescued a watch, ledger, and pen and ink from the wreck, commences, like a true-born Briton, to keep a set of books. His stock-book contains a list of the objects of utility that belong to him, of the operations necessary for their production; and lastly, of the labour time that definite quantities of those objects have, on an average, cost him. All the relations between Robinson and the objects that form this wealth of his own creation, are here so simple and clear as to be intelligible without exertion. . . . And yet those relations contain all that is essential to the determination of value.

Let us now transport ourselves from Robinson's island bathed in light to the European Middle Ages shrouded in darkness. Here, instead of the independent man, we find everyone dependent, serfs and lords, vassals and suzerains, laymen and clergy. Personal dependence here characterises the social relations of production just as much as it does the other spheres of life organised on the basis of that production. But for the very reason that personal dependence forms the groundwork of society, there is no necessity for labour and its products to assume a fantastic form different from their reality. They take the shape, in the transactions of society, of services in kind and payments in kind. Here the particular and natural form of labour, and not, as in a society based on production of commodities, its general abstract form is the immediate social form of labour. Compulsory labour is just as properly measured by time, as commodity-producing labour; but every serf knows that what he expends in the service of his lord, is a definite quantity of his own personal labour power. The tithe to be rendered to the priest is more matter of fact than his blessing. No matter, then, what we may think of the parts played by the different classes of people themselves in this society, the social relations between individuals in the performance of their labour, appear at all events as their own mutual personal relations, and are not disguised under the shape of social relations between the products of labour.

For an example of labour in common or directly associated labour, we have no occasion to go back to that spontaneously developed form which we find on the threshold of the history of all civilised races. We have one close at hand in the patriarchal industries of a peasant family, that produces corn, cattle, yarn, linen, and clothing for home use. These different articles are, as regards the family, so many products of its labour, but as between themselves, they are not commodities. The different kinds of labour, such as tillage, cattle tending, spinning, weaving and making clothes, which result in the various products, are in themselves, and such as they are, direct social functions, because functions of the family, which, just as much as a society based on the production of commodities, possesses a spontaneously developed system of division of labour. The distribution of the work within the family, and the regulation of the labour time of the several members, depend as well upon differences of age and sex as upon natural conditions varying with the seasons. The labour power of each individual, by its very nature, operates in this case merely as a definite portion of the whole labour power of the family, and therefore, the measure of the expenditure of individual labour power by its duration, appears here by its very nature as a social character of their labour.

Let us now picture to ourselves, by way of change, a community of free individuals, carrying on their work with the means of production in common, in which the labour power of all the different individuals is consciously applied as the combined labour power of the community. All the characteristics of Robinson's labour are here repeated, but with this difference, that they are social, instead of individual. Everything produced by him was exclusively the result of his own personal labour, and therefore simply an object of use for himself. The total product of our community is a social product. One portion serves as fresh means of production and remains social. But another portion is consumed by the members as means of subsistence. A distribution of this portion amongst them is consequently necessary. The mode of this distribution will vary with the productive organisation of the community, and the degree of historical development attained by the producers. We will assume, but merely for the sake of a parallel with the production of commodities, that the share of each individual producer in the means of subsistence is determined by his labour time. Labour time would, in that case, play a double part. Its apportionment in accordance with a definite social plan maintains the proper proportion between the different kinds of work to be done and the various wants of the community. On the other hand, it also serves as a measure of the portion of the common labour borne by each individual, and of his share in the part of the total product destined for individual consumption. The social relations of the individual producers, with regard both to their labour and to its products, are in this case perfectly simple and intelligible, and that with regard not only to production but also to distribution. . . .

The life-process of society, which is based on the process of material production, does not strip off its mystical veil until it is treated as production by freely associated men, and is consciously regulated by them in accordance with a settled plan. This, however, demands for society a certain material ground-work or set of conditions of existence which in their turn are the spontaneous product of a long and painful process of development.

Political economy has indeed analysed, however incompletely, value and its magnitude, and has discovered what lies beneath these forms. But it has never once asked the question why labour is represented by the value of its product and labour time by the magnitude of that value. These formulæ, which bear it stamped upon them in unmistakable letters that they belong to a state of society, in which the process of production has the mastery over man, instead of being controlled by him, such formulæ appear to the bourgeois intellect to be as much a self-evident necessity imposed by Nature as productive labour itself. Hence forms of social production that preceded the bourgeois form, are treated by the bourgeoisie in much the same way as the Fathers of the Church treated pre-Christian religions.

To what extent some economists are misled by the Fetishism inherent in commodities, or by the objective appearance of the social characteristics of labour, is shown, amongst other ways, by the dull and tedious quarrel over the part played by Nature in the formation of exchange value. Since exchange value is a definite social manner of expressing the amount of labour bestowed upon an object, Nature has no more to do with it, than it has in fixing the course of exchange.

The mode of production in which the product takes the form of a commodity, or is produced directly for exchange, is the most general and most embryonic form of bourgeois production. It therefore makes its appearance at an early date in history, though not in the same predominating and characteristic manner as now-a-days. Hence its Fetish character is comparatively easy to be seen through. But when we come to more concrete forms, even this appearance of simplicity vanishes. Whence arose the illusions of the monetary system? To it gold and silver, when serving as money, did not represent a social relation between producers, but were natural objects with strange social properties. And modern economy, which looks down with such disdain on the monetary system, does not its superstition come out as clear as noon-day, whenever it treats of capital? How long is it since economy discarded the physiocratic illusion, that rents grow out of the soil and not out of society? . . .

chapter 17

The General Formula for Capital (1867)

The circulation of commodities is the starting-point of capital. The production of commodities, their circulation, and that more developed form of their circulation called commerce, these form the historical ground-work from which it rises. The modern history of capital dates from the creation in the 16th century of a world-embracing commerce and a world-embracing market. . . .

As a matter of history, capital, as opposed to landed property, invariably takes the form at first of money; it appears as moneyed wealth, as the capital of the merchant and of the usurer. But we have no need to refer to the origin of capital in order to discover that the first form of appearance of capital is money. We can see it daily under our very eyes. All new capital, to commence with, comes on the stage, that is, on the market, whether of commodities, labour, or money, even in our days, in the shape of money that by a definite process has to be transformed into capital.

The first distinction we notice between money that is money only, and money that is capital, is nothing more than a difference in their form of circulation.

The simplest form of the circulation of commodities is $C - M - C$, the transformation of commodities into money, and the change of the money back again into commodities; or selling in order to buy. But alongside of this form we find another specifically different form: $M - C - M$, the transformation of money into commodities, and the change of commodities back again into money; or buying in order to sell. Money that circulates in the latter manner is thereby transformed into, becomes capital, and is already potentially capital. . . .

The circuit $C - M - C$ starts with one commodity, and finishes with another, which falls out of circulation and into consumption. Consumption, the satisfaction of wants, in one word, use value, is its end and aim. The circuit $M - C - M$, on the contrary, commences with money and ends with money. Its leading motive, and the goal that attracts it, is therefore mere exchange value.

In the simple circulation of commodities, the two extremes of the circuit have the same economic form. They are both commodities, and commodities of equal value. But they are also use values differing in their qualities, as, for example, corn and clothes. The exchange of products, of the different materials in which the labour of society is embodied, forms here the basis of the movement. It is otherwise in the circulation M – C – M, which at first sight appears purposeless, because tautological. Both extremes have the same economic form. They are both money, and therefore are not qualitatively different use values; for money is but the converted form of commodities, in which their particular use values vanish. To exchange £100 for cotton, and then this same cotton again for £100, is merely a roundabout way of exchanging money for money, the same for the same, and appears to be an operation just as purposeless as it is absurd. One sum of money is distinguishable from another only by its amount. The character and tendency of the process M – C – M, is therefore not due to any qualitative difference between its extremes, both being money, but solely to their quantitative difference. More money is withdrawn from circulation at the finish than was thrown into it at the start. The cotton that was bought for £100 is perhaps resold for £100 + £10 or £110. The exact form of this process is therefore M – C – M′, where M′ = M + ΔM = the original sum advanced, plus an increment. This increment or excess over the original value I call "surplus value". The value originally advanced, therefore, not only remains intact while in circulation, but adds to itself a surplus value or expands itself. It is this movement that converts it into capital.

Of course, it is also possible, that in C – M – C, the two extremes C – C, say corn and clothes, may represent different quantities of value. The farmer may sell his corn above its value, or may buy the clothes at less than their value. He may, on the other hand, "be done" by the clothes merchant. Yet, in the form of circulation now under consideration, such differences in value are purely accidental. The fact that the corn and the clothes are equivalents, does not deprive the process of all meaning, as it does in M – C – M. The equivalence of their values is rather a necessary condition to its normal course.

The repetition or renewal of the act of selling in order to buy, is kept within bounds by the very object it aims at, namely, consumption or the satisfaction of definite wants, an aim that lies altogether outside the sphere of circulation. But when we buy in order to sell, we, on the contrary, begin and end with the same thing, money, exchange value; and thereby the movement becomes interminable. . . . Money ends the movement only to begin it again. Therefore, the final result of every separate circuit, in which a purchase and consequent sale are completed, forms of itself the starting-point of a new circuit. The simple circulation of commodities – selling in order to buy – is a means of carrying out a purpose unconnected with circulation, namely, the appropriation of use values, the satisfaction of wants. The circulation of money as capital is, on the contrary, an end in itself, for the expansion of value takes place only within this constantly renewed movement. The circulation of capital has therefore no limits.

As the conscious representative of this movement, the possessor of money becomes a capitalist. His person, or rather his pocket, is the point from which the money starts and to which it returns. The expansion of value, which is the objective basis or mainspring of the circulation $M - C - M$, becomes his subjective aim, and it is only in so far as the appropriation of ever more and more wealth in the abstract becomes the sole motive of his operations, that he functions as a capitalist, that is, as capital personified and endowed with consciousness and a will. Use values must therefore never be looked upon as the real aim of the capitalist; neither must the profit on any single transaction. The restless never-ending process of profit-making alone is what he aims at. This boundless greed after riches, this passionate chase after exchange value, is common to the capitalist and the miser; but while the miser is merely a capitalist gone mad, the capitalist is a rational miser. The never-ending augmentation of exchange value, which the miser strives after, by seeking to save his money from circulation, is attained by the more acute capitalist, by constantly throwing it afresh into circulation. . . .

part 4

From Manufacture to Modern Industry: The First and Second Industrial Revolutions

In the Feuerbach essay above (chapter 1 of *The German Ideology*), young Marx and Engels already saw manufacture and large-scale industry as major phases of capitalist development. This part focuses on Marx's detailed and mature treatment of the topic in the first volume of *Capital*. His chapter on "manufacture and modern industry" elaborated sociologically and historically his broader materialist emphases on production and cooperation. Marx held that manufacture was still production by hand, and therefore merely modified, rather than revolutionized, the technologies of pre-capitalist handicraft. In his view, however, manufacture instituted major changes in the social organization of labor. Recall that he saw the emergence of the bourgeoisie and wage labor as the most essential factors in the rise of capitalism and ultimate source of its initial phase of explosive growth. His treatment of manufacture analyzed the social transformation of the work process that was wrought by, and accompanied, the changes in class structure and property relations and that accelerated greatly accumulation. Marx argued that manufacturers reorganized producers into more specialized units than those of handicraft; they forged a more consciously planned and coordinated work process, and more differentiated social division of labor. Although describing the new workplace as "despotic," Marx considered manufacture's more organized and directive form of complex cooperation and increased productivity as constituting an advance over handicraft's "simple cooperation."

According to Marx, manufacturers pumped more surplus product out of workers by keeping wages stable or reducing them while lengthening the workday ("absolute surplus value") and increasing labor's intensity or efficiency ("relative surplus value"). Marx argued that manufacturers combined separate handicrafts into larger, multiphase operations, increasing the numbers of workers and requiring longer hours than handicraft. However, he stressed especially that they decomposed generalized craft production (i.e., single producers carrying out all or most steps in making a product) into specialized detail operations, which increased efficiency by simplifying worker routines and reducing "gaps" in the labor process (i.e., specialized workers shifted steps and tools less often). The increased intensity of labor reduced the socially necessary labor time to make a commodity and produce the equivalent of the workers' wage. Marx argued that competition spurred ceaseless efforts to increase specialization, improve coordination, and refine tools to fit altered work processes. All these changes were designed to increase the intensity of labor and extract more surplus value. Portraying specialization as "crippling" workers, Marx held that increased "social productive power" came at the cost of trivialized work, reduced wages, harsh oversight, stiff penalties, and increased insecurity. Yet Marx still saw a progressive side to manufacture: its "collective worker" showed signs of superior intelligence and capacities for creating use values and reducing social misery.

Marx saw labor power as the dynamic force in the rise of manufacture, but he declared that the revolution in modern industry "begins with the instruments of labor." The selections from "Machinery and Modern Industry" explain how mechanized factories severed ties to handicraft and animated much more radical changes in the workplace. Marx held that manufacture's detail production by hand resulted in unevenly instituted, partially specialized workplaces and labor hierarchies based on skill, which put sharp limits on capitalist efforts to reorganize work and maximize accumulation. Pockets of variously skilled, male workers resisted workplace control and lacked discipline. By contrast, Marx argued that mechanization reduced work to exceptionally specialized, repetitive, simple motions, which moved all intelligence and discretion from the worker to the "collective machine." Radical splitting of mental labor from physical labor, he contended, turned the work force into a nearly homogeneous mass of unskilled labor and flattened manufacture's skill hierarchy. Marx noted traces of a "superior class" of professional and technical staff (e.g., engineers), but he considered them to be, at the time, "numerically unimportant." He focused more on "overseers," or foremen, drawn from the ranks of workers, who had the authority to fine or fire on the spot and impose "barracks discipline." However, he stressed that factory workers became appendages of the machinery, and thus were disciplined primarily automatically by its design and speed. In his view, competitive pressures that increased automation made this technical control ever more pervasive and rigid.

By reducing reliance on craft skills and physical strength, Marx held, mechanization made possible a longer workday and the employment of women and children (increasing the labor pool and reducing dependence on resistant male workers). Remember that Marx saw profit or surplus value as deriving from unpaid labor time. From this vantage point, machinery, or "constant capital," cannot create value, but merely transfers it to the product. But Marx argued that modern industry advances the expropriation of surplus value in various ways. For example, in addition to the lengthened workday, he held, industrial capitalists created a much larger scale of production and much greater mass of wage labor. Most important, however, Marx held that mechanization revolutionized productive efficiency, reducing sharply the socially necessary labor time to make a product and thus increasing the proportion of unpaid labor time and decreasing relative wages. Wage costs also dropped because unskilled factory operatives needed little training and could easily be replaced, and because increased productivity reduced the costs of necessary goods for workers' subsistence. As explained in the next part, however, Marx saw the trend toward automation and consequent growing proportion of machinery relative to living labor ("variable capital") as a major contradiction that threatened to shrink the very source of value and profit. Finally, he held that modern industry's use of "science" opens a new era in which production is planned more rationally according to technical efficiency, rather than on traditional grounds, and whereby complex cooperation becomes increasingly a "technical necessity" of the means of production. Although he saw modern industry as, by far, history's most efficient mechanism for pumping surplus out of direct producers, he also believed that it creates means to reduce necessary labor and unnecessary misery.

Marx anticipated critically trends that Frederick Winslow Taylor and other advocates of "scientific management" described, lauded, and tried to advance in the later nineteenth century and early twentieth century. They were later addressed, in various ways, by the sociology of work, organization, and economy. Harry Braverman's *Labor and Monopoly Capital* (1974) drew heavily from Marx's thought about the labor process and stimulated renewed interest in it. Following Braverman, sociologists applied Marx's ideas in diverse types of empirical-historical research, and stressed his view that genuine understanding of the financial and technical aspects of capitalism must include knowledge about the labor process. Opposing trends and critiques are numerous and varied. Focusing on the very early phase of modern industry, Marx's analyses, in this part, have mostly historical value, and do not address the modern corporate firm's highly segmented labor force and massive managerial and professional staff or constraints imposed by state regulation and powerful unions. However, many recent critics have argued that the traditional working class has disappeared or is numerically insignificant in today's service and information economy. But others counter that Marxist-type de-skilling and technical control are on the increase and pervade low-wage service work and even the activities of many lower to middle managers and professionals in diverse industries. They also argue that classical forms of industrial labor regimes and traditional working classes have not vanished, but have multiplied in globally dispersed locations and in new forms. These points are contested, but they raise crucial questions about neoliberal restructuring and globalization. As with the theory of value, Marx's analysis of the work process raises issues that are still relevant today. More generally, his view that capitalism's productive powers derive from collective labor challenges clichés about workerless progress driven by entrepreneurs and investors.

chapter 18

Division of Labour and Manufacture (1867)

That co-operation which is based on division of labour, assumes its typical form in manufacture, and is the prevalent characteristic form of the capitalist process of production throughout the manufacturing period properly so called. That period, roughly speaking, extends from the middle of the 16th to the last third of the 18th century. . . .

The mode in which manufacture arises, its growth out of handicrafts, is . . . twofold. On the one hand, it arises from the union of various independent handicrafts, which become stripped of their independence and specialised to such an extent as to be reduced to mere supplementary partial processes in the production of one particular commodity. On the other hand, it arises from the co-operation of artificers of one handicraft; it splits up that particular handicraft into its various detail operations, isolating, and making these operations independent of one another up to the point where each becomes the exclusive function of a particular labourer. On the one hand, therefore, manufacture either introduces division of labour into a process of production, or further develops that division; on the other hand, it unites together handicrafts that were formerly separate. But whatever may have been its particular starting-point, its final form is invariably the same – a productive mechanism whose parts are human beings.

For a proper understanding of the division of labour in manufacture, it is essential that the following points be firmly grasped. First, the decomposition of a process of production into its various successive steps coincides, here, strictly with the resolution of a handicraft into its successive manual operations. Whether complex or simple, each operation has to be done by hand, retains the character of a handicraft, and is therefore dependent on the strength, skill, quickness, and sureness, of the individual workman in handling his tools. The handicraft continues to be the basis. This narrow technical basis excludes a really scientific analysis of any definite process of industrial production, since it is still a condition that each detail process gone through by the product must be capable of being done by hand and of forming, in its way, a separate handicraft. It is just because handicraft skill continues, in this way, to be the foundation of the process of production, that each workman becomes exclusively assigned to a partial function, and that for the rest of his life, his labour power is turned into the organ of this detail function.

Secondly, this division of labour is a particular sort of co-operation, and many of its disadvantages spring from the general character of co-operation, and not from this particular form of it.

... [A] labourer who all his life performs one and the same simple operation, converts his whole body into the automatic, specialised implement of that operation. Consequently, he takes less time in doing it, than the artificer who performs a whole series of operations in succession. But the collective labourer, who constitutes the living mechanism of manufacture, is made up solely of such specialised detail labourers. Hence, in comparison with the independent handicraft, more is produced in a given time, or the productive power of labour is increased. Moreover, when once this fractional work is established as the exclusive function of one person, the methods it employs become perfected. The workman's continued repetition of the same simple act, and the concentration of his attention on it, teach him by experience how to attain the desired effect with the minimum of exertion. But since there are always several generations of labourers living at one time, and working together at the manufacture of a given article, the technical skill, the tricks of the trade thus acquired, become established, and are accumulated and handed down. Manufacture, in fact, produces the skill of the detail labourer, by reproducing, and systematically driving to an extreme within the workshop, the naturally developed differentiation of trades which it found ready to hand in society at large. On the other hand, the conversion of fractional work into the life-calling of one man, corresponds to the tendency shown by earlier societies, to make trades hereditary. . . .

An artificer, who performs one after another the various fractional operations in the production of a finished article, must at one time change his place, at another his tools. The transition from one operation to another interrupts the flow of his labour, and creates, so to say, gaps in his working day. These gaps close up so soon as he is tied to one and the same operation all day long; they vanish in proportion as the changes in his work diminish. The resulting increased productive power is owing either to an increased expenditure of labour power in a given time – i.e., to increased intensity of labour – or to a decrease in the amount of labour power unproductively consumed. The extra expenditure of power, demanded by every transition from rest to motion, is made up for by prolonging the duration of the normal velocity when once acquired. On the other hand, constant labour of one uniform kind disturbs the intensity and flow of a man's animal spirits, which find recreation and delight in mere change of activity.

The productiveness of labour depends not only on the proficiency of the workman, but on the perfection of his tools. Tools of the same kind . . . may be employed in different processes; and the same tool may serve various purposes in a single process. But so soon as the different operations of a labour process are disconnected the one from the other, and each fractional operation acquires in the hands of the detail labourer a suitable and peculiar form, alterations become necessary in the implements that previously served more than one purpose. The direction taken by this change is determined by the difficulties experienced in consequence of the unchanged form of the implement. Manufacture is characterised by the differentiation of the instruments of labour – a differentiation whereby implements of a given sort acquire fixed shapes, adapted to each particular application, and by the specialisation of those instruments, giving to each special implement its full play only in the hands of a specific detail labourer. In Birmingham alone 300 varieties of hammers are produced, and not only is each adapted to one particular process, but several varieties often serve exclusively for the different operations in one and the same process. The manufacturing period simplifies, improves, and multiplies the implements of labour, by adapting them to the exclusively special functions of each detail labourer. It thus creates at the same time one of the material conditions for the existence of machinery, which consists of a combination of simple instruments. . . .

The collective labourer, formed by the combination of a number of detail labourers, is the machinery specially characteristic of the manufacturing period. The various operations that are performed in turns by the producer of a commodity, and coalesce one with another during the process of production, lay claim to him in various ways. In one operation he must exert more strength, in another more skill, in another more attention; and the same individual does not possess all these qualities in an equal degree. After manufacture has once separated, made independent, and isolated the various operations, the labourers are divided, classified, and grouped according to their predominating qualities. If their natural endowments are, on the one hand, the foundation on which the division of labour is built up, on the other hand, manufacture, once introduced, develops in them new powers that are by nature fitted only for limited and special functions. The collective labourer now possesses, in an equal degree of excellence, all the qualities requisite for production, and expends them in the most economical manner, by exclusively employing all his organs, consisting of particular labourers, or groups of labourers, in performing their special functions. The one-sidedness and the deficiencies of the detail labourer become perfections when he is a part of the collective labourer. The habit of doing only one thing converts him into a never failing instrument, while his connexion with the whole mechanism compels him to work with the regularity of the parts of a machine.

Since the collective labourer has functions, both simple and complex, both high and low, his members, the individual labour powers, require different degrees of training, and must therefore have different values. Manufacture, therefore, develops a hierarchy of labour powers, to which there corresponds a scale of wages. If, on the one hand, the individual labourers are appropriated and annexed for life by a limited function; on the other hand, the various operations of the hierarchy are parcelled out among the labourers according to both their natural and their acquired capabilities. Every process of production, however, requires certain simple manipulations, which every man is capable of doing. They too are now severed from their connexion with the more pregnant moments of activity, and ossified into exclusive functions of specially appointed labourers. Hence, manufacture begets, in every handicraft that it seizes upon, a class of so-called unskilled labourers, a class which handicraft industry strictly excluded. If it develops a one-sided speciality into a perfection, at the expense of the whole of a man's working capacity, it also begins to make a speciality of the absence of all development. Alongside of the hierarchic gradation there steps the simple separation of the labourers into skilled and unskilled. For the latter, the cost of apprenticeship vanishes; for the former, it diminishes, compared with that of artificers, in consequence of the functions being simplified. In both cases the value of labour power falls. An exception to this law holds good whenever the decomposition of the labour process begets new and comprehensive functions, that either had no place at all, or only a very modest one, in handicrafts. The fall in the value of labour power, caused by the disappearance or diminution of the expenses of apprenticeship, implies a direct increase of surplus value for the benefit of capital; for everything that shortens the necessary labour time required for the reproduction of labour power, extends the domain of surplus labour. . . .

We first considered the origin of manufacture, then its simple elements, then the detail labourer and his implements, and finally, the totality of the mechanism. We shall now lightly touch upon the relation between the division of labour in manufacture, and the social division of labour, which forms the foundation of all production of commodities. . . .

. . . Division of labour in society is brought about by the purchase and sale of the products of different branches of industry, while the connexion between the detail operations in a workshop, is due to the sale of the labour power of several workmen to one capitalist, who applies it as combined labour power. The division of labour in the workshop implies concentration of the means of production in the hands of one capitalist; the division of labour in society implies their dispersion among many independent producers of commodities. While within the workshop, the iron law of proportionality subjects definite numbers of workmen to definite functions, in the society outside the workshop, chance and caprice have full play in distributing the producers and their means of production among the various branches of industry. The different spheres of production, it is true, constantly tend to an equilibrium: for, on the one hand, while each producer of a commodity is bound to produce a use value, to satisfy a particular social want, and while the extent of these wants differs quant- itatively, still there exists an inner relation which settles their proportions into a regular system, and that system one of spontaneous growth; and, on the other hand, the law of the value of commodities ultimately deter- mines how much of its disposable working time society can expend on each particular class of commodities. But this constant tendency to equilib- rium, of the various spheres of production, is exercised, only in the shape of a reaction against the constant upsetting of this equilibrium. The *a priori* system on which the division of labour, within the workshop, is regu- larly carried out, becomes in the division of labour within the society, an *a posteriori*, nature-imposed necessity, controlling the lawless caprice of the producers, and perceptible in the barometrical fluctuations of the market prices. Division of labour within the workshop implies the undis- puted authority of the capitalist over men, that are but parts of a mech- anism that belongs to him. The division of labour within the society brings into contact independent commodity producers, who acknowledge no other authority but that of competition, of the coercion exerted by the pressure of their mutual interests. . . . The same bourgeois mind which praises division of labour in the workshop, life-long annexation of the labourer to a partial operation, and his complete subjection to capital, as being an organisation of labour that increases its productiveness – that same bour- geois mind denounces with equal vigour every conscious attempt to socially control and regulate the process of production, as an inroad upon such sacred things as the rights of property, freedom and unrestricted play for the bent of the individual capitalist. It is very characteristic that the enthusiastic apologists of the factory system have nothing more damn- ing to urge against a general organisation of the labour of society, than that it would turn all society into one immense factory.

. . . [I]n a society with capitalist production, anarchy in the social division of labour and despotism in that of the workshop are mutual conditions the one of the other. . . .

An increased number of labourers under the control of one capitalist is the natural starting-point, as well of co-operation generally, as of manu- facture in particular. But the division of labour in manufacture makes this increase in the number of workmen a technical necessity. The minimum number that any given capitalist is bound to employ is here prescribed by the previously established division of labour. On the other hand, the advantages of further division are obtainable only by adding to the number of workmen, and this can be done only by adding multiples of the various detail groups. But an increase in the variable component of the capital employed necessitates an increase in its constant component, too, in the workshops, implements, &c., and, in particular, in the raw material, the call for which grows quicker than the number of workmen. The quantity of it consumed in a given time, by a given amount of labour, increases in the same ratio as does the productive power of that labour in consequence of its division. Hence, it is a law, based on the very nature of manufacture, that the minimum amount of capital, which is bound to be in the hands of each capitalist, must keep increasing; in other words, that the transformation into capital of the social means of production and subsistence must keep extending.

In manufacture, as well as in simple co-operation, the collective working organism is a form of existence of capital. The mechanism that is made up of numerous individual detail labourers belongs to the capitalist. Hence, the productive power resulting from a combination of labours appears to be the productive power of capital. Manufacture proper not only subjects the previously independent workman to the discipline and command of capital, but, in addition, creates a hierarchic gradation of the workmen themselves. While simple co-operation leaves the mode of working by the individual for the most part unchanged, manufacture thoroughly revolutionises it, and seizes labour power by its very roots. It converts the labourer into a crippled monstrosity, by forcing his detail dexterity at the expense of a world of productive capabilities and instincts. . . . Not only is the detail work distributed to the different individuals, but the individual himself is made the automatic motor of a fractional operation. . . . If, at first, the workman sells his labour power to capital, because the material means of producing a commodity fail him, now his very labour power refuses its services unless it has been sold to capital. Its functions can be exercised only in an environment that exists in the workshop of the capitalist after the sale. By nature unfitted to make anything independently, the manufacturing labourer develops productive activity as a mere appendage of the capitalist's workshop. . . .

The knowledge, the judgment, and the will, which, though in ever so small a degree, are practised by the independent peasant or handicraftsman, in the same way as the savage makes the whole art of war consist in the exercise of his personal cunning – these faculties are now required only for the workshop as a whole. Intelligence in production expands in one direction, because it vanishes in many others. What is lost by the detail labourers, is concentrated in the capital that employs them. It is a result of the division of labour in manufactures, that the labourer is brought face to face with the intellectual potencies of the material process of production, as the property of another, and as a ruling power. This separation begins in simple co-operation, where the capitalist represents to the single workman, the oneness and the will of the associated labour. It is developed in manufacture which cuts down the labourer into a detail labourer. It is completed in modern industry, which makes science a productive force distinct from labour and presses it into the service of capital.

In manufacture, in order to make the collective labourer, and through him capital, rich in social productive power, each labourer must be made poor in individual productive powers....

By decomposition of handicrafts, by specialisation of the instruments of labour, by the formation of detail labourers, and by grouping and combining the latter into a single mechanism, division of labour in manufacture creates a qualitative gradation, and a quantitative proportion in the social process of production; it consequently creates a definite organisation of the labour of society, and thereby develops at the same time new productive forces in the society. In its specific capitalist form – and under the given conditions, it could take no other form than a capitalistic one – manufacture is but a particular method of begetting relative surplus value, or of augmenting at the expense of the labourer the self-expansion of capital.... It increases the social productive power of labour, not only for the benefit of the capitalist instead of for that of the labourer, but it does this by crippling the individual labourers. It creates new conditions for the lordship of capital over labour. If, therefore, on the one hand, it presents itself historically as a progress and as a necessary phase in the economic development of society, on the other hand, it is a refined and civilised method of exploitation....

During the manufacturing period proper, i.e., the period during which manufacture is the predominant form taken by capitalist production, many obstacles are opposed to the full development of the peculiar tendencies of manufacture. Although manufacture creates, as we have already seen, a simple separation of the labourers into skilled and unskilled, simultaneously with their hierarchic arrangement in classes, yet the number of the unskilled labourers, owing to the preponderating influence of the skilled, remains very limited. Although it adapts the detail operations to the various degrees of maturity, strength, and development of the living instruments of labour, thus conducing to exploitation of women and children, yet this tendency as a whole is wrecked on the habits and the resistance of the male labourers. Although the splitting up of handicrafts lowers the cost of forming the workman, and thereby lowers his value, yet for the more difficult detail work, a longer apprenticeship is necessary, and, even where it would be superfluous, is jealously insisted upon by the workmen. In England, for instance, we find the laws of apprenticeship, with their seven years' probation, in full force down to the end of the manufacturing period; and they are not thrown on one side till the advent of modern industry. Since handicraft skill is the foundation of manufacture, and since the mechanism of manufacture as a whole possesses no framework, apart from the labourers themselves, capital is constantly compelled to wrestle with the insubordination of the workmen. . . .

Hence throughout the whole manufacturing period there runs the complaint of want of discipline among the workmen. And had we not the testimony of contemporary writers, the simple facts, that during the period between the 16th century and the epoch of modern industry, capital failed to become the master of the whole disposable working time of the manufacturing labourers, that manufactures are short-lived, and change their locality from one country to another with the emigrating or immigrating workmen, these facts would speak volumes. . . .

At the same time manufacture was unable, either to seize upon the production of society to its full extent, or to revolutionise that production to its very core. It towered up as an economic work of art, on the broad foundation of the town handicrafts, and of the rural domestic industries. At a given stage in its development, the narrow technical basis on which manufacture rested, came into conflict with requirements of production that were created by manufacture itself.

One of its most finished creations was the workshop for the production of the instruments of labour themselves, including especially the complicated mechanical apparatus then already employed. . . .

This workshop, the product of the division of labour in manufacture, produced in its turn – machines. It is they that sweep away the handicraftsman's work as the regulating principle of social production. Thus, on the one hand, the technical reason for the life-long annexation of the workman to a detail function is removed. On the other hand, the fetters that this same principle laid on the dominion of capital, fall away.

chapter 19

Machinery and Modern Industry (1867)

The Development of Machinery

. . . In manufacture, the revolution in the mode of production begins with the labour power, in modern industry it begins with the instruments of labour. Our first inquiry then is, how the instruments of labour are converted from tools into machines, or what is the difference between a machine and the implements of a handicraft? We are only concerned here with striking and general characteristics; for epochs in the history of society are no more separated from each other by hard and fast lines of demarcation, than are geological epochs. . . .

All fully developed machinery consists of three essentially different parts, the motor mechanism, the transmitting mechanism, and finally the tool or working machine. The motor mechanism is that which puts the whole in motion. It either generates its own motive power, like the steam-engine, the caloric engine, the electromagnetic machine, &c., or it receives its impulse from some already existing natural force, like the water-wheel from a head of water, the wind-mill from wind, &c. The transmitting mechanism, composed of fly-wheels, shafting, toothed wheels, pullies, straps, ropes, bands, pinions, and gearing of the most varied kinds, regulates the motion, changes its form where necessary, as for instance, from linear to circular, and divides and distributes it among the working machines. These two first parts of the whole mechanism are there, solely for putting the working machines in motion, by means of which motion the subject of labour is seized upon and modified as desired. The tool or working machine is that part of the machinery with which the industrial revolution of the 18th century started. And to this day it constantly serves as such a starting-point, whenever a handicraft, or a manufacture, is turned into an industry carried on by machinery.

. . . The machine proper is . . . a mechanism that, after being set in motion, performs with its tools the same operations that were formerly done by the workman with similar tools. Whether the motive power is derived from man, or from some other machine, makes no difference in this respect. From the moment that the tool proper is taken from man, and fitted into a mechanism, a machine takes the place of a mere implement. The difference strikes one at once, even in those cases where man himself continues to be the prime mover. The number of implements that he himself can use simultaneously, is limited by the number of his own natural instruments of production, by the number of his bodily organs. . . . The number of tools that a machine can bring into play simultaneously, is from the very first emancipated from the organic limits that hedge in the tools of a handicraftsman. . . .

As soon as tools had been converted from being manual implements of man into implements of a mechanical apparatus, of a machine, the motive mechanism also acquired an independent form, entirely emancipated from the restraints of human strength. Thereupon the individual machine, that we have hitherto been considering, sinks into a mere factor in production by machinery. One motive mechanism was now able to drive many machines at once. The motive mechanism grows with the number of the machines that are turned simultaneously, and the transmitting mechanism becomes a wide-spreading apparatus. . . .

. . . In those branches of industry in which the machinery system is first introduced, manufacture itself furnishes, in a general way, the natural basis for the division, and consequent organisation, of the process of production. Nevertheless an essential difference at once manifests itself. In manufacture it is the workmen who, with their manual implements, must, either singly or in groups, carry on each particular detail process. If, on the one hand, the workman becomes adapted to the process, on the other, the process was previously made suitable to the workman. This subjective principle of the division of labour no longer exists in production by machinery. Here, the process as a whole is examined objectively, in itself, that is to say, without regard to the question of its execution by human hands, it is analysed into its constituent phases; and the problem, how to execute each detail process, and bind them all into a whole, is solved by the aid of machines, chemistry, &c. But, of course, in this case also, theory must be perfected by accumulated experience on a large scale. Each detail machine supplies raw material to the machine next in order; and since they are all working at the same time, the product is always going through the various stages of its fabrication, and is also constantly in a state of transition, from one phase to another. Just as in manufacture, the direct co-operation of the detail labourers establishes a numerical proportion between the special groups, so in an organised system of machinery, where one detail machine is constantly kept employed by another, a fixed relation is established between their numbers, their size, and their speed. The collective machine, now an organised system of various kinds of single machines, and of groups of single machines, becomes more and more perfect, the more the process as a whole becomes a continuous one, i.e., the less the raw material is interrupted in its passage from its first phase to its last; in other words, the more its passage from one phase to another is effected, not by the hand of man, but by the machinery itself. In manufacture the isolation of each detail process is a condition imposed by the nature of division of labour, but in the fully developed factory the continuity of those processes is, on the contrary, imperative.

A system of machinery, whether it reposes on the mere co-operation of similar machines, as in weaving, or on a combination of different machines, as in spinning, constitutes in itself a huge automaton, whenever it is driven by a self-acting prime mover. But although the factory as a whole be driven by its steam-engine, yet either some of the individual machines may require the aid of the workman for some of their movements (such aid was necessary for the running in of the mule carriage, before the invention of the self-acting mule, and is still necessary in fine-spinning mills); or, to enable a machine to do its work, certain parts of it may require to be handled by the workman like a manual tool; this was the case in machine-makers' workshops, before the conversion of the slide rest into a self-actor. As soon as a machine executes, without man's help, all the movements requisite to elaborate the raw material, needing only attendance from him, we have an automatic system of machinery, and one that is susceptible of constant improvement in its details. . . .

An organised system of machines, to which motion is communicated by the transmitting mechanism from a central automaton, is the most developed form of production by machinery. Here we have, in the place of the isolated machine, a mechanical monster whose body fills whole factories, and whose demon power, at first veiled under the slow and measured motions of his giant limbs, at length breaks out into the fast and furious whirl of his countless working organs. . . .

Modern industry had therefore itself to take in hand the machine, its characteristic instrument of production, and to construct machines by machines. It was not till it did this, that it built up for itself a fitting technical foundation, and stood on its own feet. Machinery, simultaneously with the increasing use of it, in the first decades of this century, appropriated, by degrees, the fabrication of machines proper. But it was only during the decade preceding 1866, that the construction of railways and ocean steamers on a stupendous scale called into existence the cyclopean machines now employed in the construction of prime movers. . . .

The implements of labour, in the form of machinery, necessitate the substitution of natural forces for human force, and the conscious application of science, instead of rule of thumb. In manufacture, the organisation of the social labour process is purely subjective; it is a combination of detail labourers; in its machinery system, modern industry has a productive organism that is purely objective, in which the labourer becomes a mere appendage to an already existing material condition of production. In simple co-operation, and even in that founded on division of labour, the suppression of the isolated, by the collective, workman still appears to be more or less accidental. Machinery, with a few exceptions to be mentioned later, operates only by means of associated labour, or labour in common. Hence the co-operative character of the labour process is, in the latter case, a technical necessity dictated by the instrument of labour itself.

The Proximate Effects of Machinery on the Workman

a. The employment of women and children

In so far as machinery dispenses with muscular power, it becomes a means of employing labourers of slight muscular strength, and those whose bodily development is incomplete, but whose limbs are all the more supple. The labour of women and children was, therefore, the first thing sought for by capitalists who used machinery. That mighty substitute for labour and labourers was forthwith changed into a means for increasing the number of wage labourers by enrolling, under the direct sway of capital, every member of the workman's family, without distinction of age or sex. Compulsory work for the capitalists usurped the place, not only of the children's play, but also of free labour at home within moderate limits for the support of the family.

The value of labour power was determined, not only by the labour time necessary to maintain the individual adult labourer, but also by that necessary to maintain his family. Machinery, by throwing every member of that family on to the labour market, spreads the value of the man's labour power over his whole family. It thus depreciates his labour power. To purchase the labour power of a family of four workers may, perhaps, cost more than it formerly did to purchase the labour power of the head of the family, but, in return, four days' labour takes the place of one, and their price falls in proportion to the excess of the surplus labour of four over the surplus labour of one. In order that the family may live, four people must now, not only labour, but expend surplus labour for the capitalist. Thus we see, that machinery, while augmenting the human material that forms the principal object of capital's exploiting power, at the same time raises the degree of exploitation.

Machinery also revolutionises out and out the contract between the labourer and the capitalist, which formally fixes their mutual relations. Taking the exchange of commodities as our basis, our first assumption was that capitalist and labourer met as free persons, as independent owners of commodities; the one possessing money and means of production, the other labour power. But now the capitalist buys children and young persons under age. Previously, the workman sold his own labour power, which he disposed of nominally as a free agent. Now he sells wife and child. He has become a slave-dealer. The demand for children's labour often resembles in form the inquiries for negro slaves. . . .

b. Prolongation of the working day

If machinery be the most powerful means for increasing the productiveness of labour – i.e., for shortening the working time required in the production of a commodity, it becomes in the hands of capital the most powerful means, in those industries first invaded by it, for lengthening the working day beyond all bounds set by human nature. . . .

In the first place, in the form of machinery, the implements of labour become automatic, things moving and working independent of the workman. They are thenceforth an industrial *perpetuum mobile*, that would go on producing forever, did it not meet with certain natural obstructions in the weak bodies and the strong wills of its human attendants. The automaton, as capital, and because it is capital, is endowed, in the person of the capitalist, with intelligence and will; it is therefore animated by the longing to reduce to a minimum the resistance offered by that repellent yet elastic natural barrier, man. This resistance is moreover lessened by the apparent lightness of machine work, and by the more pliant and docile character of the women and children employed on it. . . .

Given the length of the working day, all other circumstances remaining the same, the exploitation of double the number of workmen demands, not only a doubling of that part of constant capital which is invested in machinery and buildings, but also of that part which is laid out in raw material and auxiliary substances. The lengthening of the working day, on the other hand, allows of production on an extended scale without any alteration in the amount of capital laid out on machinery and buildings. Not only is there, therefore, an increase of surplus value, but the outlay necessary to obtain it diminishes. It is true that this takes place, more or less, with every lengthening of the working day; but in the case under consideration, the change is more marked, because the capital converted into the instruments of labour preponderates to a greater degree. . . .

. . . [H]owever much the use of machinery may increase the surplus labour at the expense of the necessary labour by heightening the productiveness of labour, it is clear that it attains this result, only by diminishing the number of workmen employed by a given amount of capital. It converts what was formerly variable capital, invested in labour power, into machinery which, being constant capital, does not produce surplus value. It is impossible, for instance, to squeeze as much surplus value out of 2 as out of 24 labourers. If each of these 24 men gives only one hour of surplus labour in 12, the 24 men give together 24 hours of surplus labour, while 24 hours is the total labour of the two men. Hence, the application of machinery to the production of surplus value implies a contradiction which is immanent in it, since of the two factors of the surplus value created by a given amount of capital, one, the rate of surplus value, cannot be increased, except by diminishing the other, the number of workmen. This contradiction comes to light, as soon as by the general employment of machinery in a given industry, the value of the machine-produced commodity regulates the value of all commodities of the same sort; and it is this contradiction, that in its turn, drives the capitalist, without his being conscious of the fact, to excessive lengthening of the working day, in order that he may compensate the decrease in the relative number of labourers exploited, by an increase not only of the relative, but of the absolute surplus labour.

If, then, the capitalistic employment of machinery, on the one hand, supplies new and powerful motives to an excessive lengthening of the working day, and radically changes, as well the methods of labour, as also the character of the social working organism, in such a manner as to break down all opposition to this tendency, on the other hand, it produces, partly by opening out to the capitalist new strata of the working class, previously inaccessible to him, partly by setting free the labourers it supplants, a surplus working population, which is compelled to submit to the dictation of capital. Hence that remarkable phenomenon in the history of modern industry, that machinery sweeps away every moral and natural restriction on the length of the working day. Hence, too, the economic paradox, that the most powerful instrument for shortening labour time, becomes the most unfailing means for placing every moment of the labourer's time and that of his family, at the disposal of the capitalist for the purpose of expanding the value of his capital. . . .

c. Intensification of labour

. . . It is self-evident, that in proportion as the use of machinery spreads, and the experience of a special class of workmen habituated to machinery accumulates, the rapidity and intensity of labour increase as a natural consequence. Thus in England, during half a century, lengthening of the working day went hand in hand with increasing intensity of factory labour. Nevertheless the reader will clearly see, that where we have labour, not carried on by fits and starts, but repeated day after day with unvarying uniformity, a point must inevitably be reached, where extension of the working day and intensity of the labour mutually exclude one another, in such a way that lengthening of the working day becomes compatible only with a lower degree of intensity, and a higher degree of intensity, only with a shortening of the working day. So soon as the gradually surging revolt of the working class compelled Parliament to shorten compulsorily the hours of labour, and to begin by imposing a normal working day on factories proper, so soon consequently as an increased production of surplus value by the prolongation of the working day was once for all put a stop to, from that moment capital threw itself with all its might into the production of relative surplus value, by hastening on the further improvement of machinery. At the same time a change took place in the nature of relative surplus value. Generally speaking, the mode of producing relative surplus value consists in raising the productive power of the workman, so as to enable him to produce more in a given time with the same expenditure of labour. Labour time continues to transmit as before the same value to the total product, but this unchanged amount of exchange value is spread over more use values; hence the value of each single commodity sinks. Otherwise, however, so soon as the compulsory shortening of the hours of labour takes place. The immense impetus it gives to the development of productive power, and to economy in the means of production, imposes on the workman increased expenditure of labour in a given time, heightened tension of labour power, and closer filling up of the pores of the working day, or condensation of labour to a degree that is attainable only within the limits of the shortened working day. This condensation of a greater mass of labour into a given period thenceforward counts for what it really is, a greater quantity of labour. . . .

The shortening of the hours of labour creates, to begin with, the subjective conditions for the condensation of labour, by enabling the workman to exert more strength in a given time. So soon as that shortening becomes compulsory, machinery becomes in the hands of capital the objective means, systematically employed for squeezing out more labour in a given time. This is effected in two ways: by increasing the speed of the machinery, and by giving the workman more machinery to tend. Improved construction of the machinery is necessary, partly because without it greater pressure cannot be put on the workman, and partly because the shortened hours of labour force the capitalist to exercise the strictest watch over the cost of production. . . .

The Factory

At the commencement of this chapter we considered that which we may call the body of the factory, i.e., machinery organised into a system. We there saw how machinery, by annexing the labour of women and children, augments the number of human beings who form the material for capitalistic exploitation, how it confiscates the whole of the workman's disposable time, by immoderate extension of the hours of labour, and how finally its progress, which allows of enormous increase of production in shorter and shorter periods, serves as a means of systematically getting more work done in a shorter time, or of exploiting labour power more intensely. We now turn to the factory as a whole, and that in its most perfect form. . . .

Along with the tool, the skill of the workman in handling it passes over to the machine. The capabilities of the tool are emancipated from the restraints that are inseparable from human labour power. Thereby the technical foundation on which is based the division of labour in manufacture, is swept away. Hence, in the place of the hierarchy of specialised workmen that characterises manufacture, there steps, in the automatic factory, a tendency to equalise and reduce to one and the same level every kind of work that has to be done by the minders of the machines; in the place of the artificially produced differentiations of the detail workmen, step the natural differences of age and sex.

So far as division of labour reappears in the factory, it is primarily a distribution of the workmen among the specialised machines; and of masses of workmen, not however organised into groups, among the various departments of the factory, in each of which they work at a number of similar machines placed together; their co-operation, therefore, is only simple. The organised group, peculiar to manufacture, is replaced by the connexion between the head workman and his few assistants. The essential division is, into workmen who are actually employed on the machines (among whom are included a few who look after the engine), and into mere attendants (almost exclusively children) of these workmen. Among the attendants are reckoned more or less all "Feeders" who supply the machines with the material to be worked. In addition to these two principal classes, there is a numerically unimportant class of persons, whose occupation it is to look after the whole of the machinery and repair it from time to time; such as engineers, mechanics, joiners, &c. This is a superior class of workmen, some of them scientifically educated, others brought up to a trade; it is distinct from the factory operative class, and merely aggregated to it. This division of labour is purely technical.

To work at a machine, the workman should be taught from childhood, in order that he may learn to adapt his own movements to the uniform and unceasing motion of an automaton. When the machinery, as a whole, forms a system of manifold machines, working simultaneously and in concert, the co-operation based upon it, requires the distribution of various groups of workmen among the different kinds of machines. But the employment of machinery does away with the necessity of crystallising this distribution after the manner of manufacture, by the constant annexation of a particular man to a particular function. Since the motion of the whole system does not proceed from the workman, but from the machinery, a change of persons can take place at any time without an interruption of the work. The most striking proof of this is afforded by the *relays system*, put into operation by the manufacturers during their revolt from 1848–1850. Lastly, the quickness with which machine work is learnt by young people, does away with the necessity of bringing up for exclusive employment by machinery, a special class of operatives. With regard to the work of the mere attendants, it can, to some extent, be replaced in the mill by machines, and owing to its extreme simplicity, it allows of a rapid and constant change of the individuals burdened with this drudgery.

Although then, technically speaking, the old system of division of labour is thrown overboard by machinery, it hangs on in the factory, as a traditional habit handed down from manufacture, and is afterwards systematically re-moulded and established in a more hideous form by capital, as a means of exploiting labour power. The life-long speciality of handling one and the same tool, now becomes the life-long speciality of serving one and the same machine. Machinery is put to a wrong use, with the object of transforming the workman, from his very childhood, into a part of a detail-machine. In this way, not only are the expenses of his reproduction considerably lessened, but at the same time his helpless dependence upon the factory as a whole, and therefore upon the capitalist, is rendered complete. Here as everywhere else, we must distinguish between the increased productiveness due to the development of the social process of production, and that due to the capitalist exploitation of that process. In handicrafts and manufacture, the workman makes use of a tool, in the factory, the machine makes use of him. There the movements of the instrument of labour proceed from him, here it is the movements of the machine that he must follow. In manufacture the workmen are parts of a living mechanism. In the factory we have a lifeless mechanism independent of the workman, who becomes its mere living appendage. . . .

At the same time that factory work exhausts the nervous system to the uttermost, it does away with the many-sided play of the muscles, and confiscates every atom of freedom, both in bodily and intellectual activity. The lightening of the labour, even, becomes a sort of torture, since the machine does not free the labourer from work, but deprives the work of all interest. . . . By means of its conversion into an automaton, the instrument of labour confronts the labourer, during the labour process, in the shape of capital, of dead labour, that dominates, and pumps dry, living labour power. The separation of the intellectual powers of production from the manual labour, and the conversion of those powers into the might of capital over labour, is, as we have already shown, finally completed by modern industry erected on the foundation of machinery. The special skill of each individual insignificant factory operative vanishes as an infinitesimal quantity before the science, the gigantic physical forces, and the mass of labour that are embodied in the factory mechanism and, together with that mechanism, constitute the power of the "master." . . .

The technical subordination of the workman to the uniform motion of the instruments of labour, and the peculiar composition of the body of workpeople, consisting as it does of individuals of both sexes and of all ages, give rise to a barrack discipline, which is elaborated into a complete system in the factory, and which fully develops the before mentioned labour of overlooking, thereby dividing the workpeople into operatives and over-lookers, into private soldiers and sergeants of an industrial army. . . . The factory code in which capital formulates, like a private legislator, and at his own good will, his autocracy over his workpeople, unaccompanied by that division of responsibility, in other matters so much approved of by the bourgeoisie, and unaccompanied by the still more approved rep-resentative system, this code is but the capitalistic caricature of that social regulation of the labour process which becomes requisite in co-operation on a great scale, and in the employment in common, of instruments of labour and especially of machinery. The place of the slave-driver's lash is taken by the overlooker's book of penalties. All punishments naturally resolve themselves into fines and deductions from wages, and the law-giving talent of the factory Lycurgus so arranges matters, that a violation of his laws is, if possible, more profitable to him than the keeping of them.

We shall here merely allude to the material conditions under which factory labour is carried on. Every organ of sense is injured in an equal degree by artificial elevation of the temperature, by the dust-laden atmo-sphere, by the deafening noise, not to mention danger to life and limb among the thickly crowded machinery, which, with the regularity of the seasons, issues its list of the killed and wounded in the industrial battle. Economy of the social means of production, matured and forced as in a hothouse by the factory system, is turned, in the hands of capital, into systematic robbery of what is necessary for the life of the workman while he is at work, robbery of space, light, air, and of protection to his person against the dangerous and unwholesome accompaniments of the productive process, not to mention the robbery of appliances for the comfort of the workman. . . .

part 5

The Downside of Capitalist Growth: Overpopulation, Poverty, Speculative Crises, and Environmental Devastation

This part focuses on Marx's views about contradictory aspects and costs of modern industry. Several of the selections address matters related to the rising "organic composition of capital" – the increasing proportion of machinery, or fixed capital, to living labor, or variable capital. Marx argued that the first capitalist, in an industry, to mechanize or make major improvements in machinery greatly intensifies labor and produces commodities much faster than their socially necessary labor time. He held that productivity is so high, and savings in labor time so great, that the capitalist can raise money wages well above the industry average, and still hold back from workers a much higher percentage of their surplus product. Each individual product has substantially less value, or crystallized labor time, than that of backward competitors, and thus can be sold at a much lower price and reap surplus profits (far above the industry average). For example, Henry Ford's assembly line provided enormous productivity gains and huge advantages over competitors; he sold his cars at half the price, paid the highest wages, and made massive profits. This initial advantage is lost, and prices and profits equalize, when competitors adopt similar technologies and readjust downward the entire industry's socially necessary labor time. However, Marx held that renewed competition and efforts to increase productivity and profits curtail this leveling and send technical innovation and mechanization spiraling upward.

In *Capital*, Marx argued that modern industry both concentrates and centralizes capital – single capitalists control huge amounts of wealth, and each market has fewer and fewer capitalists. He held that high barriers to entry block small capitalists from competing in technically advanced sectors of modern industry, since funding expensive start-up costs, technical innovations, and an expanded scale of production requires large amounts of capital or credit. Marx claimed that large, mechanized firms beat small, backward ones and that, among major producers, multiple waves of competition, innovation, and business failure leave a few giant firms, or even a single one, dominating an entire industry. Thus, a split arises between an oligopoly sector composed of a relatively few, large, industrial firms and a competitive sector made up of a multitude of small and, usually, technically backward operations. In Marx's view, the competitive markets praised by economists as capitalism's special virtue prevail among small firms, but diminish among large ones, where "co-operation on a large scale" becomes the rule. Overall, he held that capitalism contains seeds of its own destruction, because accumulation depends ultimately on increasing the size of the proletariat and mass of unpaid labor, but that automation makes industrial productive forces less a "means of employment for laborers." Arguing that modern industry causes technology costs to soar, living labor to shrink, and commodities to lose value, he predicted "a gradual fall in the general rate of profit." Although Marx acknowledged various conditions that put a brake on this process, he still viewed it to be a "logical necessity" and the ultimate Achilles' heel of long-term capitalist development.

In the selection on "relative surplus population," also from the first volume of *Capital*, Marx focused on related, already existent problems of modern industry. Seeing "overpopulation" to be a unique product of capitalism, he argued that the laboring population was growing explosively while the relative demand for labor power was falling. Therefore, a substantial number of people were deprived of regular jobs as well as of productive forces. Marx considered the consequent mass of "unemployed or half-employed" workers to be an inherent facet of capitalist development; modern industry needs a large body of flexible workers who can be quickly hired or fired according to the fluctuating demand for labor power. In his view, the "reserve army" is mobilized to cope with sudden changes arising from the frenetic creation of new technologies, industries, and markets and from shifts in the economic "cycle." He also contended that capitalists try to perpetuate a sizable reserve army to keep wages close to subsistence. He claimed that, operating in marginal jobs and suffering periodical unemployment, even active members of the reserve army are poor. However, he held that capitalism breeds more hapless, "lazarus-layers" of unemployable "paupers" (e.g., habitual criminals, physically or mentally damaged people, demoralized workers). Being systematic facets of capitalism, he argued, this "dangerous" underclass and overall reserve army will continue to grow with accumulated wealth.

The concluding selections provide examples of Marx's views about modern industry's wide-ranging, problematic ripple effects. His newspaper article about the "lunatic poor" addressed one of the most rapidly growing segments of the new underclass. Marx attacked scathingly the warehousing of the mad in workhouses and lunatic asylums. Anticipating presciently later twentieth-century critiques, he portrayed these institutions' overcrowded and understaffed operations, their inadequate provision, ventilation, and oversight, lack of exercise, activity, and treatment, and overall emphasis on minimal expense. Marx's article on Europe's mid-1850s "economic crisis" implies an entirely different segment of superfluous or nonproductive populace, located closer to the top of the class system. He described the speculative frenzies, pyramid schemes, and financial swindling accompanying modern industry's expansion of credit, high finance, and joint-stock companies. His portrayal of financiers luring small investors with initially high dividends, fraudulent accounts, and fake reports, while draining off the capital for themselves and their families, parallels recent financial swindles. Having ambivalent feelings, Marx usually praised capitalists' contributions to material progress, while he criticized their exploitative ways. However, this essay points to a parasitic, wealthy stratum that contradicts the systematic accumulation of the captains of industry. From the first volume of *Capital*, the last selection probes another facet of capitalism's irrationality. Marx argued that mechanized agriculture was "laying waste" to the "fertility of the soil" as well as to peasants' "vitality, freedom, and independence." In his view, modern industrial technology will exact grave human and environmental costs as long as it serves capitalist accumulation.

Marx's argument about the development of a dual economy is now part of conventional thought in the sociology of the economy and institutional economics. His views about concentration and centralization, unemployment, and poverty have often been criticized; but they point to enduring problems, which continue to plague contemporary capitalism. Marx's views on these matters raise critical questions about the people left out of the late twentieth-century US economic boom (e.g., "flexible," part-time labor, the minority underclass) and about global capitalism's profound inequalities (e.g., the roughly 3 billion people who live on less than $2 a day). However, diverse critics reject Marx's argument about the falling rate of profit, contending that it lacks empirical support, and that it gravely underestimates capitalism's vibrancy and powers of self-renewal. Even Marx expressed hesitancy about this theory, referring to it as a "law" at some points and at others only as a "tendency." He also pointed to major measurement problems. Engels had much more basic reservations about the idea. Marx's argument about falling profit remains very problematic, and is extremely difficult or even impossible to test. Critics also argue that his contentions about capitalism's various harsh consequences reduce multi-faceted sociocultural matters to economic problems and blame capitalism for virtually every pathology of modernity. This critique will probably be debated as along as interest in Marx's ideas persists. However, his points about capitalism's irrational side, inherent limits, and costs offer a provocative and potentially fruitful lens whereby to analyze and discuss matters that have grave consequences or pose major threats, but are seen to be impervious to human control (e.g., inner city poverty, extreme disparities in the global distribution of wealth, and global environmental threats).

chapter 20

The General Law of Capitalist Accumulation (1867)

. . . The composition of capital is to be understood in a twofold sense. On the side of value, it is determined by the proportion in which it is divided into constant capital or value of the means of production, and variable capital or value of labour power, the sum total of wages. On the side of material, as it functions in the process of production, all capital is divided into means of production and living labour power. This latter composition is determined by the relation between the mass of the means of production employed, on the one hand, and the mass of labour necessary for their employment on the other. I call the former the *value composition*, the latter the *technical composition* of capital. Between the two there is a strict correlation. To express this, I call the value composition of capital, in so far as it is determined by its technical composition and mirrors the changes of the latter, the *organic composition* of capital. Wherever I refer to the composition of capital, without further qualification, its organic composition is always understood. . . .

Growth of capital involves growth of its variable constituent or of the part invested in labour power. A part of the surplus value turned into additional capital must always be re-transformed into variable capital, or additional labour fund. . . . As simple reproduction constantly reproduces the capital relation itself, i.e., the relation of capitalists on the one hand, and wage workers on the other, so reproduction on a progressive scale, i.e., accumulation, reproduces the capital relation on a progressive scale, more capitalists or larger capitalists at this pole, more wage workers at that. The reproduction of a mass of labour power, which must incessantly reincorporate itself with capital for that capital's self-expansion; which cannot get free from capital, and whose enslavement to capital is only concealed by the variety of individual capitalists to whom it sells itself, this reproduction of labour power forms, in fact, an essential of the reproduction of capital itself. Accumulation of capital is, therefore, increase of the proletariat. . . .

Once given the general basis of the capitalistic system, then, in the course of accumulation, a point is reached at which the development of the productivity of social labour becomes the most powerful lever of accumulation.

... [T]he degree of productivity of labour, in a given society, is expressed in the relative extent of the means of production that one labourer, during a given time, with the same tension of labour power, turns into products.... [T]he growing extent of the means of production, as compared with the labour power incorporated with them, is an expression of the growing productiveness of labour. The increase of the latter appears, therefore, in the diminution of the mass of labour in proportion to the mass of means of production moved by it....

... [T]he development of the productiveness of social labour presupposes co-operation on a large scale.... The basis of the production of commodities can admit of production on a large scale in the capitalistic form alone. A certain accumulation of capital, in the hands of individual producers of commodities, forms therefore the necessary preliminary of the specifically capitalistic mode of production. We had, therefore, to assume that this occurs during the transition from handicraft to capitalistic industry.... But all methods for raising the social productive power of labour that are developed on this basis, are at the same time methods for the increased production of surplus value or surplus product, which in its turn is the formative element of accumulation.... With the accumulation of capital ... the specifically capitalistic mode of production develops, and with the capitalist mode of production the accumulation of capital. Both these economic factors bring about, in the compound ratio of the impulses they reciprocally give one another, that change in the technical composition of capital by which the variable constituent becomes always smaller and smaller as compared with the constant.

... With the increasing mass of wealth which functions as capital, accumulation increases the concentration of that wealth in the hands of individual capitalists, and thereby widens the basis of production on a large scale and of the specific methods of capitalist production. The growth of social capital is effected by the growth of many individual capitals.... With the accumulation of capital ... the number of capitalists grows to a greater or less extent. Two points characterise this kind of concentration which grows directly out of, or rather is identical with, accumulation. First: The increasing concentration of the social means of production in the hands of individual capitalists is, other things remaining equal, limited by the degree of increase of social wealth. Second: The part of social capital domiciled in each particular sphere of production is divided among many capitalists who face one another as independent commodity producers competing with each other. Accumulation and the concentration accompanying it are, therefore, not only scattered over many points, but the increase of each functioning capital is thwarted by the formation of new and the sub-division of old capitals. Accumulation, therefore, presents itself on the one hand as increasing concentration of the means of production, and of the command over labour; on the other, as repulsion of many individual capitals one from another.

This splitting-up of the total social capital into many individual capitals or the repulsion of its fractions one from another, is counteracted by their attraction. This last does not mean that simple concentration of the means of production and of the command over labour, which is identical with accumulation. It is concentration of capitals already formed, destruction of their individual independence, expropriation of capitalist by capitalist, transformation of many small into few large capitals. This process differs from the former in this, that it only presupposes a change in the distribution of capital already to hand, and functioning; its field of action is therefore not limited by the absolute growth of social wealth, by the absolute limits of accumulation. Capital grows in one place to a huge mass in a single hand, because it has in another place been lost by many. This is centralisation proper, as distinct from accumulation and concentration.

. . . The battle of competition is fought by cheapening of commodities. The cheapness of commodities depends, *ceteris paribus*, on the productiveness of labour, and this again on the scale of production. Therefore, the larger capitals beat the smaller. It will further be remembered that, with the development of the capitalist mode of production, there is an increase in the minimum amount of individual capital necessary to carry on a business under its normal conditions. The smaller capitals, therefore, crowd into spheres of production which modern industry has only sporadically or incompletely got hold of. Here competition rages in direct proportion to the number, and in inverse proportion to the magnitudes, of the antagonistic capitals. It always ends in the ruin of many small capitalists, whose capitals partly pass into the hands of their conquerors, partly vanish. Apart from this, with capitalist production an altogether new force comes into play – the credit system. Not only is this itself a new and mighty weapon in the battle of competition. By unseen threads it, moreover, draws the disposable money, scattered in larger or smaller masses over the surface of society, into the hands of individual or associated capitalists. It is the specific machine for the centralisation of capitals. . . .

The increasing bulk of individual masses of capital becomes the material basis of an uninterrupted revolution in the mode of production itself. Continually the capitalist mode of production conquers branches of industry not yet wholly, or only sporadically, or only formally, subjugated by it. At the same time there grow up on its soil new branches of industry, such as could not exist without it. Finally, in the branches of industry already carried on upon the capitalist basis, the productiveness of labour is made to ripen, as if in a hot-house. In all these cases, the number of labourers falls in proportion to the mass of the means of production worked up by them. An ever increasing part of the capital is turned into means of production, an ever decreasing one into labour power. With the extent, the concentration and the technical efficiency of the means of production, the degree lessens progressively, in which the latter are means of employment for labourers. . . .

chapter 21

The Tendency of the Rate of Profit to Fall (1894)

. . . If it is . . . assumed that this gradual change in the composition of capital is not confined only to individual spheres of production, but that it occurs more or less in all, or at least in the key spheres of production, so that it involves changes in the average organic composition of the total capital of a certain society, then the gradual growth of constant capital in relation to variable capital must necessarily lead to *a gradual fall of the general rate of profit*, so long as the rate of surplus value, or the intensity of exploitation of labour by capital, remain the same. Now we have seen that it is a law of capitalist production that its development is attended by a relative decrease of variable in relation to constant capital, and consequently to the total capital set in motion. This is just another way of saying that owing to the distinctive methods of production developing in the capitalist system the same number of labourers, i.e., the same quantity of labour power set in motion by a variable capital of a given value, operate, work up and productively consume in the same time span an ever-increasing quantity of means of labour, machinery and fixed capital of all sorts, raw and auxiliary materials – and consequently a constant capital of an ever-increasing value. This continual relative decrease of the variable capital vis-à-vis the constant, and consequently the total capital, is identical with the progressively higher organic composition of the social capital in its average. It is likewise just another expression for the progressive development of the social productive power of labour, which is demonstrated precisely by the fact that the same number of labourers, in the same time, i.e., with less labour, convert an ever-increasing quantity of raw and auxiliary materials into products, thanks to the growing application of machinery and fixed capital in general. To this growing quantity of value of the constant capital – although indicating the growth of the real mass of use values of which the constant capital materially consists only approximately – corresponds a progressive cheapening of products. Every individual product, considered by itself, contains a smaller quantity of labour than it did on a lower level of production, where the capital invested in labour occupies a far greater place compared to the capital invested in means of production. . . . This mode of production produces a progressive relative decrease of the variable capital as compared to the constant capital, and consequently a continuously rising organic composition of the total capital. The immediate result of this is that the rate of surplus value, at the same, or even a rising, degree of labour exploitation, is represented by a continually falling general rate of profit. (. . . [T]his fall does not manifest itself in an absolute form, but rather as a tendency toward a progressive fall.) The progressive tendency of the general rate of profit to fall is, therefore, just *an expression peculiar to the capitalist mode of production* of the progressive development of the social productive power of labour. This does not mean to say that the rate of profit may not fall temporarily for other reasons. But proceeding from the nature of the capitalist mode of production, it is thereby proved a logical necessity that in its development the general average rate of surplus value must express itself in a falling general rate of profit. Since the mass of the employed living labour is continually on the decline as compared to the mass of objectified labour set in motion by it, i.e., to the productively consumed means of production, it follows that the portion of living labour, unpaid and congealed in surplus value, must also be continually on the decrease compared to the amount of value represented by the invested total capital. Since the ratio of the mass of surplus value to the value of the invested total capital forms the rate of profit, this rate must constantly fall. . . .

chapter 22

Progressive Production of a Relative Surplus Population or Industrial Reserve Army (1867)

... With the growth of the total capital, its variable constituent or the labour incorporated in it, also does increase, but in a constantly diminishing proportion. . . . This accelerated relative diminution of the variable constituent . . . takes the inverse form, at the other pole, of an apparently absolute increase of the labouring population, an increase always moving more rapidly than that of the variable capital or the means of employment. But in fact, it is capitalistic accumulation itself that constantly produces, and produces in the direct ratio of its own energy and extent, a relatively redundant population of labourers, i.e., a population of greater extent than suffices for the average needs of the self-expansion of capital, and therefore a surplus population. . . .

But if a surplus labouring population is a necessary product of accumulation or of the development of wealth on a capitalist basis, this surplus population becomes, conversely, the lever of capitalistic accumulation, nay, a condition of existence of the capitalist mode of production. It forms a disposable industrial reserve army, that belongs to capital quite as absolutely as if the latter had bred it at its own cost. Independently of the limits of the actual increase of population, it creates, for the changing needs of the self-expansion of capital, a mass of human material always ready for exploitation. With accumulation, and the development of the productiveness of labour that accompanies it, the power of sudden expansion of capital grows also; it grows, not merely because the elasticity of the capital already functioning increases, not merely because the absolute wealth of society expands, of which capital only forms an elastic part, not merely because credit, under every special stimulus, at once places an unusual part of this wealth at the disposal of production in the form of additional capital; it grows, also, because the technical conditions of the process of production themselves – machinery, means of transport, &c. – now admit of the rapidest transformation of masses of surplus product into additional means of production. The mass of social wealth, over-flowing with the advance of accumulation, and transformable into additional capital, thrusts itself frantically into old branches of production, whose market suddenly expands, or into newly formed branches, such as railways, &c., the need for which grows out of the development of the old ones. In all such cases, there must be the possibility of throwing great masses of men suddenly on the decisive points without injury to the scale of production in other spheres. Overpopulation supplies these masses. The course characteristic of modern industry, viz., a decennial cycle (interrupted by smaller oscillations), of periods of average activity, production at high pressure, crisis and stagnation, depends on the constant formation, the greater or less absorption, and the re-formation of the industrial reserve army or surplus population. In their turn, the varying phases of the industrial cycle recruit the surplus population, and become one of the most energetic agents of its reproduction. This peculiar course of modern industry, which occurs in no earlier period of human history, was also impossible in the childhood of capitalist production. . . . The whole form of the movement of modern industry depends, therefore, upon the constant transformation of a part of the labouring population into unemployed or half-employed hands. . . .

The number of labourers commanded by capital may remain the same, or even fall, while the variable capital increases. This is the case if the individual labourer yields more labour, and therefore his wages increase, and this although the price of labour remains the same or even falls, only more slowly than the mass of labour rises. Increase of variable capital, in this case, becomes an index of more labour, but not of more labourers employed. It is the absolute interest of every capitalist to press a given quantity of labour out of a smaller, rather than a greater number of labourers, if the cost is about the same. In the latter case, the outlay of constant capital increases in proportion to the mass of labour set in action; in the former that increase is much smaller. The more extended the scale of production, the stronger this motive. Its force increases with the accumulation of capital. . . .

. . . If the means of production, as they increase in extent and effective power, become to a less extent means of employment of labourers, this state of things is again modified by the fact that in proportion as the productiveness of labour increases, capital increases its supply of labour more quickly than its demand for labourers. The overwork of the employed part of the working class swells the ranks of the reserve, whilst conversely the greater pressure that the latter by its competition exerts on the former, forces these to submit to overwork and to subjugation under the dictates of capital. The condemnation of one part of the working class to enforced idleness by the overwork of the other part, and the converse, becomes a means of enriching the individual capitalists, and accelerates at the same

time the production of the industrial reserve army on a scale corresponding with the advance of social accumulation. . . .

Taking them as a whole, the general movements of wages are exclusively regulated by the expansion and contraction of the industrial reserve
army, and these again correspond to the periodic changes of the industrial cycle. They are, therefore, not determined by the variations of the
absolute number of the working population, but by the varying proportions in which the working class is divided into active and reserve army,
by the increase or diminution in the relative amount of the surplus population, by the extent to which it is now absorbed, now set free. . . .

The lowest sediment of the relative surplus population finally dwells
in the sphere of pauperism. Exclusive of vagabonds, criminals, prostitutes,
in a word, the "dangerous" classes, this layer of society consists of three
categories. First, those able to work. One need only glance superfici-
ally at the statistics of English pauperism to find that the quantity of
paupers increases with every crisis, and diminishes with every revival of
trade. Second, orphans and pauper children. These are candidates for the
industrial reserve army, and are, in times of great prosperity, as 1860, e.g.,
speedily and in large numbers enrolled in the active army of labourers.
Third, the demoralised and ragged, and those unable to work, chiefly
people who succumb to their incapacity for adaptation, due to the division of labour; people who have passed the normal age of the labourer;
the victims of industry, whose number increases with the increase of
dangerous machinery, of mines, chemical works, &c., the mutilated, the
sickly, the widows, &c. Pauperism is the hospital of the active labour army
and the dead weight of the industrial reserve army. Its production is
included in that of the relative surplus population, its necessity in theirs;
along with the surplus population, pauperism forms a condition of capitalist production, and of the capitalist development of wealth. . . .

The greater the social wealth, the functioning capital, the extent and
energy of its growth, and, therefore, also the absolute mass of the proletariat and the productiveness of its labour, the greater is the industrial reserve
army. The same causes which develop the expansive power of capital,
develop also the labour power at its disposal. The relative mass of the
industrial reserve army increases therefore with the potential energy of
wealth. But the greater this reserve army in proportion to the active labour
army, the greater is the mass of a consolidated surplus population, whose
misery is in inverse ratio to its torment of labour. The more extensive,
finally, the lazarus-layers of the working class, and the industrial reserve
army, the greater is official pauperism. *This is the absolute general law of
capitalist accumulation.* Like all other laws it is modified in its working by
many circumstances, the analysis of which does not concern us here. . . .

chapter 23

The Increase of Lunacy in Great Britain (1858)

There is, perhaps, no better established fact in British society than that of the corresponding growth of modern wealth and pauperism. Curiously enough, the same law seems to hold good with respect to lunacy. The increase of lunacy in Great Britain has kept pace with the increase of exports, and has outstripped the increase of population. Its rapid progress in England and Wales during the period extending from 1852 to 1857, a period of unprecedented commercial prosperity, [is] evident from the . . . annual returns of paupers, lunatics and idiots for the years 1852, 1854 and 1857. . . .

The proportion of acute and curable cases to those of a chronic and apparently incurable kind was, on the last day of 1856, estimated to be somewhat less than 1 in 5. . . .

There exist in England and Wales, for the accommodation of lunatics and idiots of all sorts and of all classes, 37 public asylums, of which 33 are county and 4 borough asylums; 15 hospitals; 116 private licensed houses, of which 37 are metropolitan and 79 provincial; and lastly, the workhouses. The public asylums, or lunatic asylums properly so called, were, by law, exclusively destined for the reception of the lunatic poor, to be used as hospitals for the medical treatment, not as safe places for the mere custody of the insane. On the whole, in the counties at least, they may be considered well regulated establishements, although of too extensive a construction to be properly superintended, overcrowded, lacking the careful separation of the different classes of patients, and yet inadequate to the accommodation of somewhat more than one-half of the lunatic poor. After all, the space afforded by these 37 establishments, spreading over the whole country, suffices for the housing of over 15,690 inmates. The pressure upon these costly asylums on the part of the lunatic population may be illustrated by one case. When, in 1831, Hanwell (in Middlesex) was built for 500 patients, it was supposed to be large enough to meet all the wants of the county. But, two years later, it was full; after another two years, it had to be enlarged for 300 more; and at this time (Colney Hatch having been meanwhile constructed for the reception of 1,200 lunatic paupers belonging to the same county) Hanwell contains upward of 1,000 patients. Colney Hatch was opened in 1851; within a period of less than five years, it became necessary to appeal to the rate-payers for further accommodation; and the latest returns show that at the close of 1856 there were more than 1,100 pauper lunatics belonging to the county unprovided for in either of its asylums. While the existing asylums are too large to be properly conducted, their number is too small to meet [the] rapid spread of mental disorders. Above all, the asylums ought to be separated into two distinct categories: asylums for the incurable, hospitals for the curable. By huddling both classes together, neither receives its proper treatment and cure.

The private licensed houses are, on the whole, reserved for the more affluent portion of the insane. Against these "snug retreats," as they like to call themselves, public indignation has been lately raised by the kidnapping of Lady Bulwer into Wyke House, and the atrocious outrages committed on Mrs. Turner in Acomb House, York. A Parliamentary inquiry into the secrets of the trade in British lunacy being imminent, we may refer to that part of the subject hereafter. For the present let us call attention only to the treatment of the 2,000 lunatic poor, whom, by way of contract, the Boards of Guardians and other local authorities let out to managers of private licensed houses. The weekly consideration per head for maintenance, treatment and clothing, allotted to these private contractors, varies from five to twelve shillings, but the average allowance may be estimated from 5s. to 8s. 4d. The whole study of the contractors consists, of course, in the one single point of making large profits out of these small receipts, and consequently of keeping the patient at the lowest possible expense. In their latest report the Commissioners of Lunacy state that even where the means of accommodation in these licensed houses are large and ample, the actual accommodation afforded is a mere sham, and the treatment of the inmates a disgrace.

It is true that a power is vested in the Lord Chancellor of revoking a license or preventing its renewal, on the advice of the Commissioners in Lunacy; but, in many instances, where there exists no public asylum in the neighborhood, or where the existing asylum is already overcrowded, no alternative was left the Commissioners but to prevent the license to continue, or to throw large masses of the insane poor into their several workhouses. Yet, the same Commissioners add that great as are the evils of the licensed houses, they are not so great as the danger and evil combined of leaving those paupers almost uncared for in workhouses. In the latter about 7,000 lunatics are at present confined. At first the lunatic wards in workhouses were restricted to the reception of such pauper lunatics as required little more than ordinary accommodation, and were capable of associating with the other inmates. What with the difficulty of obtaining admission for their insane poor into properly regulated asylums, what

with motives of parsimony, the parochial boards are more and more transforming the workhouses into lunatic asylums, but into asylums wanting
in the attendance, the treatment and the supervision which form the
principal safeguard of patients detained in asylums regularly constituted.
Many of the larger workhouses have lunatic wards containing from 40 to
120 inmates. The wards are gloomy and unprovided with any means for
occupation, exercise or amusement. The attendants for the most part are
pauper inmates totally unfitted for the charge imposed upon them. The
diet, essential above everything else to the unhappy objects of mental disease, rarely exceeds in any case that allowed for the healthy and able-
bodied inmates. Hence, it is a natural result that detention in workhouses
not only deteriorates the cases of harmless imbecility for which it was
originally intended, but has the tendency to render chronic and permanent cases that might have yielded to early care. The decisive principle for
the Boards of Guardians is economy.

According to law, the insane pauper should come at first under the care
of the district parish surgeon, who is bound to give notice to the relieving officers, by whom communication is to be made to the magistrate,
upon whose order they are to be conveyed to the asylum. In fact, these
provisions are disregarded altogether. The pauper lunatics are in the first
instance hurried into the workhouses, there to be permanently detained,
if found to be manageable. The recommendation of the Commissioners
in Lunacy, during their visits to the workhouses, of removing to the
asylums all inmates considered to be curable, or to be exposed to treatment unsuited to their state, is generally outweighed by the report of the
medical officer of the Union, to the effect that the patient is "harmless."
What the workhouse accommodation is, may be understood from the
following illustrations described in the last Lunacy Report as "faithfully
exhibiting the general characteristics of workhouse accommodation."

In the Infirmary Asylum of Norwich the beds of even the sick and feeble
patients were of straw. The floors of thirteen small rooms were of stone.
There were no water-closets. The nightwatch on the male side had been
discontinued. There was a great deficiency of blankets, of toweling, of
flannels, of waistcoats, of washing basins, of chairs, of plates, of spoons
and of dining accommodation. The ventilation was bad. . . .

It would be too loathsome even to give extracts from the Commissioners' report on the St. Pancras Workhouse at London, a sort of low
Pandemonium. Generally speaking, there are few English stables which,
at the side of the lunatic wards in the workhouses, would not appear
boudoirs, and where the treatment received by the quadrupeds may not
be called sentimental when compared to that of the poor insane.

chapter 24

The Economic Crisis in Europe (1856)

What distinguishes the present period of speculation in Europe is the universality of the rage. There have been gambling manias before – corn manias, railway manias, mining manias, banking manias, cotton-spinning manias – in short, manias of every possible description; but at the epochs of the great commercial crises of 1817, 1825, 1836, 1846–'47, although every branch of industrial and commercial enterprise was affected, one leading mania gave to each epoch its distinct tone and character. Every department being invaded by the spirit of speculation, every speculator still confined himself within his department. On the contrary, the ruling principle of the Crédit Mobilier, the representative of the present mania, is not to speculate in a given line, but to speculate in speculation, and to universalize swindling at the same rate that it centralizes it. There is, besides, this further difference in the origin and growth of the present mania, that it did not begin in England, but in France. . . . The British are prone to congratulate themselves upon the removal of the focus of speculation from their free and sober island to the muddled and despot-ridden Continent; but then they forget the intense anxiety with which they watch the monthly statement of the Bank of France as influencing the heap of bullion in the sanctum of the Bank of England; they forget that it is English capital, to a great extent, which supplies the great arteries of the European Crédits Mobiliers with the heavenly moisture; they forget that the "sound" over-trading and over-production in England, which they are now extolling as having reached the figure of nearly £110,000,000 of exports, is the direct offspring of the "unsound" speculation they denounce on the Continent, as much as their liberal policy of 1854 and 1856 is the offspring of the coup d'état of Bonaparte. Yet it cannot be denied that they are innocent of the breeding of that curious mixture of Imperial Socialism, St. Simonistic stock-jobbing and philosophical swindling which makes up what is called the Crédit Mobilier. In strong contradistinction to this continental refinement, English speculation has gone back to its coarsest and most primitive form of fraud, plain, unvarnished and unmitigated. Fraud was the mystery of

Paul, Strahan & Bates; of the Tipperary Bank of Sadleir memory; of the great City operations of Cole, Davidson & Gordon; and fraud is the sad but simple tale of the Royal British Bank of London.

For a set of directors to eat up a company's capital, while cheering on its shareholders by high dividends, and inveigling depositors and fresh shareholders by fraudulent accounts, no high degree of refinement is necessary. Nothing is wanted but English law. The case of the Royal British Bank has caused a sensation, not so much on account of the capital as on account of the number of small people involved, both among the shareholders and depositors. The division of labor in this concern appears to have been very simple, indeed. There were two sets of directors, the one content to pocket their salary of $10,000 a year for knowing nothing of the affairs of the Bank and keeping their consciences clear, the other intent upon the real direction of the Bank, only to be its first customers or rather plunderers. The latter class being dependent for accommodation upon the manager, at once begin with letting the manager accommodate himself. Beside the manager they must take into the secret the auditor and solicitor of the Company, who consequently receive bribes in the shape of advances. In addition to advances made to themselves and relatives in their own names, the directors and manager proceed to set up a number of men of straw, in whose names they pocket further advances. The whole paid-up capital amounts now to £150,000, of which £121,840 were swallowed directly and indirectly by the directors. The founder of the Company, Mr. McGregor, M.P. for Glasgow, the celebrated statistical writer, saddled the Company with £7,362; another director and Member of Parliament, Mr. Humphrey Brown of Tewkesbury, who used the bank to pay his electioneering expenses, incurred at one time a liability to it of £70,000, and appears to be still in its debt to the tune of £50,000. Mr. Cameron, the manager, had advances to the amount of £30,000.

Every year since the bank went in operation, it had been losing £50,000, and yet the directors came forward every year to congratulate the shareholders upon their prosperity. Dividends of six per cent were paid quarterly, although by the declaration of the official accountant, Mr. Coleman, the shareholders ought never to have had a dividend at all. Only last Summer, fallacious accounts to the extent of over £370,000 were presented to the shareholders, the advances made to McGregor, Humphrey Brown, Cameron & Co., figuring under the abstract head of Convertible Securities. When the bank was completely insolvent, new shares were issued, amid glowing reports of its progress and a vote of confidence in the directors. This issue of new shares was by no means contemplated as a desperate means of relieving the position of the bank, but simply to furnish fresh material for directorial fraud. Although it was one of the rules of the charter that the bank was not to traffic in its own shares, it appears to have been the constant practice to saddle it, by way of security, with its own shares whenever they had become depreciated in the directors' hands. . . .

It is due to Mr. Cameron to say that, without waiting for the consequences of these discoveries, he, with great prudence and promptitude, expatriated himself from England.

One of the most extraordinary and characteristic transactions of the Royal British Bank was its connection with some Welsh Iron Works. At a time when the paid-up capital of the Company amounted to but £50,000, the advances made to these Iron Works alone reached the sum of £70,000 to £80,000. When the Company first got possession of this iron establishment it was an unworkable concern. Having become workable after an investment of something like £50,000, we find the property in the hands of a Mr. Clarke, who, after having worked it "for some time," threw it back upon the bank, while "expressing his conviction that he was throwing up a large fortune," leaving the bank, however, to bear an additional debt of £20,000 upon the "property." Thus, this concern kept going out of the hands of the bank whenever profits seemed likely to come in, and kept coming back to the bank when fresh advances were required to go out. This practical joke the Directors were endeavoring to continue even at the last moment of their confession, still holding up the profitable capacities of the works, which they say might yield £16,000 per annum, forgetting that they have cost the shareholders £17,742 during every year of the Company's existence. The affairs of the Company are now to be wound up in the Court of Chancery. Long before that can be done, however, the whole adventures of the Royal British Bank will have been drowned amid the deluge of the general European crisis.

chapter 25

Modern Industry and Agriculture (1867)

... If the use of machinery in agriculture is for the most part free from the injurious physical effect it has on the factory operative, its action in superseding the labourers is more intense, and finds less resistance. . . .

In the sphere of agriculture, modern industry has a more revolutionary effect than elsewhere, for this reason, that it annihilates the peasant, that bulwark of the old society, and replaces him by the wage labourer. Thus the desire for social changes, and the class antagonisms are brought to the same level in the country as in the towns. The irrational, old-fashioned methods of agriculture are replaced by scientific ones. Capitalist production completely tears asunder the old bond of union which held together agriculture and manufacture in their infancy. . . . Capitalist production, by collecting the population in great centres, and causing an ever-increasing preponderance of town population, on the one hand concentrates the historical motive power of society; on the other hand, it disturbs the circulation of matter between man and the soil, i.e., prevents the return to the soil of its elements consumed by man in the form of food and clothing; it therefore violates the conditions necessary to lasting fertility of the soil. By this action it destroys at the same time the health of the town labourer and the intellectual life of the rural labourer. . . . In agriculture as in manufacture, the transformation of production under the sway of capital, means, at the same time, the martyrdom of the producer; the instrument of labour becomes the means of enslaving, exploiting, and impoverishing the labourer; the social combination and organisation of labour processes is turned into an organised mode of crushing out the workman's individual vitality, freedom, and independence. The dispersion of the rural labourers over larger areas breaks their power of resistance while concentration increases that of the town operatives. In modern agriculture, as in the urban industries, the increased productiveness and quantity of the labour set in motion are bought at the cost of laying waste and consuming by disease labour power itself. Moreover, all progress in capitalistic agriculture is a progress in the art, not only of robbing the labourer, but of robbing the soil; all progress in increasing the fertility of the soil for a given time, is a progress towards ruining the lasting sources of that fertility. The more a country starts its development on the foundation of modern industry, like the United States, for example, the more rapid is this process of destruction. Capitalist production, therefore, develops technology, and the combining together of various processes into a social whole, only by sapping the original sources of all wealth – the soil and the labourer.

part 6

Globalization and Colonialism: The New International Division of Labor

In the 1840s, when modern industry was in its very early phase, young Marx and Engels asserted emphatically that a capitalist world market was on the rise, and that the spread of capitalist class relations would eventually eradicate national differences. Even before manufacture was well established, they contended, European powers were engaged in major colonial ventures to expand their emerging markets (e.g., plundering South America for its precious metals). Marx's mature work tempered his earlier views about the rise of a homogeneous or universal form of global capitalism, but he still argued that a boundless drive to accumulate and competitive pressure drove capitalists to seek "an ever-expansive market." He held that falling profits would accelerate globalization even as monopolistic tendencies diminish competition at home. The consequent pattern of global capitalist development, he argued, would be very uneven.

In the two selections from *Capital* given below, Marx portrayed industrial countries extracting surpluses from the less developed world and fashioning a global capitalism that perpetuates their dominance and subordinates poor regions. Marx held that modern industry's advanced forms of transportation, communication, and general technology provide means to expand capitalism rapidly and extensively. He also argued that its much enlarged scale of production creates pressure to seek global sources of raw materials and global outlets for its commodities. Producing much more efficiently, or far below the socially necessary labor time of backward handicraft production and simple manufacture, Marx contended, industrial capitalists are able to trade their commodities substantially above their value in a poor region. He also held that they gain from the region's lower living standards and reduced labor costs (slavery and serfdom often persist). Asserting that rich countries benefit from an unequal exchange (i.e., receiving goods with more crystallized labor in exchange for those with less), Marx believed that the consequent surplus profits counter falling profits at home. Overall, he argued that the poor regions are developed to suit modern industry. For example, he stated that Great Britain destroyed India's handicrafts and developed its cotton and other raw material production to meet British industry's needs. In his view, these practices were giving rise to a "new international division of labor" – an interdependent social formation with wealthy industrial centers extracting surplus from, and dominating, peripheral regions. Poor countries and colonies supply the core with raw materials and agricultural goods, and serve as markets for cheap, mass-produced goods.

Marx's newspaper article about the impact of the American Civil War on British industry draws out consequences of the emergent world economy's growing interdependence. Early in the war, Marx worried that dependence on American cotton might draw Great Britain into the conflict on the side of the slave states. The Union's navel blockade, which aimed to choke the Confederacy economically, cut off the flow of cotton to British factories. Marx thought that a severe cotton shortage would devastate this crucial sector of British industry, and perhaps the entire British economy. But he feared that the British working class would suffer the most. Marx also explained that the crisis was forcing Great Britain to increase reliance on cotton from distant India and to reorganize haphazard production there. Marx demonstrated that crisis conditions, in a single location of the global capitalist system, can have worldwide ripple effects, and that conditions in dependent agricultural regions may have dire consequences for rich as well as for poor regions. The piece also implies that global capitalism breeds, among the industrial powers, global geopolitical interests, which open the possibility of military interventions in widespread parts of the world.

In the newspaper article on "British Incomes in India," Marx challenged the view that the colonial regime benefited the British people as a whole. He contended that costs of colonial administration and the military exceeded the revenues that the colony produced for the British Treasury. By contrast, Marx demonstrated that the British East India Company provided huge financial benefits to a tiny number of wealthy stockholders and top administrators. He also showed that a substantially larger group of British business people and middling civil service and military personnel also benefited. His main point was that colonialism serves primarily upper-class economic interests and those of allied fragments of the middle class, while other British taxpayers and, especially, the colonized people bear the costs. For Marx, however, the "endless conquest and aggression" of British imperialism had much more than economic costs.

In "The Indian Revolt," Marx reported on the insurrection of Indian troops, or "Sepoys," employed by Great Britain's East India Company. A rumor that cartridges for new guns had been greased with cow or pig fat offended the religious convictions of Hindu and Muslim troops. This story arose in the broader context of the colonial regime's repeated insensitivity to the Indian people's religious and cultural traditions. The violent revolt against British rule started shortly after 85 Sepoys were tried for mutiny and imprisoned for refusing to use the cartridges. Marx's newspaper article portrays the racist side of colonialism, attacking scathingly the British Press's double standard – moral outrage about Sepoy violence and an all too casual and even cheery attitude to the brutality of British troops. Marx attacked the reportage for failing to probe the wider context of the violence and to recognize that British rule was responsible for the revolt. As indicated by the other essays in this part, Marx saw colonialism as driven primarily by ruling-class economic interests. However, he did not reduce British racism and cruelty or Sepoy violence to economic causes. This piece counters critics who claim that Marx was oblivious to cultural conflicts or treated them in a reductionist manner.

Early twentieth-century Marxists fashioned more detailed theories of imperialism. However, classical colonialism collapsed after the Second World War. In the optimistic climate of rapid, postwar economic growth, many Western intellectuals and policymakers, especially in the United States, adopted "modernization theory," which saw backwardness as deriving from the attributes of poor regions and their peoples, rather than from their dependent relations with rich countries. Modernization theorists held that the postwar era's Keynesian or Social Democratic capitalism put "developing nations" on a convergent developmental path with rich countries. In their view, poor countries that resisted communism and adopted capitalism and modern Western values would advance economically and socially. The most famous American modernization theorist, Talcott Parsons, posed a quasi-evolutionary theory of progress which held that the United States was leading global modernization. By contrast, American Marxist Paul Baran portrayed the United States as draining resources from the poor regions of the world and creating backwardness. Building on Marxian ideas about uneven development, he argued, more sweepingly than did Marx, that advanced capitalist countries' exploitative economic relations with the Third World produce "underdevelopment" there. Diverging from earlier Marxists, Baran implied that capitalism and Third World development are contradictory.

By the 1970s, certain "newly industrialized countries" (e.g., South Korea) proved that capitalist industrialism could arise in the less developed world. However, such progress stalled in much of Africa and South America; economic growth slowed, socioeconomic infrastructure eroded, authoritarianism and corruption became rampant, severe environmental and health problems arose, poverty was widespread, and the gap between poor and rich countries grew wider. Moreover, Communist nations stagnated, and their Third World interventions seemed bankrupt. Thinkers from both Left and Right attacked modernization theory. Following Baran, "dependency theorists" and "world systems theorists" revived Marx's ideas about unequal exchange and dependent relations between the advanced capitalist center and the less developed periphery. However, by the 1980s, neoliberal, or revived free-market, thought began to dominate policymaking in the United States and Great Britain and in the American-dominated International Monetary Fund, World Bank, and World Trade Organization. These leading capitalist financial institutions required Third World and former Communist nations seeking loans to embrace free-market policies. Overall, Third World countries were pressed to adopt forms of production, trade, and policy that meet rich countries' demands. In this climate, socialist strategies seemed moribund, and even social democracies drifted toward neoliberal policy. Consequently, dependency theory and world systems theory faded from popularity.

After the collapse of Eastern European communism and the end of wars of national liberation, books such as Francis Fukuyama's *The End of History* (1992) and Thomas L. Friedman's *The Lexus and the Olive Tree* (2000) celebrated the consolidation of deregulated global capitalism. They abandoned postwar liberalism's emphases on expanding welfare, regulation, and planning, as well as its high hopes about reducing economic inequality and about convergence between rich and poor countries. Recent globalization of production, finance, and consumption has created a much more complex and interdependent international division of labor and capitalist system than even Marx imagined. But many facets of his arguments about global capitalist development have been upheld. Moreover, the collapse of communism and spread of neoliberal policy is fashioning a global capitalism that looks more and more like the highly uneven type that Marx predicted. Recent protesters against the World Trade Organization and diverse anti-corporate movements criticize the neoliberal pattern of globalization and revive themes from Marx, fusing them with cultural politics. New Marxist theories of globalized capitalism are on the rise. Critics of modernization theory and Marxism raise a strong point that socioeconomic development is a multifaceted process that cannot be explained satisfactorily by a single theory. However, Marxism's emphases on the expansionary, extractive, and class nature of capitalism raise empirical questions that remain vital.

chapter 26

Foreign Trade (1894)

Since foreign trade partly cheapens the elements of constant capital, and partly the necessities of life into which the variable capital is converted, it tends to raise the rate of profit by increasing the rate of surplus value and lowering the value of constant capital. It generally acts in this direction by permitting an expansion of the scale of production. It thereby hastens the process of accumulation, on the one hand, but causes the variable capital to shrink in relation to the constant capital, on the other, and thus hastens a fall in the rate of profit. In the same way, the expansion of foreign trade, although the basis of the capitalist mode of production in its infancy, has become its own product, however, with the further progress of the capitalist mode of production, through the innate necessity of this mode of production, its need for an ever-expanding market. Here we see once more the dual nature of this effect. . . .

. . . Is the general rate of profit raised by the higher rate of profit produced by capital invested in foreign, and particularly colonial, trade?

Capitals invested in foreign trade can yield a higher rate of profit, because, in the first place, there is competition with commodities produced in other countries with inferior production facilities, so that the more advanced country sells its commodities above their value even though cheaper than the competing countries. In so far as the labour of the more advanced country is here realised as labour of a higher specific weight, the rate of profit rises, because labour which has not been paid as being of a higher quality is sold as such. The same may obtain in relation to the country, to which commodities are exported and to that from which commodities are imported; namely, the latter may offer more objectified labour *in natura* than it receives, and yet thereby receive commodities cheaper than it could produce them. Just as a manufacturer who employs a new invention before it becomes generally used, undersells his competitors and yet sells his commodity above its individual value, that is, realises the specifically higher productiveness of the labour he employs as surplus labour. He thus secures a surplus profit. As concerns capitals invested in colonies, etc., on the other hand, they may yield higher rates of profit for the simple reason that the rate of profit is higher there due to backward development, and likewise the exploitation of labour, because of the use of slaves, coolies, etc. It is hard to see why these higher rates of profit, realised by capitals invested in certain lines and sent home by them, should not, unless monopolies stand in the way, enter here into the equalisation of the general rate of profit and thus tend, *pro tanto*, to raise it. It is hard to see this in particular if these spheres of investment of capital are subject to the laws of free competition. . . . The favoured country recovers more labour in exchange for less labour, although this difference, this excess is pocketed, as in any exchange between labour and capital, by a certain class. Since the rate of profit is higher, therefore, because it is generally higher in a colonial country, it may, provided natural conditions are favourable, go hand in hand with low commodity prices. . . .

This same foreign trade develops the capitalist mode of production in the home country, which implies the decrease of variable capital in relation to constant, and, on the other hand, causes overproduction in respect to foreign markets, so that in the long run it again has an opposite effect.

We have thus seen in a general way that the same influences which produce a tendency in the general rate of profit to fall, also call forth countereffects, which hamper, retard, and partly paralyse this fall. The latter do not do away with the law, but impair its effect. Otherwise, it would not be the fall of the general rate of profit, but rather its relative slowness, that would be incomprehensible. Thus, the law acts only as a tendency. And it is only under certain circumstances and only after long periods that its effects become strikingly pronounced. . . .

chapter 27

Repulsion and Attraction of Workpeople (1867)

. . . So long as, in a given branch of industry, the factory system extends itself at the expense of the old handicrafts or of manufacture, the result is as sure as is the result of an encounter between an army furnished with breach-loaders, and one armed with bows and arrows. This first period, during which machinery conquers its field of action, is of decisive importance owing to the extraordinary profits that it helps to produce. These profits not only form a source of accelerated accumulation, but also attract into the favoured sphere of production a large part of the additional social capital that is being constantly created, and is ever on the look-out for new investments. The special advantages of this first period of fast and furious activity are felt in every branch of production that machinery invades. So soon, however, as the factory system has gained a certain breadth of footing and a definite degree of maturity, and, especially, so soon as its technical basis, machinery, is itself produced by machinery; so soon as coal mining and iron mining, the metal industries, and the means of transport have been revolutionised; so soon, in short, as the general conditions requisite for production by the modern industrial system have been established, this mode of production acquires an elasticity, a capacity for sudden extension by leaps and bounds that finds no hindrance except in the supply of raw material and in the disposal of the produce. On the one hand, the immediate effect of machinery is to increase the supply of raw material in the same way, for example, as the cotton gin augmented the production of cotton. On the other hand, the cheapness of the articles produced by machinery, and the improved means of transport and communication furnish the weapons for conquering foreign markets. By ruining handicraft production in other countries, machinery forcibly converts them into fields for the supply of its raw material. In this way East India was compelled to produce cotton, wool, hemp, jute, and indigo for Great Britain. By constantly making a part of the hands "supernumerary", modern industry, in all countries where it has taken root, gives a spur to emigration and to the colonisation of foreign lands, which are thereby converted into settlements for growing the raw material of the mother country; just as Australia, for example, was converted into a colony for growing wool. A new and international division of labour, a division suited to the requirements of the chief centres of modern industry springs up, and converts one part of the globe into a chiefly agricultural field of production, for supplying the other part which remains a chiefly industrial field. This revolution hangs together with radical changes in agriculture which we need not here further inquire into. . . .

The enormous power, inherent in the factory system, of expanding by jumps, and the dependence of that system on the markets of the world, necessarily beget feverish production, followed by overfilling of the markets, whereupon contraction of the markets brings on crippling of production. The life of modern industry becomes a series of periods of moderate activity, prosperity, overproduction, crisis and stagnation. The uncertainty and instability to which machinery subjects the employment, and consequently the conditions of existence, of the operatives become normal, owing to these periodic changes of the industrial cycle. Except in the periods of prosperity, there rages between the capitalists the most furious combat for the share of each in the markets. This share is directly proportional to the cheapness of the product. Besides the rivalry that this struggle begets in the application of improved machinery for replacing labour power, and of new methods of production, there also comes a time in every industrial cycle, when a forcible reduction of wages beneath the value of labour power, is attempted for the purpose of cheapening commodities. . . .

chapter 28

The Crisis in England (1857)

Today, as fifteen years ago, England faces a catastrophe that threatens to strike at the root of her entire economic system. As is known, the *potato* formed the exclusive food of Ireland and a not inconsiderable section of the English working people when the potato blight of 1845 and 1846 struck the root of Irish life with decay. The results of this great catastrophe are known. The Irish population declined by two million, of whom one part died of starvation and the other fled across the Atlantic Ocean. At the same time, this dreadful misfortune helped the English Free Trade party to triumph; the English landed aristocracy was compelled to sacrifice one of its most lucrative monopolies, and the abolition of the Corn Laws assured a broader and sounder basis for the reproduction and maintenance of the working millions.

What the *potato* was to Irish agriculture, *cotton* is to the dominant branch of Great Britain's industry. On its manufacture depends the subsistence of a mass of people greater than the total number of inhabitants of Scotland and than two-thirds of the present number of inhabitants of Ireland. For according to the census of 1861, the population of Scotland consisted of 3,061,117 persons, that of Ireland now only 5,764,543, whilst more than four million in England and Scotland live directly or indirectly by the cotton industry. Now the cotton plant is not, indeed, diseased. Just as little is its production the monopoly of a few regions of the earth. On the contrary, no other plant that yields clothing material thrives in equally extensive areas of America, Asia and Africa. The cotton monopoly of the slave states of the American Union is not a natural, but an historical monopoly. It grew and developed simultaneously with the monopoly of the English cotton industry on the world market. In the year 1793, shortly after the time of the great mechanical inventions in England, a Quaker of Connecticut, Ely Whitney, invented the cotton gin, a machine for cleaning cotton, which separates the cotton fibre from the cotton seed. Prior to this invention, a day of a Negro's most intensive labour barely sufficed to separate a pound of cotton fibre from the cotton seed. After the invention of the cotton gin, an old Negrowoman could comfortably supply fifty pounds of cotton daily, and gradual improvements have subsequently doubled the efficiency of the machine. The fetters on the cultivation of cotton in the United States were now burst asunder. Hand in hand with the English cotton industry, it grew swiftly to a great commercial power. Now and then in the course of development, England seemed to take fright at the monopoly of American cotton, as at a spectre that threatened danger. Such a moment occurred, for example, at the time when the emancipation of the Negroes in the English colonies was purchased for £20,000,000. It was a matter for misgiving that the industry in Lancashire and Yorkshire should rest on the sovereignty of the slave-whip in Georgia and Alabama, whilst the English nation imposed on itself so great a sacrifice to abolish slavery in its own colonies. Philanthropy, however, does not make history, least of all commercial history. Similar doubts arose as often as a cotton crop failure occurred in the United States and as, in addition, such a natural phenomenon was exploited by the slaveholders to artificially raise the price of cotton still higher through combination. The English cotton spinners and weavers then threatened rebellion against "King Cotton". Manifold projects for procuring cotton from Asiatic and African sources came to light. This was the case, for example, in 1850. However, the following good crop in the United States triumphantly dispelled such yearnings for emancipation. Indeed, in the last few years the American cotton monopoly attained dimensions scarcely dreamt of before, partly in consequence of the free trade legislation, which repealed the hitherto existing differential tariff on the cotton grown by slaves; partly in consequence of the simultaneous giant strides made by the English cotton industry and American cotton cultivation during the last decade. In the year 1857 the consumption of cotton in England already amounted to nearly 1,500 million pounds.

Now, all of a sudden, the American Civil War menaces this great pillar of English industry. Whilst the Union blockades the harbours of the Southern states, in order to cut off the secessionists' chief source of income by preventing the export of their cotton crop of this year, the Confederacy lends compelling force to this blockade with the decision not to export a bale of cotton of its own accord, but rather to compel England to come and fetch her cotton from the Southern harbours herself. England is to be driven to the point of forcibly breaking through the blockade, of then declaring war on the Union and so of throwing her sword into the scale of the slave states.

From the beginning of the American Civil War the price of cotton in England rose continuously; for a considerable time, however, to a less degree than was to be expected. On the whole, the English commercial world appeared to look down very phlegmatically on the American crisis. The cause of this cold-blooded way of viewing things was unmistakable. The whole of the last American crop was long ago in Europe. The yield of a new crop is never shipped before the end of November, and this shipment seldom attains considerable dimensions before the end of December. Till then, therefore, it remained pretty much a matter of indifference whether the cotton bales were held back on the plantations or forwarded to the harbours of the South immediately after their packing. Should the blockade cease at any time before the end of the year, England could safely count on receiving her customary cotton imports in March or April, quite as if the blockade had never taken place. The English commercial world, in large measure misled by the English press, succumbed, however, to the delusion that a spectacle of about six months' war would end with recognition of the Confederacy by the United States. But at the end of August, North Americans appeared in the market of Liverpool to buy cotton, partly for speculation in Europe, partly for reshipment to North America. This unheard-of event opened the eyes of the English. They began to understand the seriousness of the situation. The Liverpool cotton market has since been in a state of feverish excitement; the prices of cotton were soon driven 100 per cent above their average level; the speculation in cotton assumed the same wild features that characterised the speculation in railways in 1845. The spinning and weaving mills in Lancashire and other seats of the British cotton industry limited their labour time to three days a week; a number of mills stopped their machines altogether; the disastrous reaction on other branches of industry was not wanting, and at this moment all England trembles at the approach of the greatest economic catastrophe that has yet threatened her.

The consumption of *Indian* cotton is naturally increasing, and the rising prices will ensure further increase of importation from the ancient home of cotton. Nevertheless, it remains impossible radically to change the conditions of production and the course of trade at, so to speak, a few months' notice. England is, in fact, now expiating her long mismanagement of India. Her present spasmodic attempts to replace American cotton by Indian encounter two great obstacles: the lack of means of communication and transport in India, and the miserable condition of the Indian peasant, which prevents him from taking advantage of the momentarily favourable circumstances. But, apart from this, apart from the process of improvement that Indian cotton has still to go through to be able to take the place of American, even under the most favourable circumstances it will be *years* before India can produce for export the requisite quantity of cotton. It is statistically established, however, that in *four months* the stocks of cotton in Liverpool will be exhausted. They will hold out even as long as this only if the limitation of the labour time to three days a week and the complete stoppage of a part of the machinery is effected by the British cotton spinners and weavers to a still greater extent than hitherto. Such a procedure is already exposing the factory districts to the greatest social sufferings. But if the American blockade continues over January! What then?

chapter 29

British Incomes in India (1887)

The present state of affairs in Asia suggests the inquiry, What is the real value of their Indian dominion to the British nation and people? Directly, that is in the shape of tribute, of surplus of Indian receipts over Indian expenditures, nothing whatever reaches the British Treasury. On the contrary, the annual outgo is very large. From the moment that the East India Company entered extensively on the career of conquest – now just about a century ago – their finances fell into an embarrassed condition, and they were repeatedly compelled to apply to Parliament, not only for military aid to assist them in holding the conquered territories, but for financial aid to save them from bankruptcy. And so things have continued down to the present moment, at which so large a call is made for troops on the British nation, to be followed, no doubt, by corresponding calls for money. In prosecuting its conquests hitherto, and building up its establishments, the East India Company has contracted a debt of upward of £50,000,000 sterling, while the British Government has been at the expense, for years past, of transporting to and from and keeping up in India, in addition to the forces, native and European, of the East India Company, a standing army of thirty thousand men. Such being the case, it is evident that the advantage to Great Britain from her Indian empire must be limited to the profits and benefits which accrue to individual British subjects. These profits and benefits, it must be confessed, are very considerable.

First, we have the stockholders in the East India Company, to the number of about 3,000 persons, to whom under the recent charter there is guaranteed, upon a paid-up capital of six millions of pounds sterling, an annual dividend of ten and a half per cent, amounting to £630,000 annually. As the East India stock is held in transferable shares, anybody may become a stockholder who has money enough to buy the stock, which, under the existing charter, commands a premium of from 125 to 150 per cent. Stock to the amount of £500, costing say $6,000, entitles the holder to speak at the Proprietors' meetings, but to vote he must have £1,000 of stock. Holders of £3,000 have two votes, of £6,000 three votes, and of £10,000 or upward four votes. The proprietors, however, have but little voice, except in the election of the Board of Directors, of whom they choose twelve, while the Crown appoints six; but these appointees of the Crown must be qualified by having resided for ten years or more in India. One third of the Directors go out of office each year, but may be re-elected or reappointed. To be a Director, one must be a proprietor of £2,000 of stock. The Directors have a salary of £500 each, and their Chairman and Deputy Chairman twice as much; but the chief inducement to accept the office is the great patronage attached to it in the appointment of all Indian officers, civil and military – a patronage, however, largely shared, and, as to the most important offices, engrossed substantially, by the Board of Control. This Board consists of six members, all Privy Councilors, and in general two or three of them Cabinet Ministers – the President of the Board being always so, in fact a Secretary of State for India.

Next come the recipients of this patronage, divided into five classes – civil, clerical, medical, military and naval. For service in India, at least in the civil line, some knowledge of the languages spoken there is necessary, and to prepare young men to enter their civil service, the East India Company has a college at Haileybury. A corresponding college for the military service, in which, however, the rudiments of military science are the principal branches taught, has been established at Addiscombe, near London. Admission to these colleges was formerly a matter of favor on the part of the Directors of the Company, but under the latest modifications of the charter it has been opened to competition in the way of a public examination of candidates. On first reaching India, a civilian is allowed about $150 a month, till having passed a necessary examination in one or more of the native languages (which must be within twelve months after his arrival), he is attached to the service with emoluments which vary from $2,500 to near $50,000 per annum. The latter is the pay of the members of the Bengal Council; the members of the Bombay and Madras Councils receive about $30,000 per annum. No person not a member of Council can receive more than about $25,000 per annum, and, to obtain an appointment worth $20,000 or over, he must have been a resident in India for twelve years. Nine years' residence qualifies for salaries of from $15,000 to $20,000, and three years' residence for salaries of from $7,000 to $15,000. Appointments in the civil service go nominally by seniority and merit, but really to a great extent by favor. As they are the best paid, there is great competition to get them, the military officers leaving their regiments for this purpose whenever they can get a chance. The average of all the salaries in the civil service is stated at about $8,000, but this does not include perquisites and extra allowances, which are often very considerable. These civil servants are employed as Governors, Councilors, Judges, Embassadors, Secretaries, Collectors of the Revenue, &c. – the number in the whole being generally about 800. The salary of the Governor-General of India is $125,000, but the extra allowances often amount to a still larger sum. The Church service includes three bishops and about one hundred and sixty chaplains. The Bishop of Calcutta has $25,000 a year; those of Madras and Bombay half as much; the chaplains from $2,500 to $7,000, beside fees. The medical service includes some 800 physicians and surgeons, with salaries of from $1,500 to $10,000.

The European military officers employed in India, including those of the contingents which the dependent princes are obliged to furnish, number about 8,000. The fixed pay in the infantry is, for ensigns, $1,080; lieutenants, $1,344; captains, $2,226; majors, $3,810; lieutenant colonels, $5,520; colonels, $7,680. This is the pay in cantonment. In active service, it is more. The pay in the cavalry, artillery and engineers, is somewhat higher. By obtaining staff situations or employments in the civil service, many officers double their pay.

Here are about ten thousand British subjects holding lucrative situations in India, and drawing their pay from the Indian service. To these must be added a considerable number living in England, whither they have retired upon pensions, which in all the services are payable after serving a certain number of years. These pensions, with the dividends and interest on debts due in England, consume some fifteen to twenty millions of dollars drawn annually from India, and which may in fact be regarded as so much tribute paid to the English Government indirectly through its subjects. Those who annually retire from the several services carry with them very considerable amounts of savings from their salaries, which is so much more added to the annual drain on India.

Beside those Europeans actually employed in the service of the Government, there are other European residents in India, to the number of 6,000 or more, employed in trade or private speculation. Except a few indigo, sugar and coffee planters in the rural districts, they are principally merchants, agents and manufacturers, who reside in the cities of Calcutta, Bombay and Madras, or their immediate vicinity. The foreign trade of India, including imports and exports to the amount of about fifty millions of dollars of each, is almost entirely in their hands, and their profits are no doubt very considerable.

It is thus evident that individuals gain largely by the English connection with India, and of course their gain goes to increase the sum of the national wealth. But against all this a very large offset is to be made. The military and naval expenses paid out of the pockets of the people of England on Indian account have been constantly increasing with the extent of the Indian dominion. To this must be added the expense of Burmese, Afghan, Chinese and Persian wars. In fact, the whole cost of the late Russian war may fairly be charged to the Indian account, since the fear and dread of Russia, which led to that war, grew entirely out of jealousy as to her designs on India. Add to this the career of endless conquest and perpetual aggression in which the English are involved by the possession of India, and it may well be doubted whether, on the whole, this dominion does not threaten to cost quite as much as it can ever be expected to come to.

chapter 30

The Indian Revolt (1857)

London, Sept. 4, 1857

The outrages committed by the revolted Sepoys in India are indeed appalling, hideous, ineffable – such as one is prepared to meet only in wars of insurrection, of nationalities, of races, and above all of religion; in one word, such as respectable England used to applaud when perpetrated by the Vendeans on the "Blues," by the Spanish guerrillas on the infidel Frenchmen, by Servians on their German and Hungarian neighbors, by Croats on Viennese rebels, by Cavaignac's Garde Mobile or Bonaparte's Decembrists on the sons and daughters of proletarian France. However infamous the conduct of the Sepoys, it is only the reflex, in a concentrated form, of England's own conduct in India, not only during the epoch of the foundation of her Eastern Empire, but even during the last ten years of a long-settled rule. To characterize that rule, it suffices to say that torture formed an organic institution of its financial policy. There is something in human history like retribution; and it is a rule of historical retribution that its instrument be forged not by the offended, but by the offender himself.

The first blow dealt to the French monarchy proceeded from the nobility, not from the peasants. The Indian revolt does not commence with the Ryots, tortured, dishonored and stripped naked by the British, but with the Sepoys, clad, fed, petted, fatted and pampered by them. To find parallels to the Sepoy atrocities, we need not, as some London papers pretend, fall back on the middle ages, nor even wander beyond the history of contemporary England. All we want is to study the first Chinese war, an event, so to say, of yesterday. The English soldiery then committed abominations for the mere fun of it; their passions being neither sanctified by religious fanaticism nor exacerbated by hatred against an overbearing and conquering race, nor provoked by the stern resistance of a heroic enemy. The violations of women, the spittings of children, the roastings of whole villages, were then mere wanton sports, not recorded by Mandarins, but by British officers themselves.

Even at the present catastrophe it would be an unmitigated mistake to suppose that all the cruelty is on the side of the Sepoys, and all the milk of human kindness flows on the side of the English. The letters of the British officers are redolent of malignity. An officer writing from Peshawur gives a description of the disarming of the 10th irregular cavalry for not charging the 55th native infantry when ordered to do so. He exults in the fact that they were not only disarmed, but stripped of their coats and boots, and after having received 12d. per man, were marched down to the river side, and there embarked in boats and sent down the Indus, where the writer is delighted to expect every mother's son will have a chance of being drowned in the rapids. Another writer informs us that, some inhabitants of Peshawur having caused a night alarm by exploding little mines of gunpowder in honor of a wedding (a national custom), the persons concerned were tied up next morning, and

"received such a flogging as they will not easily forget."

News arrived from Pindee that three native chiefs were plotting. Sir John Lawrence replied by a message ordering a spy to attend to the meeting. On the spy's report, Sir John sent a second message, "Hang them." The chiefs were hanged. An officer in the civil service, from Allahabad, writes:

"We have power of life and death in our hands, and we assure you we spare not."

Another, from the same place:

"Not a day passes but we string up from ten to fifteen of them (non-combatants)."

One exulting officer writes:

"Holmes is hanging them by the score, like a 'brick.'"

Another, in allusion to the summary hanging of a large body of the natives:

"Then our fun commenced."

A third:

"We hold court-martials on horseback, and every nigger we meet with we either string up or shoot."

From Benares we are informed that thirty Zemindars were hanged on the mere suspicion of sympathizing with their own countrymen, and whole villages were burned down on the same plea. An officer from Benares, whose letter is printed in *The London Times*, says:

"The European troops have become fiends when opposed to natives."

And then it should not be forgotten that, while the cruelties of the English are related as acts of martial vigor, told simply, rapidly, without dwelling on disgusting details, the outrages of the natives, shocking as they are, are still deliberately exaggerated. For instance, the circumstantial account first appearing in *The Times*, and then going the round of the London press, of the atrocities perpetrated at Delhi and Meerut, from whom did it proceed? From a cowardly parson residing at Bangalore, Mysore, more than a thousand miles, as the bird flies, distant from the scene of action. Actual accounts of Delhi evince the imagination of an English parson to be capable of breeding greater horrors than even the wild fancy of a Hindoo mutineer. The cutting of noses, breasts, &c., in one word, the horrid mutilations committed by the Sepoys, are of course more revolting to European feeling than the throwing of red-hot shell on Canton dwellings by a Secretary of the Manchester Peace Society, or the roasting of Arabs pent up in a cave by a French Marshal, or the flaying alive of British soldiers by the cat-o'-nine-tails under drum-head court-martial, or any other of the philanthropical appliances used in British penitentiary colonies. Cruelty, like every other thing, has its fashion, changing according to time and place. Caesar, the accomplished scholar, candidly narrates how he ordered many thousand Gallic warriors to have their right hands cut off. Napoleon would have been ashamed to do this. He preferred dispatching his own French regiments, suspected of republicanism, to St. Domingo, there to die of the blacks and the plague.

The infamous mutilations committed by the Sepoys remind one of the practices of the Christian Byzantine Empire, or the prescriptions of Emperor Charles V.'s criminal law, or the English punishments for high treason, as still recorded by Judge Blackstone. With Hindoos, whom their religion has made virtuosi in the art of self-torturing, these tortures inflicted on the enemies of their race and creed appear quite natural, and must appear still more so to the English, who, only some years since, still used to draw revenues from the Juggernaut festivals, protecting and assisting the bloody rites of a religion of cruelty.

The frantic roars of the "bloody old *Times*," as Cobbett used to call it – its playing the part of a furious character in one of Mozart's operas, who indulges in most melodious strains in the idea of first hanging his enemy, then roasting him, then quartering him, then spitting him, and then flaying him alive – its tearing the passion of revenge to tatters and to rags – all this would appear but silly if under the pathos of tragedy there were not distinctly perceptible the tricks of comedy. *The London Times* overdoes its part, not only from panic. It supplies comedy with a subject even missed by Molière, the Tartuffe of Revenge. What it simply wants is to write up the funds and to screen the Government. As Delhi has not, like the walls of Jericho, fallen before mere puffs of wind, John Bull is to be steeped in cries for revenge up to his very ears, to make him forget that his Government is responsible for the mischief hatched and the colossal dimensions it has been allowed to assume.

First published unsigned in the *New-York Daily Tribune*, No. 5119,
September 16, 1857

part 7

New Society Rising in the Old: Socially Regulated Capitalism and a Third Industrial Revolution

According to Marx's materialism, progressively developing productive forces triumph eventually over a society's backward features and bring a new social world into being. Drawn from *Capital* and the *Grundrisse* (the notebooks for his masterwork), the following selections express Marx's views about modern industry producing, in addition to exploitation and disintegration, progressive social reforms and the seeds of an emancipated post-capitalist society. Recall his point that intense competition spurs mechanization, but that it also generates concentration and centralization, and therefore is a self-terminating process. This part of the book explores Marx's ideas about the progressive side of this contradictory development – that concentration and centralization increase general social interdependence, and thus extend planned social cooperation, which previously was limited to the individual firm, to capitalism's heretofore "anarchic" and conflictive societal division of labor, and that automation's sharp reduction of necessary labor time makes possible a new mode of production in which material subsistence and overall social well-being can be decoupled from wage labor or private wealth.

The selection on the British Factory Acts addresses the first broad social legislation aimed at reducing the human costs of·unregulated capitalism (e.g., restricting child labor and protecting workplace safety and ventilation). Marx explained that capitalists opposed these laws for undermining "free trade." He argued that legislators, bending to this complaint, designed the Factory Acts to keep regulation weak and permit avoidance. For example, rather than eliminating child labor, they required compulsory education for young workers that took only half the standard hours and allowed them to work the rest of the day. Marx was critical of the change, but still argued that this modest regulation contained the "germ" of a future, elevated type of working-class education that would integrate work and study in a manner that would produce "fully developed human beings." He also held that the shuttling of reserve army workers from job to job, although ruthless and harsh, prefigured a new world in which varied work would cultivate and satisfy "varied aptitudes." Similarly, he argued that employment of female factory workers was brutally exploitative, but that it eroded the "traditional" family and forged the economic basis for a more "humane" form of working group and a "higher" type of family and gender relations. Marx argued that modern industry necessitated the Factory Acts, but that continued development would require much more comprehensive, "conscious" intervention by "society." Anticipating recent conservative critics, he held that increased state regulation would accelerate concentration and centralization, because big business bears the costs much more easily than small business. However, Marx embraced this trend, believing that it would contribute to exploding the old world and ushering in the new.

In the selection on the formation of stock companies, Marx described large-scale firms that could not be funded by family wealth alone and had to borrow from commercial banks and sell stocks. He argued that large capitalists' access to credit and finance capital helped them swallow up small and medium-sized capitalists at an ever greater rate, and gave rise to a new "financial aristocracy" whose swindling and gambling on the stock market led to greatly increased economic instability and the possibility of sudden speculative crises. Replacing the earlier, prudent type of capitalist owner, or "rational miser," Marx held, these "pure adventurers" forged a faster, more irrational capitalism. By contrast, however, Marx praised the heads of stock companies for transforming private productive property into "social capital." He explained that these firms' day-to-day operations were run by a new form of "skilled labor," or salaried managers, rather than owners. He also said that owners were reduced to "mere money capitalists," who receive dividends, but relinquish effective control of production. Overall, Marx saw these new firms as creating "associated production" on a societal-wide scale, which required increased "state interference." He asserted that they were effectively abolishing capitalism "within the capitalist mode of production." He held that capitalist property rights, although circumscribed, still allowed "parasitic" speculators to set the general direction of how social labor was utilized and to appropriate most of its fruits for themselves. But he asserted that such capitalism was becoming harder and harder to justify.

In the third selection, from the *Grundrisse*, we find Marx claiming that modern industry was bringing into being a new capitalism, in which "general science" and "accumulated knowledge" are the leading productive forces. In his view, the emergent system of production decouples the creation of "real wealth," or use values that satisfy human wants and needs, from living labor. Marx contended that living labor is being reduced to a briefer and briefer moment of a highly automated, scientifically mediated productive process, and that workers become its regulators, rather than its agents. He envisioned a future time when automation would be so advanced that the wage labor system would be a mere vestige, perpetuating capitalist property relations and class power, but contributing little to the provisioning of human needs and even fettering the process. Marx implied that distinctly capitalist surplus extraction, as portrayed by his labor theory of value, would be so outmoded and contradictory that it would collapse of its own accord. In his view, this last stage of capitalism would initiate an epochal break from all past modes of production, providing the means to reduce labor time to a minimum and to create free time and resources for "development of individuals."

An often-repeated, standard critique of Marx stresses the absence of a revolutionary proletariat in rich countries and the repression and inefficiencies of Communist regimes. These critics tend to ignore the fact that he dwelled primarily on capitalism and dealt only passingly with communism. They also fail to stress his striking foresight regarding major features of twentieth-century capitalism. This part illustrates that he prophesied, in the very early phase of modern industry (before it spread beyond England), the rise of corporate capitalism and the Second Industrial Revolution; the complex of highly mechanized, managerial firms and interventionist states that came to dominate Europe and North America by 1920 and that blossomed and spread internationally after the Second World War. Parallel arguments about a new "socialized" or "collectivized" capitalism, employing ever more scientific methods of automated production, appeared in much later non-Marxist works, stretching from Adolf A. Berle's and Gardiner C. Means's *The Modern Corporation and Private Property* (1932) to Alfred D. Chandler's *The Visible Hand* (1977). These thinkers portrayed a "corporate" or "managerial" phase of capitalism, in which planning by corporate managers and state officials replaces unregulated free-market competition (or Adam Smith's "invisible hand"), and property rights are qualified by limited shareholder benefits and privileges and by government regulation.

Ironically, the revolutionary class struggles that Marx also predicated have been deflected or moderated in the most developed capitalist countries, in part by the type of state regulation and reformist social change that he pointed to perceptively in these selections and that he argued rightly would be broadened – wider regulation of working conditions, expanded educational opportunity, erosion of the traditional family, much increased female participation in the work force, and, at least for the middle class, many more opportunities for varied and rich work experiences. Critics stress, however, that Marx failed to foresee the massive middle classes and well-provisioned working classes that arose in the richest countries during the postwar era and that largely opposed Socialism. Others respond that the late twentieth-century erosion of the welfare state and unregulated global markets are regenerating, on a worldwide basis, the types of class splits that Marx predicted, and that political responses will one day follow. Putting this debate aside, recent globalization and financial deregulation have increased greatly the importance of the stock market and finance capital, generated many new, often instant credit mechanisms, stimulated increased speculation, and, overall, fashioned a much faster capitalism. Marx's vision of emergent, knowledge-based capitalism, with enormous productive power and very unevenly distributed benefits, anticipated the broad outlines of today's so-called New Economy, especially its new computer and communication technologies, which greatly extend automation and make knowledge a most important commodity, as well as a fundamental productive force.

Marx's last stage of capitalism, in which labor time becomes superfluous, is no more a reality today than it was in his time. But his ideas, in this part, still raise critical questions about the intensity of today's work (e.g., could France's 35-hour week be extended to other rich countries?) and about views that equate wider stock-market participation, expanded stockholders' rights, and increased wealth from dividends as unequivocally good trends and as democratization. Numerous postwar critics, from Left and Right, attack Marx's "economism" and "productivism," arguing that his vision of post-capitalism promised to make the world a workhouse. This critique was, in part, a response to facets of his work, but perhaps even more to Communist Party clichés about heroic workers, which employed his name and phrases to justify repressive, workaday regimes. By contrast, in the above selections, Marx's hopes for reducing unnecessary labor and drudgery suggested something more than life governed by prosaic economic ends and work. Rather, he dreamed of a new world in which the top priority would be developing human individuality and nurturing artistic, scientific, and other cultural values as ends in themselves. However distant, this scenario offers an alternative goal for lives now centered in enforced work, private consumption, and restless accumulation.

chapter 31

The Factory Acts (1867)

Factory legislation, that first conscious and methodical reaction of society against the spontaneously developed form of the process of production, is . . . just as much the necessary product of modern industry as cotton yarn, self-actors, and the electric telegraph. . . .

Apart from their wording, which makes it easy for the capitalist to evade them, the sanitary clauses are extremely meagre, and, in fact, limited to provisions for whitewashing the walls, for insuring cleanliness in some other matters, for ventilation, and for protection against dangerous machinery. . . . [W]e shall return again to the fanatical opposition of the masters to those clauses which imposed upon them a slight expenditure on appliances for protecting the limbs of their workpeople, an opposition that throws a fresh and glaring light on the Free-trade dogma, according to which, in a society with conflicting interests, each individual necessarily furthers the common weal by seeking nothing but his own personal advantage! . . .

What could possibly show better the character of the capitalist mode of production, than the necessity that exists for forcing upon it, by Acts of Parliament, the simplest appliances for maintaining cleanliness and health? . . .

Paltry as the education clauses of the Act appear on the whole, yet they proclaim elementary education to be an indispensable condition to the employment of children. The success of those clauses proved for the first time the possibility of combining education and gymnastics with manual labour, and, consequently, of combining manual labour with education and gymnastics. The factory inspectors soon found out by questioning the schoolmasters, that the factory children, although receiving only one half the education of the regular day scholars, yet learnt quite as much and often more. . . .

Further information on this point will be found in [a] speech at the Social Science Congress at Edinburgh in 1863. [The author] there shows, amongst other things, how the monotonous and uselessly long school hours of the children of the upper and middle classes, uselessly add to the labour of the teacher, "while he not only fruitlessly but absolutely injuriously, wastes the time, health, and energy of the children". From the Factory system budded . . . the germ of the education of the future, an education that will, in the case of every child over a given age, combine productive labour with instruction and gymnastics, not only as one of the methods of adding to the efficiency of production, but as the only method of producing fully developed human beings.

Modern industry, as we have seen, sweeps away by technical means the manufacturing division of labour, under which each man is bound hand and foot for life to a single detail operation. At the same time, the capitalistic form of that industry reproduces this same division of labour in a still more monstrous shape; in the factory proper, by converting the workman into a living appendage of the machine; and everywhere outside the Factory, partly by the sporadic use of machinery and machine workers, partly by reestablishing the division of labour on a fresh basis by the general introduction of the labour of women and children, and of cheap unskilled labour. . . .

. . . Modern industry rent the veil that concealed from men their own social process of production, and that turned the various, spontaneously divided branches of production into so many riddles, not only to outsiders, but even to the initiated. The principle which it pursued, of resolving each process into its constituent movements, without any regard to their possible execution by the hand of man, created the new modern science of technology. The varied, apparently unconnected, and petrified forms of the industrial processes now resolved themselves into so many conscious and systematic applications of natural science to the attainment of given useful effects. Technology also discovered the few main fundamental forms of motion, which, despite the diversity of the instruments used, are necessarily taken by every productive action of the human body; just as the science of mechanics sees in the most complicated machinery nothing but the continual repetition of the simple mechanical powers.

Modern industry never looks upon and treats the existing form of a process as final. The technical basis of that industry is therefore revolutionary, while all earlier modes of production were essentially conservative. By means of machinery, chemical processes and other methods, it is continually causing changes not only in the technical basis of production, but also in the functions of the labourer, and in the social combinations of the labour process. At the same time, it thereby also revolutionises the division of labour within the society, and incessantly launches masses of capital and of workpeople from one branch of production to another. But if modern industry, by its very nature, therefore necessitates variation of labour, fluency of function, universal mobility of the labourer, on the other hand, in its capitalistic form, it reproduces the old division of labour with its ossified particularisations. We have seen how this absolute contradiction between the technical necessities of modern industry, and the social character inherent in its capitalistic form, dispels all fixity and security in the situation of the labourer; how it constantly threatens, by taking away the instruments of labour, to snatch from his hands his means of subsistence, and, by suppressing his detail-function, to make him superfluous. We have seen, too, how this antagonism vents its rage in the creation of that monstrosity, an industrial reserve army, kept in misery in order to be always at the disposal of capital; in the incessant human sacrifices from among the working class, in the most reckless squandering of labour power, and in the devastation caused by a social anarchy which turns every economic progress into a social calamity. This is the negative side. But if, on the one hand, variation of work at present imposes itself after the manner of an overpowering natural law, and with the blindly destructive action of a natural law that meets with resistance at all points, modern industry, on the other hand, through its catastrophes imposes the necessity of recognising, as a fundamental law of production, variation of work, consequently fitness of the labourer for varied work, consequently the greatest possible development of his varied aptitudes. It becomes a question of life and death for society to adapt the mode of production to the normal functioning of this law. Modern industry, indeed, compels society, under penalty of death, to replace the detail-worker of to-day, crippled by life-long repetition of one and the same trivial operation, and thus reduced to the mere fragment of a man, by the fully developed individual, fit for a variety of labours, ready to face any change of production, and to whom the different social functions he performs, are but so many modes of giving free scope to his own natural and acquired powers.

One step already spontaneously taken towards effecting this revolution is the establishment of technical and agricultural schools, and of *"écoles d'enseignement professionnel"*, in which the children of the workingmen receive some little instruction in technology and in the practical handling of the various implements of labour. Though the Factory Act, that first and meagre concession wrung from capital, is limited to combining elementary education with work in the factory, there can be no doubt that when the working class comes into power, as inevitably it must, technical instruction, both theoretical and practical, will take its proper place in the working-class schools. There is also no doubt that such revolutionary ferments, the final result of which is the abolition of the old division of labour, are diametrically opposed to the capitalistic form of production, and to the economic status of the labourer corresponding to that form. But the historical development of the antagonisms, immanent in a given form of production, is the only way in which that form of production can be dissolved and a new form established. . . .

So long as Factory legislation is confined to regulating the labour in factories, manufactories, &c., it is regarded as a mere interference with the exploiting rights of capital. But when it comes to regulating the so-called "home-labour", it is immediately viewed as a direct attack on the *patria potestas*, on parental authority. The tender-hearted English Parliament long affected to shrink from taking this step. The force of facts, however, compelled it at last to acknowledge that modern industry, in overturning the economic foundation on which was based the traditional family, and the family labour corresponding to it, had also unloosened all traditional family ties. The rights of the children had to be proclaimed. . . .

It was not, however, the misuse of parental authority that created the capitalistic exploitation, whether direct or indirect, of children's labour; but, on the contrary, it was the capitalistic mode of exploitation which, by sweeping away the economic basis of parental authority, made its exercise degenerate into a mischievous misuse of power. However terrible and disgusting the dissolution, under the capitalist system, of the old family ties may appear, nevertheless, modern industry, by assigning as it does an important part in the process of production, outside the domestic sphere, to women, to young persons, and to children of both sexes, creates a new economic foundation for a higher form of the family and of the relations between the sexes. It is, of course, just as absurd to hold the Teutonic-Christian form of the family to be absolute and final as it would be to apply that character to the ancient Roman, the ancient Greek, or the Eastern forms which, moreover, taken together form a series in historical development. Moreover, it is obvious that the fact of the collective working group being composed of individuals of both sexes and all ages, must necessarily, under suitable conditions, become a source of humane development; although in its spontaneously developed, brutal, capitalistic form, where the labourer exists for the process of production, and not the process of production for the labourer, that fact is a pestiferous source of corruption and slavery. . . .

If the general extension of factory legislation to all trades for the purpose of protecting the working class both in mind and body has become inevitable, on the other hand, as we have already pointed out, that extension hastens on the general conversion of numerous isolated small industries into a few combined industries carried on upon a large scale; it therefore accelerates the concentration of capital and the exclusive predominance of the factory system. It destroys both the ancient and the transitional forms, behind which the dominion of capital is still in part concealed, and replaces them by the direct and open sway of capital; but thereby it also generalises the direct opposition to this sway. While in each individual workshop it enforces uniformity, regularity, order, and economy, it increases by the immense spur which the limitation and regulation of the working day give to technical improvement, the anarchy and the catastrophes of capitalist production as a whole, the intensity of labour, and the competition of machinery with the labourer. By the destruction of petty and domestic industries it destroys the last resort of the "redundant population", and with it the sole remaining safety-valve of the whole social mechanism. By maturing the material conditions, and the combination on a social scale of the processes of production, it matures the contradictions and antagonisms of the capitalist form of production, and thereby provides, along with the elements for the formation of a new society, the forces for exploding the old one.

chapter 32

The Role of Credit in Capitalist Production (1894)

... Formation of stock companies. Thereby:

1) An enormous expansion of the scale of production and of enterprises, that was impossible for individual capitals. At the same time, enterprises that were formerly government enterprises, become public.

2) The capital, which in itself rests on a social mode of production and presupposes a social concentration of means of production and labour power, is here directly endowed with the form of social capital (capital of directly associated individuals) as distinct from private capital, and its undertakings assume the form of social undertakings as distinct from private undertakings. It is the abolition of capital as private property within the framework of the capitalist mode of production itself.

3) Transformation of the actually functioning capitalist into a mere manager, administrator of other people's capital, and of the owner of capital into a mere owner, a mere money capitalist. Even if the dividends which they receive include the interest and the profit of enterprise, i.e., the total profit (for the salary of the manager is, or should be, simply the wage of a specific type of skilled labour, whose price is regulated in the labour market like that of any other labour), this total profit is henceforth received only in the form of interest, i.e., as mere compensation for owning capital that now is entirely divorced from the function in the actual process of reproduction, just as this function in the person of the manager is divorced from ownership of capital. Profit thus appears (no longer only that portion of it, the interest, which derives its justification from the profit of the borrower) as a mere appropriation of the surplus labour of others, arising from the conversion of means of production into capital, i.e., from their estrangement vis-à-vis the actual producer, from their antithesis as another's property to every individual actually at work in production, from manager down to the last day labourer. In stock companies the function is divorced from capital ownership, hence also labour is entirely divorced from ownership of means of production and surplus labour. This result of the ultimate development of capitalist production is a necessary

transitional phase towards the reconversion of capital into the property of producers, although no longer as the private property of the individual producers, but rather as the property of associated producers, as direct social property. On the other hand, the stock company is a transition toward the conversion of all functions in the reproduction process which still remain linked with capitalist property, into mere functions of associated producers, into social functions. . . .

This is the abolition of the capitalist mode of production within the capitalist mode of production itself, and hence a self-dissolving contradiction, which *prima facie* represents a mere phase of transition to a new form of production. It manifests itself as such a contradiction in its effects. It establishes a monopoly in certain spheres and thereby requires state interference. It reproduces a new financial aristocracy, a new variety of parasites in the shape of promoters, speculators and simply nominal directors; a whole system of swindling and cheating by means of corporation promotion, stock issuance, and stock speculation. It is private production without the control of private property.

. . . Aside from the stock-company business, which represents the abolition of capitalist private industry on the basis of the capitalist system itself and destroys private industry as it expands and invades new spheres of production, credit offers to the individual capitalist, or to one who is regarded a capitalist, absolute control within certain limits over the capital and property of others, and thereby over the labour of others. The control over social capital, not the individual capital of his own, gives him control over social labour. The capital itself, which a man really owns or is supposed to own in the opinion of the public, becomes purely a basis for the superstructure of credit. This is particularly true of wholesale commerce, through which the greatest portion of the social product passes. All standards of measurement, all excuses more or less still justified under capitalist production, disappear here. What the speculating wholesale merchant risks is social property, not *his own*. Equally sordid becomes the phrase relating the origin of capital to savings, for what he demands is that *others* should save for him. . . . The other phrase concerning abstention is squarely refuted by his luxury, which is now itself a means of credit. Conceptions which have some meaning on a less developed stage of capitalist production, become quite meaningless here. Success and failure both lead here to a centralisation of capital, and thus to expropriation on the most enormous scale. Expropriation extends here from the direct producers to the smaller and the medium-sized capitalists themselves. It is the point of departure for the capitalist mode of production; its accomplishment is the goal of this production. In the last instance, it aims at the expropriation of the means of production from all individuals. With the development of social production the means of production cease to be means of private production and products of private production, and can thereafter be only means of production in the hands of associated producers, i.e., the latter's social property, much as they are their social products. However, this expropriation appears within the capitalist system in a contradictory form, as appropriation of social property by a few; and credit lends the latter more and more the aspect of pure adventurers. Since property here exists in the form of stock, its movement and transfer become purely a result of gambling on the stock exchange, where the little fish are swallowed by the sharks and the lambs by the stock-exchange wolves. There is antagonism against the old form in the stock companies, in which social means of production appear as individual property; but the conversion to the form of stock still remains ensnared in the trammels of capitalism; hence, instead of overcoming the antithesis between the character of wealth as social and as private wealth, the stock companies merely develop it in a new form.

The cooperative factories of the labourers themselves represent within the old form the first sprouts of the new, although they naturally reproduce, and must reproduce, everywhere in their actual organisation all the shortcomings of the prevailing system. But the antithesis between capital and labour is overcome within them, if at first only by way of making the associated labourers into their own capitalist, i.e., by enabling them to use the means of production for the employment of their own labour. They show how a new mode of production naturally grows out of an old one, when the development of the material forces of production and of the corresponding forms of social production have reached a particular stage. Without the factory system arising out of the capitalist mode of production there could have been no cooperative factories. Nor could these have developed without the credit system arising out of the same mode of production. The credit system is not only the principal basis for the gradual transformation of capitalist private enterprises into capitalist stock companies, but equally offers the means for the gradual extension of cooperative enterprises on a more or less national scale. The capitalist stock companies, as much as the cooperative factories, should be considered as transitional forms from the capitalist mode of production to the associated one, with the only distinction that the antagonism is resolved negatively in the one and positively in the other. . . .

The credit system appears as the main lever of overproduction and overspeculation in commerce solely because the reproduction process, which is elastic by nature, is here forced to its extreme limits, and is so forced because a large part of the social capital is employed by people who do not own it and who consequently tackle things quite differently than the owner, who anxiously weighs the limitations of his private capital in so far as he handles it himself. This simply demonstrates the fact that the self-expansion of capital based on the contradictory nature of capitalist production permits an actual free development only up to a certain point, so that in fact it constitutes an immanent fetter and barrier to production, which are continually broken through by the credit system. Hence, the credit system accelerates the material development of the productive forces and the establishment of the world market. It is the historical mission of the capitalist mode of production to raise these material foundations of the new form of production to a certain degree of perfection. At the same time credit accelerates the violent eruptions of this contradiction – crises – and thereby the elements of disintegration of the old mode of production.

The two characteristics immanent in the credit system are, on the one hand, to develop the incentive of capitalist production, enrichment through exploitation of the labour of others, to the purest and most colossal form of gambling and swindling, and to reduce more and more the number of the few who exploit the social wealth; on the other hand, to constitute the form of transition to a new mode of production. It is this ambiguous nature, which endows the principal spokesmen of credit . . . with the pleasant character mixture of swindler and prophet.

chapter 33

Fixed Capital and the Development of the Productive Forces of Society (1857–8)

. . . Once included into the production process of capital . . . the means of labour passes through a series of metamorphoses until it ends up as the *machine*, or rather as an *automatic system of machinery*. . . . That system is set in motion by an automaton, self-moved motive power; this automaton consists of a large number of mechanical and intellectual organs. . . .

. . . The production process has ceased to be a labour process in the sense that it is no longer embraced by labour as the unity which dominates it. Now, on the contrary, labour appears merely as a conscious organ, dispersed at many points of the mechanical system in isolated living workers. It is subsumed under the overall process of the machinery itself, and is merely a member of the system, whose unity exists not in living workers but in the living (active) machinery. The latter confronts the isolated, insignificant activity of the worker as a mighty organism. . . .

As we have seen, it is the necessary tendency of capital to increase the productive power of labour and to bring about the greatest possible negation of necessary labour. This tendency is realised by the transformation of the means of labour into machinery. . . .

. . . [T]o the extent that machinery develops with the accumulation of social knowledge and productive power in general, it is not in the worker but in capital that general social labour is represented. The productive power of society is measured in terms of *fixed capital*, exists in it in the form of objects; and conversely the productive power of capital develops with this general progress, which is appropriated gratis by capital. . . .

. . . The entire production process then appears no longer as subsumed under the immediate skill of the worker, but as technological application of science. Capital thus tends to impart a scientific character to production, and immediate labour is reduced to a mere moment of this process. . . .

In the same measure as labour time – the simple quantity of labour – is posited by capital as the sole determinant of value, immediate labour and its quantity disappear as the determining principle of production, of the creation of use values. It is reduced both quantitatively, in that its proportion declines, and qualitatively, in that it, though still indispensable, becomes a subaltern moment in comparison to general scientific work, the technological application of the natural sciences, on the one hand, and also in comparison to the general productive power originating from the organisation of society in overall production, a productive power which appears as a natural gift of social labour (although it is an historical product). Thus capital works to dissolve itself as the form which dominates production. . . .

Capital employs the machine, rather, only in so far as it enables the worker to work a larger part of his time for capital, to relate to a larger part of his time as not belonging to him, to work a longer time for another. By this process, the quantity of labour necessary for the production of a certain object is in fact reduced to the minimum, but only in order that a maximum of labour can be valorised in a maximum of such objects. The first aspect is important because capital in this way – quite unintentionally – reduces human labour, the expenditure of [human] energy, to a minimum. This will be to the advantage of emancipated labour and is the condition for its emancipation. . . .

. . . [T]he appropriation of living labour by capital takes on an immediate reality in machinery: on the one hand, it is the analysis and application of mechanical and chemical laws – originating directly from science – that enables the machine to perform the same labour as was previously performed by the worker. However, the development of machinery takes this course only when large-scale industry has already attained a high level of development and all the sciences have been forced into the service of capital, and when, on the other hand, the machinery already in existence itself affords great resources. At this point, invention becomes a business, and the application of science to immediate production itself becomes a factor determining and soliciting science.

However, this is not the way in which machinery has come into being on a general basis; and still less is it the way in which it develops in detail. The actual way is that of analysis – through the division of labour, which increasingly transforms the workers' operations into mechanical ones, so that at a certain point the workers can be replaced by a mechanism. . . . Therefore, a definite mode of labour appears here to be directly transferred from the worker to capital in the form of the machine, and this transposition devalues his own labour capacity. Hence the workers' struggle against machinery. What was the activity of a live worker now becomes an activity of the machine. . . .

The exchange of living labour for objectified, i.e. the positing of social labour in the form of the antithesis of capital and wage labour, is the ultimate development of the *value relationship* and of production based on value. Its presupposition is and remains the sheer volume of immediate labour time, the quantity of labour employed, as the decisive factor in the production of wealth. But in the degree in which large-scale industry develops, the creation of real wealth becomes less dependent upon labour time and the quantity of labour employed than upon the power of the agents set in motion during labour time. And their power – their POWER-FUL EFFECTIVENESS – in turn bears no relation to the immediate labour time which their production costs, but depends, rather, upon the general level of development of science and the progress of technology, or on the application of science to production. . . .

Real wealth manifests itself rather – and this is revealed by large-scale industry – in the immense disproportion between the labour time employed and its product, and similarly in the qualitative disproportion between labour reduced to a pure abstraction and the power of the production process which it oversees. Labour no longer appears so much as included in the production process, but rather man relates himself to that process as its overseer and regulator. (What is true of machinery is equally true of the combination of human activities and the development of human intercourse.) No longer does the worker interpose a modified natural object as an intermediate element between the object and himself; now he interposes the natural process, . . . which he transforms into an industrial one, as an intermediary between himself and inorganic nature, which he makes himself master of. He stands beside the production process, rather than being its main agent.

Once this transformation has taken place, it is neither the immediate labour performed by man himself, nor the time for which he works, but the appropriation of his own general productive power, his comprehension of Nature and domination of it by virtue of his being a social entity – in a word, the development of the social individual – that appears as the corner-stone of production and wealth. The *theft of alien labour time, which is the basis of present wealth*, appears to be a miserable foundation compared to this newly developed one, the foundation created by large-scale industry itself. As soon as labour in its immediate form has ceased to be the great source of wealth, labour time ceases and must cease to be its measure, and therefore exchange value [must cease to be the measure] of use value. The *surplus labour of the masses* has ceased to be the condition for the development of general wealth, just as the *non-labour of a few* has ceased to be the condition for the development of the general powers of the human mind. As a result, production based upon exchange value collapses, and the immediate material production process itself is stripped of its form of indigence and antagonism. Free development of individualities, and hence not the reduction of necessary labour time in order to posit surplus labour, but in general the reduction of the necessary labour of society to a minimum, to which then corresponds the artistic, scientific, etc., development of individuals, made possible by the time thus set free and the means produced for all of them.

By striving to reduce labour time to a minimum, while, on the other hand, positing labour time as the sole measure and source of wealth, capital itself is a contradiction-in-process. It therefore diminishes labour time in the form of necessary labour time in order to increase it in the form of superfluous labour time; it thus posits superfluous labour time to an increasing degree as a condition . . . for necessary labour time. On the one hand, therefore, it calls into life all the powers of science and Nature, and of social combination and social intercourse, in order to make the creation of wealth (relatively) independent of the labour time employed for that purpose. On the other hand, it wishes the enormous social forces thus created to be measured by labour time and to confine them within the limits necessary to maintain as value the value already created. The productive forces and social relations – two different aspects of the development of the social individual – appear to capital merely as the means, and *are* merely the means, for it to carry on production on its restricted basis. IN FACT, however, they are the material conditions for exploding that basis. . . .

Nature does not construct machines, locomotives, railways, ELECTRIC TELE-GRAPHS, SELF-ACTING MULES, etc. They are products of human industry; natural material transformed into organs of man's will over Nature, or of man's activity in Nature. They are *organs of the human mind which are created by the human hand*, the objectified power of knowledge. The development of fixed capital shows the degree to which society's general science, KNOWLEDGE, has become an *immediate productive force*, and hence the degree to which the conditions of the social life process itself have been brought under the control of the GENERAL INTELLECT and remoulded according to it. It shows the degree to which the social productive forces are produced not merely in the form of knowledge but as immediate organs of social praxis, of the actual life process. . . .

part 8

The Revolutionary Proletariat and the Vicissitudes of History: Counterrevolution, Dictatorship, or Radical Democracy?

More than any other part of Marx's work, his ideas about revolution and communism have had historical impact outside academe. Communist regimes and left-wing insurgencies have often embraced these ideas in a quasi-religious manner, while critics have attacked them strenuously for legitimating communism. Critics have pointed repeatedly to communism's repression and inefficiency, and to the fact that proletarian revolution failed to occur in the most industrialized countries as Marx had predicted. The same problems caused "Western Marxists" to revise their tradition and frame new theories. However, critics and allies alike usually draw selectively from Marx's ideas on revolution and communism, and often overstate the certainty and consistency of these views. As stated above, Marx anticipated reforms that would blunt revolutionary change in advanced capitalist societies. This part probes his divergent and sometimes ambiguous or contradictory views on revolution and communism.

The opening selection, from the *Manifesto of the Communist Party*, is the classic expression of Marx's and Engels's optimistic narrative of proletarian revolution. They argued that capitalist property relations fetter modern industrial production; cyclical crises worsen, and the economy and culture run out of control, because the productive forces are governed

by private interests, and thus lack the overall social coordination that capitalists impose in their individual firms and that is needed to regulate the
society's complex, interdependent forms of cooperation. Remember that
Marx and Engels saw the bourgeoisie as early capitalism's revolutionary
class (ending feudal property relations and leading productive force revolution). Claiming that capitalists had become modern industry's ruling
class, Marx and Engels argued that concentrated, centralized ownership
makes their ranks ever smaller and richer, and creates an ever larger pool
of unemployed, propertyless workers. They believed that polarized conditions were forging a unified proletariat that one day would seize state
power and advance the progressive, cooperative aspects of industrial productive forces. By contrast to all previous revolutionary classes, Marx and
Engels held, proletarians lack productive property, and thus represent the
vast majority of the populace. Marx and Engels concluded that the soon
to be empowered proletariat would forge communal cooperation and begin
a new classless historical epoch. They insisted that the Communist Party,
enlightened by historical materialist theory, grasps the key historical
contradictions and possibilities, and will insure that the revolution stays
on its emancipatory course.

Also drawn from the *Manifesto*, Marx's and Engels's ten-point program
concerning the transition to communism illustrates poignantly some problematic aspects of their revolutionary vision. They asserted that by wresting control of the state from the bourgeoisie, the proletariat would put
itself in a position to "win the battle for democracy," or to turn society
into a "vast association" that would eliminate class hierarchy and harmonize individual freedom with collective well-being. In this regime, they
held, "public power would lose its political character," meaning that
its extensive publicly owned operations and administrative mechanisms
would serve everyone, and that debates would center on their technical
efficiency and social utility, rather than on their legitimacy as public goods
(i.e., they would be no more controversial than one of today's successful
public transportation systems). Thus, the state would fade away as a
coercive apparatus. However, Marx and Engels argued that such fundamental changes must be preceded by a historical phase in which the
proletariat organizes itself as a "ruling class," imposing a near total centralization of power, or proletarian dictatorship, to eradicate the taints of
capitalism and to develop productive forces and new institutions as rapidly
as possible. But they did not explain why the new ruling class would ever
come to give up the reins of power, or how such a regime could ever
nurture the democratic self-management that, they implied, would flour-
ish under fully developed communism.

Marx's optimism faded when the democratic upheavals that were
sweeping across Europe gave way to counterrevolution. The third selection is drawn from a work, published a few years after the *Manifesto*,

on the creation by Louis Napoleon (Napoleon Bonaparte's nephew) of a total power state foreshadowing twentieth-century dictatorships. Louis Napoleon became France's president in a landslide election, which had support from the lower classes, and especially from the peasantry. He promised to restore order, but also to institute social reform. Marx focused on his later *coup d'état* that ended parliamentary democracy. The events that Marx described reversed the *Manifesto*'s emancipatory scenario: the dictatorship pushed aside the proletariat as well as the bourgeoisie; it was supported in the streets by the poorest segments of the proletariat; and it served the interests of the semi-feudal peasantry. Marx held that the parliamentary regime's massive state bureaucracy, which the bourgeoisie employed against the proletariat, paved the way for dictatorship. In Marx's view, Louis Napoleon simply dismissed the parliament and took control of the power machine, creating a new type of repressive, total power state. It returned to ancient rule by "the saber and the cowl," but now executed by a top-to-bottom bureaucracy that had relative autonomy from the class system. By contrast to the *Manifesto*'s effusive faith in progress, science, and modernity, Marx now saw history as shaped by unforeseen circumstances and irrational forces and impulses. Voicing eloquently a theoretical about-face, he declared that "The tradition of all the dead generations weighs like a nightmare on the brain of the living."

The fourth selection is drawn from Marx's report on the 1871 proletarian revolt in Paris following France's loss of its war with Prussia and the fall of Emperor Louis Napoleon. It is Marx's only sustained comment on participatory socialist democracy. He argued that the Parisian working class and important segments of other classes broke suddenly and radically with the preexisting authoritarian culture and shifted almost instantly to democratic self-management. Moreover, Marx contended that the new government was cheaper and more efficient than the old, and was more open about its mistakes. He argued emphatically that the "incubation of a new society" was under way, and that the heroic resistance to the brutal repression of the regime by the national army was a measure of people's loyalty to the new order. He held that the Communards were creating communism through participatory democratic means, rather than through the despotic centralization that he called for in the *Manifesto* and certain other places.

The last selection comes from Marx's *Critique of the Gotha Programme*, which had been formulated to unify two organizations of radical German workers. He argued against what he considered to be the excessive promises of Ferdinand Lassalle's followers. Marx's somber realist and gradualist tone contrasts sharply with his ebullient description of the Paris Commune and revolutionary optimism in the *Manifesto*. Attacking claims that a new Communist regime would return workers' total product to them, Marx held that it would have to hold back much surplus product to develop productive forces, provide for social welfare and education, and manage and improve other public institutions and infrastructure. He also warned that such a regime would retain major features of the old bourgeois order (e.g., it would still have to provide unequal rewards for unequal tasks). Marx argued that a "higher phase" of communism would eradicate all taints of capitalism, but he suggested that it awaited development of extremely advanced productive forces and the elimination of the division of labor. Thus, it was merely a far-off possibility. Marx stressed that progress toward fully developed communism depends on a society's "economic structure" and level of "cultural development." In the *Manifesto*, he argued that even early communism would vary "in different countries." This is one reason, as Engels later stressed, why historical materialism must interrogate history ever anew. Marx's second-phase communism is little more than a very general normative vision. He understood that making it a reality requires entirely new types of people and of material and cultural resources. Knowing that they were not close at hand, he was aware that the emancipatory path would not be easy or short.

Marx did not live long enough to see the massive twentieth-century expansion of the middle class and the complex segmentation of nearly all classes, including the working class. He framed his materialist viewpoint in light of modes of production that did not generate sufficient surpluses to free up massive numbers of people from direct production and support large, differentiated middle classes. However revolutionary, even the early phase of modern industry, when Marx wrote, did not alter this condition immediately, and was characterized by a relatively simple type of class polarization. A few decades after his death, however, modern corporations emerged, which employed huge numbers of highly specialized, professionally educated, salaried managers, technicians, and financial and marketing experts. Recall Marx's passing comment that these types of personnel were numerically insignificant in the largest firms of his time. Moreover, his description of early modern industry's trend toward a relatively homogenous mass of factory operatives soon gave way to much more divergent grades of specialized blue-collar and service workers. And early twentieth-century mass production and mass distribution began a basic trajectory of change that culminated in post-Second World War consumer capitalism. Much more elaborate class structures and patterns of class conflict were complicated by diverse status groupings (e.g., based on race, ethnicity, gender, religion) and divergent material and cultural interests that cut across class. The later twentieth-century's global division of labor, with its exceptionally diverse workers and workplaces, made matters even more complex. The scenario of the *Manifesto* and of certain parts of Marx's and Engels's other work, pitting the industrial working class against industrial capitalists, was framed for a different era and is now dated. The working class and the bourgeoisie are still fundamental classes, but they are much more segmented, are part of much more differentiated class structures, and operate in much more diverse, greatly transformed, scattered workplaces and sociocultural, technical, and political contexts. The conditions require fresh analyses of class structure and class conflict.

Twentieth-century Marxist discourse about the so-called Asiatic mode of production debated the claim that Communist regimes tend to devolve into total power states. By the 1970s, communism was plagued generally by repressive, corrupt, backward bureaucracy; it arguably resembled Marx's description of the Napoleonic dictatorship more closely than his visions of first-phase or second-phase communism. Marx probably understood that his emancipatory hopes framed a very complex, contingent, long-term, risky project. However, his faith in the Communist Party and, more generally, in the process of centralization should be critiqued. He failed to anticipate conditions that could derail the moderating effect which he expected wider social cooperation and socialist cultural sensibilities to exert on centralized power. The shortcomings of Marx's ideas about revolution and communism, however, should not be attributed exclusively to theoretical "error." They also manifest the inherently complex, problematic nature of efforts to institute radical change and egalitarian democracy. Radical democratic theorists today are probably no closer to knowing how to create or sustain the type of participatory sociopolitical climate that Marx described as characterizing the Paris Commune, or even if it is possible on a wider basis.

As I have argued, Marx's extensive analysis of capitalism constitutes his main thrust, and is the facet of his work that has the most enduring theoretical importance and the most relevance for contemporary affairs. By contrast, his comments about revolution and communism are for the most part brief and sketchy. Moreover, they have been used to justify some of the twentieth century's sorriest events and regimes. However, his dream of eliminating unnecessary suffering and emancipating society gave direction to his studies of capitalism, and made such knowledge worth having. It also posed a normative goal that is still embraced by many people. Thus, serious inquiry into Marx's ideas requires engaging critically his political ideals. Finally, it still remains to be seen if today's class divides will revive his Socialist project.

chapter 34

The Rise of the Revolutionary Proletariat (with Engels) (1848)

... Modern bourgeois society with its relations of production, of exchange and of property, a society that has conjured up such gigantic means of production and of exchange, is like the sorcerer, who is no longer able to control the powers of the nether world whom he has called up by his spells. For many a decade past the history of industry and commerce is but the history of the revolt of modern productive forces against modern conditions of production, against the property relations that are the conditions for the existence of the bourgeoisie and of its rule. It is enough to mention the commercial crises that by their periodical return put on its trial, each time more threateningly, the existence of the entire bourgeois society. In these crises a great part not only of the existing products, but also of the previously created productive forces, are periodically destroyed. In these crises there breaks out an epidemic that, in all earlier epochs, would have seemed an absurdity – the epidemic of over-production. Society suddenly finds itself put back into a state of momentary barbarism; it appears as if a famine, a universal war of devastation had cut off the supply of every means of subsistence; industry and commerce seem to be destroyed; and why? Because there is too much civilisation, too much means of subsistence, too much industry, too much commerce. The productive forces at the disposal of society no longer tend to further the development of the conditions of bourgeois property; on the contrary, they have become too powerful for these conditions, by which they are fettered, and so soon as they overcome these fetters, they bring disorder into the whole of bourgeois society, endanger the existence of bourgeois property. The conditions of bourgeois society are too narrow to comprise the wealth created by them. And how does the bourgeoisie get over these crises? On the one hand by enforced destruction of a mass of productive forces; on the other, by the conquest of new markets, and by the more thorough exploitation of the old ones. That is to say, by paving the way for more extensive and more destructive crises, and by diminishing the means whereby crises are prevented.

The weapons with which the bourgeoisie felled feudalism to the ground are now turned against the bourgeoisie itself.

But not only has the bourgeoisie forged the weapons that bring death to itself; it has also called into existence the men who are to wield those weapons – the modern working class – the proletarians.

In proportion as the bourgeoisie, i.e., capital, is developed, in the same proportion is the proletariat, the modern working class, developed – a class of labourers, who live only so long as they find work, and who find work only so long as their labour increases capital. These labourers, who must sell themselves piecemeal, are a commodity, like every other article of commerce, and are consequently exposed to all the vicissitudes of competition, to all the fluctuations of the market.

Owing to the extensive use of machinery and to division of labour, the work of the proletarians has lost all individual character, and, consequently, all charm for the workman. He becomes an appendage of the machine, and it is only the most simple, most monotonous, and most easily acquired knack, that is required of him. Hence, the cost of production of a workman is restricted, almost entirely, to the means of subsistence that he requires for his maintenance, and for the propagation of his race. But the price of a commodity, and therefore also of labour, is equal to its cost of production. In proportion, therefore, as the repulsiveness of the work increases, the wage decreases. Nay more, in proportion as the use of machinery and division of labour increases, in the same proportion the burden of toil also increases, whether by prolongation of the working hours, by increase of the work exacted in a given time or by increased speed of the machinery, etc.

Modern industry has converted the little workshop of the patriarchal master into the great factory of the industrial capitalist. Masses of labourers, crowded into the factory, are organised like soldiers. As privates of the industrial army they are placed under the command of a perfect hierarchy of officers and sergeants. Not only are they slaves of the bourgeois class, and of the bourgeois State; they are daily and hourly enslaved by the machine, by the overlooker, and, above all, by the individual bourgeois manufacturer himself. The more openly this despotism proclaims gain to be its end and aim, the more petty, the more hateful and the more embittering it is.

The less the skill and exertion of strength implied in manual labour, in other words, the more modern industry becomes developed, the more is the labour of men superseded by that of women. Differences of age and sex have no longer any distinctive social validity for the working class. All are instruments of labour, more or less expensive to use, according to their age and sex.

No sooner is the exploitation of the labourer by the manufacturer, so far, at an end, and he receives his wages in cash, than he is set upon by the other portions of the bourgeoisie, the landlord, the shopkeeper, the pawnbroker, etc.

The lower strata of the middle class – the small tradespeople, shopkeepers, and retired tradesmen generally, the handicraftsmen and peasants – all these sink gradually into the proletariat, partly because their diminutive capital does not suffice for the scale on which Modern Industry is carried on, and is swamped in the competition with the large capitalists, partly because their specialised skill is rendered worthless by new methods of production. Thus the proletariat is recruited from all classes of the population.

The proletariat goes through various stages of development. With its birth begins its struggle with the bourgeoisie. At first the contest is carried on by individual labourers, then by the workpeople of a factory, then by the operatives of one trade, in one locality, against the individual bourgeois who directly exploits them. They direct their attacks not against the bourgeois conditions of production, but against the instruments of production themselves; they destroy imported wares that compete with their labour, they smash to pieces machinery, they set factories ablaze, they seek to restore by force the vanished status of the workman of the Middle Ages.

At this stage the labourers still form an incoherent mass scattered over the whole country, and broken up by their mutual competition. If anywhere they unite to form more compact bodies, this is not yet the consequence of their own active union, but of the union of the bourgeoisie, which class, in order to attain its own political ends, is compelled to set the whole proletariat in motion, and is moreover yet, for a time, able to do so. At this stage, therefore, the proletarians do not fight their enemies, but the enemies of their enemies, the remnants of absolute monarchy, the landowners, the non-industrial bourgeois, the petty bourgeoisie. Thus the whole historical movement is concentrated in the hands of the bourgeoisie; every victory so obtained is a victory for the bourgeoisie.

But with the development of industry the proletariat not only increases in number; it becomes concentrated in greater masses, its strength grows, and it feels that strength more. The various interests and conditions of life within the ranks of the proletariat are more and more equalised, in proportion as machinery obliterates all distinctions of labour, and nearly everywhere reduces wages to the same low level. The growing competition among the bourgeois, and the resulting commercial crises, make the wages of the workers ever more fluctuating. The unceasing improvement of machinery, ever more rapidly developing, makes their livelihood more and more precarious; the collisions between individual workmen and individual bourgeois take more and more the character of collisions between two classes. Thereupon the workers begin to form combinations (Trades' Unions) against the bourgeois; they club together in order to keep up the rate of wages; they found permanent associations in order to make provision beforehand for these occasional revolts. Here and there the contest breaks out into riots.

Now and then the workers are victorious, but only for a time. The real fruit of their battles lies, not in the immediate result, but in the ever-expanding union of the workers. This union is helped on by the improved means of communication that are created by modern industry and that place the workers of different localities in contact with one another. It was just this contact that was needed to centralise the numerous local struggles, all of the same character, into one national struggle between classes. But every class struggle is a political struggle. And that union, to attain which the burghers of the Middle Ages, with their miserable highways, required centuries, the modern proletarians, thanks to railways, achieve in a few years.

This organisation of the proletarians into a class, and consequently into a political party, is continually being upset again by the competition between the workers themselves. But it ever rises up again, stronger, firmer, mightier. It compels legislative recognition of particular interests of the workers, by taking advantage of the divisions among the bourgeoisie itself. Thus the ten-hours' bill in England was carried.

Altogether collisions between the classes of the old society further, in many ways, the course of development of the proletariat. The bourgeoisie finds itself involved in a constant battle. At first with the aristocracy; later on, with those portions of the bourgeoisie itself, whose interests have become antagonistic to the progress of industry; at all times, with the bourgeoisie of foreign countries. In all these battles it sees itself compelled to appeal to the proletariat, to ask for its help, and thus, to drag it into the political arena. The bourgeoisie itself, therefore, supplies the proletariat with its own elements of political and general education, in other words, it furnishes the proletariat with weapons for fighting the bourgeoisie.

Further, as we have already seen, entire sections of the ruling classes are, by the advance of industry, precipitated into the proletariat, or are at least threatened in their conditions of existence. These also supply the proletariat with fresh elements of enlightenment and progress.

Finally, in times when the class struggle nears the decisive hour, the process of dissolution going on within the ruling class, in fact within the whole range of old society, assumes such a violent, glaring character, that a small section of the ruling class cuts itself adrift, and joins the revolutionary class, the class that holds the future in its hands. Just as, therefore, at an earlier period, a section of the nobility went over to the bourgeoisie, so now a portion of the bourgeoisie goes over to the proletariat, and in particular, a portion of the bourgeois ideologists, who have raised themselves to the level of comprehending theoretically the historical movement as a whole.

Of all the classes that stand face to face with the bourgeoisie today, the proletariat alone is a really revolutionary class. The other classes decay and finally disappear in the face of Modern Industry; the proletariat is its special and essential product.

The lower middle class, the small manufacturer, the shopkeeper, the artisan, the peasant, all these fight against the bourgeoisie, to save from extinction their existence as fractions of the middle class. They are therefore not revolutionary, but conservative. Nay more, they are reactionary, for they try to roll back the wheel of history. . . .

The "dangerous class", the social scum, that passively rotting mass thrown off by the lowest layers of old society may, here and there, be swept into the movement by a proletarian revolution; its conditions of life, however, prepare it far more for the part of a bribed tool of reactionary intrigue.

In the conditions of the proletariat, those of old society at large are already virtually swamped. The proletarian is without property; his relation to his wife and children has no longer anything in common with the bourgeois family relations; modern industrial labour, modern subjection to capital, the same in England as in France, in America as in Germany, has stripped him of every trace of national character. Law, morality, religion, are to him so many bourgeois prejudices, behind which lurk in ambush just as many bourgeois interests.

All the preceding classes that got the upper hand, sought to fortify their already acquired status by subjecting society at large to their conditions of appropriation. The proletarians cannot become masters of the productive forces of society, except by abolishing their own previous mode of appropriation, and thereby also every other previous mode of appropriation. They have nothing of their own to secure and to fortify; their mission is to destroy all previous securities for, and insurances of, individual property.

All previous historical movements were movements of minorities, or in the interest of minorities. The proletarian movement is the self-conscious, independent movement of the immense majority, in the interest of the immense majority. The proletariat, the lowest stratum of our present society, cannot stir, cannot raise itself up, without the whole superincumbent strata of official society being sprung into the air.

Though not in substance, yet in form, the struggle of the proletariat with the bourgeoisie is at first a national struggle. The proletariat of each country must, of course, first of all settle matters with its own bourgeoisie.

In depicting the most general phases of the development of the proletariat, we traced the more or less veiled civil war, raging within existing society, up to the point where that war breaks out into open revolution, and where the violent overthrow of the bourgeoisie lays the foundation for the sway of the proletariat.

Hitherto, every form of society has been based, as we have already seen, on the antagonism of oppressing and oppressed classes. But in order to oppress a class, certain conditions must be assured to it under which it can, at least, continue its slavish existence. The serf, in the period of serfdom, raised himself to membership in the commune, just as the petty bourgeois, under the yoke of feudal absolutism, managed to develop into a bourgeois. The modern labourer, on the contrary, instead of rising with the progress of industry, sinks deeper and deeper below the conditions of existence of his own class. He becomes a pauper, and pauperism develops more rapidly than population and wealth. And here it becomes evident, that the bourgeoisie is unfit any longer to be the ruling class in society, and to impose its conditions of existence upon society as an overriding law. It is unfit to rule because it is incompetent to assure an existence to its slave within his slavery, because it cannot help letting him sink into such a state, that it has to feed him, instead of being fed by him. Society can no longer live under this bourgeoisie, in other words, its existence is no longer compatible with society.

The essential condition for the existence, and for the sway of the bourgeois class, is the formation and augmentation of capital; the condition for capital is wage-labour. Wage-labour rests exclusively on competition between the labourers. The advance of industry, whose involuntary promoter is the bourgeoisie, replaces the isolation of the labourers, due to competition, by their revolutionary combination, due to association. The development of Modern Industry, therefore, cuts from under its feet the very foundation on which the bourgeoisie produces and appropriates products. What the bourgeoisie, therefore, produces, above all, is its own grave-diggers. Its fall and the victory of the proletariat are equally inevitable.

chapter 35

Proletarians and Communists (with Engels) (1848)

... [T]he first step in the revolution by the working class is to raise the proletariat to the position of ruling class, to win the battle of democracy.

The proletariat will use its political supremacy to wrest, by degrees, all capital from the bourgeoisie, to centralise all instruments of production in the hands of the State, i.e., of the proletariat organised as the ruling class; and to increase the total of productive forces as rapidly as possible.

Of course, in the beginning, this cannot be effected except by means of despotic inroads on the rights of property, and on the conditions of bourgeois production; by means of measures, therefore, which appear economically insufficient and untenable, but which, in the course of the movement, outstrip themselves, necessitate further inroads upon the old social order, and are unavoidable as a means of entirely revolutionising the mode of production.

These measures will of course be different in different countries.

Nevertheless in the most advanced countries, the following will be pretty generally applicable:

1. Abolition of property in land and application of all rents of land to public purposes.
2. A heavy progressive or graduated income tax.
3. Abolition of all right of inheritance.
4. Confiscation of the property of all emigrants and rebels.
5. Centralisation of credit in the hands of the State, by means of a national bank with State capital and an exclusive monopoly.
6. Centralisation of the means of communication and transport in the hands of the State.
7. Extension of factories and instruments of production owned by the State; the bringing into cultivation of waste-lands, and the improvement of the soil generally in accordance with a common plan.

8. Equal liability of all to labour. Establishment of industrial armies, especially for agriculture.
9. Combination of agriculture with manufacturing industries; gradual abolition of the distinction between town and country, by a more equable distribution of the population over the country.
10. Free education for all children in public schools. Abolition of children's factory labour in its present form. Combination of education with industrial production, &c., &c.

When, in the course of development, class distinctions have disappeared, and all production has been concentrated in the hands of a vast association of the whole nation, the public power will lose its political character. Political power, properly so called, is merely the organised power of one class for oppressing another. If the proletariat during its contest with the bourgeoisie is compelled, by the force of circumstances, to organise itself as a class, if, by means of a revolution, it makes itself the ruling class, and, as such, sweeps away by force the old conditions of production, then it will, along with these conditions, have swept away the conditions for the existence of class antagonisms and of classes generally, and will thereby have abolished its own supremacy as a class.

In place of the old bourgeois society, with its classes and class antagonisms, we shall have an association, in which the free development of each is the condition for the free development of all.

chapter 36

From The Eighteenth Brumaire of Louis Bonaparte *(1852)*

I

Hegel remarks somewhere that all facts and personages of great importance in world history occur, as it were, twice. He forgot to add: the
first time as tragedy, the second as farce. Caussidière for Danton, Louis
Blanc for Robespierre, the Montagne of 1848 to 1851 for the Montagne of
1793 to 1795, the Nephew for the Uncle. And the same caricature occurs
in the circumstances attending the second edition of the eighteenth
Brumaire!

Men make their own history, but they do not make it just as they
please; they do not make it under circumstances chosen by themselves,
but under circumstances directly encountered, given and transmitted
from the past. The tradition of all the dead generations weighs like a nightmare on the brain of the living. And just when they seem engaged in
revolutionising themselves and things, in creating something that has
never yet existed, precisely in such periods of revolutionary crisis they
anxiously conjure up the spirits of the past to their service and borrow
from them names, battle-cries and costumes in order to present the new
scene of world history in this time-honoured disguise and this borrowed
language. . . .

Consideration of this world-historical necromancy reveals at once a salient
difference. Camille Desmoulins, Danton, Robespierre, Saint-Just, Napoleon,
the heroes as well as the parties and the masses of the old French Revolution, performed the task of their time in Roman costume and with Roman
phrases, the task of unchaining and setting up modern *bourgeois* society.
The first ones knocked the feudal basis to pieces and mowed off the
feudal heads which had grown on it. The other created inside France the

conditions under which free competition could first be developed, parcelled landed property exploited and the unchained industrial productive forces of the nation employed; and beyond the French borders he everywhere swept the feudal institutions away, so far as was necessary to furnish bourgeois society in France with a suitable up-to-date environment on the European Continent. The new social formation once established, the antediluvian Colossi disappeared and with them resurrected Romanity – the Brutuses, Gracchi, Publicolas, the tribunes, the senators, and Caesar himself. Bourgeois society in its sober reality had begotten its true interpreters and mouthpieces in the Says, Cousins, Royer-Collards, Benjamin Constants and Guizots; its real commanders sat behind the counter, and the hogheaded Louis XVIII was its political chief. Wholly absorbed in the production of wealth and in peaceful competitive struggle, it no longer comprehended that ghosts from the days of Rome had watched over its cradle. But unheroic as bourgeois society is, it nevertheless took heroism, sacrifice, terror, civil war and battles of peoples to bring it into being. And in the classically austere traditions of the Roman Republic its gladiators found the ideals and the art forms, the self-deceptions that they needed in order to conceal from themselves the bourgeois limitations of the content of their struggles and to maintain their passion on the high plane of great historical tragedy. . . .

From 1848 to 1851 only the ghost of the old revolution walked about, from Marrast, . . . who disguised himself as the old Bailly, down to the adventurer who hides his commonplace repulsive features under the iron death mask of Napoleon. An entire people, which had imagined that by means of a revolution it had imparted to itself an accelerated power of motion, suddenly finds itself set back into a defunct epoch and, in order that no doubt as to the relapse may be possible, the old dates arise again, the old chronology, the old names, the old edicts, which had long become a subject of antiquarian erudition, and the old myrmidons of the law, who had seemed long decayed. . . . The French, so long as they were engaged in revolution, could not get rid of the memory of Napoleon, as the election of December 10 proved. . . . They have not only a caricature of the old Napoleon, they have the old Napoleon himself, caricatured as he must appear in the middle of the nineteenth century. . . .

The February revolution was a surprise attack, a *taking* of the old society *unawares*, and the people proclaimed this unexpected *coup de main* as a deed of historic importance, ushering in the new epoch. On December 2 the February revolution is conjured away by a cardsharper's trick, and what seems overthrown is no longer the monarchy but the liberal concessions that were wrung from it by centuries of struggle. Instead of *society* having conquered a new content for itself, it seems that the *state* only returned to its oldest form, to the shamelessly simple domination of the sabre and the cowl. . . .

VII

On the threshold of the February revolution, the *social republic* appeared as a phrase, as a prophecy. In the June days of 1848, it was drowned in the blood of the *Paris proletariat*, but it haunts the subsequent acts of the drama like a ghost. The *democratic republic* announces its arrival. On June 13, 1849 it is dissipated together with its *petty bourgeois*, who have taken to their heels, but in its flight it blows its own trumpet with redoubled boastfulness. The *parliamentary republic*, together with the bourgeoisie, takes possession of the entire stage; it enjoys its existence to the full, but December 2, 1851 buries it to the accompaniment of the anguished cry of the coalitioned royalists: "Long live the Republic!"

The French bourgeoisie balked at the power of the working proletariat; it has brought the lumpenproletariat to power, with the chief of the Society of December 10 at the head. The bourgeoisie kept France in breathless fear of the future terrors of red anarchy; Bonaparte discounted this future for it when, on December 4, he had the eminent bourgeois of the Boulevard Montmartre and the Boulevard des Italiens shot down at their windows by the liquor-inspired army of order. The bourgeoisie apotheosised the sword; the sword rules it. It destroyed the revolutionary press; its own press has been destroyed. It placed popular meetings under police supervision; its salons are under the supervision of the police. It disbanded the democratic National Guards; its own National Guard is disbanded. It imposed a state of siege; a state of siege is imposed upon it. It supplanted the juries by military commissions; its juries are supplanted by military commissions. It subjected public education to the sway of the priests; the priests subject it to their own education. It transported people without trial; it is being transported without trial. It repressed every stirring in society by means of the state power; every stirring in its society is suppressed by the state power. Out of enthusiasm for its purse, it rebelled against its own politicians and men of letters; its politicians and men of letters are swept aside, but its purse is being plundered now that its mouth has been gagged and its pen broken. The bourgeoisie never wearied of crying out to the revolution what Saint Arsenius cried out to the Christians: "*Fuge, tace, quiesce!* Flee, be silent, keep still!" Bonaparte cries to the bourgeoisie: "*Fuge, tace, quiesce!* Flee, be silent, keep still!"

. . . No Circe, by means of black magic, has distorted that work of art, the bourgeois republic, into a monstrous shape. That republic has lost nothing but the semblance of respectability. Present-day France was contained in a finished state within the parliamentary republic. It only required a bayonet thrust for the abcess to burst and the monster to spring forth before our eyes.

Why did the Paris proletariat not rise in revolt after December 2?

The overthrow of the bourgeoisie had as yet been only decreed: the decree had not been carried out. Any serious insurrection of the proletariat would at once have put fresh life into the bourgeoisie, would have reconciled it with the army and ensured a second June defeat for the workers. . . .

By a *coup de main* during the night of December 1 to 2, Bonaparte had robbed the Paris proletariat of its leaders, the barricade commanders. An army without officers, averse to fighting under the banner of the Montagnards because of the memories of June 1848 and 1849 and May 1850, it left to its vanguard, the secret societies, the task of saving the insurrectionary honour of Paris, which the bourgeoisie had so unresistingly surrendered to the soldiery that, later on, Bonaparte could sneeringly give as his motive for disarming the National Guard – his fear that its arms would be turned against itself by the anarchists!

. . . But if the overthrow of the parliamentary republic contains within itself the germ of the triumph of the proletarian revolution, its immediate and palpable result was *the victory* of *Bonaparte over parliament, of the executive power over the legislative power, of force without words over the force of words*. In parliament the nation made its general will the law, that is, it made the law of the ruling class its general will. Before the executive power it renounces all will of its own and submits to the superior command of an alien will, to authority. The executive power, in contrast to the legislative power, expresses the heteronomy of a nation, in contrast to its autonomy. France, therefore, seems to have escaped the despotism of a class only to fall back beneath the despotism of an individual, and, what is more, beneath the authority of an individual without authority. The struggle seems to be settled in such a way that all classes, equally impotent and equally mute, fall on their knees before the rifle butt.

But the revolution is thorough. It is still journeying through purgatory. It does its work methodically. By December 2, 1851 it had completed one half of its preparatory work; it is now completing the other half. First it perfected the parliamentary power, in order to be able to overthrow it. Now that it has attained this, it perfects the *executive power*, reduces it to its purest expression, isolates it, sets it up against itself as the sole target, in order to concentrate all its forces of destruction against it. And when it has done this second half of its preliminary work, Europe will leap from its seat and exultantly exclaim: Well burrowed, old mole!

This executive power with its enormous bureaucratic and military organisation, with its extensive and artificial state machinery, with a host of officials numbering half a million, besides an army of another half million, this appalling parasitic body, which enmeshes the body of French society like a net and chokes all its pores, sprang up in the days of the absolute monarchy, with the decay of the feudal system, which it helped to hasten. The seignorial privileges of the landowners and towns became

transformed into so many attributes of the state power, the feudal dignitaries into paid officials and the motley pattern of conflicting medieval
plenary powers into the regulated plan of a state authority whose work
is divided and centralised as in a factory. The first French Revolution, with
its task of breaking all separate local, territorial, urban and provincial
powers in order to create the civil unity of the nation, was bound to develop
what the absolute monarchy had begun: the centralisation, but at the same
time the extent, the attributes and the agents of governmental power.
Napoleon perfected this state machinery. The Legitimist monarchy and
the July monarchy added nothing but a greater division of labour, growing in the same measure as the division of labour within bourgeois society
created new groups of interests, and, therefore, new material for state
administration. Every *common* interest was straightway severed from
society, counterposed to it as a higher, *general* interest, snatched from the
activity of society's members themselves and made an object of government activity, whether it was a bridge, a schoolhouse and the communal
property of a village community, or the railways, the national wealth and
the national university of France. Finally, in its struggle against the revolution, the parliamentary republic found itself compelled to strengthen,
along with the repressive measures, the resources and centralisation of
governmental power. All revolutions perfected this machine instead of
breaking it. The parties that contended in turn for domination regarded
the possession of this huge state edifice as the principal spoils of the
victor.

But under the absolute monarchy, during the first revolution, under
Napoleon, bureaucracy was only the means of preparing the class rule
of the bourgeoisie. Under the Restoration, under Louis Philippe, under
the parliamentary republic, it was the instrument of the ruling class, however much it strove for power of its own.

Only under the second Bonaparte does the state seem to have made
itself completely independent. As against civil society, the state machine
has consolidated its position so thoroughly that the chief of the Society
of December 10 suffices for its head, a casual adventurer from abroad,
raised up as leader by a drunken soldiery, which he has bought with liquor
and sausages, and which he must continually ply with more sausage. Hence
the downcast despair, the feeling of most dreadful humiliation and
degradation that oppresses the breast of France and makes her catch her
breath. She feels dishonoured.

And yet the state power is not suspended in mid air. Bonaparte
represents a class, and the most numerous class of French society at that,
the *small-holding peasantry*.

Just as the Bourbons were the dynasty of big landed property and
just as the Orleans were the dynasty of money, so the Bonapartes are
the dynasty of the peasants, that is, the mass of the French people. Not

the Bonaparte who submitted to the bourgeois parliament, but the Bonaparte who dispersed the bourgeois parliament is the chosen man of the peasantry....

The small-holding peasants form a vast mass, the members of which live in similar conditions but without entering into manifold relations with one another. Their mode of production isolates them from one another instead of bringing them into mutual intercourse. The isolation is increased by France's bad means of communication and by the poverty of the peasants. Their field of production, the smallholding, admits of no division of labour in its cultivation, no application of science and, therefore, no diversity of development, no variety of talent, no wealth of social relationships. Each individual peasant family is almost self-sufficient; it itself directly produces the major part of its consumption and thus acquires its means of life more through exchange with nature than in intercourse with society.... Insofar as millions of families live under economic conditions of existence that separate their mode of life, their interests and their culture from those of the other classes, and put them in hostile opposition to the latter, they form a class. Insofar as there is merely a local interconnection among these small-holding peasants, and the identity of their interests begets no community, no national bond and no political organisation among them, they do not form a class. They are consequently incapable of enforcing their class interests in their own name, whether through a parliament or through a convention. They cannot represent themselves, they must be represented. Their representative must at the same time appear as their master, as an authority over them, as an unlimited governmental power that protects them against the other classes and sends them rain and sunshine from above. The political influence of the small-holding peasants, therefore, finds its final expression in the executive power subordinating society to itself.

Historical tradition gave rise to the belief of the French peasants in the miracle that a man named Napoleon would bring all the glory back to them. And an individual turned up who gives himself out as the man because he bears the name of Napoleon, as a result of the *Code Napoléon*. ... After a vagabondage of twenty years and after a series of grotesque adventures, the legend finds fulfilment and the man becomes Emperor of the French. The fixed idea of the Nephew was realised, because it coincided with the fixed idea of the most numerous class of the French people.

chapter 37

From The Civil War in France *(1871)*

III

On the dawn of the 18th of March, Paris arose to the thunderburst of "Vive la Commune!" What is the Commune, that sphinx so tantalizing to the bourgeois mind?

> "The proletarians of Paris," said the Central Committee in its manifesto of the 18th March, "amidst the failures and treasons of the ruling classes, have understood that the hour has struck for them to save the situation by taking into their own hands the direction of public affairs.... They have understood that it is their imperious duty and their absolute right to render themselves masters of their own destinies, by seizing upon the governmental power."

But the working class cannot simply lay hold of the ready-made State machinery, and wield it for its own purposes.

The centralized State power, with its ubiquitous organs of standing army, police, bureaucracy, clergy, and judicature – organs wrought after the plan of a systematic and hierarchic division of labour – originates from the days of absolute monarchy, serving nascent middle-class society as a mighty weapon in its struggles against feudalism. Still, its development remained clogged by all manner of mediaeval rubbish, seignorial rights, local privileges, municipal and guild monopolies and provincial constitutions. The gigantic broom of the French Revolution of the eighteenth century swept away all these relics of bygone times, thus clearing simultaneously the social soil of its last hindrances to the superstructure of the modern State edifice raised under the First Empire, itself the offspring of the coalition wars of old semi-feudal Europe against modern France. During the subsequent *régimes* the Government, placed under parliamentary control – that is, under the direct control of the propertied classes – became not only a hotbed of huge national debts and crushing taxes; with its irresistible allurements of place, pelf, and patronage, it became not only the bone of contention between the rival factions and adventurers of the ruling classes; but its political character changed simultaneously with the economic changes of society. At the same pace at which the progress of modern industry developed, widened, intensified the class antagonism between capital and labour, the State power assumed more and more the character of the national power of capital over labour, of a public force organized for social enslavement, of an engine of class despotism. After every revolution marking a progressive phase in the class struggle, the purely repressive character of the State power stands out in bolder and bolder relief. The Revolution of 1830, resulting in the transfer of Government from the landlords to the capitalists, transferred it from the more remote to the more direct antagonists of the working men. . . . However, after their one heroic exploit of June, the bourgeois Republicans had, from the front, to fall back to the rear of the "Party of Order" – a combination formed by all the rival fractions and factions of the appropriating class in their now openly declared antagonism to the producing classes. The proper form of their joint-stock Government was the *Parliamentary Republic*, with Louis Bonaparte for its President. Theirs was a *régime* of avowed class terrorism and deliberate insult towards the "vile multitude." If the Parliamentary Republic, as M. Thiers said, "divided them (the different fractions of the ruling class) least," it opened an abyss between that class and the whole body of society outside their spare ranks. The restraints by which their own divisions had under former *régimes* still checked the State power, were removed by their union; and in view of the threatening upheaval of the proletariate, they now used that State power mercilessly and ostentatiously as the national war-engine of capital against labour. In their uninterrupted crusade against the producing masses they were, however, bound not only to invest the executive with continually increased powers of repression, but at the same time to divest their own parliamentary stronghold – the National Assembly – one by one, of all its own means of defence against the Executive. The Executive, in the person of Louis Bonaparte, turned them out. The natural offspring of the "Party-of-Order" Republic was the Second Empire.

The Empire, with the *coup d'état* for its certificate of birth, universal suffrage for its sanction, and the sword for its sceptre, professed to rest upon the peasantry, the large mass of producers not directly involved in the struggle of capital and labour. It professed to save the working class by breaking down Parliamentarism, and, with it, the undisguised subserviency of Government to the propertied classes. It professed to save the propertied classes by upholding their economic supremacy over the working class; and, finally, it professed to unite all classes by reviving for all the chimera of national glory. In reality, it was the only form of government possible at a time when the bourgeoisie had already lost, and the working class had not yet acquired, the faculty of ruling the nation. It was acclaimed throughout the world as the saviour of society. Under its sway, bourgeois society, freed from political cares, attained a development unexpected even by itself. Its industry and commerce expanded to colossal dimensions; financial swindling celebrated cosmopolitan orgies; the misery of the masses was set off by a shameless display of gorgeous, meretricious, and debased luxury. The State power, apparently soaring high above society, was at the same time itself the greatest scandal of that society and the very hotbed of all its corruptions. Its own rottenness, and the rottenness of the society it had saved, were laid bare by the bayonet of Prussia, herself eagerly bent upon transferring the supreme seat of that *régime* from Paris to Berlin. Imperialism is, at the same time, the most prostitute and the ultimate form of the State power which nascent middle-class society had commenced to elaborate as a means of its own emancipation from feudalism, and which full-grown bourgeois society had finally transformed into a means for the enslavement of labour by capital.

The direct antithesis to the Empire was the Commune. The cry of "Social Republic," with which the revolution of February was ushered in by the Paris proletariate, did but express a vague aspiration after a Republic that was not only to supersede the monarchical form of class-rule, but class-rule itself. The Commune was the positive form of that Republic.

Paris, the central seat of the old governmental power, and, at the same time, the social stronghold of the French working class, had risen in arms against the attempt of Thiers and the Rurals to restore and perpetuate that old governmental power bequeathed to them by the Empire. Paris could resist only because, in consequence of the siege, it had got rid of the army, and replaced it by a National Guard, the bulk of which consisted of working men. This fact was now to be transformed into an institution. The first decree of the Commune, therefore, was the suppression of the standing army, and the substitution for it of the armed people.

The Commune was formed of the municipal councillors, chosen by universal suffrage in the various wards of the town, responsible and revocable at short terms. The majority of its members were naturally working men, of acknowledged representatives of the working class. The Commune was to be a working, not a parliamentary, body, executive and legislative at the same time. Instead of continuing to be the agent of the Central Government, the police was at once stripped of its political attributes, and turned into the responsible and at all times revocable agent of the Commune. So were the officials of all other branches of the Administration. From the members of the Commune downwards, the public service had to be done at *workmen's wages*. The vested interests and the representation allowances of the high dignitaries of State disappeared along with the high dignitaries themselves. Public functions ceased to be the private property of the tools of the Central Government. Not only municipal administration, but the whole initiative hitherto exercised by the State was laid into the hands of the Commune.

Having once got rid of the standing army and the police, the physical force elements of the old Government, the Commune was anxious to break the spiritual force of repression, the "parson-power," by the disestablishment and disendowment of all churches as proprietary bodies. The priests were sent back to the recesses of private life, there to feed upon the alms of the faithful in imitation of their predecessors, the Apostles. The whole of the educational institutions were opened to the people gratuitously, and at the same time cleared of all interference of Church and State. Thus, not only was education made accessible to all, but science itself freed from the fetters which class prejudice and governmental force had imposed upon it.

The judicial functionaries were to be divested of that sham independence which had but served to mask their abject subserviency to all succeeding governments to which, in turn, they had taken, and broken, the oaths of allegiance. Like the rest of public servants, magistrates and judges were to be elective, responsible, and revocable.

The Paris Commune was, of course, to serve as a model to all the great industrial centres of France. The communal *régime* once established in Paris and the secondary centres, the old centralized Government would in the provinces, too, have to give way to the self-government of the producers. In a rough sketch of national organization which the Commune had no time to develop, it states clearly that the Commune was to be the political form of even the smallest country hamlet, and that in the rural districts the standing army was to be replaced by a national militia, with an extremely short term of service. The rural communes of every district were to administer their common affairs by an assembly of delegates in the central town, and these district assemblies were again to send deputies to the National Delegation in Paris, each delegate to be at any time revocable and bound by the *mandat impératif* (formal instructions) of his constituents. The few but important functions which still would remain for a central government were not to be suppressed, as has been intentionally mis-stated, but were to be discharged by Communal, and therefore strictly responsible agents. The unity of the nation was not to be broken, but, on the contrary, to be organized by the Communal constitution, and to become a reality by the destruction of the State power which claimed to be the embodiment of that unity independent of, and superior to, the nation itself, from which it was but a parasitic excrescence. While the merely repressive organs of the old governmental power were to be amputated, its legitimate functions were to be wrested from an authority usurping pre-eminence over society itself, and restored to the responsible agents of society. Instead of deciding once in three or six years which member of the ruling class was to misrepresent the people in Parliament, universal suffrage was to serve the people, constituted in Communes, as individual suffrage serves every other employer in the search for the workmen and managers in his business. And it is well known that companies, like individuals, in matters of real business generally know how to put the right man in the right place, and, if they for once make a mistake, to redress it promptly. On the other hand, nothing could be more foreign to the spirit of the Commune than to supersede universal suffrage by hierarchic investiture.

. . . In reality, the Communal Constitution brought the rural producers under the intellectual lead of the central towns of their districts, and there secured to them, in the working men, the natural trustees of their interests. – The very existence of the Commune involved, as a matter of course, local municipal liberty, but not longer as a check upon the, now superseded, State power. . . . The Commune made that catch-word of bourgeois revolutions, cheap government, a reality, by destroying the two greatest sources of expenditure – the standing army and State functionarism. Its very existence presupposed the non-existence of monarchy, which, in Europe at least, is the normal incumbrance and indispensable cloak of class-rule. It supplied the Republic with the basis of really democratic institutions. But neither cheap government nor the "true Republic" was its ultimate aim; they were its mere concomitants.

The multiplicity of interpretations to which the Commune has been subjected, and the multiplicity of interests which construed it in their favour, show that it was a thoroughly expansive political form, while all previous forms of government had been emphatically repressive. Its true secret was this. It was essentially a working-class government, the produce of the struggle of the producing against the appropriating class, the political form at last discovered under which to work out the economical emancipation of Labour.

Except on this last condition, the Communal Constitution would have been an impossibility and a delusion. The political rule of the producer cannot coexist with the perpetuation of his social slavery. The Commune was therefore to serve as a lever for uprooting the economical foundations upon which rests the existence of classes, and therefore of class rule. With labour emancipated, every man becomes a working man, and productive labour ceases to be a class attribute.

. . . [I]he Commune intended to abolish that class-property which makes the labour of the many the wealth of the few. It aimed at the expropriation of the expropriators. It wanted to make individual property a truth by transforming the means of production, land and capital, now chiefly the means of enslaving and exploiting labour, into mere instruments of free and associated labour. – But this is Communism, "impossible" Communism! . . . If co-operative production is not to remain a sham and a snare; if it is to supersede the Capitalist system; if united co-operative

societies are to regulate national production upon a common plan, thus
taking it under their own control, and putting an end to the constant
anarchy and periodical convulsions which are the fatality of Capitalist production – what else, gentlemen, would it be but Communism,
"possible" Communism?

The working class did not expect miracles from the Commune. They
have no ready-made utopias to introduce. . . . They know that in order to
work out their own emancipation, and along with it that higher form to
which present society is irresistibly tending by its own economical agencies, they will have to pass through long struggles, through a series of
historic processes, transforming circumstances and men. They have no
ideals to realize, but to set free elements of the new society with which old
collapsing bourgeois society itself is pregnant. In the full consciousness
of their historic mission, and with the heroic resolve to act up to it, the
working class can afford to smile at the coarse invective of the gentlemen's
gentlemen with the pen and inkhorn, and at the didactic patronage of well-
wishing bourgeois-doctrinaires, pouring forth their ignorant platitudes and
sectarian crotchets in the oracular tone of scientific infallibility.

When the Paris Commune took the management of the revolution in
its own hands; when plain working men for the first time dared to infringe
upon the Governmental privilege of their "natural superiors," and, under
circumstances of unexampled difficulty, performed their work modestly,
conscientiously, and efficiently, – performed it at salaries the highest of
which barely amounted to one-fifth of what, according to high scientific
authority, is the minimum required for a secretary to a certain metropolitan school-board, – the old world writhed in convulsions of rage at
the sight of the Red Flag, the symbol of the Republic of Labour, floating
over the Hôtel de Ville.

And yet, this was the first revolution in which the working class was
openly acknowledged as the only class capable of social initiative, even
by the great bulk of the Paris middle class – shopkeepers, tradesmen,
merchants – the wealthy capitalists alone excepted. The Commune had saved
them by a sagacious settlement of that ever-recurring cause of dispute
among the middle classes themselves – the debtor and creditor accounts.
The same portion of the middle class, after they had assisted in putting
down the working men's insurrection of June, 1848, had been at once uncer-
emoniously sacrificed to their creditors by the then Constituent Assembly.
But this was not their motive for now rallying round the working class.
They felt that there was but one alternative – the Commune, or the Empire
– under whatever name it might reappear. The Empire had ruined them
economically by the havoc it made of public wealth, by the wholesale financial swindling it fostered, by the props it lent to the artificially accelerated
centralization of capital, and the concomitant expropriation of their own
ranks. It had suppressed them politically, it had shocked them morally

by its orgies, it had insulted their Voltairianism by handing over the education of their children to the *frères Ignorantins*, it had revolted their national feeling as Frenchmen by precipitating them headlong into a war which left only one equivalent for the ruins it made – the disappearance of the Empire. In fact, after the exodus from Paris of the high Bonapartist and capitalist *Bohême*, the true middle-class Party of Order came out in the shape of the "Union Républicaine," enrolling themselves under the colours of the Commune and defending it against the wilful misconstruction of Thiers. Whether the gratitude of this great body of the middle class will stand the present severe trial, time must show.

The Commune was perfectly right in telling the peasants that "its victory was their only hope." Of all the lies hatched at Versailles and re-echoed by the glorious European penny-a-liner, one of the most tremendous was that the Rurals represented the French peasantry. Think only of the love of the French peasant for the men to whom, after 1815, he had to pay the milliard of indemnity! In the eyes of the French peasant, the very existence of a great landed proprietor is in itself an encroachment on his conquests of 1789. The bourgeois, in 1848, had burthened his plot of land with the additional tax of forty-five cents in the franc; but then he did so in the name of the revolution; while now he had fomented a civil war against the revolution, to shift on to the peasant's shoulders the chief load of the five milliards of indemnity to be paid to the Prussians. The Commune, on the other hand, in one of its first proclamations, declared that the true originators of the war would be made to pay its cost. The Commune would have delivered the peasant of the blood tax, – would have given him a cheap government, – transformed his present blood-suckers, the notary, advocate, executor, and other judicial vampires, into salaried communal agents, elected by, and responsible to, himself. It would have freed him of the tyranny of the *garde champêtre*, the gendarme, and the prefect, would have put enlightenment by the schoolmaster in the place of stuntification by the priest. And the French peasant is, above all, a man of reckoning. He would find it extremely reasonable that the pay of the priest, instead of being extorted by the tax-gatherer, should only depend upon the spontaneous action of the parishioners' religious instincts. Such were the great immediate boons which the rule of the Commune – and that rule alone – held out to the French peasantry. It is, therefore, quite superfluous here to expatiate upon the more complicated but vital problems which the Commune alone was able, and at the same time compelled, to solve in favour of the peasant, viz., the hypothecary debt, lying like an incubus upon his parcel of soil, the *prolétariat foncier* (the rural proletariate), daily growing upon it, and his expropriation from it enforced, at a more and more rapid rate, by the very development of modern agriculture and the competition of capitalist farming.

The French peasant had elected Louis Bonaparte president of the Republic; but the Party of Order created the Empire. What the French peasant really wants he commenced to show in 1849 and 1850, by opposing his maire to the Government's prefect, his schoolmaster to the Government's priest, and himself to the Government's gendarme. All the laws made by the Party of Order in January and February, 1850, were avowed measures of repression against the peasant. The peasant was a Bonapartist, because the great Revolution, with all its benefits to him, was, in his eyes, personified in Napoleon. This delusion, rapidly breaking down under the Second Empire (and in its very nature hostile to the Rurals), this prejudice of the past, how could it have withstood the appeal of the Commune to the living interests and urgent wants of the peasantry?

The Rurals – this was, in fact, their chief apprehension – knew that three months' free communication of Communal Paris with the provinces would bring about a general rising of the peasants, and hence their anxiety to establish a police blockade around Paris, so as to stop the spread of the rinderpest.

If the Commune was thus the true representative of all the healthy elements of French society, and therefore the truly national Government, it was, at the same time, as a working men's Government, as the bold champion of the emancipation of labour, emphatically international. Within sight of the Prussian army, that had annexed to Germany two French provinces, the Commune annexed to France the working people all over the world. . . .

The great social measure of the Commune was its own working existence. Its special measures could but betoken the tendency of a government of the people by the people. Such were the abolition of the nightwork of journeymen bakers; the prohibition, under penalty, of the employers' practice to reduce wages by levying upon their workpeople fines under manifold pretexts, – a process in which the employer combines in his own person the parts of legislator, judge, and executor, and filches the money to boot. Another measure of this class was the surrender, to associations of workmen, under reserve of compensation, of all closed workshops and factories, no matter whether the respective capitalists had absconded or preferred to strike work.

The financial measures of the Commune, remarkable for their sagacity and moderation, could only be such as were compatible with the state of a besieged town. Considering the colossal robberies committed upon the city of Paris by the great financial companies and contractors . . . the Commune would have had an incomparably better title to confiscate their property than Louis Napoleon had against the Orléans family. . . .

While the Versailles Government, as soon as it had recovered some spirit and strength, used the most violent means against the Commune; while it put down the free expression of opinion all over France, even to the

forbidding of meetings of delegates from the large towns; while it subjected Versailles and the rest of France to an espionage far surpassing that
of the Second Empire; while it burned by its gendarme inquisitors all papers
printed at Paris, and sifted all correspondence from and to Paris; while
in the National Assembly the most timid attempts to put in a word for
Paris were howled down. . . .

. . . [T]he Commune dismissed and arrested its generals whenever they
were suspected of neglecting their duties. The expulsion from, and arrest
by, the Commune of one of its members who had slipped in under a false
name, and had undergone at Lyons six days' imprisonment for simple
bankruptcy, was it not a deliberate insult hurled at the forger, Jules
Favre, then still the foreign minister of France, still selling France to
Bismarck, and still dictating his orders to that paragon Government of
Belgium? But indeed the Commune did not pretend to infallibility, the
invariable attribute of all governments of the old stamp. It published its
doings and sayings, it initiated the public into all its shortcomings.

In every revolution there intrude, at the side of its true agents, men of
a different stamp; some of them survivors of and devotees to past revolutions, without insight into the present movement, but preserving popular influence by their known honesty and courage, or by the sheer force
of tradition; others mere bawlers, who, by dint of repeating year after year
the same set of stereotyped declamations against the Government of the
day, have sneaked into the reputation of revolutionists of the first water.
After the 18th of March, some such men did also turn up, and in some
cases contrived to play pre-eminent parts. As far as their power went, they
hampered the real action of the working class, exactly as men of that sort
have hampered the full development of every previous revolution. They
are an unavoidable evil; with time they are shaken off; but time was not
allowed to the Commune.

Wonderful, indeed, was the change the Commune had wrought in Paris!
No longer any trace of the meretricious Paris of the Second Empire. No
longer was Paris the rendezvous of British landlords, Irish absentees,
American ex-slaveholders and shoddy men, Russian ex-serfowners, and
Wallachian boyards. No more corpses at the Morgue, no nocturnal bur-
glaries, scarcely any robberies; in fact, for the first time since the days of
February, 1848, the streets of Paris were safe, and that without any police
of any kind. . . .

The *cocottes* had refound the scent of their protectors – the abscond-
ing men of family, religion, and, above all, of property. In their stead, the
real women of Paris showed again at the surface – heroic, noble, and
devoted, like the women of antiquity. Working, thinking, fighting,
bleeding Paris – almost forgetful, in its incubation of a new society,
of the cannibals at its gates – radiant in the enthusiasm of its historic
initiative!

Opposed to this new world at Paris, behold the old world at Versailles – that assembly of the ghouls of all defunct *régimes*, Legitimists and Orleanists, eager to feed upon the carcass of the nation, – with a tail of antediluvian Republicans, sanctioning, by their presence in the Assembly, the slaveholders' rebellion, relying for the maintenance of their Parliamentary Republic upon the vanity of the senile mountebank at its head. . . . There it was, this Assembly, the representative of everything dead in France, propped up to the semblance of life by nothing but the swords of the generals of Louis Bonaparte. Paris all truth, Versailles all lie. . . .

IV

The first attempt of the slaveholders' conspiracy to put down Paris by getting the Prussians to occupy it, was frustrated by Bismarck's refusal. The second attempt, that of the 18th of March, ended in the rout of the army and the flight to Versailles of the Government, which ordered the whole administration to break up and follow in its track. By the semblance of peace-negotiations with Paris, Thiers found the time to prepare for war against it. But where to find an army? The remnants of the line regiments were weak in number and unsafe in character. His urgent appeal to the provinces to succour Versailles, by their National Guards and volunteers, met with a flat refusal. Brittany alone furnished a handful of *Chouans* fighting under a white flag, every one of them wearing on his breast the heart of Jesus in white cloth, and shouting "Vive le Roi!" (Long live the King!) Thiers was, therefore, compelled to collect, in hot haste, a motley crew, composed of sailors, marines, Pontifical Zouaves, Valentin's gendarmes, and Piétri's sergents-de-ville and *mouchards*. This army, however, would have been ridiculously ineffective without the instalments of imperialist war-prisoners, which Bismarck granted in numbers just sufficient to keep the civil war a-going, and keep the Versailles Government in abject dependence on Prussia. During the war itself, the Versailles police had to look after the Versailles army, while the gendarmes had to drag it on by exposing themselves at all posts of danger. The forts which fell were not taken, but bought. The heroism of the Federals convinced Thiers that the resistance of Paris was not to be broken by his own strategic genius and the bayonets at his disposal. . . .

On the arrival at Frankfort of [an] exquisite pair of plenipotentiaries [selected by Thiers], bully Bismarck at once met them with the imperious alternative: Either the restoration of the Empire, or the unconditional acceptance of my own peace terms! These terms included a shortening of the intervals in which the war indemnity was to be paid, and the continued occupation of the Paris forts by Prussian troops until Bismarck should feel satisfied with the state of things in France; Prussia thus being recognized as the supreme arbiter in internal French politics! In return for this he offered to let loose, for the extermination of Paris, the captive Bonapartist army, and to lend them the direct assistance of Emperor William's troops. He pledged his good faith by making payment of the first instalment of the indemnity dependent on the "pacification" of Paris. Such a bait was, of course, eagerly swallowed by Thiers and his plenipotentiaries. They signed the treaty of peace on the 10th of May, and had it endorsed by the Versailles Assembly on the 18th. . . .

So it was. The civilization and justice of bourgeois order comes out in its lurid light whenever the slaves and drudges of that order rise against their masters. Then this civilization and justice stand forth as undisguised savagery and lawless revenge. Each new crisis in the class struggle between the appropriator and the producer brings out this fact more glaringly. Even the atrocities of the bourgeois in June, 1848, vanish before the ineffable infamy of 1871. The self-sacrificing heroism with which the population of Paris – men, women, and children – fought for eight days after the entrance of the Versaillese, reflects as much the grandeur of their cause, as the infernal deeds of the soldiery reflect the innate spirit of that civilization of which they are the mercenary vindicators. A glorious civilization, indeed, the great problem of which is how to get rid of the heaps of corpses it made after the battle was over!

To find a parallel for the conduct of Thiers and his bloodhounds we must go back to the times of Sulla and the two Triumvirates of Rome. The same wholesale slaughter in cold blood; the same disregard, in massacre, of age and sex; the same system of torturing prisoners; the same proscriptions, but this time of a whole class; the same savage hunt after concealed leaders, lest one might escape; the same denunciations of political and private enemies; the same indifference for the butchery of entire strangers to the feud. . . .

That after the most tremendous war of modern times, the conquering and the conquered hosts should fraternize for the common massacre of the proletariate – this unparalleled event does indicate, not, as Bismarck thinks, the final repression of a new society upheaving, but the crumbling into dust of bourgeois society. The highest heroic effort of which old society is still capable is national war; and this is now proved to be a mere governmental humbug, intended to defer the struggle of classes, and to be thrown aside as soon as that class struggle bursts out into civil war. Class rule is no longer able to disguise itself in a national uniform; the national Governments are *one* as against the proletariate! . . .

. . . Wherever, in whatever shape, and under whatever conditions the class struggle obtains any consistency, it is but natural that members of our association should stand in the foreground. The soil out of which it grows is modern society itself. It cannot be stamped out by any amount of carnage. To stamp it out, the Governments would have to stamp out the despotism of capital over labour – the condition of their own parasitical existence.

Working men's Paris, with its Commune, will be for ever celebrated as the glorious harbinger of a new society. Its martyrs are enshrined in the great heart of the working class. Its exterminators history has already nailed to that eternal pillory from which all the prayers of their priests will not avail to redeem them.

chapter 38

From Critique of the Gotha Programme *(1875)*

... What is "fair" distribution?

Do not the bourgeois assert that present-day distribution is "fair"? And is it not, in fact, the only "fair" distribution on the basis of the present-day mode of production? Are economic relations regulated by legal concepts or do not, on the contrary, legal relations arise from economic ones? Have not also the socialist sectarians the most varied notions about "fair" distribution?

... [The Lassallean idea of fair distribution] presupposes a society wherein "the means of labour are common property and the total labour is collectively regulated" ... [Also] "the proceeds of labour belong undiminished with equal right to all members of society".

"To all members of society"? To those who do not work as well? What remains then of "the undiminished proceeds of labour"? Only to those members of society who work? What remains then of "the equal right" of all members of society?

But "all members of society" and "equal right" are obviously mere phrases. The crucial point is this, that in this communist society every worker must receive his "undiminished" Lassallean "proceeds of labour".

Let us take first of all the words "proceeds of labour" in the sense of the product of labour; then the collective proceeds of labour are the *total social product*.

From this must now be deducted:

First, cover for replacement of the means of production used up.

Secondly, additional portion for expansion of production.

Thirdly, reserve or insurance funds to provide against accidents, disturbances caused by natural factors, etc.

These deductions from the "undiminished proceeds of labour" are an economic necessity and their magnitude is to be determined according to available means and forces, and party by computation of probabilities, but they are in no way calculable by equity.

There remains the other part of the total product, intended to serve as means of consumption.

Before this is divided among the individuals, there has to be again deducted from it:

First, the general costs of administration not directly appertaining to production.

This part will, from the outset, be very considerably restricted in comparison with present-day society and it diminishes in proportion as the new society develops.

Secondly, that which is intended for the common satisfaction of needs, such as schools, health services, etc.

From the outset this part grows considerably in comparison with present-day society and it grows in proportion as the new society develops.

Thirdly, funds for those unable to work, etc., in short, for what is included under so-called official poor relief today.

Only now do we come to the "distribution" which the programme, under Lassallean influence, has alone in view in its narrow fashion, namely, to that part of the means of consumption which is divided among the individual producers of the collective.

The "undiminished proceeds of labour" have already unnoticeably become converted into the "diminished" proceeds, although what the producer is deprived of in his capacity as a private individual benefits him directly or indirectly in his capacity as a member of society.

Just as the phrase of the "undiminished proceeds of labour" has disappeared, so now does the phrase of the "proceeds of labour" disappear altogether.

Within the collective society based on common ownership of the means of production, the producers do not exchange their products; just as little does the labour employed on the products appear here *as the value* of these products, as a material quality possessed by them, since now, in contrast to capitalist society, individual labour no longer exists in an indirect fashion but directly as a component part of the total labour. The phrase "proceeds of labour", objectionable even today on account of its ambiguity, thus loses all meaning.

What we are dealing with here is a communist society, not as it has *developed* on its own foundations, but on the contrary, just as it *emerges* from capitalist society, which is thus in every respect, economically, morally and intellectually, still stamped with the birth-marks of the old society from whose womb it emerges. Accordingly, the individual producer receives back from society – after the deductions have been made – exactly what he gives to it. What he has given to it is his individual quantum of labour. For example, the social working day consists of the sum of the individual hours of work; the individual labour time of the individual producer is the part of the social working day contributed by him, his share in it. He receives a certificate from society that he has furnished such and such an amount of labour (after deducting his labour for the common funds), and with this certificate he draws from the social stock of means of consumption as much as the same amount of labour costs. The same amount of labour which he has given to society in one form he receives back in another.

Here obviously the same principle prevails as that which regulates the exchange of commodities, as far as this is the exchange of equal values. Content and form are changed, because under the altered circumstances no one can give anything except his labour, and because, on the other hand, nothing can pass to the ownership of individuals except individual means of consumption. But, as far as the distribution of the latter among the individual producers is concerned, the same principle prevails as in the exchange of commodity-equivalents: a given amount of labour in one form is exchanged for an equal amount of labour in another form.

Hence, *equal right* here is still in principle – *bourgeois right*, although principle and practice are no longer at loggerheads, while the exchange of equivalents in commodity exchange only exists *on the average* and not in the individual case.

In spite of this advance, this *equal right* is still constantly encumbered by a bourgeois limitation. The right of the producers is *proportional* to the labour they supply; the equality consists in the fact that measurement is made with an *equal standard*, labour. But one man is superior to another physically or mentally and so supplies more labour in the same time, or can work for a longer time; and labour, to serve as a measure, must be defined by its duration or intensity, otherwise it ceases to be a standard of measurement. This *equal* right is an unequal right for unequal labour. It recognises no class distinctions, because everyone is only a worker like everyone else; but it tacitly recognises the unequal individual endowment and thus productive capacity of the workers as natural privileges. *It is, therefore, a right of inequality, in its content, like every right.* Right by its nature can exist only as the application of an equal standard; but unequal individuals (and they would not be different individuals if they were not unequal) are measurable by an equal standard only insofar as they are made subject to an equal criterion, are taken from a *certain* side only, for instance, in the present case, are regarded *only as workers* and nothing more is seen in them, everything else being ignored. Besides, one worker is married, another not; one has more children than another, etc., etc. Thus, given an equal amount of work done, and hence an equal share in the social consumption fund, one will in fact receive more than another, one will be richer than another, etc. To avoid all these defects, right would have to be unequal rather than equal.

But these defects are inevitable in the first phase of communist society as it is when it has just emerged after prolonged birth-pangs from capitalist society. Right can never be higher than the economic structure of society and its cultural development which this determines.

In a higher phase of communist society, after the enslaving sub-ordination of the individual to the division of labour, and thereby also the antithesis between mental and physical labour, has vanished; after labour has become not only a means of life but life's prime want; after the productive forces have also increased with the all-round development of the individual, and all the springs of common wealth flow more abundantly – only then can the narrow horizon of bourgeois right be crossed in its entirety and society inscribe on its banners: From each according to his abilities, to each according to his needs!

I have dealt at greater length with the "undiminished proceeds of labour", on the one hand, and with "equal right" and "fair distribution", on the other, in order to show what a crime it is to attempt, on the one hand, to force on our Party again, as dogmas, ideas which in a certain period had some meaning but have now become obsolete verbal rubbish, while again perverting, on the other, the realistic outlook, which it cost so much effort to instil into the Party but which has now taken root in it, by means of ideological, legal and other trash so common among the Democrats and French Socialists.

Quite apart from the analysis so far given, it was in general a mistake to make a fuss about so-called *distribution* and put the principal stress on it.

Any distribution whatever of the means of consumption is only a consequence of the distribution of the conditions of production themselves. The latter distribution, however, is a feature of the mode of production itself. The capitalist mode of production, for example, rests on the fact that the material conditions of production are in the hands of non-workers in the form of capital and land ownership, while the masses are only owners of the personal condition of production, of labour power. If the elements of production are so distributed, then the present-day distribution of the means of consumption results automatically. If the material conditions of production are the collective property of the workers themselves, then there likewise results a distribution of the means of consumption different from the present one. The vulgar socialists (and from them in turn a section of the Democrats) have taken over from the bourgeois economists the consideration and treatment of distribution as independent of the mode of production and hence the presentation of socialism as turning principally on distribution. After the real relation has long been made clear, why retrogress again? . . .

SECTION II: CONTEMPORARY READINGS

part 9

After Communism: The Death or Return of Marx?

During the post-Second World War era, many people associated Marx with growing "socialist tendencies" (e.g., powerful labor unions, strong Social Democratic parties, and expansive welfare and regulatory states) in advanced capitalist countries and with expanding Communist regimes and insurgencies in other parts of the world. Centrist and right-wing thinkers attacked Marx often, albeit usually passingly, as the ultimate root of the Communist or Socialist threat. By the early 1990s, however, Eastern European communism had collapsed, Communist insurgencies had greatly diminished, and most surviving Communist regimes had shifted to more market-based policies. In leading capitalist countries, union power, social regulation, and social welfare came under threat or were scaled back. Pessimistic left-wing critics agreed with neoconservative Francis Fukuyama's claim that neoliberalism, or revived free-market capitalism, was now so dominant globally that one could not imagine an alternative to it.

In this climate, the Right ignored Marx, shifting their attacks to ascendant forms of left-leaning cultural politics, centering on race, ethnicity, gender, and sexual orientation. These successors to the New Left usually broke sharply with Marxism. Leading thinkers from this "post-Marxist" camp, new cultural theorists and postmodernists saw Marx as the master theorist of Eurocentric modernization and the originator of later Marxist scientism, workerism, and productivism. They argued that his one-sided class analysis dismissed cultural forms of domination. Seldom engaging Marx's work directly, post-Marxist critiques pointed out limitations of postwar Marxism (especially its orthodox forms) and of related labor movements and political parties. Aspects of these problems were foreshadowed in Marx's thought, but their pervasiveness and seriousness in his texts is open to debate. Although post-Marxists brought forward important problems and issues that went beyond Marx's focus, few of these critics entertained the question of whether materialist analysis of capitalism could

accommodate cultural questions, or whether it could be employed in concert with separate cultural approaches which address different types of
issues. Too often, post-Marxists substituted an all-encompassing cultural
approach for what they believed to be an all-encompassing materialism,
dismissing Marx *in toto* and scrapping materialism's valuable tools for analyzing and critiquing capitalism. The main point, however, is that major
factions of the Left and Right in the 1990s considered Marx and Marxism
to have been surpassed and to be irrelevant to current affairs. But opposing thinkers, in the later 1990s, countered that neoliberal hegemony
recreates the types of social problems discussed by Marx, and that his
thought is more relevant to today's conditions than to those in the postwar era. This part focuses on the question of whether Marx has left the
historical stage permanently or is poised for a return.

The selection by post-Marxist Ronald Aronson contends that the primary postwar, Marxist political projects are exhausted. In highly industrialized countries, New Left protests have fizzled; in the Communist world,
Marxism has failed as an alternative theory of modernization; and in the
Third World, Marxist insurgencies have diminished. Aronson argues that
Marxism has too often served repressive political regimes, and no longer
inspires progressive social movements. Also, he holds that Marxism's recent
failures manifest deeply rooted problems that plagued the tradition from
the start. Aronson declares unequivocally that Marxism is over. However,
he expresses some ambivalence about its demise, because he believes that
it has been accompanied by a loss of "hope." He sees as illusory Marx's
claims that history is coherent and can be understood, that workers will
unite and control their destiny, and that they will liberate everyone. Yet
he holds that such views supported the idea that social justice and social
equality can be achieved and should be fought for. Aronson states that
the belief in these values has dimmed, and that the most pressing social
problems now seem intractable. He asserts that "radical opposition"
must somehow be recreated *de novo* "after Marxism."

David Harvey compares his experience teaching Marx's *Capital* 30 years
ago with his recent experience. During the early 1970s, he explains,
radical graduate students and younger faculty sat in on the course,
believing that Marx's work would provide insight into then rampant, left-
wing, revolutionary insurgencies and protest movements and lay bare the
forces that shaped that turbulent time. However, Harvey implies that the
interest in Marx derived more from his status as a subversive figure than
from *Capital*'s capacity to illuminate the pressing issues of that day. He
contends that, 30 years ago, the nineteenth-century type of unregulated
capitalism analyzed by Marx, appeared to be moribund, and that his ideas
in *Capital* had to be revised sharply and extended to fit the new conditions. Today, Harvey explains, the course on *Capital* enrolls mostly undergraduates, and few of them have radical political views. But he states that

the majority of students find *Capital* to be a powerfully engaging text; they connect it easily to current conditions, because they live under a transformed neoliberal or deregulated capitalism that has many of the features and problems predicted by Marx.

John Cassidy provides a broad argument about the relevance of Marx for contemporary life. Like Aronson, he sees proletarian revolution and communism as over. However, he contends that Marx is primarily a theorist of capitalism, and that his views on this topic are today extremely timely. He holds that Marx's portrayal of capitalists' relentlessly rational orientation to material acquisition now applies to wider circles of people than ever, and that it suffuses popular culture. Cassidy asserts that Marx identified core tendencies of capitalism – concentration, centralization, globalization, and class polarization – that have been accelerated greatly under neoliberalism. In his view, however, Marx's "most enduring" contribution is his argument about where power lies in capitalism – with capitalists rather than with consumers. This seemingly simple insight is of utmost importance, because it poses critical questions about power and inequality, which are beyond the scope of bourgeois economics' and the neoliberal media's and policymakers' vision of consumer sovereignty, or the rule of free, rational, individual choice.

chapter 39

Mourning Marxism

Ronald Aronson

These are the reasons why I say Marxism is over now, and was not over until now. In 1975 the New Left, the Third World struggle against imperialism, and the Communist world seemed to belong to the same complex and contradictory, but ascendant, field of force, while the capitalist world appeared more vulnerable than ever. Today this field of force has disintegrated, and the deeper structural issues plaguing Marxism for nearly one hundred years appear as the underlying cause. One could have said that the Marxian project had been over for several generations, because almost none of its reformulations seemed able to revive a sense of revolutionary possibility in the industrialized societies. But having traveled the earth and been recast time and again, only today has Marxism finally exhausted its possibilities.

Marxist renewals are not conceivable in the former and still-Communist world where Marxism served a vital role as the theory and practice of anticapitalist "modernization." Marxist-led struggles for national liberation have run their course and were by and large about neither socialism nor the working class. The New Left was unable to successfully unite its undoctrinaire and dialectical Marxism with its various social movements; and even the most ideologically radical of advanced industrial proletariats, the French and Italian, have overwhelmingly abandoned Marxism. The one-hundred-year wave has spent its force: just as all radical thought and action between 1891 and 1991 took place within the field Marxism shaped and defined, so today must all radical thought and action take place *after* Marxism. It is finally time to declare that, whatever value its intellectual tools may still have, the Marxian project has been tried everywhere and reveals no remaining possibilities. It is over.

Should we mourn its passing? There are powerful reasons not to. After all, its end is as much a relief as a loss, freeing those of us who have been radical and socialist from the endless burden of explaining away the Soviet Union and its satellites. It ends the hours many of us have spent in study groups, in discussions, in arguments, learning and explaining why Soviet

Communism did not reflect the original Marxian project, why its political structure was not socialist. Freed from our albatross, are we not, as André Codrescu said in celebrating the fall of the Romanian leader Ceausescu, finally free once again to dream of socialism?

Another reason to not mourn is to show sympathy for the millions who died in the name of Marxism – in the Soviet Union, of course, but also in China, in Kampuchea, in flimsy boats in the South China Sea. We should also remember all those who have not only been killed but oppressed and bullied and straitjacketed in its name – throughout Eastern Europe, in Cuba, elsewhere in Asia. If Marxism became the ruling ideology in all those societies, there must have been something about it that can be linked to how and where and why it was used as it was. It may not have caused Stalinism, but Stalinism was after all a form that the Marxian project assumed under certain determinate conditions. It is absurd to argue that nothing about the one is implicated in the other.

Another reason for not mourning Marxism's demise is the fact that many millions more have felt and thought and lived Marxism's vision of human liberation through solidarity and have been disillusioned by their leaders, their hope destroyed. If we still wish to pursue that vision, at the very least we need to share and understand their loss. And to see how frail hope is, and that it must be forever renewed; something vital is lost when it dies.

Yet was the Marxian project to blame for this wreckage, and not those on the other side, who fought with all the weapons at their disposal to retain every last one of their class privileges? And not the social systems that made these privileges seem like second nature? Should the countless millions not have struggled against capitalism, colonialism, and imperialism over the past hundred years? Should they not have taken this radical vision to their heart as a coherent and meaningful project? Should they instead have accepted lives of oppression and exploitation, for themselves and their children? Once deciding to fight, could they have devised a better project, one not needing power to fight power, one not susceptible to corruption, one immune to defeat, and worse, to defeat in victory? Could their revolutionary project have avoided the illusions and evils of their world while they were in and of that world? Should they have not hoped so powerfully?

Even under Communism, its dogmatic texts, imposed and learned by rote, travestied daily, contained revolutionary messages about human life and human dignity. Some learned them well, well enough to overthrow Communism. And even its most corrupt, nepotistic, cynical hierarchies served, along with themselves, a sense of community, the destruction of which is disastrous. What now will happen to the hope that Marxism inspired as that vision of community is torn apart by nationalisms, as the former Marxist societies are delivered over to the mercies of a new war of all against all?

No, do not regret Marxism, in spite of all the regrettable acts committed in its name. For there are reasons to mourn its end: it gave hope; it made sense of the world; it gave direction and meaning to many and countless lives. As the twentieth century's greatest call to arms, it inspired millions to stand up and fight, to believe that humans could one day shape their lives and their world to meet their needs.

It lent coherence to human history, explained inequality and privilege – regarding these as the fundamental social evils – projected a meaningful future, and shaped and guided millions of lives. Committed to the view that humans were at bottom cooperative, rational, and equal, it said that all of human history could be deciphered not only as a story of human and technical development, but of progress in overcoming oppression. Now, after Marxism, most of this has vanished. Without it, without the sense of collective might it gave, of a coherent and shared picture of the universe, of all humanity joined together pursuing right, can we help but be forlorn? Scattered groups will continue to fight for their good, but will we ever again see people regarding themselves as no more and no less than people, fighting for a common good? And we have lost, along with this vision of universal solidarity, the sense that its victory is possible. Optimism about where history is headed is denied us after Marxism, as social orders predominate that give most people just enough, that are just flexible enough at the last minute to avoid fundamental change. A world racked with pain, its people mystified, lost to themselves, with its evils having become more and more acceptable: is this our fate?

Marxism nourished a sense of human collectivity, of humanity capable of becoming a vast *we* – and thus the sense that the problems facing us could be solved. This is no longer the case. Without it we are alone against profound inequity and oppression – our sense of justice diminished, our strength sapped, our self-confidence undermined, our picture of the universe shattered into multiple, contending, and overlapping perspectives, lacking even the right to talk about *we*. After Marxism we are, cannot help but be, desolate.

But perhaps we have lost no more and no less than our illusions. After all, those who presided over the *we* silenced many voices and gave us the humanity of a specific culture, race, and gender masquerading as humanity in general. And wasn't this humanity's confidence in history mythical, and its sense of coherence based on erasing all that didn't conform to its simplified picture? Didn't reducing human activity to labor, and deriving culture from the socioeconomic process, drastically misrepresent and misunderstand all that humans do? And didn't the particular universal good being pursued leave out many less privileged goods of particular people? In short, weren't the comforts and hopes of this *we* bought at too great a cost, and isn't its end, however sad, to be welcomed as is the loss of any great illusion?

Ronald Aronson

For all its negative aspects, Marxism was nevertheless a powerful, positive reality with powerful, positive effects. The sense of collective strength it encouraged and tapped was real. It might not have been enough to solve all of the problems all of the time, and it might not have even been enough, at any given moment, to win specific demands over the ruling powers, given their control over the means of survival, culture, values, and state apparatuses. But its vision of collective solidarity was made into reality, not only in song and incantation but, time and again, in struggle. Its strength became real, as did its hopes, as did its sense of right and justice. Even if the *we* it nourished and from time to time realized was not broad enough, or diverse enough, or complex enough, it was more and other than an illusion.

We can see how much more by glancing at the collective gloom and loss of energy after Marxism. The strength of its universal vision, it turns out, encouraged strength; the depth and breadth of its hope encouraged hope; it was the main alternative, and its ending leaves us with no alternative. We now lack the sense that the victory of justice and equality is likely, or even possible. Without its collective strength, anger, and sense of justice we now lack a sense of how our world may be significantly improved.

As a result, Marxists or not, we all suffer from the end of Marxism, at least for the time being, until other visions and projects rekindle the sense that we can tackle, and solve, our most pressing problems. The end of Marxism is accompanied by a general loss of social will: we are left with overwhelming social difficulties, no sense of amelioration, no paths to solution, no identifiable force capable and willing to act. If we have no feeling that good is winning out, neither do we any longer believe even that it *can* win out, or what it is, or how to find it. We do not even have a sense of the collective body that could do this. Marxists or not, with the end of Marxism we have lost all this. Alone among evils, with no clear answer to them or comprehension of them, for everyone's sake we will have to reconstitute the who and how and why and "we" of radical opposition. Until then we are at a loss.

chapter 40

Marx Redux

David Harvey

Every year since 1971 (with the exception of one) I have run either a read-ing group or a course on Marx's *Capital* (Volume 1). While this may reasonably be taken as the mark of a peculiarly stodgy academic mind, it has allowed me to accumulate a rare time-series of reactions to this particular text.

In the early 1970s there was great political enthusiasm for it on the part of at least a radical minority. Participation was understood as a political act. Indeed, the course was set up . . . to try to find a theoretical basis, a way of understanding all of the chaos and political disruption evident in the world (the civil rights movement of the 1960s and the urban upris-ings that followed the assassination of Martin Luther King in the United States, the growing opposition to the imperialist war in Vietnam, the massive student movements of 1968 that shook the world from Paris to Mexico City, from Berkeley and Berlin to Bangkok, the Czech "Spring" and its subsequent repression by the Soviets, the "Seven Days War" in the Middle East, the dramatic events that occurred at the Democratic National Convention in Chicago, just to name a few of the signal events that made it seem as if the world as we knew it was falling apart).

In the midst of all this turmoil there was a crying need for some sort of political and intellectual guidance. Given the way in which Marx's works had effectively been proscribed through the long history of McCarthyite repression in the United States, it seemed only right and proper to turn to Marx. He must have had something important to say, we reasoned, otherwise his works would not have been suppressed for so long. This presumption was given credibility by the icy reception to our efforts on many a campus. I disguised the name of the course, often ran it on an evening and gave "independent study" credit for those who did not want any mention of it on their transcript (I later learned from someone high up in the administration that since the course was taught in the geography program and was called "Reading Capital" it took them nearly a decade to figure out it was Marx's *Capital* that was being taught!) . . .

In these early years many young faculty members participated as did many graduate students. Some of them have gone on to be famous (and though some have changed their stripes most will generously acknowledge the formative nature of the whole experience). They came from all manner of disciplines (Philosophy, Math Sciences, Political Theory, History of Science, English, Geography, History, Sociology, Economics . . .). In retrospect I realize what an incredible privilege it was to work through this text with people armed with so many different intellectual skills and political perspectives. This was how I learned my Marx, through a process of mutual self-education that obeyed little or no particular disciplinary logic let alone party political line. I soon found myself teaching the text well beyond the confines of the university, in the community (with activists, teachers, unionists). I even got to teach some of it (not very successfully) in the Maryland penitentiary.

Teaching undergraduates was somewhat more fraught. The dominant tone of undergraduate radicalism in those days was anti-intellectual. For them, the academy seemed the center of ideological repressions; book learning of any sort was inherently suspect as a tool of indoctrination and domination. Many undergraduate student activists (and these were, of course, the only ones who would ever think of taking the course) thought it rather unradical to demand that they read let alone understand and write about such a long and tortuous book. Not many of them lasted the course. . . .

The situation is radically different now. I teach *Capital* purely as a respectable regular course. I rarely if ever see any faculty members and the graduate student audience has largely disappeared (except for those few who plan to work with me and who take the course as some kind of "rite of passage" before they go on to more important things). Most of the graduate survey courses in other departments now allot Marx a week or two, sandwiched in between, say, Darwin and Weber. Marx gets attention. But in academia, this is devoted either to putting him in his place as, say, a "minor post-Ricardian" or passing him by as an out-moded "structuralist" or "modernist." Marx is, in short, largely written off as the weaver of an impossibly huge masternarrative of history and an advocate of some totally impossible historical transformation that has in any case been proven by events to be just as fallacious politically and practically as it always was theoretically.

Even before the collapse of the Berlin Wall, in the early 1980s, Marx was definitely moving out of academic and political fashion. In the halcyon years of identity politics and the famous "cultural turn" the Marxian tradition assumed an important negative role. It was ritualistically held up (incorrectly) as a dominant ideology that had to be fought against. Marx and "traditional" Marxism were systematically criticized and denigrated as insufficiently concerned with more important questions of gender, race, sexuality, human desires, religion, ethnicity, colonial dominations, environment, or whatever. Cultural powers and movements were just as important if not more so than those of class and what was class anyway if not one out of many different and cross-cutting cultural configurations. All of that might have been fair enough (there were plenty of grounds for such criticisms) if it had not also been concluded that Marxism as a mode of thought was inherently antagonistic towards any such alternative formulations and therefore a totally lost cause. In particular, cultural analysis supplanted political economy (the former, in any case, being much more fun than being absorbed in the dour world and crushing realities of capitalist exploitation).

And then came the collapse of the Wall, the last nail in the coffin of any sort of Marxist credibility even if many of a Marxian persuasion had long distanced themselves (some as long ago as the Hungarian uprising of 1956 and still more with the crushing of the Czech Spring in 1968) from actually existing socialism of the Soviet-Chinese sort. To pretend there was anything interesting about Marx after 1989 was to sound more and more like an all-but extinct dinosaur whimpering its own last rites. Free-market capitalism rode triumphantly across the globe, slaying all such old dinosaurs in its path. "Marx talk" was increasingly confined to what might best be described as an increasingly geriatric "New Left" (I myself passed none too gently into that night known as "senior citizen"). By the early 1990s the intellectual heft of Marxian theory seemed to be terminally in decline.

But some undergraduates still continue to take the *Capital* course. For most of them this is no longer a political act. The fear of communism has largely dissipated. The course has a good reputation. A few students are curious to see what all the fuss with Marxism was about. And a few still have some radical instincts left to which they feel Marx might add an extra insight or two. So, depending on their timetable and their requirements, some undergraduates end up in Marx's *Capital* rather than in Aristotle's *Ethics* or Plato's *Republic*. . . .

But there is another tale to be told that makes matters rather more confusing. In the early 1970s it was hard to find the direct relevance of Volume 1 of *Capital* to the political issues that dominated the day. We needed Lenin to get us from Marx to an understanding of the imperialist war that so unnerved us in Vietnam. We needed a theory of civil society (Gramsci at least) to get us from Marx to civil rights, and a theory of the state (such as Miliband or Poulantzas) to get us to a critique of state repressions and welfare state expenditures manipulated to requirements of capital accumulation. We needed the Frankfurt School to understand questions of legitimacy, technological rationality, the state and bureaucracy, and the environment.

But then consider the historical-geographical conditions. In much of the advanced capitalist world, the trade union movement (often far too reformist for our radical tastes) was still strong, unemployment was broadly contained, everywhere (except in the United States) nationalization and public ownership was still on the agenda and the welfare state had been built up to a point where it seemed unassailable if flawed. Elsewhere in the world movements were afoot that seemed to threaten the existence of capitalism. Mao was a pre-eminent revolutionary leader in China while many other charismatic revolutionaries from Che Guevara and Castro in the Latin American context to Cabral and Nyerere in Africa actively held out the possibility of a socialist or communist alternative.

Revolution seemed imminent and we have subsequently learned that it was actively feared among many of the rulers of the time. . . . How that revolution might occur and the kind of society to which it might lead were not topics even remotely touched upon in Marx's *Capital* (though there were plenty of other texts of Marx and the Marxists to which we could turn for enlightenment).

In short, we needed a whole host of mediations to get from Marx's *Capital* to the political issues that concerned us. And it frequently entailed an act of faith in the whole history of the Marxist movement (or in some charismatic figure like Mao or Castro) to believe in the inner connection between Marx's *Capital* and all that we were interested in. This is not to say there was nothing in the text to fascinate and delight – the extraordinary insights that came from consideration of the commodity fetish, the wonderful sense of how class struggle had altered the world from the pristine forms of capital accumulation that Marx described. And once one got used to it, the text provided its own peculiar and beguiling pleasures. But the plain fact was that *Capital* did not have that much direct relevance to daily life. It described capitalism in its raw, unmodified, and most barbaric nineteenth-century state.

The situation today is radically different. The text teems with ideas as to how to explain our current state. There is the fetish of the market that caught out that lover of children Kathy Lee Gifford when she was told that the line of clothing she was selling through Wal-Mart was made either by thirteen-year-olds in Honduras paid a mere pittance or by sweated women workers in New York who had not been paid for weeks. There is also the whole savage history of downsizing (prominently reported on in the *New York Times*), the scandals over child labor in Pakistan in the manufacture of carpets and soccer balls (a scandal that was forced upon FIFA's attention), and Michael Jordan's $30 million retainer for Nike, set against press accounts of the appalling conditions of Nike workers in Indonesia and Vietnam. The press is full of complaints as to how technological change is destroying employment opportunities, weakening the institutions of organized labor and increasing rather than lightening the intensity and hours of labor (all central themes of Marx's chapter on "Machinery and Modern Industry"). And then there is the whole question of how an "industrial reserve army" of labor has been produced, sustained and manipulated in the interests of capital accumulation these last decades, including the public admission by Alan Budd, an erstwhile advisor to Margaret Thatcher, that the fight against inflation in the early 1980s was a cover for raising unemployment and reducing the strength of the working class. "What was engineered," he said, "in Marxist terms – was a crisis in capitalism which re-created a reserve army of labour, and has allowed the capitalists to make high profits ever since." . . .

All of this now makes it all too easy to connect Marx's text to daily life. Students who stray into the course soon feel the heat of what amounts to a devastating critique of a world of free-market neoliberalism run riot. For their final paper I give them bundles of cuttings from the *New York Times* (a respectable source, after all) and suggest they use them to answer an imaginary letter from a parent/relative/friend from home that says:

> I hear you are taking a course on Marx's Das Kapital. I have never read it myself though I hear it is both interesting and difficult. But thank heavens we have put that nineteenth century nonsense behind us now. Life was hard and terrible in those days, but we have come to our collective senses and made a world that Marx would surely never recognize . . .

They write illuminating and often devastatingly critical letters in reply. Though they dare not send them, few finish the course without having their views disrupted by the sheer power of a text that connects so trenchantly with conditions around us.

Herein, then, lies a paradox. This text of Marx's was much sought after and studied in radical circles at a time when it had little direct relationship to daily life. But now, when the text is so pertinent, scarcely anyone cares to consider it. Why?

chapter 41

The Return of Karl Marx

John Cassidy

Early this summer, I enjoyed a weekend at the Long Island vacation home of a college friend – a highly intelligent and levelheaded Englishman whose career has taken him . . . to a big Wall Street investment bank. There he has spent the last few years organizing stock issues and helping his firm milk the strongest market in living memory. Between dips in his pool, we discussed the economy and speculated about how long the current financial boom would last.

To my surprise, he brought up Karl Marx. "The longer I spend on Wall Street, the more convinced I am that Marx was right," he said.

I assumed he was joking.

"There is a Nobel Prize waiting for the economist who resurrects Marx and puts it all together in a coherent model," he continued, quite seriously. "I am absolutely convinced that Marx's approach is the best way to look at capitalism."

I didn't hide my astonishment. We had both studied economics during the early eighties at Oxford, where most of our teachers agreed with Keynes that Marx's economic theories were "complicated hocus-pocus" and Communism was "an insult to our intelligence." The prevailing attitude among bright students of our generation was that Marx's arguments were fit only for polytechnic lecturers and aspiring Labour Party politicians (many of whom are now right-wing Blairites). In the years since, his reputation has fallen lower still: Moscow's Institute of Marxism-Leninism is gone; the Chinese Red Army has retooled itself into a manufacturing business; even Fidel Castro is looking for outside investors. Nonetheless, I decided that if my host, with all his experience of global finance, reckoned Marx had something worthwhile to say, perhaps it was time to take a look.

Gathering the material proved easy. Hardly anybody reads Marx these days, so secondhand bookstores are overflowing with moldy translations of "The Communist Manifesto" and "Das Kapital." . . . I took the books with me on my August vacation and nibbled at them on the beach – plums like "Theories of Surplus Value," "The German Ideology," and "The Eighteenth Brumaire of Louis Bonaparte."

More than fifty years ago, Edmund Wilson noted that much of Marx's prose "hypnotizes the reader with its paradoxes and eventually puts him to sleep." The passing decades have not made the going any easier. Marx was ludicrously prolix (even Engels complained that his chapters were too long) and often willfully obscure. . . . Not that Marx couldn't write. When he felt like it, he could compose simple declarative sentences that were, in Wilson's words, "dense with the packed power of high explosives." Parts of the "Manifesto" and "The Eighteenth Brumaire" are brilliantly written, and Marx's journalistic dispatches for Charles Dana's New York *Tribune* were eminently readable. . . .

In spite of this, I gradually began to grasp what my friend had been talking about. In many ways, Marx's legacy has been obscured by the failure of Communism, which wasn't his primary interest. In fact, he had little to say about how a socialist society should operate, and what he did write, about the withering away of the state and so on, wasn't very helpful – something Lenin and his comrades quickly discovered after seizing power. Marx was a student of capitalism, and that is how he should be judged. Many of the contradictions that he saw in Victorian capitalism and that were subsequently addressed by reformist governments have begun reappearing in new guises, like mutant viruses. When he wasn't driving the reader to distraction, he wrote riveting passages about globalization, inequality, political corruption, monopolization, technical progress, the decline of high culture, and the enervating nature of modern existence – issues that economists are now confronting anew, sometimes without realizing that they are walking in Marx's footsteps. . . .

Like many thinkers, Marx did his most novel cogitating in his twenties and thirties, then spent decades expanding ideas that he had developed as a young man. His basic insight, which he introduced in "The German Ideology" (1846), was reintroduced in recent times by James Carville: "It's the economy, stupid." Marx's own term for this theory was "the materialist conception of history," and it is now so widely accepted that analysts of all political views use it, like Carville, without any attribution. When conservatives argue that the welfare state is doomed because it stifles private enterprise, or that the Soviet Union collapsed because it couldn't match the efficiency of Western capitalism, they are adopting Marx's argument that economics is the driving force in human development. Indeed, as Sir John Hicks, a Nobel Prize-winning British economist, noted in 1969, when it comes to theories of history Karl Marx still has the field pretty much to himself. It is, Hicks wrote, "extraordinary that one hundred years after *Das Kapital* . . . so little else should have emerged."

Marx wasn't a crude reductionist, but he did believe that the way in which society organized production ultimately shaped people's attitudes

and beliefs. Capitalism, for example, made human beings subjugate themselves to base avarice. "Money is the universal, self-constituted value of
all things. It has therefore robbed the whole world, human as well as
natural, of its own values," he wrote when he was twenty-five. "Money
is the alienated essence of man's work and being. This alien essence dominates him, and he adores it." The language may be a bit strong, but has
anything changed? The magazine racks are packed with titles like *Money*,
Smart Money, *Worth*, and *Fortune*; it is difficult to turn on a television without hearing financial advice; and successful investors like Warren Buffett
and George Soros are regularly lionized by the media.

The money-driven debasement of popular culture, epitomized by
most of Hollywood's output, was also foreshadowed by Marx. In the
"Grundrisse" (1857), he argued that the quality of the art a society produces is a reflection of the material conditions present at the time. Homer
and Virgil reflected a naïve mythological view of nature, which wasn't
sustainable in an age of machinery, railways, and electric telegraphs. "Where
does Vulcan come in as against Roberts & Co.? Jupiter as against the
lightning conductor? Hermes as against the Crédit Mobilier?" Marx
asked. "What becomes of the Goddess Fama side by side with Printing
House Square?" When these words were written, Dickens and Thackeray
were writing for monthly magazines, most educated people had studied
Latin, and capitalism hadn't yet demonstrated its ability to produce "The
Jenny Jones Show."

"The Communist Manifesto," of which Marx was the co-author with
Friedrich Engels . . . almost didn't get written. Engels wrote a first draft
in late 1847, but Marx, who was busy, sat down to complete it only after
receiving a desperate plea from his colleagues in the Communist League.
Perhaps because of this deadline pressure, his language was much
nattier than usual, and the final version, which appeared in February, 1848,
contained some of his sharpest phrases: "A spectre is haunting Europe –
the spectre of Communism," "The history of all hitherto existing society
is the history of class struggles," "What the bourgeoisie produces, above
all, is its own grave-diggers".

The book's misguided prophecies about capitalism's imminent demise
have obscured a far more durable intellectual achievement: Marx's explanation in the "Manifesto" of how capitalism works. Unlike many of his
followers, he never underestimated the power of the free market. "The
bourgeoisie, during its rule of scarcely one hundred years, has created
more massive and more colossal productive forces than have all preceding generations together," he wrote. "It has accomplished wonders far surpassing Egyptian pyramids, Roman aqueducts, and Gothic cathedrals; it
has conducted expeditions that put in the shade all former Exoduses of
nations and crusades." Moreover, this unprecedented productive spurt,

otherwise known as the industrial revolution, was not confined to any one country, since the ever-present need for new markets "chases the bourgeoisie over the whole surface of the globe." Wherever the bourgeoisie go, Marx said, they undermine traditional ways of doing things. "All old-established national industries have been destroyed or are daily being destroyed," he wrote. "They are dislodged by new industries, whose introduction becomes a life-and-death question for all civilized nations." It wasn't just local businesses that suffered. Entire cultures were swept aside by the relentless forces of modernization and international integration. "The intellectual creations of individual nations become common property," he noted. "National one-sidedness and narrow-mindedness become more and more impossible, and from the numerous national and local literatures, there arises a world literature."

"Globalization" is the buzzword of the late twentieth century, on the lips of everybody from Jiang Zemin to Tony Blair, but Marx predicted most of its ramifications a hundred and fifty years ago. Capitalism is now well on its way to transforming the world into a single market, with the nations of Europe, Asia, and the Americas evolving into three rival trading blocs within that market. John Grisham's novels are translated into dozens of languages, teen-agers in Australia wear Chicago Bulls caps, and almost everybody in business speaks English, the global language of money. Occasionally, some embattled group – French farmers, British miners, American autoworkers – puts up a fight for traditional interests, but its efforts always prove fruitless. Nothing can stop the permanent revolution that capitalism represents. "Uninterrupted disturbance of all social conditions, everlasting uncertainty and agitation distinguish the bourgeois epoch from all earlier ones," Marx wrote. "All that is solid melts into air, all that is holy is profaned, and man is at last compelled to face with sober senses his real conditions of life and his relations with his kind."

Globalization is set to become the biggest political issue of the next century. Richard Gephardt is already running for President on a "fair trade" platform, and populist, xenophobic parties are emerging in Russia, France, and many other countries. According to a recent World Bank study, Russia, China, India, Indonesia, and Brazil will all become major industrial powers within the next twenty-five years, and this will only increase the competitive pressures on other advanced nations. Even economists, who traditionally have been globalization's biggest defenders (on the ground that it creates more winners than losers), are now having second thoughts about its impact. Contemporary critics tend to use drier language than Marx did, but their message is similar. "The international integration of markets for goods, services, and capital is pressuring societies to alter their traditional practices, and, in return, broad segments of these societies are putting up a fight," Dani Rodrik, a Harvard economist, wrote in a path-breaking book, published earlier this year, entitled "Has Globalization Gone

Too Far?" Rodrik pointed out that child labor, corporate tax avoidance, and shuttered American factories are all features of globalization. He didn't mention Marx directly – citations of his work are not good for the career prospects of an Ivy League economist – but he concluded that failure to meet the global challenge could lead to "social disintegration." . . .

In one way, Marx's efforts were a failure. His mathematical model of the economy, which depended on the idea that labor is the source of all value, was riven with internal inconsistencies and is rarely studied these days. Many of the constructs used by modern economists – such as supply-and-demand curves, production functions, and game theory – hadn't been conceived in the eighteen-sixties. A new textbook, "Principles of Economics," by N. Gregory Mankiw, a Harvard professor, mentions Marx just once in eight hundred pages, and that reference is pejorative.

Mankiw, quoting the turn-of-the-century economist Alfred Marshall, says that economics is "a study of mankind in the ordinary business of life," which answers questions like "Why are apartments so hard to find in New York City?" and "Why do airlines charge less for a round-trip ticket if the traveller stays over a Saturday night?" and "Why is Jim Carrey paid so much to star in movies?" Marx didn't dismiss such questions – although his labor theory of value was ill equipped to address them – but he considered them secondary to the real task of economics, which was to explain how society evolved over time.

One important lesson Marx taught is that capitalism tends toward monopoly – an observation that was far from obvious in his day – giving rise to a need for strong regulation. This problem subsequently seemed to have been taken care of by the reforms of Teddy Roosevelt and F.D.R., but the last decade has witnessed an unprecedented wave of mergers in sectors as diverse as entertainment, medicine, defense, and financial services. At the same time, budget cuts and conservative court rulings have undermined the effectiveness of government regulatory agencies, such as the Federal Trade Commission. Unless these trends are reversed, the inevitable result will be more mergers, higher prices, and fewer choices for consumers.

Marx's primary achievement as an economist was placing the entrepreneur and the profit motive front and center in the study of economic development. To the layman who reads the business pages, this may seem obvious, but it isn't obvious to professional economists. In neoclassical economics – the sort taught by Mankiw – consumers are the main focus of attention, while firms are merely "black boxes" that transform raw material and labor into commodities that people want to buy. In the world envisioned by this theory, the economy grows at a pace determined by the expansion of the labor force and the rate of technical progress, which appears like manna from Heaven and is not governed by market forces.

Marx's view of economic growth was darker and more complex. In his model, capitalists were a beleaguered species, constantly under pressure from competitors trying to enter their markets and steal their profits. Given such pressure, firms had to cut costs by investing in labor-saving machinery, forcing their employees to work harder, and developing new products. This process, which Marx called "accumulation," was the main reason that capitalism was so much more productive than previous social systems. In feudal times, the nobles consumed the economic "surplus" created by the peasants, but in the industrial society capitalists were forced to invest the surplus created by their employees or risk being swept aside by their rivals. "Accumulate! Accumulate! Accumulate! That is Moses and the Prophets," Marx declared.

This vision of economic growth was largely forgotten by the economics profession after Marx's death, but it was resurrected in the nineteen-forties by Joseph Schumpeter, a former Austrian finance minister turned Harvard academic. He labelled it "creative destruction." In recent years, Schumpeter's work has been formalized by a group of eminent and mathematically inclined theorists, including Paul Romer, of Stanford, and Philippe Aghion, of the University of London. Economists working in this field, which calls itself endogenous-growth theory, usually fail to credit Marx as their intellectual forefather (to do so would invite ridicule), but their models are undoubtedly Marxist in spirit, since their main aim is to demonstrate how technical progress emerges from the competitive process, and not from Heaven, as in the neoclassical model.

Marx's version of free enterprise also chimes with the views of many contemporary businessmen, who would rather be flogged than labelled Marxists. In the nineteen-eighties, for instance, Jack (Neutron Jack) Welch, Jr., the flinty but highly respected chairman of General Electric, transformed the company, closing down dozens of plants and firing tens of thousands of employees. The reasons he did so would have been familiar to any reader of Marx. "The events we see rushing toward us make the rough, tumultuous eighties look like a decade at the beach," Welch said at a shareholders' meeting in 1989. "Ahead of us are Darwinian shake-outs in every major maketplace, with no consolation prizes for the losing companies and nations."

In 1881, Jenny Marx died. Marx never got over loss – "The Moor is dead, too," he said to Engels – and two years later he followed his wife to the grave. At his funeral, Engels eulogized him in a way that Marx would have liked, declaring, "Just as Darwin discovered the law of evolution in organic nature, so Marx discovered the law of evolution in human history." This wasn't quite true, but it wasn't altogether false. Capitalism certainly wasn't succeeded by Communism, but, just as certainly, it didn't survive in the Dickensian form that Marx had witnessed. During the century following his death, governments in industrialized countries introduced numerous reforms designed to improve the living standard of working people: labor laws, minimum-wage legislation, welfare benefits, public housing, public-health systems, inheritance levies, progressive income taxes, and so on. These ameliorative measures would have been labelled "socialism" in Marx's day; indeed, he prescribed many of them in the "Manifesto," and it is difficult to see how capitalism could have survived without them.

It is only in the past two decades that a systematic assault on social democracy has been carried out in the name of "economic efficiency." This right-wing backlash has produced a sharp upsurge in inequality, just as Marx would have predicted. Between 1980 and 1996, the share of total household income going to the richest five per cent of the families in the country increased from 15.3 per cent to 20.3 per cent, while the share of the income going to the poorest sixty per cent of families fell from 34.2 per cent to 30 per cent. These changes represent an unprecedented redistribution of resources from poor to rich – each shift of one per cent represents about thirty-eight billion dollars.

Marx believed that the fundamental divide in any society is between the people who own the machinery and the factories used to make commodities (the "bourgeoisie") and the people whose only marketable asset is their capacity for work (the "proletarians"). This split is too rigid – it doesn't account for self-employed people, public-sector employees, and workers who own shares in their employer's firm – but there is no doubt that the biggest winners, by far, during the past two decades have been the people who control the means of production: chief executives and shareholders. In 1978, a typical chief executive at a big company earned about sixty times what a typical worker earned; in 1995, he took home about a hundred and seventy times as much. Shareholders have also done fabulously, and this has accentuated the increase in inequality. According to Edward Wolff, a professor of economics at New York University, half of all financial assets in the country are owned by the richest one per cent of the population, and more than three-quarters of them are owned by the richest ten per cent. A Federal Reserve Board survey shows that six in ten American families still own no stocks whatever, either directly or via 401(k) pension plans. And most families who do own stocks have total holdings worth less than two thousand dollars.

These figures suggest that one of Marx's most controversial ideas, the "theory of immiseration," may be making a comeback. He didn't believe, as some critics suggest, that wages could never rise under capitalism, but he did say that profits would increase faster than wages, so that workers would become poorer relative to capitalists over time, and this is what has happened during the last two decades. Inflation-adjusted average hourly wages are still below their 1973 levels, but profits have soared. In 1979, sixteen per cent of all the money produced by the corporate sector went to profits and interest; today the figure is twenty-one per cent.

A key question for the future, the answer to which will determine the fate of the soaring stock market and much else, is whether capital can hold on to its recent gains. The United Parcel Service strike and the raising of the minimum wage both suggest that workers are starting to recover some losses, but their bargaining power is limited, because many firms can easily relocate to countries where labor is cheaper. Marx, for one, had no doubt which side held the upper hand. "The worshipful capitalists will never want for fresh exploitable flesh and blood, and will let the dead bury their dead," he noted in "Wage-Labour and Capital."

Highgate Cemetery is just a short stroll from the bijou urban village of the same name in north London. To get there, you stroll past a row of designer stores and a bunch of English schoolchildren in blue-and-gray uniforms, turn left down a narrow lane, pass some tennis courts, and turn left again at a set of tall black gates. There to meet you is an elderly English lady named Kathleen, who is clad in a tweed skirt, a woolly sweater, and sensible shoes. With her strangled vowels, she might have just stepped out of an Agatha Christie novel. One afternoon last month, I took the bus from central London to Highgate and walked down to the cemetery to see her.

"Do many people come to visit Marx these days?" I asked as I handed over the admission fee of two pounds (one for entry, the other for a map of the graveyard).

"Oh, yes, some do, but I can't say why," Kathleen replied. "We've got a lot more interesting people here, you know. George Eliot, Sir Ralph Richardson. Are you sure you don't want to see them?"

I said I was sure, and Kathleen reluctantly directed me down a path to the cemetery's northwest corner, where I found a large marble tombstone topped with an imposing statue of Marx's head and the inscription "Workers of all lands unite." There were fresh flowers next to the grave, but only three people: two bearded students from Turkey and a young woman from South Korea who said she was a socialist. All were in London studying English.

"Marx is very big in Turkey, although Communism is illegal," one of the Turks told me. He added that he had been imprisoned briefly in Ankara for his socialist activities. He and his friend were tickled to be smoking Camels in front of Marx's grave.

I asked the visitors whether they had read any of Marx's works – "Das Kapital," in particular.

The young South Korean socialist said she hadn't.

"I tried it, but it is very big," the Turk who had been arrested volunteered.

"I started it, but I didn't understand it," his friend said.

We talked for about twenty minutes, and then I made my way back to Kathleen and asked her if Highgate was still a working cemetery. (It is. Rod Stewart's parents are buried there.) On the bus for central London, I wondered again why Marx is so little read these days.

Maybe it is because the economy is doing well, but even in good times he has lessons to teach us, such as the fact that raising workers' living standards depends on maintaining a low rate of unemployment – something that many orthodox economists denied until recently. Marx believed that wages were held down by the presence of a "reserve army" of unemployed workers who attempt to underbid the employed. Reduce the ranks of this army, he said, and wages would rise – just as they have started to do in the last year. Since the middle of 1996, the unemployment rate has averaged about five per cent, its lowest level in twenty-four years, and inflation-adjusted median hourly wages have risen by 1.4 per cent, their first appreciable rise in almost a decade.

Perhaps the most enduring element of Marx's work is his discussion of where power lies in a capitalist society. This is a subject that economists, with their fixation on consumer choice, have neglected for decades, but recently a few of them have returned to Marx's idea that the circumstances in which people are forced to make choices are often just as important as the choices. (Take the case of a robbery victim who is given the "choice" of handing over his money or being stabbed.) At Harvard, for example, Oliver Hart has developed a new theory of how firms operate which depends on the power struggle among shareholders, managers, and workers. Other economists are looking critically at the exercise of political power. Elhanan Helpman, another Harvard professor, and Gene Grossman, of Princeton, have constructed a formal model illustrating the way that the government is encouraged to introduce damaging trade policies by pressure from rival business lobbyists.

Marx, of course, delighted in declaring that politicians merely carry water for their corporate paymasters. "The executive of the modern State is but a committee for managing the common affairs of the bourgeoisie," he wrote in the "Manifesto," and he later singled out American politicians, saying they had been "subordinated" to "bourgeois production" ever since the days of George Washington. The sight of a President granting shady businessmen access to the White House in return for campaign contributions would have shocked him not at all. Despite his errors, he was a man for whom our economic system held few surprises. His books will be worth reading as long as capitalism endures.

part 10

New Economy or Old? Information Capitalism and the Polarization of Class, Race, and Ethnicity

In the late 1970s and early 1980s, American corporations began restructuring in response to a profitability crisis and severe erosion of the leading manufacturing sector. Many large firms "downsized" and "re-engineered" their "vertically integrated" operations. The older, "Fordist" organization usually owned the means of production for its product lines, employed full-time labor forces, cooperated with unions, and provided job security, timely promotions, and ample benefit packages. By contrast, new, "post-Fordist" firms typically sold off key parts of their facilities and used "outsourcing" to fill gaps, reduced full-time labor forces, and supplemented them with part-time, contingent, and contract workers, weakened or avoided unions, and streamlined operations (thus reducing bureaucratic steps and paperwork and speeding up operations). Restructuring also generated a wave of corporate takeovers, increased emphasis on finance capital, and, especially, elevated stockholder interests to first priority. Although too complex to summarize briefly, the changes were substantial, and depended upon new information and communications technologies. American corporations made major investments in electronic means to coordinate dispersed operations, streamline and automate administrative and retail activities, execute instant global transactions, and create a "fast capitalism" that shortens the time from initial investment to realization of profit and overcomes geographical barriers. These and other changes increased productivity, reduced labor costs, extended markets, restored profitability, and perpetuated their global economic dominance, which had been threatened. Leading the "digital revolution" and dominating the fastest

growth sector of the economy, the United States strengthened its hegemonic position at a time when other countries were restructuring and glob-
alizing, and thus were adopting the new technologies.

Responding to the soaring NASDAQ index of technology stocks and
the stunning success of 1990s dot.com entrepreneurs, pundits celebrated the
rise of a "New Economy" that shifted production from goods to information and revolutionized wealth creation. They held that neoliberal deregulation and the new technologies removed political and spatiotemporal
limits to information and made it the chief commodity, creating near
"perfect markets" and transcending "Old Economy" limits and laws. New
Economy advocates trumpeted the start of a "long boom" of permanent
growth and easy wealth that promised to solve capitalism's most pressing historic problems. Stressing an emerging, middle-class "information
society," they ignored the underside of the New Economy – the fate of
its many low-wage service workers and its underclasses. However, their
utopian hopes were punctuated by the 2001 economic slowdown and NAS-
DAQ crash. The selections below explore the changes that have accompanied the "New Economy." They address matters anticipated in Marx's
arguments about emergent knowledge-based, automated production and
about the increased class divisions, employment problems, and poverty
that accompany the accelerated accumulation of wealth.

In the first selection, Jeremy Rifkin argues that the United States has
shifted from industrial to cultural production – it leads the world in entertainment and information products. He states that mid-1990s deregulation
of global telecommunications markets has sharply increased privatization
and commodification of the media. Neoliberals equate the reduced government ownership and control with democracy and freedom. By contrast,
Rifkin argues that the changes have permitted unparalleled global
concentration of the entertainment and information industries through
merger, takeovers, strategic alliances, and joint ventures. He claims that
ten corporate giants (including Disney, Time Warner, Sony) control much
of the global production and dissemination of media products. Because
cultural participation depends on having the resources to be wired and
to afford the various goods and programs, he argues, the thoroughly
commercialized media create "electronic gates" between the classes. Rifkin
holds that a very substantial part of the global populace is desperately
poor, and that the great majority lack access to electronic cultural and
information portals. He sees the privatized media to be widening the gap
between the richer and poorer classes in the United States and in other
rich countries, and increasing and hardening the already very steep divisions between rich and poor countries. Rifkin argues that the state's
capacity to regulate its economic and social environments and protect its
people have been weakened by the new deregulated and concentrated
form of capital. Like Marx, Rifkin portrays the rise of a knowledge-based

capitalism characterized by extremely concentrated wealth and gross economic inequality. But the electronically gated forms of cultural isolation and exclusion and profound differences in cultural experience and knowledge were beyond Marx's horizon.

In the second selection, Thomas Frank describes how late 1990s American popular culture fawned over the heroic virtues of CEOs, and embraced avidly the society's plutocratic tendencies. Like Mike Davis in the selection below, Frank executes a type of cultural critique that counters those post-Marxist approaches that pit cultural analysis against materialism and ignore today's growing class differences. In his view, even portions of the cultural Left have come to embrace free-market thinking. By contrast to postwar culture, which stressed expanding the middle class and eliminating poverty, Frank argues, 1990s "market populism" equates deregulated markets with democracy, and accepts extreme economic inequalities as a normal and tolerable condition. He holds that this "new consensus" sees the upper class as overworked and the working class as a "leisure class," and treats the much-increased wealth of the rich as a well-deserved reward that outweighs problems that less-advantaged people might suffer under the New Economy. New Economy boosters claimed that the low inflation rate during the rapid economic growth of the middle and later 1990s manifested the magical powers of deregulated markets and new technologies. However, Frank asserts that the same people urged that wages be suppressed to avert inflation. In his view, the secret of the so-called New Economy – its really new facet – is the stagnation of working-class and lower middle-class wages and the monopolization of surpluses from productivity gains by predominantly well-off stockholders. Frank implies that the stock-market boom and upscale life-styles derive largely from traditional forms of accumulation and the increased power of capital over labor.

William Julius Wilson portrays a sharp decline of economic opportunity in poor inner-city neighborhoods. He sees this trend to be part of a nationwide erosion of the condition of low-skilled workers (falling full-time, year-around work, reductions in real wages, decreased chances for advancement, and increased joblessness) and a consequence of globalization, weaker unions, and increased wage and benefit gaps between skilled and unskilled workers. He argues that high school dropouts and people who did not attend college have suffered especially from the loss of manufacturing jobs, but that African-American males from the poorest areas have suffered the greatest loss of opportunity and have not been absorbed into the economy's new growth sectors. Impoverished Black neighborhoods not only lost manufacturing; they did not benefit from the national expansion of the low-wage service sector. Wilson describes the staggering job losses in an inner-city neighborhood of Chicago, which middle-class African-Americans have deserted and is now a poverty-ridden "war zone." In such economically devastated areas, demoralized black males drop out of the legitimate labor force. Wilson's arguments overlap Marx's points about the "reserve army," and about the tendency of the numbers of destitute and permanently unemployed people to grow with capitalism. However, he also describes racially segmented class relations, which were not yet a prominent feature of the capitalism of Marx's time.

The selection by Mike Davis describes spatial politics in Los Angeles' polarized, multicultural environment, portraying a shift from later nineteenth-century urban spaces, which were designed to encourage mixing of classes and races, to planned "spatial apartheid." He portrays social and residential gating that parallels and goes hand in hand with the electronic gating described by Rifkin. The sharp divides between wealth and poverty and between lower-class minorities and predominantly white middle classes are readily visible in Los Angeles. This transnational business and investment center is also home to an enormous Third World, immigrant proletariat, who provide inexpensive services for the professional middle classes and the rich. Davis's vision of Los Angeles is reminiscent of the high-tech, "postmodern" garrison state fantasized in the movie *Blade Runner*. Although mapping the type of profoundly unequal urban world that Marx predicted, Davis portrays a postmodern condition in which classical Marxist hopes for social progress and emancipation have crashed. He describes a metropolitan context in which the downtown's gleaming development projects and suburban affluence stands alongside grim environmental devastation, social degradation, and a prison-house climate in the space occupied by the poor, predominantly minority and immigrant populace. In the absence of an organized and politically conscious working class or any other effective opposition, big capital and its powerful police arms function in almost unchallenged fashion. Davis holds that security concerns pervade Los Angeles' "bad edge of postmodernity" – lower-class and minority neighborhoods are sealed off from middle-class enclaves, and upscale areas of the city are heavily policed, electronically monitored, and designed to discourage entry of the undesirable classes. He explains that genuinely open public spaces are being destroyed, while very generous public subsidies are provided for costly downtown projects. Publicized as an "urban renaissance," these "public–private partnerships" produce gentrified, privatized spaces that exclude the majority of the inner-city populace and enrich developers and the corporate sector. Davis sees in this phenomenon the type of extreme polarization that Marx predicted, but Los Angeles' postmodern condition, exceptional diversity, garrison state tendencies, affluent upper middle classes, and spatial exclusion add new twists to Marx's scenario.

chapter 42

The Connected and the Disconnected

Jeremy Rifkin

The question of access is likely to be as passionately debated in the coming century as questions of property rights were during the whole of the modern era. That's because access is a potentially more encompassing phenomenon. While property dealt with the narrow material question of what's mine and thine, access deals with the broader cultural question of who controls lived experience itself.

The shift from geographic markets to cyberspace, made possible by the digital communications revolution, opens up new ways to organize human relationships. The coming together of computers, telecommunications, cable television, consumer electronics, broadcasting, publishing, and entertainment in an integrated communications web allows commercial enterprises to exercise unprecedented control over the ways human beings communicate with one another.

More than twenty years ago, Daniel Bell made the observation that in the coming era, "control over communication services [will be] a source of power, and access to communication [will be] a condition of freedom." The French philosopher Jean-François Lyotard tightened Bell's observation by suggesting that "increasingly, the central question is becoming who will have access" in this new postmodern world.

The New Corporate Moguls

A handful of global media companies are locked in an epic struggle to control the communications channels and cultural resources that together will make up much of the commercial sphere in the twenty-first century. Whereas in the twentieth century, companies like Standard Oil, DuPont, Ford, U.S. Steel, and Sears were at the center of a marketplace dedicated to the production and sale of propertied goods, in the twenty-first century it's companies like Disney, Time Warner, Bertelsmann, Viacom, Sony, News Corporation, TCI, General Electric, PolyGram, and Seagram who will dominate the global media market and determine the conditions by which the public gains access to cultural resources and commodified experiences. These ten companies alone enjoyed annual sales ranging from $10 billion to $25 billion in 1997. A second tier of forty or so regional media giants from Western Europe, the United States, Asia, and Latin America controls much of the remaining communications channels and content, with annual sales of between $1 billion and $5 billion.

U.S.-based media companies are the world leaders and have set the ground rules for the global contest to control communications and commodified cultural resources. The editors of *Vanity Fair* recently reflected on the historic importance of the post–Cold War shift from industrial to cultural production in the United States. They wrote:

> The power center of America . . . has moved from its role as military-industrial giant to a new supremacy as the world's entertainment-information superpower.[1]

The Disney empire is a prime example of the new commercial forces that are consolidating their control over large swathes of the media and cultural markets. Disney merged with Capital Cities/ABC in 1995. The $19 billion deal created a global entertainment production and distribution company with combined revenue of $16.5 billion. Disney also has interests in Hyperion and Chilton book publishing; 4 magazine publishing groups, including *Women's Wear Daily*; 681 Disney retail stores; and interest in television and cable networks, including Lifetime, A&E, The History Channel, and ESPN. Disney also owns a National Hockey League team, a major league baseball franchise, 11 newspapers, and 4 music companies.

Other companies have entered into similar megadeals designed to control much of the communications and cultural landscape. Paramount and Viacom's merger brought together Paramount's library of 50,000 films, Simon & Schuster's 300,000 book titles, Blockbuster Entertainment's 500 music stores, Nickelodeon and MTV, as well as several theme parks and television and radio stations all under one roof, giving this single company vast power in the cultural production industry. Adding to its clout, Viacom merged again in the fall of 1999, this time with CBS. The new merger makes Viacom the industry leader in the media and entertainment fields. The $36 billion deal creates a global enterprise worth $80 billion, with revenues of more than $20 billion per year.

The transformation to cultural capitalism was helped along in 1996 with the passage of the Telecommunications Act, a landmark piece of legislation that opened the media field to new competitors, including the large regional telephone companies and cable companies. Now, telephone companies, Hollywood studios, television companies, cable companies, and software companies are creating strategic alliances and entering into megamergers to control as much of the communications market as they can. The goal for each is to become the single provider for homes and businesses for the full range of communications and cultural services. For example, immediately after the passage of the Telecommunications Act, U.S. West, one of the largest telephone companies, acquired Continental Cablevision, the nation's third-largest cable system. Sprint, the long-distance telephone company, scurried to catch up with the competition by forming a joint venture with the cable companies TCI, Comcast, and Cox.

Meanwhile, local telephone and cable companies are beginning to understand the strategic advantage of controlling the last mile of wire that goes to customers' homes and businesses. Controlling wired access to the customer puts the regional telephone companies in a particularly favorable position to market a variety of services from data delivery to entertainment. A few years ago, Pacific Telesis, Bell Atlantic, and Nynex entered into a joint venture with what was then Michael Ovitz's Creative Artists Agency to create video entertainment for distribution over their VDT lines. The local phone companies realize that success depends on controlling both the pipeline and the content. The former gives them access to the customer, while the latter is where the profits are made. Says Paris Burstyn, an analyst with GeoPartners Research, Inc., in Cambridge, Massachusetts, "Delivery is a commodity. Content is a value-added service, and profits are higher on a value-added."

In the global arena, the media giants are either acquiring one another outright or entering into joint ventures to share market opportunities. The ten largest global media companies have, on the average, joint ventures of one kind or another with six or more of the other companies. They also enjoy various strategic partnerships with smaller media firms in regional markets. Seagram, for example, which owns Universal, also owns 15 percent of Time Warner. TCI, on the other hand, is also a major shareholder in Time Warner. In a network economy based on short-term alliances, "nobody can really afford to get mad with their competitors," says TCI chairman John Malone, "because they are partners in one area and competitors in another."

Until 1997, it was difficult for global companies to enter into joint ventures and mergers because of the many restrictions imposed on the telecommunications industry in each country. In some countries, telecommunications were government-owned utilities. In others, the companies were privately owned but publicly regulated monopolies. In 1997, however, officials from sixty countries signed an accord, through the auspices of the World Trade Organization, to end state monopolies and open up the $600 billion global telecommunications market to free competition and foreign investment in domestic markets. Renato Ruggiero, then director general of the WTO, heralded the accord, saying it is "good news for the international economy, it is good news for businesses and it is good news for ordinary people around the world who use telephones or who want to use them." President Clinton echoed the enthusiasm, saying the pact would "spread the benefits of a technology revolution to citizens around the world." While some critics questioned whether the deregulation of state telephone monopolies and their entrance into an unfettered world market would appreciably benefit the world's less advantaged populations, especially in the developing nations, everyone agreed that the pact would hasten mergers.

Under the terms of the Global Telecommunications Agreement, a foreign carrier can, for example, own 100 percent of an American telephone company if its native country provides reciprocal access to its domestic markets. (Some countries, like Japan and Canada, have set somewhat more restrictive conditions). During the early stages of deregulation, much of the effort is aimed at securing access to the lucrative global business markets – some 5,000 corporate customers – who spend more than $90 billion per year on sophisticated telecommunications services to maintain their commercial networks and operations. Typical of the powerful new joint ventures being assembled in the aftermath of the WTO accord is the partnership announced in July 1998 between AT&T and British Telecom, two of the largest phone companies in the world. They have formed a jointly owned company that will provide $10 billion worth a year of telephone, Internet, and data services to multinational companies in more than 100 countries.

Even before the WTO accord was signed, MCI's president Gerald H. Taylor was predicting, "There's probably going to be only four to six global gangs to emerge over the next five years as all of this sorts out." The *Financial Times* agrees with Taylor's forecast, saying that at the end of the day there will likely be only "a handful of giants straddling the world market." The stakes are huge. The telecommunications market now ranks third in the world behind health care and banking and is growing at twice the rate of the global economy. With revenues expected to exceed $1 trillion by 2010, the battle for market share is going to be hard fought and intense.

The telecommunications companies are targeting much of their efforts on securing the gateways to the Internet and cyberspace, hoping to control the electronic worlds in which hundreds of millions of people will be spending much of their personal and business time in the coming century. Like the telecommunications industry, cyberspace was deregulated in 1995 when the government-sponsored NSFnet turned over operating functions to commercial vendors. Today, access to cyberspace is secured through commercial network providers. Tomorrow it will be the captive of "global gangs" of telecommunications giants, broadcasters, and computer companies. The goal, once again, is to control digital voice, data and video transmissions, and products in every region and market of the world. Most of the major television broadcasters, including CNN, NBC, ABC, and Fox, have launched online services. Meanwhile Microsoft has integrated its Web browser into its Windows operating system and begun to acquire content companies.

Much of the early enthusiasm for the Internet's potential to create a more participatory public sphere has been dampened in the rush to commercialize the medium. Commercial advertising is rampant on the Net. With consumers simply unwilling to pay higher access fees, the portal companies have little choice but to connect with commercial advertisers to underwrite their operations. Customers already are being exposed to a blitz of commercial messages when they log on as part of the price they have to pay for securing access to cyberspace.

Being able to control both the communications infrastructure and access to the portals and gateways that hundreds of millions of people will use to communicate with one another, as well as much of the cultural content that flows over the wires and spectrum, gives global media companies unparalleled power. Media historian and critic Ben Bagdikian observes:

> Nothing in earlier history matches this corporate group's power to penetrate the social landscape. Using both old and new technology, by owning each other's shares, engaging in joint ventures as partners, and other forms of cooperation, this handful of giants has created what is, in effect, a new communications cartel. . . . At issue is not just a financial statistic, like production numbers or ordinary industrial products like refrigerators or clothing. At issue is the possession of power to surround almost every man, woman, and child . . . with controlled images and words, to socialize each new generation of Americans, to alter the political agenda of the country. And with that power comes the ability to exert influence that in many ways is greater than that of schools, religion, parents, and even government itself.[2]

The End of the Nation-State

The deregulation and commercialization of the world's telecommunications and broadcasting systems is stripping nation-states of their ability to oversee and control communications within their borders. Global media companies are establishing a worldwide network of communications that bypasses political boundaries altogether and, in the process, changing the fundamental character of political life on earth.

At the dawn of the global media age more than twenty years ago, an American government official remarked that "trade doesn't follow the flag anymore; it follows the communications systems." Private communications networks are forging new communities of interest that have fewer and fewer ties to geography. Many professionals now spend more time in cyberspace than in geographic space, and identify more with their virtual addresses than their geographic ones. Today, the larger multinational companies rely on sophisticated communications technologies to maintain their networks of worldwide operations. Their global reach is impressive. Less than 500 transnational companies now account for $\frac{1}{3}$ of all manufacturing exports, $\frac{3}{4}$ of commodity trade, and $\frac{4}{5}$ of the total trade in technology and management services. The partnership between global media companies and the world's largest manufacturing and service-based companies is a powerful one. Their combined ability to control the flow of communications, goods, and services represents a formidable challenge to the traditional political powers exercised by states.

Market libertarians argue that the deregulation of telecommunications, broadcasting, and other media services is the most efficient way to reduce barriers to entry into markets and to spawn innovations. Encouraging competition, they believe, will ensure commercial opportunity and result in greater access to the many new networks that are being forged. Esther Dyson, George Gilder, George Keyworth, and Alvin Toffler, four of the leading proselytizers of the cyberspace revolution, argue that "technological progress is turning the telecommunications marketplace from one characterized by 'economies of scale' and 'natural monopolies' into a prototypical competitive market. The challenge for government," they say, "is to encourage this shift – to create the circumstances under which new competitors and new technologies will challenge the natural monopolies of the past."

Lending institutions, like the World Bank, have made deregulation of telecommunications a quid pro quo for extending loans to developing countries in the belief that the marketization of media is the most effective way to spur development. Others argue that such policies only encourage a new form of colonialism, further impoverishing the most disadvantaged countries. Jill Hills, professor of international political economy at City University in London, says that when a Third World country hands over its telecommunications networks to a foreign operator, it often results in "the loss of ongoing network revenues and capital outflow in the repatriation of profits." The bottom line, say the critics, is that "where private companies own both the domestic infrastructure and international links, developing countries are returned to their prewar situation of colonial appendages."

The international telecommunications accord of 1997 went a long way toward weakening national governments by taking away from them one of the most basic regulatory powers in their political arsenal: the right to determine the terms and conditions on how communications are structured and accessed within their borders. Now, a new proposal being floated in U.S. policy circles threatens to complete the deregulation process altogether. If it succeeds, governments around the world will have lost the last remaining vestige of power they have over communications within their borders.

The electromagnetic spectrum is the entire range of radio frequencies in the earth's atmosphere, which is used to transmit radio, television, and other broadcast media. In each country, the spectrum is treated as a "commons" and controlled and administered by government on behalf of its citizenry. The United States was one of the first governments to take ownership of the spectrum in 1927 with the establishment of the Federal Communications Commission (FCC). Since then, the FCC has allocated parts of the spectrum to radio, television, cellular telephone communications, paging and messaging, satellite services, point-to-point microwave and taxi dispatching, and other media, and licensed it to broadcasters for fixed durations, subject to renewal. To keep their licenses, local broadcasters have to comply with government regulations designed to safeguard the "public interest." Now a coalition of some of the nation's most powerful public policy think tanks have suggested that the FCC relinquish its long-standing control over all spectrum frequencies and institute a one-time massive sell-off of the entire band to private broadcasters, who would then own and trade the frequencies in the open marketplace in the form of private "electronic real estate."

The suggestion that spectrum frequencies be enclosed in the form of private property was first made by attorney Leo Herzel in the 1950s in an article in the *University of Chicago Law Review*. In the 1990s, the idea was resurrected by the Progress and Freedom Foundation, a Washington think tank with close ties to the former Republican speaker of the U.S. House of Representatives Newt Gingrich. The foundation makes the point that the global information industry is expected to be a $3 trillion market by the early twenty-first century. Yet, they argue, the government's statutes and regulatory regime now in place was established in the 1930s and is so antiquated and outmoded that it is acting as an impediment to innovation. The think tank cites what it calls procrastination and endless delays in assigning frequencies and granting licenses, all of which, it contends, undermines the entrepreneurial spirit.

The solution, say the architects of the foundation's spectrum report – entitled *The Telecom Revolution: An American Opportunity* – is to convert the entire electromagnetic spectrum to private property to be freely used, sold, leased, or otherwise developed. The FCC itself would be eliminated altogether and replaced by a small government agency inside the executive branch, to be called the Office of Communication, whose responsibilities would be limited to auctioning off the spectrum and certain administrative chores. Under the plan, broadcasters holding existing licenses would be granted title to the spectrums they currently use and would henceforth be free to use, transfer, and develop them as they see fit. Shortly thereafter, applicants whose licenses are pending before the FCC would be granted title, and nonallocated parts of the spectrum would be sold to private bidders. "The key," says the report, "is to sell title in property, not in mere licenses." The authors of the report make it clear that the spectrum is to be treated exactly like any other property, and owners would have exclusive rights to control its use, exclude others from using it, and determine the conditions upon which it can be sold to another party. The foundation concludes with a plea to restore "ownership of the entire electromagnetic spectrum to America's entrepreneurial, innovative private sector, where it can contribute to the prosperity potential of the information revolution."

The U.S. Congress has already held hearings on the sell-off proposal, and observers close to the communications industry believe that it is only a matter of time before the spectrum is transferred into private electronic real estate. Once that happens, other nations will be encouraged to follow suit, eventually transferring the entire spectrum around the world to privately traded spectrum real estate. In the Age of Access, spectrum real estate is likely to be the single most important asset in the world. Only a handful of global media players will be able to afford to buy large parts of the electromagnetic spectrum. Owning the global frequencies will allow these companies to control access to the channels of communication over which millions of people conduct their day-to-day lives.

The transformation of the spectrum from public commons – held in trust by government on behalf of its citizenry – to private electronic real estate – controlled by global media giants – fundamentally changes the relationship between the people and global commercial enterprises. Without public ownership over the spectrum, the citizenry becomes beholden to a handful of media companies for access to the means of communicating with one another in a highly sophisticated network-based civilization.

What, then, are we to make of the fate of the nation-state in this new era? Up to now, governments have been rooted in geography. They are institutions designed to control and administer land. But with so much of the commercial and social life of humanity migrating to the nonmaterial world of cyberspace, will political institutions wedded in geography become increasingly less important and less viable?

In a world in which more and more first-tier economic and social activity takes place in cyberspace in the form of commodified cultural experiences, governments find themselves with a greatly diminished role to play. That role is further eroded as governments give up their authority to control the frequencies and communications channels that are the pipelines to cyberspace. In cyberspace, the only megaproperties really worth owning are the radio frequencies, the fiber optic cable, the communications satellites, the hardware and software technologies that make up the channels of communication, and the content that flows through the pipelines. With these forms of property firmly in the hands of a few global commercial networks, other forms of property become less important. While personal property and even commercial property continue to exist, they become ancillary to the more important requisite of securing access to the communications channels and content that link people together in networks of shared meaning.

The decline of the nation-state is becoming most apparent in issues of trade. Global companies have successfully lobbied governments for major concessions that have further weakened traditional rights of sovereignty. International treaties and conventions like NAFTA and GATT have stripped governments of their right to impose domestic restrictions on such things as unfair labor practices or egregious environmental violations, if they interfere with the free exercise of global trade. New institutions like the World Trade Organization, whose officials are unaccountable to any specific government, can impose sanctions on countries who violate trade agreements and norms.

Nowhere, however, is the diminished nature of nation-states becoming more at issue than in the question of tax collection. With a growing amount of personal and commercial business being conducted in cyberspace, it becomes more difficult to assess and collect taxes. In a network economy, in which so much commercial activity is "broken up into small packets of information which do not mean anything until reassembled," says Diane Coyle, economic editor of the *Independent* in London, "it will be impossible for tax authorities to monitor all transactions." Coyle adds that "it would be impossible to say where those transactions had taken place even if they could be monitored and therefore knotty to decide which government is entitled to any tax on them." Then too, when so many products and services are the result of small, value-added contributions made by many players scattered over time and space but working together in shared networks and joint ventures, how does any particular government make the determination about exactly how much value added is assignable to taxation within its geographic borders? Finally, in a market economy made up of the production of things, taxing the labor that went into the process and the value added at each step of the manufacturing and sale of the products is a relatively easy undertaking. In a network economy made up of the commodification of connections, relationships, and lived experiences, how does the government determine gradations and value added for the purposes of taxation?

As long as human activity was grounded in geography, governments made sense. But now that economic and social life is becoming increasingly spaceless, do governments still matter? And when communities are no longer grounded in geography but rather defined by temporary, shared interests among people who interact with one another in virtual worlds, how does one retain any notion of collective solidarity and loyalty to place and country, long regarded as requisites for maintaining any sense of national cohesion? Jean-Marie Guéhenno, in his book *The End of the Nation-State*, makes the point that "in the age of networks, the relationship of the citizens to the body politic is in competition with the infinity of connections they establish outside it. So politics, far from being the organizing principle of life in society, appears as a secondary activity, if not an artificial construct poorly suited to the resolution of the practical problems of the modern world."

Living Outside the Electronic Gates

While nation-states are beginning to buckle under the pressure of a new global economic and social order made up of vast networks of shared interests that bypass national boundaries, eclipse geography, and exist in cyberspace, we need to understand that most people on earth are not connected to these new worlds. They exist outside the electronic gates in another world of poverty and despair, in which sheer physical survival dictates the terms of daily life. For them, life is one of toil and drudgery made up of modest efforts to eke out an existence. In an era in which the affluent fifth of the population is leaving property behind in search of cultural experiences and personal transformation, the remaining four-fifths have meager belongings and still wish to be propertied.

Despite all of the euphoria surrounding the communications revolution and the bold projections about a future wired world, the realities are that 65 percent of the human population today have never made a single telephone call and 40 percent have no access to electricity. There are more telephone lines in Manhattan than in all of sub-Saharan Africa.

Access to electricity, telephone lines, radio and television broadcasting, and the Internet has understandably become the litmus test for connectivity in a wired world. The twenty-four OECD countries – the wealthiest nations in the world – make up less than 15 percent of the world's population but account for 71 percent of all telephone lines. Together, Europe and North America own $\frac{2}{3}$ of the world's radios and TVs, even though they make up only 20 percent of the global population. In the Pacific Rim, Hong Kong is the most wired city, with 59 phones per 100 people, putting it slightly ahead of Singapore, which boasts 49 phones per 100 people. Taiwan and South Korea each has 35 phones per 100 people, while Thailand has only 3 lines per 100 people. Indonesia has only 6 phones per 1,000 people, and China has 9 phones per 1,000 people. The most wired place in the world is the island of Bermuda. With its off-shore insurance companies, investment brokerage houses, and accounting firms, it has become the prototype market in the new commercial world of electronic communications. Meanwhile, Africa represents the other extreme – a continent virtually disconnected from the global network economy. Africa has only 37 televisions and 172 radios per 1,000 people, a stark contrast to North America, where there are 798 television sets and 2,017 radios per every 1,000 people.

Meanwhile, the highly industrial countries accounted for more than 88 percent of Internet users in 1998, even though they make up less than 15 percent of the human population on earth. North America alone, with less than 5 percent of the global population, boasted more than half of the Internet users. South Asia, with 20 percent of the world's human population, accounted for less than 1 percent of the Internet users.

The communications gap between the developed nations and the developing nations is so great that many observers believe that the world is fast dividing into the informationally rich and the informationally poor. Columnist David Kline, writing in the high-tech magazine *Hot Wired*, worries that "the future may become a wonderland of opportunity only for the minority among us who are affluent, mobile, and highly educated. And it may at the same time become a digital dark age for the majority of citizens – the poor, the non-college educated, and the so-called unnecessary."

With governments around the world deregulating and selling off their telecommunications and broadcasting infrastructures, the commercial sphere becomes the ultimate arbiter of who is connected in a wired global economy. Those who can afford access to cyberspace and the shared networks and virtual worlds that make up the new ethereal plane of human existence will be connected, and everyone else will remain outside the electronic gates.

The disparity in income and wealth between the top fifth of the world's population – who already are beginning to live in simulated worlds – and everyone else is increasing so rapidly that any talk of guaranteeing universal access is likely to be greeted with deep suspicion and cynicism by most observers. According to a study conducted by the United Nations Development Program, the world's 358 billionaires now have combined assets that exceed the total annual income of nearly half the people who live on earth. While Bill Gates is now richer than half the American people put together, more than a third of the world's 3 billion workers find themselves without jobs or underemployed, according to a 1998 report of the International Labor Organization. The result is that while the wealthiest human beings on earth are increasingly preoccupied with entertainment and living creative and expressive lives, nearly 1 billion other human beings are living in poverty and several billion more are barely making ends meet. And the projections for the immediate future are even more grim. More than 100 countries, with a combined population of 1.6 billion people – more than a quarter of the world's population – continue to experience economic decline. Eighty-nine countries are worse off now in terms of income than ten years ago, and thirty-five have experienced a greater fall in per capita income than occurred at the height of the Great Depression in the 1930s. In Africa the average household consumes 20 percent less today than it did twenty-five years ago.

Worldwide, more than 600 million people are homeless or living in unsafe and unhealthy housing, and the World Bank estimates that by the year 2010, more than 1.4 billion people will live without safe water and sanitation. Meanwhile, the top 20 percent of high-income earners in the world now account for 86 percent of all the private consumption, while the poorest 20 percent consume only 1.3 percent of the global economic output. The reality is that Americans spend more on cosmetics – $8 billion annually – and Europeans on ice cream – $11 billion (in U.S. dollars) – than it would cost to provide basic education, clean water, and sanitation for the 2 billion people in the world who currently go without schooling or even toilets.

The growing disparity in income between rich and poor is affecting the developed nations as well as the developing countries. In Britain, for example, income inequality has risen faster in the past twenty years than in any other industrialized nation. In the U.S. the Census Bureau reports that income disparity between rich and poor is higher now than at any time since the end of World War II in 1945. Today, the top 20 percent of Americans receive half the income in the country, while 50 percent of American families have less than $1,000 in financial assets. Middle- and working-class families have been particularly hard hit. The median household income in 1996 was 4 percent below where it was in 1989.

At the same time that the more affluent part of the population is migrating behind electronic gates, many of the nation's poorest and least educated citizens are being put behind prison gates. More than 1.5 million Americans are currently behind bars, making the U.S. the most incarcerated population in the world. In California, the state legislature, which used to spend a mere 2 percent of its budget on prisons in 1980, spent 9 percent in 1995 and is projected to spend nearly 18 percent of its funds on prisons by the year 2002. California now spends more public funds on prisons than on higher education.

All the talk about access to global networks, cultural production, cyberspace, and simulated lived experiences falls largely on deaf ears for the millions of Americans who have yet to experience even the rudimentary benefits of ownership and a propertied way of life. Bill Gates's vision of a wired world is meaningless to the more than 7 million American families who are without even basic telephone service. Millions of others – the working poor and lower-middle-income families – lack the financial resources, educational skills, and time to become active players in the new electronically mediated network worlds. They risk being left even farther behind as the more affluent connect with one another, erect commercial and social networks of shared interest, and leave everyone else isolated, alone, and forced to fend for him- or herself in an increasingly inhospitable and impoverished world.

The disenfranchised and dispossessed also are becoming the disconnected in the Age of Access. *Time* magazine glimpsed their plight in a special issue dedicated to cyberspace. The editors noted that access to electronically mediated worlds will be essential to one's "ability to function in a democratic society."

The Right and Left of Access

Access issues are not new in the communications arena. Questions surrounding access were raised when the telephone was first introduced, and later when radio and television appeared. Debates on how best to guarantee universal access to phone lines and broadcasting technologies have reared up periodically throughout the whole of the twentieth century. Federal laws in the U.S. were passed early on to ensure rural households cheap and affordable access to telephone service. When the FCC began to regulate radio, provisions were written into the legislation to make sure license holders served local community needs. The public interest, however, quickly capitulated to commercial interests. The Communications Act of 1934 handed over vast control of the airwaves to communications companies like RCA, General Electric, and Westinghouse, who wasted little time converting the new medium to an advertising forum for commercial sponsors. Lee de Forest, the inventor of the vacuum tube that made radio broadcasting a reality, was so upset by the way the new medium was being used that he openly condemned the industry in a letter to the National Association of Broadcasters in 1946. He complained that "you have made of [radio] a laughing stock to intelligence . . . you have cut time into tiny segments called spots (more rightly stains) wherewith the occasional fine program is periodically smeared with impudent insistence to buy and try."

The advent of television in the 1940s led to similar public calls to advance popular education and the community interest. Television stations were expected by law to provide public service announcements, local public affairs shows, and children's programming. They also were required to provide equal time to people and groups in the community to air differing views on topics covered by the station management. In addition, the Fairness Doctrine required every station to present programs on controversial topics and make sure to provide a balanced set of opposing views. By the 1980s, however, most of the Fairness Doctrine had been

whittled away in the wake of the deregulating fervor spawned by the
Reagan administration. As was the case earlier with radio, commercial interests were able to thwart any effort to make television an instrument to
serve public education and community interests. While public television
has attempted to fill that role, even it has had to compromise along the
way. Although in theory public television is free of advertising, in practice it relies heavily on the private sector to underwrite and sponsor its
programming and has become increasingly subject to market pressures
to beef up its entertainment content, often at the expense of its educational content.

Again, with the birth of cable television, the issue of public access
was raised once more – this time in the halls of Congress and state
legislatures and by professional and community organizations. Many
championed the new medium as a powerful tool to serve communities.
The National Science Foundation's report on the future of cable television
was bullish over the possibilities. The foundation wrote:

> Public access channels can be made available to individual citizens and
> community groups. . . . Churches, Boy Scouts, minority groups, high school
> classes, crusaders for causes – can create and show their own programs.
> With public access, cable can become a medium for local action instead
> of a distributor of prepackaged mass-consumption programs to a passive
> audience.[3]

The NSF envisioned cable TV performing a broad educational mission,
including offering "instruction for homebound and institutionalized
persons, preschool eduction, high school and post-secondary degree
courses in the home, career education and in-service training, and community
information programming . . ." Although some vestiges of community
programming still can be found on cable, most of the fare is commercial
in nature and driven by advertising.

Today, the issue of access has become far more significant. The digital
revolution is bringing all of the major forms of technologically mediated
communications – voice, data, video – together in an integrated web.
More and more personal and commercial communications take place in
electronic networks, making them indispensable to survival in a wired
world. The issue is no longer simply one of access to the mediums themselves but rather access – through the mediums – to the culture. Our very
abilities to connect with our fellow human beings, to engage in commerce,
to create communities of shared interests, and to establish meaning in our
lives are increasingly mediated by these powerful new forms of electronic
communications. While cyberspace may not be a place in the traditional
sense, it is a social arena in which millions of people are beginning
to engage one another in human discourse. Much of the life of human

civilization is going to occur in electronic worlds in the future. The question of access, then, becomes one of the most important considerations of the coming age.

NOTES

1   "The Power Center," *Vanity Fair*, Sept. 1995, p. 271.
2   Ben Bagdikian, *The Media Monopoly*, 5th edn. (Boston: Beacon Press, 1997), p. ix.
3   Howard Besser, "From Internet to Information Superhighway," in James Brook and Iain A. Boal (eds.), *Resisting the Virtual Life: The Culture and Politics of Information* (San Francisco: City Lights Books, 1995), p. 60.

chapter 43

The Architecture of a New Consensus

Thomas Frank

. . . The formalities of democracy seemed to hold little charm for We the People in the 1990s. Election turnouts dwindled through the decade, hitting another humiliating new low every couple of years. Any cynic could tell you the reason why: Politics had once again become a sport of kings, with "soft money" and corporate contributions, spun into the pure gold of TV advertising, purchasing results for the billionaires' favorites as effectively as had the simple payoffs of the age of boodle. . . . We voted less and less, and the much-discussed price tags of electoral victory soared like the NASDAQ.

Maybe the amounts our corporate friends were spending to court us should have been a source of national pride; maybe those massive sums constituted a sort of democratic triumph all by themselves. Certainly everything else that money touched in the nineties shined with a kind of populist glow. In the eighties, maybe, money had been an evil thing, a tool of demonic coke-snorting vanity, of hostile takeovers and S&L ripoffs. But something fundamental had changed since then, we were told: Our billionaires were no longer slave-driving martinets or pump-and-dump Wall Street manipulators. They were people's plutocrats, doing without tie and suit, chatting easily with the rank-and-file, building the new superstore just for us, seeing to it that the customer was served, wearing name tags on their work-shirts, pushing the stock prices up benevolently this time, making sure we all got to share in the profit-taking and that even the hindest hindmost got out with his or her percentage intact. These billionaires were autographing workers' hard-hats out at the new plant in Coffeyville; they were stepping right up to the podium and reciting Beatles lyrics for the cameras; they were giddy with excitement; they were even allowing all people everywhere to enjoy life with them via their greatest gift of all – the World Wide Web. Maybe what our greatest popular social theorist,

George Gilder, had said about them all those years ago was finally true: "It is the entrepreneurs who know the rules of the world and the laws of God." . . .

. . . [F]ar beyond simply being "bullish on America," it was as though the good people of Merrill Lynch, IBM, and their fellow worshipers, standing at the millennium's end, could look back over the entire sweep of human struggle and see they themselves at its climax, its very peak. They were supermen, indeed, presiding over an era of historical advance so rapid, of change so profound, that it constituted nothing less than a "New Economy," a magic time in which the ancient laws of exchange, of supply and demand, had been repealed at last. From the rousing op-eds of *Wired* and *Forbes*, from CEO conference calls, from the bubbling announcements on CNBC, from the ecstatic babel of motivational seminars, came word of the miraculous advance: Through feats of sheer positive thinking, Business Man had overturned the principles of accounting, had smashed the barriers of price-to-earnings, had redrawn the map of competition, had thrown off the dead hand of the physical world! The country's gross national product, we exulted, weighed less than ever before! We dealt in ideas rather than things! And just as the laws of Newton had given way to those of the microchip, so scarcity itself, the curse of the material world, had been overcome once and for all. Not even the Fed could call the "New Economy" back to earth. We were, as one pop-economics title put it, *Living on Thin Air*.

The race was on to describe an achievement we believed to outrank any in human history, to hail the achievements of Business Man in the most grandiose possible terms. "Is this a great time or what?" asked a series of 1996 commercials for telecom giant MCI. "Let us celebrate an American triumph," thundered a Mort Zuckerman editorial early the next year in *US News & World Report*, a "triumph" based on the solid rock of pro-business political principle: "privatize, deregulate, and do not interfere with the market." And as the logic of the "New Economy" spread over all things, the imperatives of Business Man inundated every other way of imagining the world. "Everything is now thought of as a business of a sort," wrote management theorist Charles Handy in 1994. "We are all 'in business' these days, be we doctor or priest, professor or charity-worker." This was not just metaphor, either. As the Dow mounted higher and the startups soared, every avenue of inquiry found its appointed role in the new order. . . .

"New Economy" thinking expanded geographically as well. Just as Americans had once looked to Japan for the secrets of prosperity, now we demanded that other nations follow our lead. America's business thinkers confidently diagnosed the economic ailments of their competitors and announced their findings at one international summit after another: While in America business could proudly announce "I Am," in Europe and

Japan it was "held back," as journalist Louis Uchitelle summarized the conventional thinking, "by uniform pay scales, strong unions, generous unemployment insurance, costly benefits, and anti-efficient regulations. . . ." One memorable incident, at a meeting of economic policy-makers from the largest industrialized countries that was held in Denver in June 1997, signaled the new mood. President Clinton and Larry Summers, then deputy secretary of the treasury, seized the occasion to tell the world about the miraculous new American way. They handed out pairs of cowboy boots and proceeded to entertain the foreigners with what the *Financial Times* called a steady diet of "effusive self-praise" spiced with occasional "harsh words . . . for the rigidities of French and European markets." Don your boots and down with France!

Many statistical measures could be used to compare the triumphs of "New Economy" America to the floundering old economies of Europe and Japan: American productivity was up (at least it was in the second half of 1999), American growth was up, American stock markets were way, way, way up. Perhaps the most important markers of American uniqueness, though, were the different ways in which this "New Economy" chose to dole out the benefits of prosperity to different social classes. For the majority of American workers, wages through the nineties either fell or barely kept pace with inflation. But for top corporate executives these really were years in which to stand up and say "I Am." According to *Business Week* magazine, CEO compensation during the decade went from 85 times more than what average blue-collar employees received in 1990 to some *four hundred and seventy-five times* what blue collar workers received in 1999. In Japan, meanwhile, that multiple stood at about 11 times and in Britain, the country most enamored of New Economy principles after the US itself, only 24 times. . . .

What was true for CEOs was also true for the social class to which they belonged. The wealth of America's most privileged ballooned during the age of Clinton. Thanks to the feats of the Dow, the country's richest 1 percent found themselves happily holding an estimated 40.1 percent of the country's wealth in 1997, up from 35.7 percent in 1989 (and from only 20.5 percent in 1979). By the third year of the Man from Hope's first term, the country's next richest 9 percent were the proud owners of 33.3 percent of the nation's wealth. Measured according to the more comprehensive standard of inequality known as the "Gini Index," the US was achieving levels of wealth polarization both unique among industrialized nations and . . . not seen on these shores since the 1920s.

But what made the new draughts of wealth especially sweet was the exclusion of the bulk of the population from the boom times. This was most definitely not a matter of bad luck: While the inevitable trickle-down had its predictable effects (booming service industries, great innovation in luxury products, the return of servants to the homes of the rich), many of the usual mechanisms that allowed workers to participate in boom economies had been shut down. For the boldest American thinkers this was an integral part of the "New Economy," one of the things that made it "new." Stock markets, now enthroned as the judge of all economic value, massively rewarded those companies and those CEOs most ruthlessly committed to laying off great swathes of their workforce. Or take the nation's productivity figures, of which so much was made in the late nineties. Before the nineties, productivity had been a meaningful measure precisely because it signified real economic advances for the entire population. Growing productivity was, in fact, just about the only condition under which neoclassical economics was willing to acknowledge that wage increases were justified. But while productivity numbers in the final years of the decade grew at rates not seen since the 1960s, what put them on the front page and made them the subject of breathless commentary in *Wired* and on CNBC was that this connection to higher wages no longer seemed to exist. Wages remained stagnant *even while productivity increased*; the advances were funneled directly into stock prices. This was the reason productivity announcements in the late nineties were greeted with such jubilation: The people who got richer as workers became more productive were stockholders.

Just as critical was the belief among "New Economy" economists and journalists that rising wages were by definition a form of inflation – the one thing that could conceivably dim the luster of the new millions. And as inflation was the declared mortal enemy of national economic policy, rising wages had to be constrained by any means necessary. Fortunately, one of the hallmarks of the "New Economy" was a vastly enhanced arsenal of techniques for keeping wages down. With labor unions already enfeebled by years of political assault, even run-of-the-mill CEOs found they were capable of performing such celebrated tricks as the old hire-back-the-downsized-as-temps routine. And with tariff barriers lowered, with communications technology dramatically improved, and with a vast multitude of union-free regions beckoning, American managers found they only needed to raise the subject of relocation in order to restore that much-desired "flexibility" and "discipline" to a demanding workforce. At the national level interest rates could be manipulated and immigration policies modulated to suit the needs of particular industries and even particular employers. And, of course, one should not discount the influence of prisons, which helped both to maintain the appearance of reasonable unemployment rates and to further discipline a troublesome working class. The results were gratifying indeed: Even at the height of the boom in 1998 and 1999, with unemployment at historic lows and with Merrill Lynch warning us against worshiping the wrong "New Economy" deity, wage growth dropped precipitously.

For "New Economy" ideologues, though, such trends sparked no regrets. The free market, they believed, had its own built-in devices for social redress. The new order created so much opportunity for individuals to get ahead, to leave their old lives for the instant plutocracy of Silicon Valley, that the misfortunes of broad groups, while sad, paled in insignificance. Unfortunately, the promise of vastly enhanced class mobility in the "New Economy" turned out to be another myth, easily exploded by a systematic appraisal of the data. When economists measured mobility over the period 1986–91 they found that, in comparison with low-paid workers in European countries, American workers actually enjoyed slightly *less* class mobility, not more.

But who was counting? Americans in the nineties seemed to love the rich. The robber barons of old with their miserly, ground-out fortunes, had always had to confront a hostile, suspicious world. But now it was "Who Wants to Marry a Multimillionaire?" And, hell, who didn't? This plutocracy was cool! They were flooding into bohemian neighborhoods like San Francisco's Mission District, chatting with the guys in the band, and working on their poetry in Starbucks; they were going it alone with their millions and their out-of-wedlock child; they were abjuring stodgy ties and suits for 24/7 casual; they were leaping on their trampolines, typing out a few last lines on the laptop before paragliding, riding their bicycles to work, listening to Steppenwolf while they traded, drinking beer in the office, moshing at the Motley Crue show, startling the board members with their streetwise remarks, roaring down the freeway in their Lamborghinis, snowboarding in Crested, racing their jetskis by the platform at Cannes and splashing all the uptight French people.

And when they weren't being cool, they were being just like us, only more so. One of the most treasured fantasies of the decade was that of the hardworking billionaire, the no-nonsense businessman whose pragmatic ways weren't ruined by his massive wealth. Both Bill Gates and Warren Buffett had legendary appetites for hamburgers, the food of the common man. Both men were said to work way excessive hours. The none too subtle implication, of course, was that these men deserved their riches. They were rich because they had somehow done the labor of a million other men, created all manner of good things in direct proportion to their reward. From this attitude flowed . . . a "righteous indignation toward the claims of the unrich." The slightly more subtle implication was that the rich and the poor had somehow exchanged class positions (at least for purposes of moral righteousness), a cliché that one found repeated in management literature as well as "radical" showplaces like *Wired*. "The rich, the former leisure class, are becoming the new overworked," that magazine declared in a series of late-nineties manifestos. "And those who used to be considered the working class are becoming the new leisure class." . . .

[These changes] marked a fairly radical historical shift. According to the old "consensus" ideas developed in academia in the decades after World War II, the distinguishing feature of American civilization was its great and evenly distributed wealth. Consensus intellectuals of the 1950s wrote fondly about the "People of Plenty," about the "Affluent Society," imagining America as a land whose social problems arose not from deprivation but from abundance. From Henry Ford to the United Auto Workers our economic leaders imagined America as the land of the universal middle class; Richard Nixon used the panorama of goods available to even the lowliest American worker as evidence of the righteousness of our battle with Communism. Ours was a nation of homeowners and two-car garages, American writers told us, where bus drivers and sewer workers were distinguished from their white-collar neighbors by manners and tastes, not by income . And while endless consumption might not make much aesthetic or philosophical sense, the huge and widespread demand of all Americans for new cars, suburban homes, refrigerators, and stereo systems was thought to be the secret of our global preeminence. Shared abundance was not just a nice thing; it was virtually the definition of America.

But as the "New Economy" sent us on our way back into what strategist Edward Luttwak called a "Victorian pattern of income distribution," a system without any structural need for a well-paid blue-collar class, pundits discarded the ideology of abundance as though it had never existed. Now they looked into our past and saw precisely the opposite: Our tolerance for vast inequalities of wealth was what made us who we were. In an influential but strangely misinformed British study of our excellent American ways and how they might be imported into the UK, it was noted both that "the US is surely the land of grotesque inequality" and also that this was just part of our national character, something we simply "accept," abiding extremes of wealth and poverty with an admirable tolerance that the author projected into our remotest past. One can hardly blame a foreign observer for misreading American culture so wildly, though, since everywhere one looked in late-nineties America, the same story was being sung to the skies. In enthusing over a 1999 study that purported to measure international levels of "entrepreneurship" and also to prove that this quality contributed mightily to a country's growth (naturally, the US ranked number one by this measurement), the *Wall Street Journal* focused on the study's finding that "entrepreneurial societies have *and accept* higher levels of income disparity." Once it was our rage for economic democracy that was thought to yield such spectacular growth, putting a Model T in every garage: Now it was our tolerance for plutocracy that made things go. . . .

. . . "[D]estroying the old" and making the world safe for billionaires has been as much a cultural and political operation as an economic one. Consider for a minute the factors – weak trade unions, a declining regulatory apparatus, and the outright repeal of the welfare state under presidents Reagan and Clinton – that distinguish the United States, with its "New Economy," from the other industrialized nations. Aside from the technological advances of recent years (which may or may not live up to the world-historical importance we routinely ascribe to them), very little of the "New Economy" is new. What the term describes is not some novel state of human affairs but the final accomplishment of the long-standing agenda of the nation's richest class. Industries come and industries go, but what has most changed about America in the nineties is the way we think about industries, about economies. Once Americans imagined that economic democracy meant a reasonable standard of living for all – that freedom was only meaningful once poverty and powerlessness had been overcome. Today, however, American opinion leaders seem generally convinced that democracy and the free market are simply identical. There is precious little that is new about this idea, either: For nearly a century, equating the market with democracy was the familiar defense of any corporation in trouble with union or government; it was the standard-issue patter of corporate lobbyists like the National Association of Manufacturers. What is "new" is this idea's triumph over all its rivals; the determination of American leaders to extend it to all the world; the general belief among opinion-makers that there is something natural, something divine, something inherently democratic about markets. A better term for the "New Economy" might simply be "consensus." . . .

chapter 44

Societal Changes and Vulnerable Neighborhoods

William Julius Wilson

The disappearance of work in many inner-city neighborhoods is partly related to the nationwide decline in the fortunes of low-skilled workers. Although the growing wage inequality has hurt both low-skilled men and women, the problem of declining employment has been concentrated among low-skilled men. In 1987–89, a low-skilled male worker was jobless eight and a half weeks longer than he would have been in 1967–69. Moreover, the proportion of men who "permanently" dropped out of the labor force was more than twice as high in the late 1980s than it had been in the late 1960s. A precipitous drop in real wages – that is, wages adjusted for inflation – has accompanied the increases in joblessness among low-income workers. If you arrange all wages into five groups according to wage percentile (from highest to lowest), you see that men in the bottom fifth of this income distribution experienced more than a 30 percent drop in real wages between 1970 and 1989.

Even the low-skilled workers who are consistently employed face problems of economic advancement. Job ladders – opportunities for promotion within firms – have eroded, and many less-skilled workers stagnate in dead-end, low-paying positions. This suggests that the chances of improving one's earnings by changing jobs have declined: if jobs inside a firm have become less available to the experienced workers in that firm, they are probably even more difficult for outsiders to obtain.

But there is a paradox here. Despite the increasing economic marginality of low-wage workers, unemployment dipped below 6 percent in 1994 and early 1995, many workers are holding more than one job, and overtime work has reached a record high. Yet while tens of millions of new jobs have been created in the past two decades, men who are well below retirement age are working less than they did two decades ago – and a growing percentage are neither working nor looking for work. The proportion of male workers in the prime of their life (between the ages of 22 and 58) who worked in a given decade full-time, year-round, in at least eight out of ten years declined from 79 percent during the 1970s to 71 percent in the 1980s. While the American economy saw a rapid expansion in high technology and services, especially advanced services, growth in blue-collar factory, transportation, and construction jobs, traditionally held by men, has not kept pace with the rise in the working-age population. These men are working less as a result.

The growth of a nonworking class of prime-age males along with a larger number of those who are often unemployed, who work part-time, or who work in temporary jobs is concentrated among the poorly educated, the school dropouts, and minorities. In the 1970s, two-thirds of prime-age male workers with less than a high school education worked full-time, year-round, in eight out of ten years. During the 1980s, only half did so. Prime-age black men experienced a similar sharp decline. Seven out of ten of all black men worked full-time, year-round, in eight out of ten years in the 1970s, but only half did so in the 1980s. The figures for those who reside in the inner city are obviously even lower.

One study estimates that since 1967 the number of prime-age men who are not in school, not working, and not looking for work for even a single week in a given year has more than doubled for both whites and nonwhites (respectively, from 3.3 to 7.7 percent and 5.8 percent to 13.2 percent). Data from this study also revealed that one-quarter of all male high school dropouts had no official employment at all in 1992. And of those with high school diplomas, one out of ten did not hold a job in 1993, up sharply from 1967 when only one out of fifty reported that he had had no job throughout the year. Among prime-age nonwhite males, the share of those who had no jobs at all in a given year increased from 3 percent to 17 percent during the last quarter century.

These changes are related to the decline of the mass production system in the United States. The traditional American economy featured rapid growth in productivity and living standards. . . . In this system plenty of blue-collar jobs were available to workers with little formal education. Today, most of the new jobs for workers with limited education and experience are in the service sector, which hires relatively more women. . . .

The movement of lower-educated men into the growth sectors of the economy has been slow. For example, "the fraction of men who have moved into so-called pink-collar jobs like practical nursing or clerical work remains negligible." The large concentration of women in the expanding social service sector partly accounts for the striking gender differences in job growth. Unlike lower-educated men, lower-educated women are working more, not less, than in previous years. The employment patterns among lower-educated women, like those with higher education and training, reflect the dramatic expansion of social service industries. Between

1989 and 1993, jobs held by women increased by 1.3 million, while those held by men barely rose at all (by roughly 100,000).

Although the wages of low-skilled women (those with less than twelve years of education) rose slightly in the 1970s, they flattened out in the 1980s, and continued to remain below those of low-skilled men. The wage gap between low-skilled men and women shrank not because of gains made by female workers but mainly because of the decline in real wages for men. . . . However, over the past decade their rates of participation in the labor force have stagnated and have fallen further behind the labor-force-participation rates among more highly educated women, which continue to rise. The unemployment rates among both low-skilled men and women are five times that among their college-educated counterparts. . . .

The lowering of unionization rates, which accompanied the decline in the mass production system, has also contributed to shrinking wages and nonwage compensation for less skilled workers. As the economist Rebecca Blank has pointed out, "unionized workers typically receive not only higher wages, but also more non-wage benefits. As the availability of union jobs has declined for unskilled workers, non-wage benefits have also declined."

Finally, the wage and employment gap between skilled and unskilled workers is growing partly because education and training are considered more important than ever in the new global economy. At the same time that changes in technology are producing new jobs, they are making many others obsolete. The workplace has been revolutionized by technological changes that range from the development of robotics to information highways. While educated workers are benefiting from the pace of technological change, involving the increased use of computer-based technologies and microcomputers, more routine workers face the growing threat of job displacement in certain industries. . . . In the new global economy, highly educated and thoroughly trained men and women are in demand. This may be seen most dramatically in the sharp differences in employment experiences among men. Unlike men with lower education, college-educated men are working more, not less.

The shift in demand has been especially devastating for those low-skilled workers whose incorporation into the mainstream economy has been marginal or recent. Even before the economic restructuring of the nation's economy, low-skilled African-Americans were at the end of the employment queue. Their economic situation has been further weakened because they tend to reside in communities that not only have higher jobless rates and lower employment growth but lack access to areas of higher employment and employment growth as well. Moreover, . . . they are far more likely than other ethnic and racial groups to face negative employer attitudes.

Of the changes in the economy that have adversely affected low-skilled African-American workers, perhaps the most significant have been those in the manufacturing sector. One study revealed that in the 1970s "up to half of the huge employment declines for less-educated blacks might be explained by industrial shifts away from manufacturing toward other sectors." Another study reported that since the 1960s "deindustrialization" and the "erosion in job opportunities especially in the Midwest and Northeast . . . bear responsibility for the growth of the ranks of the 'truly disadvantaged.'" The manufacturing losses in some northern cities have been staggering. In the twenty-year period from 1967 to 1987, Philadelphia lost 64 percent of its manufacturing jobs; Chicago lost 60 percent; New York City, 58 percent; Detroit, 51 percent. In absolute numbers, these percentages represent the loss of 160,000 jobs in Philadelphia, 326,000 in Chicago, 520,000 – over half a million – in New York, and 108,000 in Detroit.

Another study examined the effects of economic restructuring in the 1980s by highlighting the changes in both the variety and the quality of blue-collar employment in general. Jobs were grouped into a small number of relatively homogeneous clusters on the basis of job quality (which was measured in terms of earnings, benefits, union protection, and involuntary part-time employment). The authors found that both the relative earnings and employment rates among unskilled black workers were lower for two reasons: traditional jobs that provide a living wage (high-wage blue-collar cluster, of which roughly 50 percent were manufacturing jobs) declined, as did the quality of secondary jobs on which they increasingly had to rely, leading to lower relative earnings for the remaining workers in the labor market. As employment prospects worsened, rising proportions of low-skilled black workers dropped out of the legitimate labor market.

Data from the Chicago Urban Poverty and Family Life Survey show that efforts by out-of-school inner-city black men to obtain blue-collar jobs in the industries in which their fathers had been employed have been hampered by industrial restructuring. "The most common occupation reported by respondents at ages 19 to 28 changed from operative and assembler jobs among the oldest cohorts to service jobs (waiters and janitors) among the youngest cohort." Fifty-seven percent of Chicago's employed inner-city black fathers (aged 15 and over and without undergraduate degrees) who were born between 1950 and 1955 worked in manufacturing and construction industries in 1974. By 1987, industrial employment in this group had fallen to 31 percent. Of those born between 1956 and 1960, 52 percent worked in these industries as late as 1978. But again, by 1987 industrial employment in this group fell to 28 percent. No other male ethnic group in the inner city experienced such an overall precipitous drop in manufacturing employment. . . . These employment changes have accompanied the loss of traditional manufacturing and other blue-collar jobs in Chicago. As a result, young black males have turned increasingly to the low-wage service sector and unskilled laboring jobs for employment, or have gone jobless. The strongly held U.S. cultural and economic belief that the son will do at least as well as the father in the labor market does not apply to many young inner-city males. . . .

The structural shifts in the distribution of industrial job opportunities are not the only reason for the increasing joblessness and declining earnings among young black male workers. There have also been important changes in the patterns of occupational staffing within firms and industries, including those in manufacturing. These changes have primarily benefited those with more formal education. Substantial numbers of new professional, technical, and managerial positions have been created. However, such jobs require at least some years of post-secondary education. Young high school dropouts and even high school graduates "have faced a dwindling supply of career jobs offering the real earnings opportunities available to them in the 1960s and early 1970s." . . .

The demand in the labor market has shifted toward higher-educated workers in various industries and occupations. The changing occupational and industrial mix is associated with increases in the rates of joblessness (unemployment and "dropping out" of, or nonparticipation in, the labor force) and decreases in the relative wages of disadvantaged urban workers.

The factors contributing to the relative decline in the economic status of disadvantaged workers are not solely due to those on the demand side, such as economic restructuring. The growing wage differential in the 1980s is also a function of two supply-side factors – the decline in the relative supply of college graduates and the influx of poor immigrants. . . .

Joblessness and declining wages are also related to the recent growth in ghetto poverty. The most dramatic increases in ghetto poverty occurred between 1970 and 1980, and they were mostly confined to the large industrial metropolises of the Northeast and Midwest, regions that experienced massive industrial restructuring and loss of blue-collar jobs during that decade. But the rise in ghetto poverty was not the only problem. Industrial restructuring had devastating effects on the social organization of many inner-city neighborhoods in these regions. The fate of the West Side black community of North Lawndale vividly exemplifies the cumulative process of economic and social dislocation that has swept through Chicago's inner city.

After more than a quarter century of continuous deterioration, North Lawndale resembles a war zone. Since 1960, nearly half of its housing stock has disappeared; the remaining units are mostly run-down or dilapidated. Two large factories anchored the economy of this West Side neighborhood in its good days – the Hawthorne plant of Western Electric, which employed over 43,000 workers; and an International Harvester plant with 14,000 workers. The world headquarters for Sears, Roebuck and Company was located there, providing another 10,000 jobs. The neighborhood also had a Copenhagen snuff plant, a Sunbeam factory, and a Zenith factory, a Dell Farm food market, an Alden's catalog store, and a U.S. Post Office bulk station. But conditions rapidly changed. Harvester closed its doors in the late 1960s. Sears moved most of its offices to the Loop in downtown Chicago in 1973; a catalog distribution center with a workforce of 3,000 initially remained in the neighborhood but was relocated outside of the state of Illinois in 1987. The Hawthorne plant gradually phased out its operations and finally shut down in 1984.

The departure of the big plants triggered the demise or exodus of the smaller stores, the banks, and other businesses that relied on the wages paid by the large employers. "To make matters worse, scores of stores were forced out of business or pushed out of the neighborhoods by insurance companies in the wake of the 1968 riots that swept through Chicago's West Side after the assassination of Dr. Martin Luther King, Jr. Others were simply burned or abandoned. It has been estimated that the community lost 75 percent of its business establishments from 1960 to 1970 alone." In 1986, North Lawndale, with a population of over 66,000, had only one bank and one supermarket; but it was also home to forty-eight state lottery agents, fifty currency exchanges, and ninety-nine licensed liquor stores and bars.

The impact of industrial restructuring on inner-city employment is clearly apparent to urban blacks. The UPFLS survey posed the following question: "Over the past five or ten years, how many friends of yours have lost their jobs because the place where they worked shut down – would you say none, a few, some, or most?" Only 26 percent of the black residents in our sample reported that none of their friends had lost jobs because their workplace shut down. Indeed, both black men and black women were more likely to report that their friends had lost jobs because of plant closings than were the Mexicans and the other ethnic groups in our study. Moreover, nearly half of the employed black fathers and mothers in the UPFLS survey stated that they considered themselves to be at high risk of losing their jobs because of plant shutdowns. Significantly fewer Hispanic and white parents felt this way.

Some of the inner-city neighborhoods have experienced more visible job losses than others. But residents of the inner city are keenly aware of the rapid depletion of job opportunities. A 33-year-old unmarried black male of North Lawndale who is employed as a clerical worker stated: "Because of the way the economy is structured, we're losing more jobs. Chicago is losing jobs by the thousands. There just aren't any starting companies here and it's harder to find a job compared to what it was years ago." . . .

The increasing suburbanization of employment has accompanied industrial restructuring and has further exacerbated the problems of inner-city joblessness and restricted access to jobs. "Metropolitan areas captured nearly 90 percent of the nation's employment growth; much of this growth occurred in booming 'edge cities' at the metropolitan periphery. By 1990, many of these 'edge cities' had more office space and retail sales than the metropolitan downtowns." Over the last two decades, 60 percent of the new jobs created in the Chicago metropolitan area have been located in the northwest suburbs of Cook and Du Page counties. African-Americans constitute less than 2 percent of the population in these areas. . . .

Blacks living in central cities have less access to employment, as measured by the ratio of jobs to people and the average travel time to and from work, than do central-city whites. Moreover, unlike most other groups of workers across the urban/suburban divide, less educated central-city blacks receive lower wages than suburban blacks who have similar levels of education. And the decline in earnings of central-city blacks is related to the decentralization of employment – that is, the movement of jobs from the cities to the suburbs – in metropolitan areas. . . .

Among two-car middle-class and affluent families, commuting is accepted as a fact of life; but it occurs in a context of safe school environments for children, more available and accessible day care, and higher incomes to support mobile, away-from-home lifestyles. In a multitiered job market that requires substantial resources for participation, most inner-city minorities must rely on public transportation systems that rarely provide easy and quick access to suburban locations. . . .

But the problem is not simply one of transportation and the length of commuting time. There is also the problem of the travel expense and of whether the long trek to the suburbs is actually worth it in terms of the income earned – after all, owning a car creates expenses far beyond the purchase price, including insurance, which is much more costly for city dwellers than it is for suburban motorists. . . .

Finally, in addition to enduring the search-and-travel costs, inner-city black workers often confront racial harassment when they enter suburban communities. . . .

The increase in the proportion of jobless adults in the inner city is also related to changes in the class, racial, and age composition of such neighborhoods – changes that have led to greater concentrations of poverty. Concentrated poverty is positively associated with joblessness. That is, when the former appears, the latter is found as well. As stated previously, poor people today are far more likely to be unemployed or out of the labor force than in previous years. . . . [I]n addition to the effects of joblessness, inner-city neighborhoods have experienced a growing concentration of poverty for several other reasons, including (1) the out-migration of nonpoor black families; (2) the exodus of nonpoor white and other nonblack families; and (3) the rise in the number of residents who have become poor while living in these areas. Additional research on the growth of concentrated poverty suggests another factor: the movement of poor people into a neighborhood (inmigration). And one more factor should be added to this mix: changes in the age structure of the community. . . .

chapter 45

Fortress L. A.

Mike Davis

The carefully manicured lawns of Los Angeles's Westside sprout forests of ominous little signs warning: "Armed Response!" Even richer neighborhoods in the canyons and hillsides isolate themselves behind walls guarded by gun-toting private police and state-of-the-art electronic surveillance. Downtown, a publicly-subsidized "urban renaissance" has raised the nation's largest corporate citadel, segregated from the poor neighborhoods around it by a monumental architectural glacis. In Hollywood, celebrity architect Frank Gehry, renowned for his "humanism", apotheosizes the siege look in a library designed to resemble a foreign-legion fort. In the Westlake district and the San Fernando Valley the Los Angeles Police barricade streets and seal off poor neighborhoods as part of their "war on drugs". In Watts, developer Alexander Haagen demonstrates his strategy for recolonizing inner-city retail markets: a panoptican shopping mall surrounded by staked metal fences and a substation of the LAPD in a central surveillance tower. Finally on the horizon of the next millennium, an ex-chief of police crusades for an anti-crime "giant eye" – a geo-synchronous law enforcement satellite – while other cops discreetly tend versions of "Garden Plot", a hoary but still viable 1960s plan for a law-and-order armageddon.

Welcome to post-liberal Los Angeles, where the defense of luxury lifestyles is translated into a proliferation of new repressions in space and movement, undergirded by the ubiquitous "armed response". This obsession with physical security systems, and, collaterally, with the architectural policing of social boundaries, has become a zeitgeist of urban restructuring, a master narrative in the emerging built environment of the 1990s. Yet contemporary urban theory, whether debating the role of electronic technologies in precipitating "postmodern space", or discussing the dispersion of urban functions across poly-centered metropolitan "galaxies", has been strangely silent about the militarization of city life so grimly visible at the street level. Hollywood's pop apocalypses and pulp science fiction have been more realistic, and politically perceptive, in representing the programmed hardening of the urban surface in the wake of the social polarizations of the Reagan era. Images of carceral inner cities (*Escape from New York, Running Man*), high-tech police death squads (*Blade Runner*), sentient buildings (*Die Hard*), urban bantustans (*They Live!*), Vietnam-like street wars (*Colors*), and so on, only extrapolate from actually existing trends.

Such dystopian visions grasp the extent to which today's pharaonic scales of residential and commercial security supplant residual hopes for urban reform and social integration. The dire predictions of Richard Nixon's 1969 National Commission on the Causes and Prevention of Violence have been tragically fulfilled: we live in "fortress cities" brutally divided between "fortified cells" of affluent society and "places of terror" where the police battle the criminalized poor. The "Second Civil War" that began in the long hot summers of the 1960s has been institutionalized into the very structure of urban space. The old liberal paradigm of social control, attempting to balance repression with reform, has long been superseded by a rhetoric of social warfare that calculates the interests of the urban poor and the middle classes as a zero-sum game. In cities like Los Angeles, on the bad edge of postmodernity, one observes an unprecedented tendency to merge urban design, architecture and the police apparatus into a single, comprehensive security effort.

This epochal coalescence has far-reaching consequences for the social relations of the built environment. In the first place, the market provision of "security" generates its own paranoid demand. "Security" becomes a positional good defined by income access to private "protective services" and membership in some hardened residential enclave or restricted suburb. As a prestige symbol – and sometimes as the decisive borderline between the merely well-off and the "truly rich" – "security" has less to do with personal safety than with the degree of personal insulation, in residential, work, consumption and travel environments, from "unsavory" groups and individuals, even crowds in general.

Secondly, as William Whyte has observed of social intercourse in New York, "fear proves itself". The social perception of threat becomes a function of the security mobilization itself, not crime rates. Where there is an actual rising arc of street violence, as in Southcentral Los Angeles or Downtown Washington D.C., most of the carnage is self-contained within ethnic or class boundaries. Yet white middle-class imagination, absent from any firsthand knowledge of inner-city conditions, magnifies the perceived threat through a demonological lens. Surveys show that Milwaukee suburbanites are just as worried about violent crime as inner-city Washingtonians, despite a twenty-fold difference in relative levels of mayhem. The media, whose function in this arena is to bury and obscure the daily economic violence of the city, ceaselessly throw up spectres of criminal underclasses and psychotic stalkers. Sensationalized accounts of killer youth gangs high on crack and shrilly racist evocations of marauding Willie Hortons foment the moral panics that reinforce and justify urban apartheid.

Moreover, the neo-military syntax of contemporary architecture insinuates violence and conjures imaginary dangers. In many instances the semiotics of so-called "defensible space" are just about as subtle as a swaggering white cop. Today's upscale, pseudo-public spaces – sumptuary malls, office centers, culture acropolises, and so on – are full of invisible signs warning off the underclass "Other". Although architectural critics are usually oblivious to how the built environment contributes to segregation, pariah groups – whether poor Latino families, young Black men, or elderly homeless white females – read the meaning immediately. . . .

The universal and ineluctable consequence of this crusade to secure the city is the destruction of accessible public space. The contemporary opprobrium attached to the term "street person" is in itself a harrowing index of the devaluation of public spaces. To reduce contact with untouchables, urban redevelopment has converted once vital pedestrian streets into traffic sewers and transformed public parks into temporary receptacles for the homeless and wretched. The American city, as many critics have recognized, is being systematically turned inside out – or, rather, outside in. The valorized spaces of the new megastructures and super-malls are concentrated in the center, street frontage is denuded, public activity is sorted into strictly functional compartments, and circulation is internalized in corridors under the gaze of private police.

The privatization of the architectural public realm, moreover, is shadowed by parallel restructurings of electronic space, as heavily policed, pay-access "information orders", elite data-bases and subscription cable services appropriate parts of the invisible agora. Both processes, of course, mirror the deregulation of the economy and the recession of non-market entitlements. The decline of urban liberalism has been accompanied by the death of what might be called the "Olmstedian vision" of public space. Frederick Law Olmsted, it will be recalled, was North America's Haussmann, as well as the Father of Central Park. In the wake of Manhattan's "Commune" of 1863, the great Draft Riot, he conceived public landscapes and parks as social safety-valves, *mixing* classes and ethnicities in common (bourgeois) recreations and enjoyments. As Manfredo Tafuri has shown in his well-known study of Rockefeller Center, the same principle animated the construction of the canonical urban spaces of the La Guardia–Roosevelt era.

This reformist vision of public space – as the emollient of class struggle, if not the bedrock of the American *polis* – is now as obsolete as Keynesian nostrums of full employment. In regard to the "mixing" of classes, contemporary urban America is more like Victorian England than Walt Whitman's or La Guardia's New York. In Los Angeles, once-upon-a-time a demi-paradise of free beaches, luxurious parks, and "cruising strips", genuinely democratic space is all but extinct. The Oz-like archipelago of Westside pleasure domes – a continuum of tony malls, arts centers and

gourmet strips – is reciprocally dependent upon the social imprisonment
of the third-world service proletariat who live in increasingly repressive
ghettoes and barrios. In a city of several million yearning immigrants,
public amenities are radically shrinking, parks are becoming derelict and
beaches more segregated, libraries and playgrounds are closing, youth con-
gregations of ordinary kinds are banned, and the streets are becoming
more desolate and dangerous.

Unsurprisingly, as in other American cities, municipal policy has
taken its lead from the security offensive and the middle-class demand
for increased spatial and social insulation. De facto disinvestment in
traditional public space and recreation has supported the shift of fiscal
resources to corporate-defined redevelopment priorities. A pliant city
government – in this case ironically professing to represent a bi-racial coalition of liberal whites and Blacks – has collaborated in the massive privatization of public space and the subsidization of new, racist enclaves
(benignly described as "urban villages"). Yet most current, giddy discussions of the "postmodern" scene in Los Angeles neglect entirely these
overbearing aspects of counter-urbanization and counter-insurgency. A
triumphal gloss – "urban renaissance", "city of the future", and so on – is
laid over the brutalization of inner-city neighborhoods and the increasing South Africanization of its spatial relations. Even as the walls
have come down in Eastern Europe, they are being erected all over
Los Angeles.

The observations that follow take as their thesis the existence of this
new class war (sometimes a continuation of the race war of the 1960s) at
the level of the built environment. . . .

. . . Redeveloped with public tax increments under the aegis of the powerful and largely unaccountable Community Redevelopment Agency, [Los
Angeles's] Downtown project is one of the largest postwar urban designs
in North America. Site assemblage and clearing on a vast scale, with
little mobilized opposition, have resurrected land values, upon which big
developers and off-shore capital (increasingly Japanese) have planted a
series of billion-dollar, block-square megastructures: Crocker Center, the
Bonaventure Hotel and Shopping Mall, the World Trade Center, the
Broadway Plaza, Arco Center, CitiCorp Plaza, California Plaza, and so
on. With historical landscapes erased, with megastructures and superblocks
as primary components, and with an increasingly dense and self-contained
circulation system, the new financial district is best conceived as a single,
demonically self-referential hyperstructure, a Miesian skyscape raised to
dementia.

Like similar megalomaniac complexes, tethered to fragmented and
desolated Downtowns (for instance, the Renaissance Center in Detroit, the
Peachtree and Omni Centers in Atlanta, and so on), Bunker Hill and the
Figueroa corridor have provoked a storm of liberal objections against their

abuse of scale and composition, their denigration of street landscape, and their confiscation of so much of the vital life activity of the center, now sequestered within subterranean concourses or privatized malls. Sam Hall Kaplan, the crusty urban critic of the *Times*, has been indefatigable in denouncing the anti-pedestrian bias of the new corporate citadel, with its fascist obliteration of street frontage. In his view the superimposition of "hermetically sealed fortresses" and air-dropped "pieces of suburbia" has "dammed the rivers of life" Downtown.

Yet Kaplan's vigorous defense of pedestrian democracy remains grounded in hackneyed liberal complaints about "bland design" and "elitist planning practices". Like most architectural critics, he rails against the oversights of urban design without recognizing the dimension of foresight, of explicit repressive intention, which has its roots in Los Angeles's ancient history of class and race warfare. Indeed, when Downtown's new "Gold Coast" is viewed en bloc from the standpoint of its interactions with other social areas and landscapes in the central city, the "fortress effect" emerges, not as an inadvertent failure of design, but as deliberate sociospatial strategy.

The goals of this strategy may be summarized as a double repression: to raze all association with Downtown's past and to prevent any articulation with the non-Anglo urbanity of its future. Everywhere on the perimeter of redevelopment this strategy takes the form of a brutal architectural edge or glacis that defines the new Downtown as a citadel vis-à-vis the rest of the central city. Los Angeles is unusual amongst major urban renewal centers in preserving, however negligently, most of its circa 1900–30 Beaux Arts commercial core. At immense public cost, the corporate headquarters and financial district was shifted from the old Broadway-Spring corridor six blocks west to the greenfield site created by destroying the Bunker Hill residential neigborhood. To emphasize the "security" of the new Downtown, virtually all the traditional pedestrian links to the old center, including the famous Angels' Flight funicular railroad, were removed.

The logic of this entire operation is revealing. In other cities developers might have attempted to articulate the new skyscape and the old, exploiting the latter's extraordinary inventory of theaters and historic buildings to create a gentrified history – a gaslight district, Faneuil Market or Ghirardelli Square – as a support to middle-class residential colonization. But Los Angeles's redevelopers viewed property values in the old Broadway core as irreversibly eroded by the area's very centrality to public transport, and especially by its heavy use by Black and Mexican poor. In the wake of the Watts Rebellion, and the perceived Black threat to crucial nodes of white power . . . resegregated spatial security became the paramount concern. The Los Angeles Police Department abetted the flight of business from Broadway to the fortified redoubts of Bunker Hill by spreading scare literature typifying Black teenagers as dangerous gang members.

As a result, redevelopment massively reproduced spatial apartheid. The moat of the Harbor Freeway and the regraded palisades of Bunker Hill cut off the new financial core from the poor immigrant neighborhoods that surround it on every side. Along the base of California Plaza, Hill Street became a local Berlin Wall separating the publicly subsidized luxury of Bunker Hill from the lifeworld of Broadway, now reclaimed by Latino immigrants as their primary shopping and entertainment street. Because politically connected speculators are now redeveloping the northern end of the Broadway corridor . . . the CRA is promising to restore pedestrian linkages to the Hill in the 1990s, including the Angels' Flight incline railroad. This, of course, only dramatizes the current bias against accessibility – that is to say, against *any* spatial interaction between old and new, poor and rich, except in the framework of gentrification or recolonization. . . .

Photographs of the old Downtown in its prime show mixed crowds of Anglo, Black and Latino pedestrians of different ages and classes. The contemporary Downtown "renaissance" is designed to make such heterogeneity virtually impossible. It is intended not just to "kill the street" as Kaplan fears, but to "kill the crowd", to eliminate that democratic admixture on the pavements and in the parks that Olmsted believed was America's antidote to European class polarizations. The Downtown hyperstructure – like some Buckminster Fuller post-Holocaust fantasy – is programmed to ensure a seamless continuum of middle-class work, consumption and recreation, without unwonted exposure to Downtown's working-class street environments. Indeed the totalitarian semiotics of ramparts and battlements, reflective glass and elevated pedways, rebukes any affinity or sympathy between different architectural or human orders. . . .

. . . This conscious "hardening" of the city surface against the poor is especially brazen in the Manichaean treatment of Downtown microcosms. . . . As part of the city's policy of subsidizing white-collar residential colonization in Downtown, it has spent, or plans to spend, tens of millions of dollars of diverted tax revenue on enticing, "soft" environments in these areas. Planners envision an opulent complex of squares, fountains, world-class public art, exotic shubbery, and avant-garde street furniture along a Hope Street pedestrian corridor. In the propaganda of official boosters, nothing is taken as a better index of Downtown's "liveability" than the idyll of office workers and upscale tourists lounging or napping in the terraced gardens of California Plaza, the "Spanish Steps" or Grand Hope Park.

In stark contrast, a few blocks away, the city is engaged in a merciless struggle to make public facilities and spaces as "unliveable" as possible for the homeless and the poor. The persistence of thousands of street people on the fringes of Bunker Hill and the Civic Center sours the image of designer Downtown living and betrays the laboriously constructed illusion of a Downtown "renaissance". City Hall then retaliates with its own variant of low-intensity warfare.

Although city leaders periodically essay schemes for removing indigents *en masse* . . . such "final solutions" have been blocked by councilmembers fearful of the displacement of the homeless into their districts. Instead the city, self-consciously adopting the idiom of urban cold war, promotes the "containment" (official term) of the homeless in Skid Row along Fifth Street east of the Broadway, systematically transforming the neighborhood into an outdoor poorhouse. But this containment strategy breeds its own vicious circle of contradiction. By condensing the mass of the desperate and helpless together in such a small space, and denying adequate housing, official policy has transformed Skid Row into probably the most dangerous ten square blocks in the world – ruled by a grisly succession of "Slashers", "Night Stalkers" and more ordinary predators. Every night on Skid Row is Friday the 13th, and, unsurprisingly, many of the homeless seek to escape the "Nickle" during the night at all costs, searching safer niches in other parts of Downtown. The city in turn tightens the noose with increased police harassment and ingenious design deterrents.

One of the most common, but mind-numbing, of these deterrents is the Rapid Transit District's new barrelshaped bus bench that offers a minimal surface for uncomfortable sitting, while making sleeping utterly impossible. Such "bumproof" benches are being widely introduced on the periphery of Skid Row. Another invention . . . is the aggressive deployment of outdoor sprinklers. Several years ago the city opened a "Skid Row Park" along lower Fifth Street, on a corner of Hell. To ensure that the park was not used for sleeping – that is to say, to guarantee that it was mainly utilized for drug dealing and prostitution – the city installed an elaborate overhead sprinkler system programmed to drench unsuspecting sleepers at random times during the night. The system was immediately copied by some local businessmen in order to drive the homeless away from adjacent public sidewalks. Meanwhile restaurants and markets have responded to the homeless by building ornate enclosures to protect their refuse. Although no one in Los Angeles has yet proposed adding cyanide to the garbage, as happened in Phoenix a few years back, one popular seafood restaurant has spent $12,000 to build the ultimate bag-lady-proof trash cage: made of three-quarter inch steel rod with alloy locks and vicious outturned spikes to safeguard priceless moldering fishheads and stale french fries.

Public toilets, however, are the real Eastern Front of the Downtown war on the poor. Los Angeles, as a matter of deliberate policy, has fewer available public lavatories than any major North American city. On the advice of the LAPD . . . the Community Redevelopment Agency bulldozed the remaining public toilet in Skid Row. . . .

Where the itineraries of Downtown powerbrokers unavoidably inter-
sect with the habitats of the homeless or the working poor, as in the
previously mentioned zone of gentrification along the northern Broadway
corridor, extraordinary design precautions are being taken to ensure the
physical separation of the different humanities. For instance, the CRA
brought in the Los Angeles Police to design "24-hour, state-of-the-art
security" for the two new parking structures that serve the Los Angeles
Times and Ronald Reagan State Office buildings. In contrast to the mean
streets outside, the parking structures contain beautifully landscaped lawns
or "microparks", and in one case, a food court and a historical exhibit.
Moreover, both structures are designed as "confidence-building" circulation
systems – miniature paradigms of privatization – which allow white-
collar workers to walk from car to office, or from car to boutique, with
minimum exposure to the public street. The Broadway Spring Center, in
particular, which links the Ronald Reagan Building to the proposed "Grand
Central Square" at Third and Broadway, has been warmly praised by architectural critics for adding greenery and art . . . to parking. It also adds a
huge dose of menace – armed guards, locked gates, and security cameras
– to scare away the homeless and poor.

The cold war on the streets of Downtown is ever escalating. . . . As the
head of the city planning commission explained the official line to
incredulous reporters, it is not against the law to sleep on the street per
se, "only to erect any sort of protective shelter". To enforce this prescription
against "cardboard condos", the LAPD periodically sweep the Nickle,
confiscating shelters and other possessions, and arresting resisters. Such
cynical repression has turned the majority of the homeless into urban
bedouins. They are visible all over Downtown, pushing a few pathetic
possessions in purloined shopping carts, always fugitive and in motion,
pressed between the official policy of containment and the increasing sadism
of Downtown streets.

part 11

Neoliberal Globalization: Concentration, Proletarianization, and Dislocation in the New Transnational Order

Arguably, globalization has recently replaced postmoderism as the "big discourse" or most widely discussed topic in interdisciplinary social theory. In the 1980s, concern about globalization arose in debates over American deindustrialization and capital mobility, emergence of global markets, growth of foreign direct investment, and the collapse of communism. In the 1990s, globalization has been mentioned frequently in policy debates, a spate of new books, and in TV commercials about the new information and communications technologies and worldwide investment opportunities. Global consumer goods, increased immigration, and exotic diseases (e.g., West Nile fever and foot-and-mouth disease) have also stirred discussion of the process. At the millennium, US free-market and free-trade policy – the "Washington Consensus" – ruled among most of the world's top economic and political elites and at the World Trade Organization (WTO), International Monetary Fund (IMF), and other major United States-dominated transnational, economic governance organs. This part focuses on neoliberal globalization and its problems.

Neoliberal globalization has been marked by the freer flow of people, as well as of capital and commodities, across national borders. In the first selection, Saskia Sassen holds that recent US immigrants come increasingly from the Caribbean Basin and Asia rather than from Europe, that female immigration has grown, and that the traditional "push" factors of extreme poverty and overpopulation do not explain adequately the immigration from these newly industrialized countries. She sees US foreign direct investment as animating the new immigration. Like Marx, she holds that the new proletariat is composed of former peasants, who work in labor-intensive operations, in unsafe workplaces, under unstable conditions of employment. Also like Marx, she explains that women are seen to be more obedient, disciplined workers than men, and to be more effective in tedious labor. She argues that women compose a dispropor- tionate part of the new proletariat. When these workers are employed in the many US affiliates, Sassen contends, they become Westernized and establish linkages that favor immigration to the United States. Com- pliant immigrant workers are in high demand in the United States' labor- intensive, "downgraded" manufacturing sector and expanded low-wage service sector (especially as informal workers and servants for the profes- sional middle classes). Post-Marxist critics often argue that the working class has disappeared, and that the focus should be shifted from labor and production to culture and consumption. By contrast, Sassen suggests that globalization is characterized by a major expansion of an increas- ingly feminized working class. Her scenario is consistent with Marx's points that increase of the proletariat is a fundamental basis of capitalist accumulation, that highly developed capital seeks surplus profits in less developed regions, that investment abroad creates a new transnational division of labor, and that vulnerable, easily exploited workers produce maximum profits. However, neoliberal globalization's hypermobility of capital and people recreate Third World niches in highly developed coun- tries' predominantly immigrant and minority low-wage workplaces and neighborhoods.

William Greider describes a 1993 fire in Bangkok, Thailand's Kader Industrial Toy Company, where 188 workers died, and hundreds more were injured. Almost entirely young women, the workers were recruited from the countryside, paid extremely low wages, lacked benefits, and suf- fered terrible working conditions. The company failed to abide by minimum building and safety standards, and workers were locked in, to prevent theft. Greider states that many trapped workers burned to death and that others jumped from the third and fourth floors. He explains that such awful conditions are common throughout the newly industrialized world and even in US sweatshops. Greider holds that the Kader case bears a strik- ing similarity to the 1911 Triangle Shirtwaist Company fire in New York, in which mostly impoverished, female, immigrant workers from Europe were locked in an unsafe workplace and died from burns or leaps from higher floors. By contrast to the Triangle case, the Kader fire generated no reform or even shame from its multinational owners or American retailers. Kader toys were, by law, required to meet strict safety regulations to protect American children, but Thai producers and US retailers agree that similar protections for workers would violate free trade! Greider holds that neoliberal deregulation returns low-wage workplaces to grisly, nineteenth-century conditions, eliminating, in the name of free markets, the most basic worker protections to maximize corporate profits. Marx described similarly harsh, degrading work, but he saw counterforces on the rise – labor movements and regulatory states. Greider implies that neoliberal globalization paralyzes these forces and shifts nearly all power to capital.

In the last selection, John Gray holds that the hegemonic "Washington Consensus" calls for a single, worldwide, free market to replace regional capitalism's "social markets." He contests the idea that unregulated transnational corporations and global commerce can be self-stabilizing and avert crises. Holding that genuine "free markets" are impossible, he asserts that neoliberal deregulation empowers corporate elites, causes sociocultural dislocations, increases social inequality, and forges new, unstable forms of capitalism. He argues that the consequent harsh effects are visible in the United States, which has high levels of crime and imprisonment, weak families, employment problems, and sharp inequalities. Gray fears that efforts to impose neoliberalism in other parts of the world, where it has even less of a cultural and historical basis, will produce severe crises. He argues that neoliberalism is inherently contradictory; efforts to create free markets undermine the very conditions that insure existing markets' stability. In his view, the global free market is itself an American idea and a political project of the US state and its international economic governance arms (e.g., the WTO and IMF). Gray argues that the neoliberal vision of unified global capitalism is as misguided as Marxist one-world communism (he does not distinguish Stalinism from Marx's original vision of communism, varying with local and regional conditions). Although conflicting in many ways, Gray and Marx converge on the point that economic affairs must be socioculturally and politically regulated, and that unrestricted capitalism is a road to disaster.

Reminiscent of 1920's proto-fascism, today's European "New Right" and US "paleoconservatives" attack the idea of a global free market, calling for populist resistance to neoliberal globalization and its "New World Order" and for cessation of the free flow of unwanted immigrants, media images, and consumer goods. They point toward monocultural racial or ethnic states that would end liberal democracy. Gray does not address these tendencies directly, but he argues that unrestricted capitalism generates crises, which open the way for such populist reaction. Marx's portrayal of Louis Napoleon's imperial rule anticipated such populist currents and the dictatorship that could follow.

chapter 46

America's Immigration "Problem"

Saskia Sassen

Beginning in the late 1960s, immigration patterns to the United States began to change in several different important ways. First, there was a significant rise in overall annual entry levels. . . . At the same time, there was a dramatic change in the regional composition of migration flows. As recently as 1960, more than two-thirds of all immigrants entering the United States came from Europe. By 1985, Europe's share of annual entries had shrunk to one-ninth. . . . Today, the vast majority of immigrants to the United States originate in Asia, Latin America, and the Caribbean. . . .

Another feature of the new immigration is the growing prominence of female immigrants. . . .

Moreover, the new immigrants tend to cluster in the largest metropolitan areas, such as New York, Los Angeles, San Francisco, Chicago, Houston, and Miami. . . .

The main features of the new immigration – in particular, the growing prominence of certain Asian and Caribbean Basin countries as sources of immigrants and the rapid rise in the proportion of female immigrants – cannot be adequately explained under the prevailing assumptions of why migration occurs. Even a cursory review of emigration patterns reveals that there is no systematic relationship between emigration and what conventional wisdom holds to be the principal causes of emigration – namely overpopulation, poverty, and economic stagnation. . . .

This is not to say that overpopulation, poverty, and economic stagnation do not create pressures for migration; by their very logic, they do. But it is clear that the common identification of emigration with these conditions is overly simplistic. The evidence suggests that these conditions are not sufficient by themselves to produce large new migration flows. Other intervening factors need to be taken into account – factors that work to transform these conditions into a migration-inducing situation. . . .

. . . [I]n most of the countries experiencing large migration flows to the United States, it is possible to identify a set of conditions and linkages with the United States that, together with overpopulation, poverty, or unemployment, induce emigration. While the nature and extent of these linkages vary from country to country, a common pattern of expanding U.S. political and economic involvement with emigrant-sending countries emerges. . . .

A key element in this pattern is the presence of direct foreign investment in production for export. U.S. investment in the less developed countries quintupled between 1965 and 1980, with much of it going to a few key countries in the Caribbean Basin and Southeast Asia and a large proportion channeled into the development of consumer goods such as toys, apparel, textiles, and footwear. Industries producing for export are generally highly labor intensive (this is, of course, a primary rationale for locating factories in low-wage countries). The labor-intensive nature of these industries is one reason why several of the Asian and Caribbean Basin countries that have been major recipients of direct foreign investment have experienced rapid employment growth, especially in the manufacturing sector. . . .

Perhaps the single most important effect of foreign investment in export production is the uprooting of people from traditional modes of existence. It has long been recognized that the development of commercial agriculture tends to displace subsistence farmers, creating a supply of rural wage laborers and giving rise to mass migrations to cities. In recent years, the large-scale development of export-oriented manufacturing in Southeast Asia and the Caribbean Basin has come to have a similar effect (though through different mechanisms); it has uprooted people and created an urban reserve of wage laborers. In both export agriculture and export manufacturing, the disruption of traditional work structures as a result of the introduction of modern modes of production has played a key role in transforming people into migrant workers and, potentially, into emigrants.

In export manufacturing, the catalyst for the disruption of traditional work structures is the massive recruitment of young women into jobs in the new industrial zones. Most of the manufacturing in these zones is of the sort that employs a high proportion of female workers in industrialized countries as well: electronics assembly and the manufacture of textiles, apparel, and toys. The exodus of young women to the industrial zones typically begins when factory representatives recruit young women directly in their villages and rural schools; eventually, the establishment of continuous migration streams reduces or eliminates the need for direct recruitment. The most obvious reason for the intensive recruitment of women is firms' desire to reduce costs, but there are other considerations as well: young women in patriarchal societies are seen by foreign employers as obedient and disciplined workers, willing to do tedious, high-precision work and to submit themselves to work conditions that would not be tolerated in the highly developed countries. . . .

This mobilization of large numbers of women into waged labor has a highly disruptive effect on traditional, often unwaged, work patterns. In rural areas, women fulfill important functions in the production of goods for family consumption or for sale in local markets. Village economies and rural households depend on a variety of economic activities traditionally performed by women, ranging from food preparation to cloth weaving, basket making, and various other types of crafts. All these activities are undermined by the departure of young women for the new industrial zones.

One of the most serious – and ironic – consequences of the feminization of the new proletariat has been to increase the pool of wage laborers and thus contribute to male unemployment. Not only does competition from the increased supply of female workers make it more difficult for men to find work in the new industrial zones, but the massive departure of young women also reduces the opportunities for men to make a living in many rural areas, where women are key partners in the struggle for survival. Moreover, in some of the poorer and less developed regions and countries, export-led production employing primarily women has come to replace more diversified forms of economic growth that are oriented to the internal market and typically employ men as well. The impressive employment growth figures recorded by most of the main emigration countries in recent years have obscured the reality that export-led growth can lead to unemployment for some groups even as it creates jobs for others.

For men and women alike, the disruption of traditional ways of earning a living and the ascendance of export-led development make entry into wage labor increasingly a one-way proposition. With traditional economic opportunities in the rural areas shrinking, it becomes difficult, if not impossible, for workers to return home if they are laid off or unsuccessful in the job search. This is a particularly serious problem for female workers in the new industrial zones, who are often fired after just a short period of employment. After three to five years of assembling components under microscopes, these workers typically suffer from headaches and deteriorating eyesight. In order to keep wage levels low and replace workers whose health begins to fail, firms continually fire their older workers and hire younger, healthier, and more compliant cohorts of women. Moreover, in the late 1970s and early 1980s, many companies began to move their plants out of older export manufacturing zones, where tax concessions from local governments had been exhausted, and into "new" countries such as Sri Lanka and Indonesia, where labor was even cheaper. All these trends have contributed to the formation of a pool of potential migrants in developing countries such as the Philippines, South Korea, Taiwan, and the countries of the Caribbean Basin. People uprooted from their traditional ways of life, then left unemployed and unemployable as export firms hire younger workers or move production to other countries, may see few options but emigration, especially if an export-led growth strategy has weakened the country's domestic market oriented economy.

But the role played by foreign investment in allowing the emergence of large-scale emigration flows does not end there. In addition to eroding traditional work structures and creating a pool of potential migrants, foreign investment in production for export contributes to the development of economic, cultural, and ideological linkages with the industrialized countries. These linkages tend to promote the notion of emigration both directly and indirectly. Workers actually employed in the export sector – whether managers, secretaries, or assemblers – may experience the greatest degree of Westernization and be most closely connected to the country supplying the foreign capital; they are, after all, using their labor power to produce goods and services for people and firms in developed countries. For these workers, already oriented toward Western practices and modes of thought in their daily experience on the job, the distance between a job in the offshore plant or office and a comparable job in the industrialized country itself is subjectively reduced. It is not hard to see how such individuals might come to regard emigration as a serious option. . . .

In addition to the direct impact on workers in the export sector, the linkages created by direct foreign investment also have a generalized Westernizing effect on the less developed country and its people. This "ideological" effect in promoting emigration should not be underestimated; it makes emigration an option not just for those individuals employed in the export sector but for the wider population as well. Thus, a much larger number of people than those directly or indirectly employed by foreign-owned plants and offices become candidates for emigration. In fact, the workers actually employed in foreign plants, offices, and plantations may not be the ones most likely to make use of these linkages and emigrate. . . .

It is in this context that the 1965 liberalization of U.S. immigration law and the unfading image of the United States as a land of opportunity acquire significance. The conviction among prospective emigrants that the United States offers unlimited opportunities and plentiful employment prospects, at least relative to other countries, has had the effect of making "emigration" almost identical with "emigration to the United States." This has tended to create a self-reinforcing migration pattern to the United States. As new bridges for migrants are created by foreign investment (in conjunction with political and military activity) and strengthened by the existence of economic opportunities in the United States, the resulting new migrations create additional bridges or linkages between the United States and migrant-sending countries. These, in turn, serve to facilitate future emigration to the United States, regardless of the origin of the foreign investment that created the conditions for emigration in the first place.

Although the United States remains the most important destination for migrants, the recent experience of Japan may offer a glimpse of what the future holds. As Japan has become the leading global economic power and the major foreign investor in Southeast Asia in the 1980s, a familiar combination of migration-facilitating processes appears to have been set in motion: the creation of linkages that eventually come to serve as bridges for potential emigrants, and the emergence of emigration to Japan as something that would-be emigrants see as a real option. . . .

. . . The liberalization of immigration legislation after 1965 and the prior existence of immigrant communities in major urban centers no doubt played some role in attracting immigrants from the older, primarily European, emigration countries. But the most important reason for the continuation of large inflows among the new migrant groups has been the rapid expansion of the supply of low-wage jobs in the United States and the casualization of the labor market associated with the new growth industries, particularly in the major cities. . . .

The increase in low-wage jobs in the United States is in part a result of the same international economic processes that have channeled investment and manufacturing jobs to low-wage countries. As industrial production has moved overseas, the traditional U.S. manufacturing base has eroded and been partly replaced by a downgraded manufacturing sector, which is characterized by a growing supply of poorly paid, semi-skilled or unskilled production jobs. At the same time, the rapid growth of the service sector has created vast numbers of low-wage jobs (in addition to the better-publicized increase in highly paid investment banking and management consulting jobs). Both of these new growth sectors are largely concentrated in major cities. Such cities have seen their economic importance further enhanced as they have become centers for the management and servicing of the global economy; as Detroit has lost jobs to overseas factories, New York and Los Angeles have gained jobs managing and servicing the global network of factories. . . .

These changes have been reflected in a decline in average wages and an increasing polarization of income distribution. Inflation-adjusted average weekly wages, which rose steadily during the postwar period and peaked in 1973, stagnated during the rest of the 1970s and fell into the 1980s. This decline was accompanied by an increase in the degree of inequality in the distribution of earnings, a trend that first emerged in the 1970s and accelerated in the 1980s. . . .

As mentioned earlier, one important generator of new low-wage jobs has been the downgraded manufacturing sector. This sector of the U.S. economy was created by the convergence of three trends: the social reorganization of the work process, notably the growing practice of sub-contracting out production and service work and the expansion of sweat-shops and industrial homework (all of which have the effect of isolating workers and preventing them from joining together to defend their interests); the technological transformation of the work process, which has downgraded the skill levels required for a variety of jobs by incorporating skills into machines and computers; and the rapid growth of high-technology industries that employ large numbers of low-wage production workers. Somewhat surprising, the downgrading of the skill and wage levels of industrial production jobs has taken place across a broad spectrum of industries – from the most backward to the most modern. Thus, while the garment and electronics industries would at first glance appear to have little in common, both have produced large numbers of dead-end, low-wage jobs requiring few skills. Both industries have made use of unconventional production processes such as sweatshops and industrial homework. Moreover, both have contributed to the disenfranchisement of workers, as is evident from the decline in union membership in areas of rapid high technology growth such as Los Angeles and Orange counties in California.

More important than the downgraded manufacturing sector as a source of new low-wage jobs, however, is the growth of the service sector. Unlike traditional manufacturing, which is characterized by a preponderance of middle-income jobs, the majority of service jobs tend to be either extremely well paid or very poorly paid, with relatively few jobs in the middle-income range. The growth industries of the 1980s – finance, insurance, real estate, retail trade, and business services – feature large proportions of low-wage jobs, weak unions, if any, and a high proportion of part time and female workers. . . .

In addition to employing low-wage workers directly, the expanded service sector also creates low-wage jobs indirectly, through the demand for workers to service the lifestyles and consumption requirements of the growing high-income professional and managerial class. The concentration of these high-income workers in major cities has facilitated rapid residential and commercial gentrification, which in turn has created a need for legions of low-wage service workers – residential building attendants, restaurant workers, preparers of specialty and gourmet foods, dog walkers, errand runners, apartment cleaners, childcare providers, and so on. The fact that many of these jobs are "off the books" has meant the rapid expansion of an informal economy in several major U.S. cities. For a variety of reasons, immigrants are more likely than U.S. citizens to gravitate toward these jobs: these jobs are poorly paid, offer little employment security, generally require few skills and little knowledge of English, and frequently involve undesirable evening or weekend shifts. In addition, the expansion of the informal economy facilitates the entry of undocumented immigrants into these jobs. . . .

... Significantly, even immigrants who are highly educated and skilled when they arrive in the United States tend to gravitate toward the low-wage sectors of the economy. The growing absorption of educated immigrants is partly linked to the growth of clerical and technical jobs in the service sector and the increased casualization of the labor market for these jobs.

Thus, while the redeployment of manufacturing to less developed countries has helped promote emigration from these countries, the concentration of servicing and management functions in major U.S. cities has created conditions for the absorption of the immigrant influx in New York, Los Angeles, Miami, Chicago and Houston. The same set of processes that has promoted emigration from several rapidly industrializing countries has simultaneously promoted immigration into the United States.

chapter 47

"These Dark Satanic Mills"

William Greider

REVOLUTIONS, BY THEIR NATURE, do not operate with the consent of the governed. A revolution, whether it is driven by political ideals or economic imperatives, is always the work of a radical few who seize power and impose new values and social arrangements on the many. While the process is inescapably anti-democratic, that complaint is beside the point. Human history does, on occasion, advance by such decisive breaks from the past – epic transformations that destroy the comfortable old identities and compel people, for better or worse, to adopt new understandings of themselves. . . .

. . . [T]he essential new fact of everyone's social existence . . . is indeed revolutionary: unless one intends to withdraw from modern industrial life, there is no place to hide from the others. Major portions of the earth, to be sure, remain on the periphery of the system, impoverished bystanders still waiting to be included in the action. But the patterns of global interconnectedness are already the dominant reality. Commerce has leapt beyond social consciousness and, in doing so, opened up challenging new vistas for the human potential. Most people, it seems fair to say, are not yet prepared to face the implications.

The economic transformations have engendered a profound identity crisis for peoples and societies everywhere, though the political confusion is as yet only dimly recognized. Traditional expressions of nationhood – amassing great armies, waving flags and deploying troops – are subverted by the borderless marketplace, yet these martial activities still absorb vast public resources. The capacity of nations to control their own affairs has been checked by finance and eroded by free-roving commerce, but politicians continue to pretend they are in charge. . . .

The social question – how does a society sustain equable relations among its own people? – has been brushed aside by the economic sphere. Social cohesion and consent, even the minimal standards of human decency, are irrelevant to free markets. The essential purpose of deregulation, after all, is to free the market functions of such noneconomic considerations. This arrangement is unnatural and incendiary and cannot endure, not without provoking explosive political reactions. Yet neither can people resign from their new circumstances in "one world." . . .

Assuming that the global economic system is not redirected toward a more moderate course, . . . weary political and class conflicts are sure to ripen, leading toward the same stalemate between markets and society in which fascism arose and flourished nearly a hundred years ago. In that sense, global capitalism is a reactionary system itself despite the dazzling technologies of the so-called information age, for it drives human societies backward to face social questions people thought they had resolved.

The social context of the global revolution is easier to grasp if one understands it as divided into two distinctly different realms that, distant as they are, interact intimately with one another. The realm of the poor, industrializing nation repeats capitalism's tumultuous past but in new territory – liberating millions with new incomes but also reviving the barbarisms and exploitation that industry employed in advanced nations when they were developed eighty or a hundred or even two hundred years before.

The process of industrialization has never been pretty in its primitive stages. Americans or Europeans who draw back in horror at the present brutalities in Asia or Latin America should understand that they are glimpsing repetitions of what happened in their own national histories, practices that were forbidden as inhumane in their own countries only after long political struggle. To make that historical point complicates the moral responses, but does not extinguish the social question.

The other realm, of course, is the wealthy nation where the established social structure is under assault, both from market forces depressing wages and employment and from the political initiatives to dismantle the welfare state. The governments' obligations to social equity were erected during the upheavals of the last century to ameliorate the harsher edges of unfettered capitalism; now they are in question again. The economic pressures to shrink or withdraw public benefits are relentless, yet no one has explained how wealthy industrial nations will maintain the social peace by deepening their inequalities. . . .

Two centuries ago, when the English industrial revolution dawned with its fantastic invention and productive energies, the prophetic poet William Blake drew back in moral revulsion. Amid the explosion of new wealth, human destruction was spread over England – peasant families displaced from their lands, paupers and poorhouses crowded into London slums, children sent to labor at the belching ironworks or textile looms. Blake delivered a thunderous rebuke to the pious Christians of the English aristocracy with these immortal lines:

> *And was Jerusalem builded here*
> *Among these dark Satanic mills?*

Blake's "dark Satanic mills" have returned now and are flourishing again, accompanied by the same question.

On May 10, 1993, the worst industrial fire in the history of capitalism occurred at a toy factory on the outskirts of Bangkok and was reported on page 25 of the *Washington Post*. The *Financial Times* of London, which styles itself as the daily newspaper of the global economy, ran a brief item on page 6. The *Wall Street Journal* followed a day late with an account on page 11. The *New York Times* also put the story inside, but printed a dramatic photo on its front page: rows of small shrouded bodies on bamboo pallets – dozens of them – lined along the damp pavement, while dazed rescue workers stood awkwardly among the corpses. In the background, one could see the collapsed, smoldering structure of a mammoth factory where the Kader Industrial Toy Company of Thailand had employed three thousand workers manufacturing stuffed toys and plastic dolls, playthings destined for American children.

The official count was 188 dead, 469 injured, but the actual toll was undoubtedly higher since the four-story buildings had collapsed swiftly in the intense heat and many bodies were incinerated. Some of the missing were never found; others fled home to their villages. All but fourteen of the dead were women, most of them young, some as young as thirteen years old. Hundreds of the workers had been trapped on upper floors of the burning building, forced to jump from third- or fourth-floor windows, since the main exit doors were kept locked by the managers, and the narrow stairways became clotted with trampled bodies or collapsed. . . .

As news accounts pointed out, the Kader fire surpassed what was previously the worst industrial fire in history – the Triangle Shirtwaist Company fire of 1911 – when 146 young immigrant women died in similar circumstances at a garment factory on the Lower East Side of Manhattan. The Triangle Shirtwaist fire became a pivotal event in American politics, a public scandal that provoked citizen reform movements and energized the labor organizing that built the International Ladies Garment Workers Union and other unions. The fire in Thailand did not produce meaningful political responses or even shame among consumers. The indifference of the leading newspapers merely reflected the tastes of their readers, who might be moved by human suffering in their own communities but were inured to news of recurring calamities in distant places. A fire in Bangkok was like a typhoon in Bangladesh, an earthquake in Turkey.

The Kader fire might have been more meaningful for Americans if they could have seen the thousands of soot-stained dolls that spilled from the wreckage, macabre litter scattered among the dead. Bugs Bunny, Bart Simpson and the Muppets. Big Bird and other *Sesame Street* dolls. Playskool "Water Pets." Santa Claus. What the initial news accounts did not mention was that Kader's Thai factory produced most of its toys for American companies – Toys "R" Us, Fisher-Price, Hasbro, Tyco, Arco, Kenner, Gund and J. C. Penney – as well as stuffed dolls, slippers and souvenirs for Europe.

Globalized civilization has uncovered an odd parochialism in the American character: Americans worried obsessively over the everyday safety of their children, and the U.S. government's regulators diligently policed the design of toys to avoid injury to young innocents. Yet neither citizens nor government took any interest in the brutal and dangerous conditions imposed on the people who manufactured those same toys, many of whom were mere adolescent children themselves. Indeed, the government position, both in Washington and Bangkok, assumed that there was no social obligation connecting consumers with workers, at least none that governments could enforce without disrupting free trade or invading the sovereignty of other nations.

The toy industry, not surprisingly, felt the same. Hasbro Industries, maker of Playskool, subsequently told the *Boston Globe* that it would no longer do business with Kader, but, in general, the U.S. companies shrugged off responsibility. Kader, a major toy manufacturer based in Hong Kong, "is extremely reputable, not sleaze bags," David Miller, president of the Toy Manufacturers of America, assured *USA Today*. "The responsibility for those factories," Miller told ABC News, "is in the hands of those who are there and managing the factory."

The grisly details of what occurred revealed the casual irresponsibility of both companies and governments. The Kader factory compound consisted of four interconnected, four-story industrial barns on a three-acre lot on Buddhamondhol VI Road in the Sampran district west of Bangkok. It was one among Thailand's thriving new industrial zones for garments, textiles, electronics and toys. More than 50,000 people, most of them migrants from the Thai countryside, worked in the district at 7,500 large and small firms. Thailand's economic boom was based on places such as this, and Bangkok was almost choking on its own fantastic growth, dizzily erecting luxury hotels and office towers.

The fire started late on a Monday afternoon on the ground floor in the first building and spread rapidly upward, jumping to two adjoining buildings, all three of which swiftly collapsed. Investigators noted afterwards that the structures had been cheaply built, without concrete reinforcement, so steel girders and stairways crumpled easily in the heat. Thai law required that in such a large factory, fire-escape stairways must be sixteen to thirty-three feet wide, but Kader's were a mere four and a half feet. Main doors were locked and many windows barred to prevent pilfering by the employees. Flammable raw materials – fabric, stuffing, animal fibers – were stacked everywhere, on walkways and next to electrical boxes. Neither safety drills nor fire alarms and sprinkler systems had been provided. . . .

Similar tragedies, large and small, were now commonplace across developing Asia and elsewhere. Two months after Kader, another fire at a Bangkok shirt factory killed ten women. Three months after Kader, a six-story hotel collapsed and killed 133 people, injuring 351. The embarrassed minister of industry ordered special inspections of 244 large factories in the Bangkok region and found that 60 percent of them had basic violations similar to Kader's. Thai industry was growing explosively – 12 to 15 percent a year – but workplace injuries and illnesses were growing even faster, from 37,000 victims in 1987 to more than 150,000 by 1992 and an estimated 200,000 by 1994.

In China, six months after Kader, eighty-four women died and dozens of others were severely burned at another toy factory fire in the burgeoning industrial zone at Shenzhen. At Dongguan, a Hong Kong-owned raincoat factory burned in 1991, killing more than eighty people (Kader Industries also had a factory at Dongguan where two fires have been reported since 1990). In late 1993, some sixty women died at the Taiwanese-owned Gaofu textile plant in Fuzhou Province, many of them smothered in their dormitory beds by toxic fumes from burning textiles. In 1994, a shoe factory fire killed ten persons at Jiangmen; a textile factory fire killed thirty-eight and injured 160 at the Qianshan industrial zone.

"Why must these tragedies repeat themselves again and again?" the *People's Daily* in Beijing asked. The official *Economic Daily* complained: "The way some of these foreign investors ignore international practice, ignore our own national rules, act completely lawlessly and immorally and lust after wealth is enough to make one's hair stand on end."

America was itself no longer insulated from such brutalities. When a chicken-processing factory at Hamlet, North Carolina, caught fire in 1991, the exit doors there were also locked and twenty-five people died. A garment factory discovered by labor investigators in El Monte, California, held seventy-two Thai immigrants in virtual peonage, working eighteen hours a day in "sub-human conditions." One could not lament the deaths, harsh working conditions, child labor and subminimum wages in Thailand or across Asia and Central America without also recognizing that similar conditions have reappeared in the United States for roughly the same reasons.

Sweatshops, mainly in the garment industry, scandalized Los Angeles, New York and Dallas. The grim, foul assembly lines of the poultry-processing industry were spread across the rural South; the *Wall Street Journal*'s Tony Horwitz won a Pulitzer Prize for his harrowing description of this low-wage work. "In general," the U.S. Government Accounting Office reported in 1994, "the description of today's sweatshops differs little from that at the turn of the century."

That was the real mystery: Why did global commerce, with all of its supposed modernity and wondrous technologies, restore the old barbarisms that had long ago been forbidden by law? If the information age has enabled multinational corporations to manage production and marketing spread across continents, why were their managers unable – or unwilling – to organize such mundane matters as fire prevention?

The short answer, of course, was profits, but the deeper answer was about power: Firms behaved this way because they could, because nobody would stop them. When law and social values retreated before the power of markets, then capitalism's natural drive to maximize returns had no internal governor to check its social behavior. When one enterprise took the low road to gain advantage, others would follow.

The toy fire in Bangkok provided a dramatic illustration for the much broader, less visible forms of human exploitation that were flourishing in the global system, including the widespread use of children in manufacturing, even forced labor camps in China or Burma. These matters were not a buried secret. Indeed, American television has aggressively exposed the "dark Satanic mills" with dramatic reports. ABC's *20/20* broadcast correspondent Lynn Sherr's devastating account of the Kader fire; CNN ran disturbing footage. Mike Wallace of CBS's *60 Minutes* exposed the prison labor exploited in China. NBC's *Dateline* did a piece on Wal-Mart's grim production in Bangladesh. CBS's *Street Stories* toured the shoe factories of Indonesia.

The baffling quality about modern communications was that its images could take us to people in remote corners of the world vividly and instantly, but these images have not as yet created genuine community with them. In terms of human consciousness, the "global village" was still only a picture on the TV screen.

Public opinion, moreover, absorbed contradictory messages about the global reality that were difficult to sort out. The opening stages of industrialization presented, as always, a great paradox: the process was profoundly liberating for millions, freeing them from material scarcity and limited life choices, while it also ensnared other millions in brutal new forms of domination. Both aspects were true, but there was no scale on which these opposing consequences could be easily balanced, since the good and ill effects were not usually apportioned among the same people. Some human beings were set free, while other lives were turned into cheap and expendable commodities.

Workers at Kader, for instance, earned about 100 baht a day for sewing and assembling dolls, the official minimum wage of $4, but the constant stream of new entrants meant that many at the factory actually worked for much less – only $2 or $3 a day – during a required "probationary" period of three to six months that was often extended much longer by the managers. Only one hundred of the three thousand workers at Kader were legally designated employees; the rest were "contract workers" without permanent rights and benefits, the same employment system now popularized in the United States.

"Lint, fabric, dust and animal hair filled the air on the production floor," the International Confederation of Free Trade Unions based in Brussels observed in its investigative report. "Noise, heat, congestion and fumes from various sources were reported by many. Dust control was non-existent; protective equipment inadequate. Inhaling the dust created respiratory problems and contact with it caused skin diseases." A factory clinic dispensed antihistamines or other drugs and referred the more serious symptoms to outside hospitals. Workers paid for the medication themselves and were reimbursed, up to $6, only if they had contributed 10 baht a month to the company's health fund.

A common response to such facts, even from many sensitive people, was: yes, that was terrible, but wouldn't those workers be even worse off if civil standards were imposed on their employers since they might lose their jobs as a result? This was the same economic rationale offered by American manufacturers a century before to explain why American children must work in the coal mines and textile mills. U.S. industry had survived somehow (and, in fact, flourished) when child labor and the other malpractices were eventually prohibited by social reforms. Furthermore, it was not coincidence that industry always assigned the harshest conditions and lowest pay to the weakest members of a society – women, children, uprooted migrants. Whether the factory was in Thailand or the United States or Mexico's *maquiladora* zone, people who were already quite powerless were less likely to resist, less able to demand decency from their employers.

Nor did these enterprises necessarily consist of small, struggling firms that could not afford to treat their workers better. Small sweatshops, it was true, were numerous in Thailand, and I saw some myself in a working-class neighborhood of Bangkok. Behind iron grillwork, children who looked to be ten to twelve years old squatted on the cement floors of the open-air shops, assembling suitcases, sewing raincoats, packing T-shirts. Across the street, a swarm of adolescents in blue smocks ate dinner at long tables outside a two-story building, then trooped back upstairs to the sewing machines.

Kader Holding Company, Ltd., however, was neither small nor struggling. It was a powerhouse of the global toy industry – headquartered in Hong Kong, incorporated in Bermuda, owned by a wealthy Hong Kong Chinese family named Ting that got its start after World War II making plastic goods and flashlights under procurement contracts from the U.S. military. Now Kader controlled a global maze of factories and interlocking subsidiaries in eight countries, from China and Thailand to Britain and the United States, where it owned Bachmann toys.

After the fire Thai union members, intellectuals and middle-class activists from social rights organizations (the groups known in developing countries as nongovernmental organizations, or NGOs) formed the

Committee to Support Kader Workers and began demanding justice from the employer. They sent a delegation to Hong Kong to confront Kader officials and investigate the complex corporate linkages of the enterprise. What they discovered was that Kader's partner in the Bangkok toy factory was actually a fabulously wealthy Thai family, the Chearavanonts, ethnic Chinese merchants who own the Charoen Pokphand Group, Thailand's own leading multinational corporation.

The CP Group owns farms, feed mills, real estate, air-conditioning and motorcycle factories, food-franchise chains – two hundred companies worldwide, several of them listed on the New York Stock Exchange. The patriarch and chairman, Dhanin Chearavanont, was said by *Fortune* magazine to be the seventy-fifth richest man in the world, with personal assets of $2.6 billion. . . . Like the other emerging "Chinese multinationals," the Pokphand Group operates through the informal networks of kinfolk and ethnic contacts spread around the world by the Chinese diaspora, while it also participates in the more rigorous accounting systems of Western economies.

In the mother country, China, the conglomerate nurtured political-business alliances and has become the largest outside investor in new factories and joint ventures. In the United States, it maintained superb political connections. The Chearavanonts co-sponsored a much-heralded visit to Bangkok by ex-president George Bush, who delivered a speech before Thai business leaders in early 1994, eight months after the Kader fire. The price tag for Bush's appearance, according to the Bangkok press, was $400,000 (equivalent to one month's payroll for all three thousand workers at Kader). The day after Bush's appearance, the Chearavanonts hosted a banquet for a leading entrepreneur from China – Deng Xiaoping's daughter.

The Pokphand Group at first denied any connection to the Kader fire, but reformers and local reporters dug out the facts of the family's involvement. Dhanin Chearavanont himself owned 11 percent of Honbo Investment Company and with relatives and corporate directors held majority control. Honbo, in turn, owned half of KCP Toys (KCP stood for Kader Charoen Pokphand), which, in turn, owned 80 percent of Kader Industrial (Thailand) Company. Armed with these facts, three hundred workers from the destroyed factory marched on the Pokphand Group's corporate tower on Silom Road, where they staged a gentle sit-down demonstration in the lobby, demanding just compensation for the victims.

In the context of Thai society and politics, the workers' demonstration against Pokphand was itself extraordinary, like peasants confronting the nobility. Under continuing pressures from the support group, the company agreed to pay much larger compensation for victims and their families – $12,000 for each death, a trivial amount in American terms but more than double the Thai standard. "When we worked on Kader," said

Professor Voravidh Charoenloet, an economist at Chulalongkorn University, "the government and local entrepreneurs and factory owners didn't want us to challenge these people; even the police tried to obstruct us from making an issue. We were accused of trying to destroy the country's reputation."

The settlement, in fact, required the Thai activists to halt their agitation and fall silent. "Once the extra compensation was paid," Voravidh explained, "we were forced to stop. One of the demands by the government was that everything should stop. Our organization had to accept it. We wanted to link with the international organizations and have a great boycott, but we had to cease."

The global boycott, he assumed, was going forward anyway because he knew that international labor groups like the ICFTU and the AFL-CIO had investigated the Kader fire and issued stinging denunciations. I told him that aside from organized labor, the rest of the world remained indifferent. There was no boycott of Kader toys in America. The professor slumped in his chair and was silent, a twisted expression on his face.

"I feel very bad," Voravidh said at last. "Maybe we should not have accepted it. But when we came away, we felt that was what we could accomplish. The people wanted more. There must be something more."

In the larger context, this tragedy was not explained by the arrogant power of one wealthy family or the elusive complexities of interlocking corporations. The Kader fire was ordained and organized by the free market itself. The toy industry – much like textiles and garments, shoes, electronics assembly and other low-wage sectors – existed (and thrived) by exploiting a crude ladder of desperate competition among the poorest nations. Its factories regularly hopped to new locations where wages were even lower, where the governments would be even more tolerant of abusive practices. The contract work assigned to foreign firms, including thousands of small sweatshops, fitted neatly into the systems of far-flung production of major brand names and distanced the capital owners from personal responsibility. The "virtual corporation" celebrated by some business futurists already existed in these sectors and, indeed, was now being emulated in some ways by advanced manufacturing – cars, aircraft, computers.

Over the last generation, toy manufacturers and others have moved around the Asian rim in search of the bottom-rung conditions: from Hong Kong, Korea and Taiwan to Thailand and Indonesia, from there to China, Vietnam and Bangladesh, perhaps on next to Burma, Nepal or Cambodia. Since the world had a nearly inexhaustible supply of poor people and supplicant governments, the market would keep driving in search of lower rungs; no one could say where the bottom was located. Industrial conditions were not getting better, as conventional theory assured the innocent consumers, but in many sectors were getting much worse. In

America, the U.S. diplomatic opening to Vietnam was celebrated as progressive politics. In Southeast Asia, it merely opened another trapdoor beneath wages and working conditions.

A country like Thailand was caught in the middle: if it conscientiously tried to improve, it would pay a huge price. When Thai unions lobbied to win improvements in minimum-wage standards, textile plants began leaving for Vietnam and elsewhere or even importing cheaper "guest workers" from Burma. When China opened its fast-growing industrial zones in Shenzhen, Dongguan and other locations, the new competition had direct consequences on the factory floors of Bangkok.

Kader, according to the ICFTU, opened two new factories in Shekou and Dongguan where young people were working fourteen-hour days, seven days a week, to fill the U.S. Christmas orders for Mickey Mouse and other American dolls. Why should a company worry about sprinkler systems or fire escapes for a dusty factory in Bangkok when it could hire brand-new workers in China for only $20 a month, one fifth of the labor cost in Thailand?

The ICFTU report described the market forces: "The lower cost of production of toys in China changes the investment climate for countries like Thailand. Thailand competes with China to attract investment capital for local toy production. With this development, Thailand has become sadly lax in enforcing its own legislation. It turns a blind eye to health violations, thus allowing factory owners to ignore safety standards. Since China entered the picture, accidents in Thailand have nearly tripled."

The Thai minister of industry, Sanan Kachornprasart, described the market reality more succinctly: "If we punish them, who will want to invest here?" Thai authorities subsequently filed charges against three Kader factory managers, but none against the company itself nor, of course, the Chearavanont family. . . .

The fire in Bangkok reflected the amorality of the marketplace when it has been freed of social obligations. But the tragedy also mocked the moral claims of three great religions, whose adherents were all implicated. . . . Their shared complicity was another of the strange convergences made possible by global commerce. . . .

chapter 48

From the Great Transformation to the Global Free Market

John Gray

Mid-nineteenth century England was the subject of a far-reaching experiment in social engineering. Its objective was to free economic life from social and political control and it did so by constructing a new institution, the free market, and by breaking up the more socially rooted markets that had existed in England for centuries. The free market created a new type of economy in which prices of all goods, including labour, changed without regard to their effects on society. In the past, economic life had been constrained by the need to maintain social cohesion. It was conducted in social markets – markets that were embedded in society and subject to many kinds of regulation and restraint. The goal of the experiment that was attempted in mid-Victorian England was to demolish these social markets, and replace them by deregulated markets that operated independently of social needs. The rupture in England's economic life produced by the creation of the free market has been called the Great Transformation.

The achievement of a similar transformation is the overriding objective today of transnational organizations such as the World Trade Organisation, the International Monetary Fund and the Organisation for Economic Cooperation and Development. In advancing this revolutionary project they are following the lead of the world's last great Enlightenment regime, the United States. . . .

. . . According to the "Washington consensus", "democratic capitalism" will soon be accepted throughout the world. A global free market will become a reality. The manifold economic cultures and systems that the world has always contained will be redundant. They will be merged into a single universal free market.

Transnational organizations animated by this philosophy have sought to impose free markets onto the economic life of societies throughout the world. They have implemented programmes of policies whose ultimate objective is to incorporate the world's diverse economies into a single global free market. This is a Utopia that can never be realized; its pursuit has already produced social dislocation and economic and political instability on a large scale.

In the United States free markets have contributed to social breakdown on a scale unknown in any other developed country. Families are weaker in America than in any other country. At the same time, social order has been propped up by a policy of mass incarceration. No other advanced industrial country, aside from post-communist Russia, uses imprisonment as a means of social control on the scale of the United States. Free markets, the desolation of families and communities and the use of the sanctions of criminal law as a last recourse against social collapse go in tandem.

Free markets have also weakened or destroyed other institutions on which social cohesion depends in the US. They have generated a long economic boom from which the majority of Americans has hardly benefited. Levels of inequality in the United States resemble those of Latin American countries more than those of any European society. Yet such direct consequences of the free market have not weakened support for it. It remains the sacred cow of American politics and has become identified with America's claim to be a model for a universal civilization. The Enlightenment project and the free market have become fatefully intertwined. . . .

The Utopia of the global free market has not incurred a human cost in the way that communism did. Yet over time it may come to rival it in the suffering that it inflicts. Already it has resulted in over a hundred million peasants becoming migrant labourers in China, the exclusion from work and participation in society of tens of millions in the advanced societies, a condition of near-anarchy and rule by organized crime in parts of the post-communist world, and further devastation of the environment.

Even though a global free market cannot be reconciled with any kind of planned economy, what these Utopias have in common is more fundamental than their differences. In their cult of reason and efficiency, their ignorance of history and their contempt for the ways of life they consign to poverty or extinction, they embody the same rationalist hubris and cultural imperialism that have marked the central traditions of Enlightenment thinking throughout its history.

A global free market presupposes that economic modernization means the same thing everywhere. It interprets the globalization of the economy – the spread of industrial production into interconnected market economies throughout the world – as the inexorable advance of a singular type of western capitalism: the American free market.

The real history of our time is nearer the opposite. Economic modernization does not replicate the American free market system throughout the world. It works against the free market. It spawns indigenous types of capitalism that owe little to any western model.

The market economies of east Asia diverge deeply from one another, with those of China and Japan exemplifying different varieties of capitalism. Equally, Russian capitalism differs fundamentally from capitalism in China. All that these new species of capitalism have in common is that they are not converging on any western model.

The emergence of a truly global economy does not imply the extension of western values and institutions to the rest of humankind. It means the end of the epoch of western global supremacy. The original modern economies in England, western Europe and north America are not models for the new types of capitalism created by global markets. Most countries which try to refashion their economies on the model of Anglo-Saxon free markets will not achieve a sustainable modernity.

Today's Utopia of a single global market assumes that the economic life of every nation can be refashioned in the image of the American free market. Yet in the United States the free market has ruptured the liberal capitalist civilization, founded on Roosevelt's New Deal, on which its postwar prosperity rested. The United States is only the limiting case of a general truth. Wherever deregulated markets are promoted in late modern societies they engender new varieties of capitalism.

In China they have spawned a new variant of the capitalism practised by the Chinese diaspora throughout the world. In Russia the collapse of Soviet institutions has not produced free markets but instead a novel variety of post-communist anarcho-capitalism.

Nor is the growth of a world economy promoting the universal spread of western liberal democracy. In Russia it has produced a hybrid type of democratic government in which strong presidential power is central. In Singapore and Malaysia economic modernization and the growth have been achieved without loss of social cohesion by governments that reject the universal authority of liberal democracy. With luck, a similar government may emerge in China when it becomes fully post-communist.

A world economy does not make a single regime – "democratic capitalism" – universal. It propagates new types of regimes as it spawns new kinds of capitalism. The global economy that is presently under construction will not assure the free market's future. It will trigger a new competition between remaining social market economies and free markets in which social markets must reform themselves profoundly or be destroyed. Yet, paradoxically, free market economies will not be the winners in this contest. For they too are being transformed out of all recognition by global competition.

The free market governments of the 1980s and 1990s failed to achieve many of their objectives. In Britain, levels of taxation and state spending were as high, or higher, after eighteen years of Thatcherite rule than they were when Labour fell from power in 1979.

Free market governments model their policies on the era of *laissez-faire* – the mid-nineteenth century period in which government claimed that it did not intervene in economic life. In reality a *laissez-faire* economy – that is to say, an economy in which markets are deregulated and put beyond the possibility of political or social control – cannot be reinvented. Even in its heyday it was a misnomer. It was created by state coercion, and depended at every point in its workings on the power of government. By the First World War the free market had ceased to exist in its most extreme form because it did not meet human needs – including the need for personal freedom.

Yet, without diminishing the size of the state or reinstating the social institutions that supported the free market in its Victorian heyday, free market policies have encouraged new inequalities in income, wealth, access to work and quality of life that rival those found in the vastly poorer world of the mid-nineteenth century.

In nineteenth-century England the damage done by the free market to other social institutions and to human well-being triggered political counter-movements that changed it radically. A spate of legislation, provoked by different aspects of the free market in action, re-regulated it so that its impact on other social institutions and on human needs was tempered. Mid-Victorian *laissez-faire* showed that social stability and the free market cannot be compatible for long.

England had a market economy before and after the brief mid-Victorian experiment in *laissez-faire*. In each case markets were regulated so that their workings were less inimical to social stability. Only during these eras of *laissez-faire* – in mid-nineteenth century England and, in some parts of the world, the 1980s and 1990s of this century – has the free market been the dominant social institution.

The managed market economies of the post-war era did not emerge through a series of incremental reforms. They came about as a consequence of great social, political and military conflicts. In Britain the Keynesian and Beveridge settlement was made possible by the imperatives of a war of national survival that tore up pre-war social structures by the roots.

In nineteenth-century England, the free market ran aground on enduring human needs for economic security. In the twentieth century, the liberal international economic order perished violently in the wars and dictatorships of the 1930s. That cataclysm was the precondition of post-war prosperity and political stability. In the 1930s the free market proved to be an inherently unstable institution. Built by design and artifice, it fell apart in confusion and chaos. The history of the global free market in our time is unlikely to be much different.

There is no prospect of Britain returning to Keynesian economic management, of the United States reviving a Rooseveltian New Deal, or of any continental countries (aside perhaps from Norway and Denmark) renewing the levels of social provision associated with European Social and Christian Democracy.

The continental social market that spawned German post-war prosperity will be among the most notable casualties of global free markets. It will suffer this fate along with American liberal capitalism, which assured prosperity in the United States and throughout the world for a generation after the Second World War.

Some national governments may be able to use the freedom of manoeuvre they still retain to devise policies which in some degree reconcile the imperatives of global markets with the needs of social cohesion, but the narrow margin of reform that is still open to some sovereign states will not allow any of them a return to the past.

The transnational organizations that oversee the world economy today are vehicles of a post-Keynesian orthodoxy. At the level of sovereign states, they claim that the management of national economies by the control of demand is neither feasible nor desirable. All that is needed for free markets to coordinate economic activity is a framework providing monetary and fiscal stability. The Keynesian policies of the post-war era are rejected as unnecessary or harmful. At the global level, according to these transnational organizations, free markets are equally self-stabilizing. They need no overall governance to prevent economic and social dislocation.

Economic globalization – the worldwide spread of industrial production and new technologies that is promoted by unrestricted mobility of capital and unfettered freedom of trade – actually threatens the stability of the single global market that is being constructed by American-led transnational organizations.

The central paradox of our time can be stated thus: economic globalization does not strengthen the current regime of global *laissez-faire*. It works to undermine it. There is nothing in today's global market that buffers it against the social strains arising from highly uneven economic development within and between the world's diverse societies. The swift waxing and waning of industries and livelihoods, the sudden shifts of production and capital, the casino of currency speculation – these conditions trigger political counter-movements that challenge the very ground rules of the global free market.

Today's worldwide free market lacks the political checks and balances which allowed its mid-Victorian precursor in England to wither away. It can be made more humanly tolerable for the citizens of states which pursue innovative and resourceful policies, but such reforms at the margin will not render the global free market much less unstable. Today's regime of global *laissez-faire* will be briefer than even the *belle époque* of 1870 to 1914, which ended in the trenches of the Great War. . . .

part 12

Emergent Resistance to Neoliberal Globalization: Anti-Corporate Alliance Politics and Direct Actions

In the 1970s and early 1980s, following the Soviet invasion of Czechoslovakia, Red Guard Terrorism in Western Europe, the Cambodian "killing fields," and revelations about Soviet forced-labor camps, the Chinese Cultural Revolution, and other forms of Communist repression, critics charged that Marxists failed to address the connections between their "totalizing" theory and communism's brutal realities. They argued that Marxism's emphases on a proletarian collective subject, revolution on a worldwide scale, and the Communist Party as the infallible vanguard gave rise to and justified totalitarian regimes and insurgencies. They also claimed that Marxism's errors typified broader Enlightenment overconfidence in rationally directed social change. New cultural theorists called for a shift from universal class politics to a "local politics" stressing diverse types of domination, new social movements, and identity (e.g., environment, women, race and ethnicity, gay and lesbian). They also held that Marxists were too dismissive of popular culture, and thus ignored key forms of cultural resistance and diversity. The new approaches substituted cultural critique for the critique of capitalism, and sometimes embraced directly the market and commercial culture.

The critics pointed to serious problems within the Marxist tradition, especially with its orthodox forms, but they overstated their case and failed to take account of Marxism's diversity. Yet even critical, anti-Communist Marxists agreed that the post-Second World War Left's labor-centered, mass parties and class-based politics had fizzled. However, by the mid-1990s, the limitations of the new cultural theories (e.g., postmodernist theory, poststructuralism, cultural studies) became apparent; they gave too little systematic attention to some of the most momentous social changes of the day – neoliberal restructuring, transnational capitalism, unparalleled concentration and commodification of cultural media and goods, and global economic injustice. The related forms of cultural and identity politics often claimed to have superseded Marxism and class issues. Also, their divergent and often conflictive aims and interests blocked the sustained alliance politics that their leaders hoped would consolidate resistance against an increasingly aggressive and powerful neoconservative Right. The cultural Left raised public consciousness about the problems of culturally disparaged groups, furthered the cause of minority rights, and mounted relatively effective, if sporadic, resistance against the cultural Right. But they did not address the neoliberal Right's successful class politics from above or slow its advancing corporate juggernaut. This section focuses on a recent wave of anti-corporate protests that link labor and other class-based movements to diverse cultural movements and politics. These protests oppose the Washington Consensus and the agents of neoliberal globalization, but they connect class inequality with broader democratic concerns about environmental devastation and cultural domination.

In the first selection, Jeff Faux comments on emerging anti-corporate and anti-globalization politics, shortly before the major protest against the 1999 World Trade Organization meetings in Seattle. This protest brought together youthful activists, veterans from the New Left and civil rights movement, factions of organized labor, and diverse cultural and social movement organizations across the globe. Explaining the political and historical contexts of the protests, Faux describes the WTO's role in enforcing the Washington Consensus, deregulating global markets, shifting power from governments to multinational corporations, and insuring that corporate investors' property rights trump social policies. Redistributing wealth upward, he argues, neoliberal measures have not delivered the promised "trickle-down" benefits to less-advantaged people. In his view, neoliberal globalization weakens the state's capacity to protect workers, regulate the economy, reduce environmental damage, and nurture local culture. Moreover, he implies that nationally based labor unions are ineffective against transnational capital, which can move operations to countries where labor is weak or can employ the threat of a move to win concessions. The potential for an international mobilization against globalization is an especially daunting threat to corporate capital. Faux explains that the anti-corporate opposition poses different, sometimes conflictive strategies; but he believes that their core democratically oriented groups can forge a new social contract and sustainable, economically just globalization. Overall, he portrays "disparate groups" forging loosely coupled, nonhierarchical international networks through democratic modes of communication and direct actions. The new opposition resembles a global electronically connected, participatory community rather than the top-down, centralized national regime outlined in the *Manifesto*'s ten-point program to elevate the party vanguard to total political power.

The contribution by Jeff St. Clair, a participant in the Seattle protests, is a day-by-day report on the "direct action" or postmodern counterpart to the Paris Commune – culturally diverse forces discovered each other and were knit together and empowered by the participatory action. Although much shorter-lived than the original Parisian events, this action built connections between different groups, which were maintained electronically in Seattle's aftermath, and helped initiate a more sustained campaign against neoliberal globalization. Quoting an African-American veteran of the civil rights movement, St. Clair stresses the hopefulness and positive energy generated by the radical community forged across cultural and racial lines and the advocacy of a wider social justice that transcends the interests or identity of any one group. St. Clair's report also implies a media-oriented symbolic politics: protesters attacked outlets of the brand-name clothing and sneaker retailers that employ sweatshop labor in distant parts of the world; the Teamsters Union marched alongside environmental activists dressed as sea turtles; and a French "industrial food" critic led an assault on McDonald's (one of the most powerful symbols of globalization). These actions and engagements with Seattle's militarized police were covered by national and international media, and drew attention to neoliberal globalization and its social costs. The action disrupted the WTO talks, and built momentum for the chain of anti-corporate protests that were still continuing in 2001.

The piece by Bruce Shapiro focuses on mounting opposition to neoliberal globalization shortly before the April 2000 protests at the Washington DC meetings of the International Monetary Fund (IMF) and World Bank. He holds that the Seattle action opened debate about neoliberal globalization and the Washington Consensus, even within the IMF and World Bank. These institutions initially funded post-Second World War reconstruction and currency stabilization. However, starting in the 1970s, they loaned money to Third World countries on the condition that they adopt free-market policies, reducing wages, weakening unions, and savaging environmental regulation. As these countries fell ever deeper into debt, they had to borrow more to service the debt, and were forced to adopt ever more stringent austerity programs. Shapiro claims that American views are shifting – increasing numbers of people want globalization that protects the environment, poor people, human rights, and labor, as well as develops the economy. He holds that some members of Congress and the powerful AFL-CIO union have joined the opposition to neoliberal globalization, and that this opposition is spreading on elite college campuses and even in some corporate firms. Comparing anti-corporate protest to the civil rights movement, Shapiro states that the Washington action will be "one wave in an accumulating, rippling cascade of specific, local, hard-nosed campaigns." However, he holds, as does Faux, that opposition to globalization comes from the nationalist Right as well as from the emergent Left alliance (e.g., Pat Buchanan joined the AFL-CIO in condemning the US China Trade Bill). Shapiro warns that anti-corporate politics has multiple, uncertain directions.

Regardless of the uncertainties, growing anti-globalization forces show signs of forging a global alliance politics that overcomes the split between class-based politics and cultural politics and the limits of national borders. Having little in common with nineteenth-century visions of proletarian revolution or with twentieth-century communism, anti-corporate politics has the potential to revive a Marxian-rooted "critical theory," which anchors a critique of capitalism in nascent, radically democratic social movements. A most important possibility is a new and vital form of countervailing power – organized *transnational democratic opposition* to neoliberal multi-nationalism or unrestricted, global rule by USA-supported multinational corporations and capital.

chapter 49

Slouching toward Seattle

Jeff Faux

Every economic system develops a politics around the institutions and rules that govern it. The economic system now being created by the relentless merging of the world's markets will be no exception. But what global politics will emerge to match the new global economy?

One place to look for clues will be in Seattle this November 30, when officials representing the 134 nations of the World Trade Organization (WTO) gather to begin another round of negotiations to lower trade barriers. More than tariffs will be on the table. As Renato Ruggiero, the outgoing director-general of the WTO, put it, "We are no longer writing the rules of interaction among separate national economies. We are writing the constitution of a single global economy."

The Seattle "ministerial" conference has a largely ceremonial purpose: to approve agreements already struck in smaller, less public meetings around the globe. The official business in Seattle will therefore be much like casting votes at a U.S. political convention after the deals have been cut. As at a political convention, the business presence at the WTO meeting will be highly visible. The costs of this official gathering will be financed not by the attending governments but by a business host committee chaired by Boeing and Microsoft. A donation of $250,000 buys, among other things, the right to bring five guests to a dinner with the trade ministers.

The analogy to a political convention is apt. The corporate executives, government officials, trade lawyers, and journalists who will do business with each other at the receptions and dinners and in hotel lobbies are in many ways members of an implicit multinational political association that dominates the management of the global economy. It is the Party of the Washington Consensus.

In the world of international economic policy, the term *Washington Consensus* has come to mean the promotion of the permanent deregulation of the markets for goods, services, capital, and human labor. It is the *Washington* Consensus because it has been orchestrated by the world's remaining superpower. At a recent public conference in Washington, D.C., Michael Mussa, the chief economist of the International Monetary Fund, readily acknowledged that the IMF does not make a major decision without first checking with the U.S. Treasury.

Although made in America, the Party of the Washington Consensus includes the leading figures of the world's important economies, whatever their rivalries at home. Both Margaret Thatcher and Tony Blair are members, as are the Georges Bush and Bill Clinton, Helmut Kohl, and Gerhard Schroeder. Indeed, the leadership of most of the nations represented in Seattle have accepted – even if reluctantly – the Washington Consensus's argument that it speaks for the market. Populist candidates – from Bill Clinton to Alberto Fujimori in Peru, to Kim Dae-jung in South Korea – may gain office by criticizing the maldistribution of market-driven benefits ("Americans working harder for less"), but once elected and faced with threats of a stock market crash, capital strike, or currency flight, they quickly pledge to let the market manage their economy, convinced that – as Margaret Thatcher memorably put it – "there is no alternative."

The last trade round, completed in late 1994, was a triumph for the Washington Consensus. The negotiations yielded a major dismantling of national government power to manage foreign trade, to favor domestic over foreign-owned industries, and to protect domestic labor, the environment, and public health. The WTO was established to settle international trade disputes with a jurisprudence designed to promote the rights of private investors. Indeed, for two decades, virtually every major meeting of the institutions who are charged with managing the global economy – whether the WTO, IMF, World Bank, or G-8 economic summits – has shifted more power from governments to multinational business. Jerome Levinson, former general counsel to the Inter-American Development Bank, observes, "Years ago, investment bankers would be lined up outside the hotel suites of Third World finance and trade ministers, vying for business. Today, it's the government officials who stand in the corridors waiting for an audience with Goldman Sachs or Credit Lyonaise."

The power of private capital upon which the Washington Consensus is based has, thus far, made the current structure of international economic governance a one-party system. But in Seattle, outside the official and unofficial meetings, representatives of an embryonic global party of opposition will also be gathering. Thousands of people from diverse organizations – such as the International Confederation of Free Trade Unions, representing unions that speak for 124 million workers, the Sierra Club, and United Students Against Sweatshops – will converge on Seattle for a week of teach-ins, networking, and demonstrations.

The presence of these groups in Seattle reflects the growing internationalism of progressive and populist grass-roots organizations. Internet technology, the declining cost of travel, and rising education levels have dramatically extended their capacity to both think and act, globally. Trade unions serving workers at the same multinationals in various countries have coordinated organizing campaigns. Worldwide environmental networks have herded nations into a global warming treaty. And religious and antipoverty groups have successfully pressured the World Bank and the IMF to forgive some of the debt of some of the world's poorest nations.

In Seattle, disparate groups will hold seminars on the effect of globalization on wages and living standards, the environment, social investment, democracy, and a host of other issues they believe are given short shrift by the delegates. There will also be street theater, marches, and, perhaps, physical confrontation. The Seattle police have stockpiled pepper spray.

The Party of the Washington Consensus dismisses this opposition as an irrelevant collection of environmental extremists and protectionists who are hopelessly ignorant of economics and stuck in a nationalist past. Some of those who oppose the current form of globalization certainly fit that description (just as some who support it are sweatshop owners and industrial polluters). But the bulk of the political opposition comes from people who understand that they must live, and buy and sell, on an increasingly integrated planet. Their resistance tends not to be against globalization as the natural expansion of the market, but against the Washington Consensus's effort to impose on the global marketplace a late-nineteenth-century political economy in which the primary purpose of government is to protect the freedom and property rights of corporate investors.

For example, at the May 1999 G-8 economic summit in Cologne, a group of trade union associations, representing virtually all of the functioning independent unions in the world, sent seven recommendations to the convening heads of governments. These included policies for macroeconomic stability, debt forgiveness of the poorest nations, strengthening of social safety nets, financial market regulation, international labor standards, transition help for dislocated workers, and strategies for environmentally sustainable development.

In any national context, this would be a mainstream, liberal, or moderately social democratic political platform. But in the context of the global political economy, such ideas are rejected by U.S. officials as antithetical to either the principles of free commerce or national sovereignty. The ostensible concern for other nations' sovereignty is of course disingenuous. Using trade as leverage, the American government has pressured other nations to accept U.S. notions of corporate intellectual property rights, deregulated financial markets, privatized public services, and other surrenders of sovereignty to the interests of multinational investors.

I have asked several high-ranking trade officials whether the United States would have signed the North American Free Trade Agreement (NAFTA) if Mexico had not agreed to change its constitution to accommodate U.S. business demands. The answer is always "no." In other words, for the U.S. negotiators, a refusal of Mexico to surrender sovereignty to multinational corporate interests was a deal-breaker; the refusal to surrender sovereignty for worker or environmental interests was not.

The individuals who negotiate trade and investment agreements formally represent different national interests. But globalization has brought their perspectives and personal career paths closer together – as the parade of ex–U.S. officials lobbying for foreign countries and firms attests. At a conference in New York at the Council on Foreign Relations – an organization at the heart of the Washington Consensus – a retired State Department official bluntly underlined the fundamental reality. "What you don't understand," he said, "is that when we negotiate economic agreements with these poorer countries, we are negotiating with people from the same class. That is, people whose interests are like ours – on the side of capital."

Class politics practiced from above generally succeeds when it trickles benefits down to those below. However, the failure of globalization to deliver has caused the political ground underneath the Washington Consensus to shake.

While the debate over the costs and benefits of global deregulation is far from settled, many, if not most, of its serious supporters would agree that so far its costs have proven much higher than predicted and its benefits considerably lower. In particular the income gap between rich and poor countries, which was supposed to narrow with global deregulation, has gotten wider. And the distribution of income within most countries has gotten worse. . . .

Promoters of global deregulation often analogize to the American experience, where free movement of capital, goods, and people among the various states of our union has clearly spurred economic growth. But when the United States expanded from a series of state-regulated local markets to a continental economy, it already had a political constitution within which to set the national regulatory institutions it needed – such as a central bank, child labor laws, and bank and securities regulation.

The global economy has no such institutions. For example, the IMF is far short of being a global banking regulator or a central bank. It is rather a shallow-pockets lender, dependent on loans from its member countries and partnerships with private investors who have their own agenda. In order to ensure repayment, it conditions its loans on austerity policies that invariably fall heaviest on workers, small-business people, and peasants.

The assumption of the Washington Consensus that functioning markets could be sustained in economies without strong regulatory institutions has proven embarrassingly naïve. From Russia to Mexico to the Far East, privatizations demanded by the IMF have shifted hundreds of billions of dollars in public assets to crooks and oligarchs. And crony capitalism does not stop at foreign borders; evidence mounts of the looting of aid to postcommunist eastern Europe that involved New York banks, Harvard consultants, and contributors to U.S. presidential campaigns.

In its defense, the Washington Consensus now pleads ignorance. Stanley Fischer, the American economist who is second in command at the IMF, says that despite its army of a thousand economists, his agency does not have the capacity to monitor the global banking system effectively: "The amount of detailed knowledge it takes to understand a system is beyond the capacity of a single multinational organization to deal with."

As a result, the global economy is now governed by ad hoc crisis management and high-wire policy acrobatics: IMF officials flying to Third World capitals in disguise, multibillion-dollar loans made in New York hotel suites, and late-night phone calls from vacationing U.S. Treasury officials to the world's financial tycoons. . . .

The Party of the Washington Consensus is still very much in charge, but its moral authority and its claim to competence have been shaken. As the political champion of multinational capital mobility, it has succeeded in crippling the power of governments to regulate markets or to buffer their people against capitalism's excesses. The result is a global economy that is increasingly volatile and generates an upward redistribution of income and wealth. Particularly undermined is the credibility of the Third Way faction of the Washington Consensus, whose support for global deregulation has been rationalized by the assertion that government would help the "losers." It turns out that winners are not eager to help losers. Global laissez-faire generates political pressure for tax cuts and smaller, not larger, public budgets. In nation after nation, social safety nets and human investments have been shredded on the grounds that the world's investors would disapprove.

The stream of opposition activists converging on Seattle is betting that this arrangement is not sustainable and that, therefore, they on the outside – not the trade ministers and corporate lobbyists on the inside – represent the global economic future.

But what kind of a future? As with most parties in opposition, the coalition partners mostly agree on what they don't want. On the question of what they want, the answers tend to be woven out of at least one of three implicit ideological strands.

One is economic nationalism. In America this is the cause of industrial workers concerned about the decline of manufacturing and conservatives who don't like the WTO or the IMF any better than they like the UN. It is also shared by workers in other advanced nations and by political leaders in nations as diverse as Russia, India, and Venezuela, who see the global financial system as an obstacle to their development. . . .

In modest doses, nationalism has supported the development of many individual economies – including that of the United States. But it does not address the question of how to manage the global marketplace, which, as currently organized, is relentlessly eroding the flexibility and authority of most nation-states.

Another economic vision is that of the global village – the implicit, and often explicit, projection by environmentalists of a future characterized by small-scale sustainable development, cultural and biological diversity, and limits to commercial growth. Global villagers disdain big institutions, global or corporate. They tend to believe that the vacuum created by the weakening nation-state can be filled by decentralized civic institutions linked together and empowered by the Internet. But NGOs, however humanistic their ideals, are no substitute for democratic government. "Our challenge," says Mike Dolan, Public Citizen's Seattle organizer, "is to have a seat at the table, and not merely near the table." "But," sniffs a former White House trade official: "who elected them?"

The third vision of the future is that of the global New Deal – the application of the social contract that remains intact, if somewhat tattered, in advanced nations to the global economy. . . .

. . . [I]f the essential notion of the Washington Consensus is to export the American economic model to the rest of the world, why not export all of it – not just accounting rules, but the whole package of a mixed economy in which nonmarket values such as the dignity of labor, ecological balance, and democratic community have enforceable claims? To flesh out this vision, small groups have sprung up in various parts of the world, putting together blueprints of specific proposals, including "Tobin-type" taxes on financial transactions, international sanctions against labor and environmental abuse, and bankruptcy protection for insolvent countries. Implicit in some of the thinking is the possibility of a bargain in which less-developed nations would accept minimal social standards calibrated to their level of development in return for long-term investment aid.

For many in the economic-nationalist and global-village camps, the global New Dealers are hopelessly naïve. Indeed, the latter do seem caught in a political catch-22: (1) A global social contract must be brokered and enforced by global economic institutions. (2) In the absence of world government, global economic institutions are captured by global business interests. (3) But global business interests are opposed to a global social contract.

The only way out of this trap for global New Dealers is to develop a cross-border opposition politics to force individual governments to support an international social contract. But so far, at least, it is hard going. The less technocratic and complicated visions of the nationalists and global villagers have sparked the political passions feeding the opposition to the Washington Consensus, not notions of alternative world governance.

... As so often happens in *national* political life, the opposition will have nowhere to go but into the streets, where political theater trumps political discussion. In that case, Seattle will be a lost opportunity for the Party of the Washington Consensus to diffuse the pressures building up in different parts of the world against globalization itself – from angry steelworkers in the American rust belt to unemployed rioters in Jakarta, from skinheads in Brandenburg to Zapatista peasants in Chiapas. In the United States, the politics of globalization will become more polarized. Ultimately, in its effort to avoid negotiating over the moderate proposals of the world's John Sweeneys, the Party of the Washington Consensus may find itself confronted with the demands of the world's Pat Buchanans.

The future shape of the politics of globalization in a world without a constitution remains hazy. But politics is about "who gets what." So long as the Washington Consensus does not produce stable, sustainable, and widely shared prosperity, its one-party hegemony will continue to be challenged by an increasingly sophisticated if disparate opposition. The gathering inside the meeting rooms in foggy Seattle will tell us something about the direction in which the global political economy will be going in the next century. To get the clearest picture, watch what goes on outside as well.

chapter 50

Seattle Diary

Jeffrey St. Clair

... Seattle is ... a city that hides its past in the underground. It is literally built on layers of engineered muck, like a soggy Ilium. The new opulence brought by the likes of Microsoft, Boeing, Starbucks and REI is neatly segregated from the old economic engines, the working docks and the steamy mills of chemical plants of south Seattle and Tacoma. It is a city that is both uptight and laid-back, a city of deeply repressed desires and rages. It was the best and the worst of places to convene the World Trade Organization (WTO), that Star Chamber for global capitalists. This week, Seattle was so tightly wound that it was primed to crack. The city, which practised drills to prepare itself against possible biological or chemical warfare by WTO opponents, was about to witness its own police department gas its streets and neighbourhoods. By the end of the week, much of Seattle's shiny veneer had been scratched off, the WTO talks had collapsed in futility and acrimony and a new multinational popular resistance had blackened the eyes of global capitalism and its shock troops, if only for a few raucous days and nights.

Sunday, 28 November 1999

I arrived in Seattle at dusk and settled into the King's Inn, my ratty hotel on Fifth Avenue, two blocks up from the ugly Doric column of the Westin, the HQ of the US trade delegation and, on Tuesday and Wednesday nights, the high-rise hovel of Bill Clinton. On the drive up from Portland, I had decided to forego the press briefings, NGO policy sessions and staged debates slated at dozens of venues around Seattle. Instead, I was determined to pitch my tent with the activists who had vowed in January to shut down Seattle during WTO week. After all, the plan seemed remotely possible. . . .

Monday, 29 November 1999

And the revolution will be started by . . . sea turtles. At noon, about 2,000 people massed at the United Methodist Church, the HQ of the grassroots NGOs, for a march to the Convention Center. It was environment day and the Earth Island Institute had prepared more than 500 sea turtle costumes for marchers to wear. The sea turtle became the prime symbol of the WTO's threats to environmental laws, when the WTO tribunal ruled that the US Endangered Species Act, which requires shrimp to be caught with turtle-excluder devices, was an unfair trade barrier.

But the environmentalists weren't the only ones on the street on Monday morning. In the first display of a new solidarity, trade union members from amongst the steelworkers and the longshore-men showed up to join the march. In fact, steelworker Don Kegley led the march, alongside environmentalist Ben White. . . . The throng of sea turtles and blue-jacketed union folk took off to the rhythm of a chant that would echo down the streets of Seattle for days: "The people united will never be divided!"

I walked next to Brad Spann, a burly longshoreman from Tacoma, who held up one of my favourite signs of the entire week: "Teamsters and Turtles . . . Together At Last!" Brad winked at me and said, "What the hell do you think old Hoffa thinks of that?"

The march, which was too fast and courteous for my taste, was escorted by motorcycle police and ended essentially in a cage, a fenced-in area next to a construction site near the Convention Center. A small stage had been erected there hours earlier and Carl Pope, a director of the Sierra Club, was called forth to give the opening speech.

. . . I couldn't follow much of what Pope had to say, except that he failed to utter the names of Clinton or Gore. The speech was delivered with a smugness that most of the labour people must have heard as confirmation of their worst fears about the true nature of environmentalists in suits. . . .

After the speechifying, most of the marchers headed back to the Church. But a contingent of about 200 ended up in front of McDonald's, where a group of French farmers had mustered to denounce US policy on biotech foods. Their leader was José Bové, a sheep farmer from Millau in southwest France and a leader of Confédération Paysanne, a French trade union for farmers. In August, Bové had been jailed in France for leading a raid on a McDonald's restaurant under construction in Larzac. At the time, Bové was awaiting trial on charges that he destroyed a cache of Novartis's genetically engineered corn. Bové said that his raid on the Larzac McDonald's was in response to the US's decision to impose a heavy tariff on Roquefort cheese in retaliation for the European Union's refusal to import American hormone-treated beef. Bové's act of defiance earned him the praise of Jacques Chirac and Friends of the Earth. Bové said he was prepared to start a militant worldwide campaign against "Frankenstein" foods. "These actions will only stop when this mad logic comes to a halt", said Bové. "I don't demand clemency but justice."

Bové showed up at the Seattle McDonald's with rounds of Roquefort cheese, which he handed out to the crowd. After a rousing speech against the evils of Monsanto, and its bovine growth hormone and Round-Up Ready soybeans, the crowd stormed the McDonald's, breaking its windows and urging the customers and workers to join the marchers on the streets. This was the first shot in the battle for Seattle. Moments later, the block was surrounded by Seattle police, attired in full riot gear. Many of them arrived on armoured personnel carriers, a black military truck referred to affectionately by the TV anchors on the nightly news as "the Peacekeeper". But, this time, the cops held their distance, merely making sure that no one had been injured. They cordoned off the block until the crowd dispersed on its own in about an hour. At this point, there was still lightness in the air. . . .

I returned to my hotel early that night. Too exhilarated and exhausted to sleep, I fell back on the bed and flipped on the television. A newscaster was interviewing Michael Moore, the podgy-faced director of the WTO. "I've always been on the side of the little guy", Moore proclaimed.

Tuesday, 30 November 1999

Less than twelve hours later, Seattle was under civic emergency, a step away from martial law. National Guard helicopters hovered over downtown, sweeping the city with searchlights. A 7 p.m. curfew had been imposed and was being flouted by thousands – those same thousands who captured the streets, sustained clouds of tear gas, volleys of rubber bullets, concussion grenades, high-powered bean cannons and straightforward beatings with riot batons. The bravery of the street warriors had its tremendous triumph: they held the streets long enough to force the WTO to cancel their opening day. This had been the stated objective of the direct-action strategists, and they attained it. . . .

Who were these direct-action warriors on the front lines? Earth First!, the Alliance for Sustainable Jobs and the Environment (the new envirosteelworker alliance), the Ruckus Society (a direct-action training center), Food Not Bombs, Global Exchange and a small contingent of anarchists, dressed in black, with black masks, plus a hefty international contingent including French farmers, Korean greens, Canadian wheat growers and British campaigners against genetically modified foods. . . .

Even in the run-up to WTO week in Seattle, the genteel element – foundation careerists, NGO bureaucrats, policy wonks – were all raising cautionary fingers, saying that the one thing to be feared in Seattle this week was active protest. The internet was thick with tremulous admonitions about the need for good behaviour, the perils of playing into the enemies' hands, the profound necessity for decorous – that is, passive – comportment. Their fondest hope is to attend – in mildly critical posture – not only the WTO conclave in Seattle, but all future ones. This, too, is the posture of labour. In answer to a question from CNN's Bernard Shaw, whether labour wanted to kill the WTO, James Hoffa Jr. replied, "No. We want to get labour a seat at the table."

By noon, around the Convention Center, the situation was desperate. The Seattle police, initially comparatively restrained, were now losing control. They were soon supplemented by the King County sheriffs' department, a rough mob, which seem to get their kicks from throwing concussion grenades into crowds, with the M-80-like devices often exploding only inches above the heads of people.

As the day ticked away, the street protesters kept asking, "Where are the labour marchers?", expecting that, at any moment, thousands of longshoremen and teamsters would reinforce them in the fray. The absent masses never came. The marshals for the union march steered the big crowds away from the action and the isolation of the street protesters allowed the cops to become far more violent. Eventually, several phalanxes of union marchers skirted their herders and headed up 4th Avenue to the battlegrounds at Pine and Pike. Most of them seemed to be from the more militant unions, the Steelworkers, IBEW and the Longshoremen. And they seemed to be pissed off at the political penury of their leaders. . . .

By darkness on Tuesday, the 2,000 or so street warriors had won the day, even though they were finally forced to retreat north and east out of the Center. Suppose 30,000 union people had reinforced them? Downtown could have been held all night, and the Convention Center sealed off. Maybe even President Bill would have been forced to stay away. . . .

Wednesday, 1 December 1999

Wednesday was the turning point of the week. After the vicious crackdown of Tuesday night, where even Christmas carollers in a residential area were gassed, many of us wondered who would show up to confront the WTO, Bill Clinton, the police and the National Guard the next morning. More than a thousand, it turned out. And the numbers grew as the day wore on. The resistance had proved its resilience.

The morning's first march headed down Denny Street from Seattle Community College toward downtown. The 250 marchers were met at about 7 a.m. by a line of cops in riot gear at 8th avenue. A sobering sign that things had become more serious was the sight of cops armed with AR-15 assault rifles. Some brave soul went up to one of the deputies and asked, "Do those shoot rubber bullets?" "Nope", the cop replied through a Darth Vader-like microphone embedded in his gas mask. "This is the real thing." Dozens of protesters were arrested immediately, placed in plastic wrist-cuffs and left sitting on the street for hours – more than had been arrested all day on Tuesday. . . .

On Wednesday afternoon, I encountered Kirk Murphy, the doctor. His Earth First! T-shirt had been replaced by a business suit and a rain jacket. I raised my eyebrows at him. He said, "I'm trying hard not to look like part of the support team. They've arrested a lot of our medics and I need to stay out of jail to help the injured."

These targeted arrests may have been meant to turn the protests into the chaotic mess the city's PR people were characterizing it as to the media. But it didn't happen. The various groups of protesters, sometimes in the hundreds, huddled together and decided their next course of action by a rudimentary form of consensus. Everyone was given a chance to have a say and then a vote was taken on what to do next and, usually, the will of the majority was followed without significant disruptions. The problem was that it slowed down the marches, allowing the police and National Guard troops to box in the protesters, most tragically later on Wednesday evening at Pike's Place Market.

As the march turned up toward the Sheraton and was beaten back by cops on horses, I teamed up with Etienne Vernet and Ronnie Cummings. Cummings is the head of one of the feistiest groups in the US, the PureFood Campaign, Monsanto's chief pain in the ass. Cummings hails from the oil town of Port Arthur, Texas. He went to Cambridge with that other great foe of industrial agriculture, Prince Charles. Cummings was a civil rights organizer in Houston during the mid-sixties. "The energy here is incredible. Black and white, labour and green, Americans, Europeans, Africans and Asians arm-in-arm. It's the most hopeful I've felt since the height of the civil rights movement."

Vernet lives in Paris, where he is a leading organiser for the radical green group EcoRopa. At that very moment, the European Union delegates inside the convention were capitulating on a key issue: the EU, which had banned import of genetically engineered crops and hormone-treated beef, had agreed to a US proposal to establish a scientific committee to evaluate the health and environmental risks of biotech foods, a sure first step toward undermining the moratorium. Still, Vernet was in a jolly mood, lively and invigorated, if a little bemused by the decorous nature of the crowd. "Americans seem to have been out of practice in these things", he told me. "Everyone's so polite. The only things that are burning are dumpsters filled with refuse." He pointed to a shiny black Lexus parked on Pine Street, which the throngs of protesters had scrupulously avoided. In the wind-shield was a placard identifying it as belonging to a WTO delegate. "In Paris, that car would be burning." . . .

Clinton called the events outside his suite in the Westin "a rather interesting hoopla". The president expressed sympathy for the views of those in the streets at the very moment his aides were ordering Seattle Mayor Paul Schell . . . to use all available force to clear the streets. There is now no question but that the most violent attacks by the police and the National Guard came at the request of the White House and not the mayor or the police chief. And, in fact, CNN has reported that Clinton has once again flouted the Posse Comitatus Act by sending in a contingent from the US military to the scene, More than 160 members of the Domestic Military Support Force were sent to Seattle on Tuesday, including troops from the Special Forces division. Clinton, of course, has been quite happy to blame Mayor Schell, the Seattle police, and the WTO itself, for both the chaos and the crack-down, while offering himself as a peacemaker to the very battle he provoked.

Eventually, Clinton shut up and Brower [an old friend] and Foster [a steelworker] walked into the room. Brower was breaking new ground once again by pulling together a new group of trade unionists and greens. . . . "Today, the police in Seattle have proved they are the handmaidens of the corporations", said Brower. "But something else has been proved. And that's that people are starting to stand up and say: we won't be transnational victims."

Brower was joined by David Foster, director for District 11 of the United Steelworkers of America, one of the most articulate and unflinching labour leaders in America. Earlier this year, Brower and Foster formed an unlikely alliance, a coalition of radical environmentalists and steelworkers called the Alliance for Sustainable Jobs and the Environment. . . . The groups had found they had a common enemy: Charles Hurwitz, the corporate raider. Hurwitz owns the Pacific Lumber Company, the northern California timber firm that is slaughtering some of the last stands of ancient redwoods on the planet. At the same time, Hurwitz, who also controls Kaiser Aluminium, had locked out 3,000 steelworkers at Kaiser's factories in Washington, Ohio and Louisiana. "The companies that attack the environment most mercilessly are often also the ones that are the most anti-union", Foster told me. "More unites us than divides us." . . .

When the rally broke up, hundreds of steelworkers joined with other protesters in an impromptu march down 1st Avenue. As the crowd reached Pike Place Market, they found paramilitary riot squads waiting for them and were rocked with volleys of military-strength CS gas, flash bombs, and larger rubber bullets, about a half-inch in diameter. The carnage was indiscriminate. Holiday shoppers and Metro buses were gassed. In an effort to jack up the intimidation, the cop squads were marching in almost goosestepping fashion, smacking their riot clubs against their shin-guards to create a sinister sound with echoes back to Munich. This was the most violent of the street battles that I witnessed, involving hundreds of police and more than twenty tear gas attacks.

The Ruckus Society had trained hundreds of the demonstrators in the techniques and disciplines of non-violent direct action, to considerable effect, though with occasional exaggerations. Thus it was that demonstrators at nearly every corner and barricade were being cautioned "not to retaliate" against police attacks. They were even warned not to throw the tear gas cans back toward the police lines. But, of course, that was the safest place for them. They weren't going to hurt the cops, who were decked out in the latest chemical warfare gear. . . .

Seattle police said they responded aggressively only when their officers were hit with rocks and bottles. Well, frankly, this is bullshit. Seattle isn't Beirut. There's no rocky rubble on the streets of the Emerald City. In fact, there weren't any glass bottles, either. In the eight or nine confrontations I witnessed, the most the cops were hit with were some half-full plastic water bottles and a few lightweight sticks that had been used to hold cardboard signs.

In the end, what was vandalized? Mainly the boutiques of Sweatshop Row: Nordstrom's, Adidas, The Gap, Bank of America, Niketown, Old Navy, Banana Republic and Starbucks. The expressions of destructive outrage weren't anarchic, but extremely well-targeted. The manager of Starbucks whined about how "mindless vandals" destroyed his window and tossed bags of French roast onto the street. But the vandals weren't mindless. They didn't bother the independent streetside coffee shop across the road. Instead, they lined up and bought cup after cup. No good riot in Seattle could proceed without a cup of espresso.

These minor acts of retribution served as a kind of Gulf of Tonkin incident. They were used to justify the repressive and violent onslaughts by the police and the National Guard. Predictably, the leaders of the NGOs were fast to condemn the protesters. The *World Trade Observer* is a daily tabloid produced during the convention by the mainstream environmental groups and the Nader shop. Its Wednesday morning edition contained a stern denunciation of the direct-action protests that had shut down the WTO the day before. Pope repudiated the violence of the protests, saying it delegitimized the position of the NGOs. He did not see fit to criticize the actions of the police. . . .

The assault on Niketown didn't begin with the anarchists, but with protesters who wanted to get a better view of the action. They got the idea from Rainforest Action Network activists who had free-climbed the side of a building across the street and unfurled a huge banner depicting a rattlesnake, coiled and ready to strike, with the slogan, "Don't Trade on Me".

Occupying the intersection in front of Niketown was a group of Korean farmers and greens, several were dressed in their multicoloured traditional garb. It's no secret why they picked this corner. For decades, Nike has exploited Korean workers in its Asian sweatshops. These folks cheered wildly and banged their copper kettles when a climber scaled the façade of Nike's storefront, stripped the chrome letters off the Niketown sign and tossed them to the crowd, as Nike store managers in the window a floor above ate their lunch. The action should have warmed the hearts of nearly everyone, even the Seattle Downtown Beautification Association. For one brief moment, the city of Seattle had been rid of an architectural blight. As *Harper's* magazine reported a few years ago, the black-and-silver neo-noir styling of Niketown outlets bear an eerie resemblance to the designs concocted by Albert Speer for the Third Reich.

That night I went to sleep with the words of John Goodman, a locked-out steelworker from Spokane, ringing in my head. "The things I've seen here in Seattle I never thought I'd see in America." . . .

Thursday and beyond

By Thursday morning, I was coughing up small amounts of blood, 600 demonstrators were in jail, the police were on the defensive over their tactics and the WTO conference itself was coming apart at the seams. Inside the WTO, the African nations were showing the same solidarity as the protesters on the streets. They refused to buckle to US demands and coaxing from US Trade Rep. Charlene Barshevsky: "I reiterated to the ministers that if we are unable to achieve that goal I fully reserve the right to also use an exclusive process to achieve a final outcome. There's no question about my right as a chair to do it or my intention to do it, but it is not the way I want this to be done." Despite the heavy-handed bluster, the African delegates hung together and the talks collapsed.

Beyond the wildest hopes of the street warriors, five days in Seattle have brought us one victory after another. The protesters initially shunned and denounced by the respectable "inside strategists", scorned by the press, gassed and bloodied by the cops and National Guard had:

- shut down the opening ceremony;
- prevented Clinton from addressing the WTO delegates at the Wednesday night gala;
- turned the corporate press from prim denunciations of "mindless anarchy" to bitter criticisms of police brutality;
- forced the WTO to cancel its closing ceremonies and to adjourn in disorder and confusion, without an agenda for the next round.

In the annals of popular protest in America, these have been shining hours, achieved entirely outside the conventional arena of orderly protest and white-paper activism and the timid bleats of the professional leadership of big labour and environmentalism. This truly was an insurgency from below, in which all those who strove to moderate and deflect the turbulent flood of popular outrage managed to humiliate themselves. Of course, none of this seemed to deter the capitalists. On the week, the Dow shot up more than 500 points, because of a report about a downturn in inflation and an uptick in unemployment.

I walked out to the street one last time. The sweet stench of CS gas still flavoured the morning air. As I turned to get into my car for the journey back to Portland, a black teenager grabbed my arm. Smiling, he said, "Hey, man, does this WTO thing come to town every year?" I knew immediately how the kid felt. Along with the poison, the flash bombs and the rubber bullets, there was an optimism, energy and camaraderie on the streets of Seattle that I hadn't felt in a long time. It was the perfect antidote to crackdown by the cops and to the gaseous rhetoric of Clinton, Carl Pope and John Sweeney.

chapter 51

Not just a Seattle Sequel

Bruce Shapiro

The protests surrounding this weekend's meetings of the IMF and World Bank are the next step in the backlash to globalization.

Lately, my friend Jim Schultz has been sending out a lot of e-mail. Schultz, a former San Franciscan, helps run an orphanage in Cochabamba, Bolivia, the poorest country in South America. Last year, Bolivia's government, under pressure from the World Bank, decided to privatize Cochabamba's municipal water company, selling it to a subsidiary of Bechtel Corp. Overnight, Bechtel doubled Cochabamba's water rates and Schultz witnessed the results: "Families earning a minimum wage of less than $100 per month were told to fork over $20 and more or have the tap shut off," he writes. He talks about a mother of five, an employee of a knitting factory, whose bill for drinking water amounted to the equivalent of her family's food budget for a week and a half.

At the turn of the year, Cochabamba exploded in protest, which escalated until last week, when Bolivia's government declared a state of siege, rousted protest leaders from their beds and fatally shot a 17-year-old demonstrator. When last heard from, Bechtel was packing its bags and trading blame with the Bolivian government for the debacle.

Cochabamba may seem far from Washington. But thousands of demonstrators are descending on the U.S. capital this weekend for precisely the reason that Cochabamba's angry peasants sent Bechtel packing: the one-size-fits-all, corporate-friendly dictates of the World Bank and International Monetary Fund, which hold their joint spring meeting there Sunday and Monday. Cochabamba is far, too, from New Haven, where I write this in a library at Yale University.

But a few yards outside the library doors, Yale students have been sleeping out in a plywood shanty for the past several weeks to pressure the university into higher standards for its apparel contractors – for the sake of sweatshop workers like Schultz's friend in Cochabamba – companies operating in the laissez-faire environment demanded by the IMF. The price of water in Bolivia might seem to have as little to do with American politics as, well, the price of tea in China. But Bolivian water, Chinese tea, Ivy League athletic gear – not to mention the presidential race – are increasingly part of the same story.

That story comes to the forefront again as the IMF and World Bank meet in Washington this weekend. Anti-globalization protestors are descending on the nation's capital, hoping to maintain the momentum from the protests at last year's World Trade Organization meeting in Seattle. The coming confrontation in Washington is being portrayed as the Seattle sequel – the next foray for the "Teamsters and turtles" coalition of labor, environmental and consumer advocates who paralyzed the WTO meeting.

But while Washington's protestors plan civil disobedience, the real crisis in Washington this weekend is not in the streets – it is in the conference rooms where finance ministers are meeting at a time of profound uncertainty about the future of the IMF and World Bank.

The IMF is at odds over the choice of its next managing director, but the real issue is how far and in what direction both institutions will be reformed. U.S. Treasury Secretary Lawrence Summers is pushing the institutions to get out of the long-term investment business altogether. France and Germany now call openly for trade policies that recognize social priorities beyond foreign-investment orthodoxy. Joseph Stiglitz, the former chief economist of the World Bank, denounces the IMF for imposing its political and economic agenda on developing countries. Stiglitz now calls for the kind of inclusive, locally driven development policy that only wild-eyed radicals envisioned a few years ago.

And like the first wave of protestors to arrive in Washington this week – the "*Jubilee 2000*" *movement* of Catholic activists – Stiglitz now calls upon the World Bank and IMF to write off most Third World debt. The international-finance establishment is beginning to fracture over the global economy, just as America's foreign-policy establishment tore itself apart over Vietnam.

And while the international financial institutions fracture from within, from without the protest movement gathering in Washington is not only *against* global corporations, it is also actively envisioning a pragmatic alternative to the current financial order, one that was marked by instability as the world's markets fluctuated wildly this week.

The roots of this weekend's protest are not in November's protests, but in the mid-1970s. The World Bank and IMF had been founded by the victorious allies after World War II for the modest but important job of stabilizing international currency and sponsoring post-war reconstruction. But in the '70s, both institutions took on a new and broader mission – lending money to desperately indebted Third World countries and sponsoring big-time development projects like dams and railways.

But those loans came with a price: that Third World governments privatize state industry, lower wages and generally make their nations friendlier toward foreign investment.

Instead of freeing Third World nations from debt, the measures pushed them further into the hole. The money for most of those dams and railways lined the pockets of corrupt officials, the competition for Western corporate investment drove wages in countries like Bolivia even lower. The result was not trickle-down success, but the economic culture of maquiladores – those self-contained free-trade zones in which foreign investors can evade unions, the minimum wage and environmental regulation.

A few people picked up on this crisis early, especially those on the receiving end. I remember more than 20 years ago being part of a group at the University of Chicago protesting a peace prize to Robert McNamara, then head of the World Bank. Most of us were angry about McNamara's record as secretary of defense during the Vietnam War.

But a graduate student from Mexico, a former seminarian named Primitivo Rodriguez (today one of his country's most inventive and visionary reformers), insisted that the harsh new economic order being imposed by the World Bank was as noteworthy a crime. Unfortunately, Rodriguez was the exception. Most analysts didn't wake up to the IMF–World Bank's blunders until the late-'90s Asian economic crisis, when even Business Week and Morgan Stanley could smell the coffee and proclaimed the international financial regime a debacle.

But Seattle brought the issue of globalization to the front pages and quickly got the attention of a number of people on Capitol Hill. On Thursday, five members of Congress released a sweeping "Global Sustainable Development Resolution" originally drafted by Rep. Bernie Sanders, I-Vt., incorporating a wide range of steps to stem the worldwide "race to the bottom," a race even corporate-globalization champion President Clinton now warns against.

The bill calls for the United States to renegotiate trade agreements to include worker rights and environmental protections. It calls for reining in the IMF and World Bank to their original roles as guarantors of international financial stability and proposes United Nations oversight of international lending.

Washington, in other words, is no Seattle rerun. The issues, the players and the American public itself were all changed by Seattle, in ways few would have predicted a year ago.

There is, for instance, the hot issue of the moment, most-favored trading status for China, which Clinton is trying to push through as his final foreign-policy achievement. Until recently, opponents of China's entry into the World Trade Organization – including both the AFL-CIO and Pat Buchanan, who addressed the federation's China-trade rally this week – framed their argument in the language of economic nationalism, pitting American jobs against the Chinese economy. The question still divides the broad Seattle coalition, with the AFL-CIO's critics claiming that defeating the China trade bill will only hurt Chinese workers.

But since Seattle, a growing body of evidence has emerged suggesting that Chinese workers as well as American jobs are at risk from unrestricted trade, accelerating the so-called "race to the bottom" in wages, and environmental and human-rights standards. The South China Business Post estimates that if China joins the WTO, the already-low wages of rural workers will drop by an average of 2 percent over the next five years. Economist Nicholas Lardy of the Brookings Institution, hardly a rabble-rouser, predicts that the WTO agreement will lead to a 33 percent decline in output of Chinese agriculture. The National Labor Committee reports that some regions of China are already lowering their wages to attract or keep American investors like Wal-Mart.

This data has emboldened the AFL-CIO's rhetorical shift from jobs for Americans to international workers' rights, and driven it into a closer relationship with environmental and human rights groups. Indeed, no institution better symbolizes the shift in the parameters of debate than the labor federation, which is either the dinosaur or 800-pound gorilla of American social-change politics. For months, the AFL refused to join in this weekend's demonstrations against the IMF, sticking to its narrow China demonstration Wednesday. Just a year ago, the labor federation supported the Clinton administration's call for an $18 billion increase in IMF funding. But at the last minute, AFL-CIO president John Sweeney shifted course, not only throwing his weight behind the weekend's protest but signing an angry statement against IMF lending policies in the Third World.

Sweeney is not the only person whose views have shifted since Seattle. In this presidential year, the American public's views have changed dramatically from the free-market orthodoxy of a few years ago. A recent study of U.S. attitudes toward globalization conducted by the University of Maryland found that overwhelmingly, Americans support global economic integration, but that they want it managed to protect the environment, labor and the poor.

The protests, meanwhile, are having measurable effect. Major universities – including such high-profile, high-endowment institutions as Brown and Cornell – have pledged to void their apparel contracts with companies that fail sweatshop evaluations, for instance. (Yale isn't yet one of them, which is why those students are camped out on the plaza.) Global protest recently drove the chemical giant Monsanto out of the genetically engineered food business. Starbucks has promised to buy so-called *Fair Trade coffee* from growers who respect workers' rights.

As dramatic as last year's Seattle protests were, this week's events in Washington cut closer to the bone in some ways. The WTO is a murky and ambiguous rule-making body, but all but the most ardent localists approve the general concept of regulating trade; the only argument is over whether labor, environmental and human-rights standards are part of the picture. On the other hand, to reform international financial institutions is to reform the bodies that have imposed a specific economic model world-wide, creating the greatest gulf between rich and poor in human history.

What matters about this weekend's demonstrations is not the number of protestors. These day, anyone with a bus, a driver's license and an e-mail list can get bodies to Washington. Instead, this weekend's events are important because they represent – like the 1963 civil rights march on Washington – one wave in an accumulating, rippling cascade of specific, local, hard-nosed campaigns. "Only connect," the novelist E. M. Forster once demanded. Water in Cochabamba, sweatshirts in New Haven, loans in Washington – if last fall the world came to Seattle, this weekend in Washington marks the moment that Seattle goes global, connecting and unleashing worldwide anti-corporate passions whose outcome cannot be foreseen.

part 13

Rethinking Class and Class Politics after Communism: Avoiding Marxist Determinism and Totalization

Starting with Max Weber, diverse thinkers have seen Marx as a polestar of modern social theory – his challenge to capitalist modernity is so fundamental that later generations of theorists, such as today's postmodernists and other new cultural theorists, have felt compelled to situate themselves vis-à-vis his views in debates over the historical direction and ethical or aesthetic worth of modern culture. It is no surprise that critiques of his ideas outnumber applications of them. Marx's most central category, class, has been a major point of debate in twentieth-century social science and social theory, and has had enormous impact in diverse fields. As explained above, his class analysis focuses on the ways in which property-holders extract surpluses from direct producers. However, Marx saw class as a historical matter – forms of property holding, production, and extraction vary with a society's level and unique pattern of development and with its consequent ensemble of productive forces, forms of association, types of organization, and patterns of culture. The epochal revolution of productive forces and sociocultural life that Marx stressed, and that accelerated greatly after his death, has made class issues much more complex and much less transparent today than they were in his day. Moreover, the parallel rise of more inclusive citizenship rights, more multicultural societies, and new forms of mass media and mass politics have also increased greatly the diversity and complexity of sociocultural conflicts. Stressing cultural repression and exclusion, new social movements operate alongside of, compete with, and interpenetrate labor movements and class politics. The two selections below illustrate attempts to reconceptualize Marxist views of class in response to the changed historical situation and increased social complexity.

Sociologist Erik Olin Wright operates in the tradition of "scientific Marxism," and qualifies its determinist thrust. He states that Marxists sometimes grant class *a priori* primacy over other types of domination, or presume it to be the root of all oppression. He argues that we know, from research and experience, that class is an important factor in most social arrangements and in most forms of domination, and thus should be an important concern of emancipatory movements. However, he rejects positions that would grant automatic primacy to class, and he stresses that its relation to other social conditions and forms of domination is a contingent matter and a topic of empirical inquiry. Engaging indirectly feminist critiques of Marxism's alleged, totalizing economic determinism, Wright illustrates how his qualified view of class operates in the case of gender–class relations. He aims to rethink class in a way that averts Marxism's sometimes overly deterministic, abstract, and macroscopic tendencies. Wright provides extensive examples of how to reconceptualize the middle-class, underclass, and class alliances – problematic areas for Marxist theory. For example, he argues that Marxists usually presume that individuals have a single class position. By contrast, he holds that middle-class individuals often occupy "contradictory class locations" – a manager may operate both as exploited producer and exploitative capitalist. Referring to William Julius Wilson's work on the underclass, Wright distinguishes exploitative economic oppression of workers from nonexploitative oppression of the underclass. Because capitalists need workers, he explains, proletarians have leverage to limit exploitation, and capitalists feel pressure to gain their consent and avoid costly repression. By contrast, he holds that the underclass has little leverage beyond disruption by crime and violence. Wright also argues that class alliances, formed by reaching compromises on conflicting interests, are harder to form, but more durable than multiclass alliances, which leave conflicting interests unresolved. Overall, Wright revises the concept of class to grasp its changing historical forms and the shifting conditions that affect emancipatory politics.

The approach of the feminist philosopher Nancy Fraser is rooted, at least partially, in the neo-Marxian tradition of Critical Theory, which historically has been more receptive to cultural issues and fusions with other approaches. She addresses a political climate in which public support for redistributing wealth and eliminating poverty has waned and waging "struggles for recognition" and fighting cultural domination (e.g., based on race, nationality, ethnicity, gender, sexuality) have become the main form of political conflict. But Fraser argues that this cultural turn occurs at a time when "material inequality" is increasing (e.g., growing income and wealth disparities and increasingly unequal access to health, education, jobs, safe environment contexts). Thus, she focuses on redistribution as well as recognition. For theoretical purposes, Fraser contrasts a hypothetical, pure class politics addressing exclusively economic injustice and requiring only redistribution of income, burdens, and social benefits with a cultural politics aiming exclusively at altering values and attaining recognition. Employing the example of gays and lesbians, she explains that they can be found in all classes, and that they are victimized by social norms that devalue their sexuality and open them to prejudice, discrimination, and violence. She holds that cultural change, or recognition, rather than redistribution, is needed to solve their problems. Her point is that class inequality and cultural inequality have autonomous or irreducible facets that should be distinguished empirically and analytically. However, Fraser contends that class and culture are almost always entwined in real historical situations. Using gender and race as examples, she demonstrates how cultural disrespect and exclusion usually accompany economic inequality and injustice, and how the two forms of domination mutually reinforce each other. She holds that Critical Theory should seek to redress both economic injustice and cultural injustice, but also recognize their basic differences and employ appropriate methods to cope with each.

Wright and Fraser see the concept of class as an essential – albeit not the only – analytical tool for analyzing the ordering of contemporary societies and rethinking emancipatory politics. Their suggested revisions amplify critical points that have been raised in the previous part introductions and contemporary selections. However, recall especially the early selection by Engels (chapter 7) that criticized early Marxism's dogmatic strains and that asserted that he and Marx intended their materialist approach to be nothing more than a means for inquiry about historical change. History must always be studied anew, Engels declared. Wright and Fraser revise the concept of class in the same spirit. Although coming from different, sometimes opposed traditions, both thinkers want to take account of culture and still bring the economy back in. But theory lags behind history. As stressed above, the shape of global capitalism has been changing rapidly, and perhaps fundamentally, for more than a decade. The revisions by Wright and Fraser are important and constructive, but more basic theoretical changes and different forms of appropriation of Marx and Marxism may arise in the wake of ongoing neoliberal globalization and its emerging forms of crisis and opposition.

chapter 52

Class Analysis, History, and Emancipation

Erik Olin Wright

Marxism as class analysis

To understand the tasks facing a reconstructed class analysis it is useful to distinguish between two understandings of what class analysis can realistically hope to achieve. Consider the problem of explaining various aspects of gender oppression, let's say the unequal division of labour in the home. One view is that Marxists should aspire to a general class *theory* of gender and thus of gender inequalities. . . . [A] class theory of gender oppression implies that class is in some sense understood as the most fundamental or important cause of gender oppression. This need not imply that all aspects of gender oppression are explainable by class, but that at an appropriate level of abstraction, class explains the most important properties of gender oppression.

An alternative view is that Marxists should engage in the class *analysis* of gender oppression without prejudging ahead of time whether or not a fully fledged class theory of gender is achievable. A class analysis implies examining the causal connections between class and gender and their mutual impacts on various explananda, such as gender ideologies, women's poverty, or sexual violence. This implies a provisional recognition that gender processes are rooted in autonomous causal mechanisms irreducible to class, and that the task of class analysis is to deepen our understanding of their interactions in explaining specific social phenomena. Now it may happen that out of the discoveries of the class analysis of gender oppression, it may eventually be possible to construct a class theory of such oppression. While such an eventuality seems unlikely given our present knowledge of these processes, it is not logically precluded.

Reconstructing class analysis, therefore, involves a shift from an a priori belief in the primacy of class in social explanations to a more open stance in exploring the causal importance of class. It might appear that this way of treating class analysis relegates class to the status of simply one factor among many. . . . The fact is . . . that we know a great deal about social life, both from casual observation and systematic research, and one of the things we know is that class is massively important for understanding many social phenomena. Class is a powerful causal factor because of the way in which class determines access to material resources and thus affects the use of one's time, the resources available to pursue one's interests and the character of one's life experiences within work and consumption. Class thus pervasively shapes both material interests and capacities for action. This is not to suggest that class is universally the most important determinant of everything social, rather that it is presumptively important for a very wide range of phenomena. More specifically, class is likely to be especially important in explaining the possibilities for and obstacles to human emancipation, since on virtually any construal of the problem, emancipation requires fundamental reorientations of the use of society's material resources, surplus and time. Such projects, therefore, inevitably involve in a central way class politics – political struggles over property relations and control of the social surplus. The central task of class analysis, then, is to give greater precision to the causal structure of class phenomena and the relationship between class and other social phenomena relevant to the normative goals of Marxism.

Elements of a Reconstructed Class Analysis

My work on reconstructing class analysis has revolved around a relatively simple model of the interconnections among the core concepts of class analysis: class structure, class formation and class struggle. . . . The basic idea of this model is that class structures impose *limits* upon, but do not uniquely determine, both class formations (i.e. the collective organization of class forces) and class struggles; class formations *select* class struggles within the limits imposed by class structures; class struggles in turn have *transformative* impacts on both class structures and class formations. This is not a purely structural model, for the conscious practices of actors – class struggles – transform the social structures which limit those practices. But it is also not an agent-centred model, for those struggles are seen as systematically constrained by the structures within which people live and act. Structures limit practices but within those limits practices transform structures.

. . . My own work on these issues has been preoccupied primarily with one element of the model: class structure. I have argued that in order to have a solid foundation for understanding the relationship between class structure and class formation and both of these to class struggles, we first need a coherent concept of class structure. Traditional Marxist concepts of class structure suffered, I have argued, from two major problems. First, they were too *abstract* for many empirical problems. The conventional Marxist concept of class structure posits polarized, antagonistic classes defined within pure modes of production – slaves and slave-owners, lords and serfs, capitalists and workers. But for many concrete empirical problems, many locations in the class structure, especially those loosely called the "middle class", do not seem to fit such a polarized view of classes. Second, traditional Marxist concepts of class structure tended to be too macro. They described the overall structures of societies, but did not adequately map onto the lives of individuals. My objective, then, was to produce a Marxist concept of class structure which would link concrete and micro levels of analysis to the more abstract macro concepts.

I will illustrate this problem of concept formation through three specific conceptual issues: the problem of the *middle class*, the problem of the (so-called) *underclass* and the problem of *class alliances*.

The middle class

The "middle class" poses an immediate problem for Marxist class analysis: if the abstract concept of class structure is built around polarized classes, what does it mean to be in the "middle"? In the 1970s when I began work on this problem, there was, in my judgement, no satisfactory answer to this question. I proposed a new concept as a way of dealing with these kinds of location: *contradictory locations within class relations*. The basic logic was quite simple. Previous attempts at solving the problem of the middle class all worked on the assumption that a given micro *location* within the class structure (a location filled by an individual) had to be in one and only one class. Thus the middle class was treated as part of the working class (a new working class), part of the petty bourgeoisie (a new petty bourgeoisie) or as an entirely new class in its own right (a professional-managerial class). I argued that there was no need to make this assumption. Why not entertain the possibility that some class locations – jobs actually performed by individuals – were simultaneously located in more than one class? Managers, for example, could be viewed as simultaneously capitalists and workers – capitalists insofar as they dominated the labour of workers, workers insofar as they did not own the means of production and sold their labour-power to capitalists.

The idea of contradictory locations seemed to provide a more coherent solution to the problem of the middle class, a solution that was consistent with both the abstract polarized class concept and the concrete complexities of real class structures. Nevertheless, there were a number of significant conceptual problems with this approach. This led me in the mid 1980s to propose a second solution to the problem of the middle class. This solution revolved around the concept of "exploitation". Exploitation can be loosely defined as a process by which one group is able to appropriate part of the social surplus produced by another group. Any society, I argued, is characterized by a variety of mechanisms of exploitation. Capitalist societies do not simply have distinctively capitalist forms of exploitation based on unequal ownership of means of production. They also contain what I called . . . "skill exploitation" and "organization exploitation". In skill exploitation, owners of scarce skills are able to extract a rent component in their wages. This is basically a component of the wage above and beyond the costs of producing and reproducing the skills themselves. It thus embodies part of the social surplus. In organization exploitation, managers are able to appropriate part of the surplus through the power which they command inside the bureaucratic structures of capitalist production. Using this notion of differentiated mechanisms of exploitation, the "middle class" could be defined as those locations in the class structure which were exploited on one mechanism of exploitation but exploiters on another. Professional and technical employees, for example, can be seen as capitalistically exploited but skill exploiters. They thus constitute "contradictory locations within exploitation relations".

Both of these proposals break with the idea that individual class locations must have a homogeneous class character, and in this way they introduce greater concrete complexity than earlier concepts of "class location". In other respects, however, both of these proposals still adopt a quite restricted view of what it means to occupy a class "location". In particular, they both define locations statically and they restrict the concept of class location to jobs. A fully elaborated micro-concept of how individual lives are tied to class structures needs to break with these restrictions by developing the idea of *mediated* class locations and *temporal* class locations.

The concept of mediated class location recognizes that people are linked to the class structure through social relations other than their immediate "jobs". People live in families, and via their social relations to spouses, parents and other family members, they may be linked to different class interests and capacities. This problem is particularly salient in households within which both husbands and wives are in the labour force but may occupy different job-classes. A schoolteacher married to a business executive has a different "mediated" class location than a schoolteacher married to a factory worker. For certain categories of people – housewives and children, for example – mediated class locations may be the decisive way in which their lives are linked to class. For others, mediated class locations may be less salient. In any case, the patterning of mediated class locations is potentially an important way in which class structures vary.

Temporal class locations refer to the fact that many jobs are embedded in career trajectories which in various ways involve changes in class character. Many managers, for example, begin as nonmanagerial employees, but the fact that they are on a managerial career track changes the class interests tied to their statically defined location. Moreover, many middle-class employees have a sufficiently high rent component in their wage (i.e. earnings above what is needed to reproduce their labour-power) that they can turn a significant amount of savings into capital through various kinds of investment. Such a capitalization of employment rents is itself a special kind of temporal dimension to class locations for it enables highly paid middle-class employees over time to directly tie their class interests to the bourgeoisie. This does not mean that they become capitalists, but rather that their class location assumes an increasingly capitalist character over time.

All of these complexities are attempts at defining systematically the linkages between individual lives and the class structure in ways that enrich the general model. . . . In that model class structures are seen as imposing limits on the process of class formation. There are two basic mechanisms through which this limitation occurs: first, class structures shape the material interests of individuals and thus make it more or less difficult to organize certain arrays of class locations into collective organizations; and second, class structures shape the access to material resources and thus affect the kinds of resources that can be deployed by collective organizations within class struggles. Both of the proposed concepts of the middle class as well as the concepts of mediated class locations and temporal class locations attempt to provide a more fine-grained map of the nature of the material interests and resources available to individuals by virtue of their linkage to the class structure and thereby to facilitate the analysis of the process of class formation.

The underclass

A second problem in the analysis of class structures that has become especially important in recent years is the issue of the "underclass". This concept was popularized in William Julius Wilson's work on the interconnection between race and class in American society. Wilson argues that as legal barriers to racial equality have disappeared and class differentiation within the black population has increased, the central determining structure of the lives of many African-Americans is no longer race as such, but class. More specifically, he argues that there has been a substantial growth of what can be called an urban "underclass" of people without marketable skills and with very weak attachments to the labour force, living in crumbling central cities isolated from the mainstream of American life and institutions.

How can this concept be given some precision within the framework of a reconstructed Marxist class analysis? One strategy for doing this is to introduce a distinction between what might be termed *nonexploitative economic oppression* and *exploitative economic oppression* (or simply "exploitation" for short). To get at this distinction, we first need to define the general concept of economic oppression. As a first approximation, economic oppression can be defined as a situation in which (a) the material welfare of one group of people is causally related to the material deprivations of another, and (b) the causal relation involves morally indictable coercion. . . . "Economic oppression" is thus a situation in which the material benefits of one group are acquired at the expense of another and in which unjust coercion is an essential part of the process by which this occurs. . . .

Economic oppression defined in this way can take many forms. Of particular salience to class analysis is the distinction between exploitative and nonexploitative economic oppression. Economic exploitation is a specific form of economic oppression defined by a particular kind of mechanism through which the welfare of exploiters is causally related to the deprivations of the exploited. In exploitation, *the material well-being of the exploiter causally depend upon their ability to appropriate the fruits of labour of the exploited.* The welfare of the exploiter therefore depends upon the *effort* of the exploited, not merely the deprivations of the exploited. In nonexploitative economic oppression there is no transfer of the fruits of labour from the oppressed to the oppressor; the welfare of the oppressor depends on the exclusion of the oppressed from access to certain resources, but not on their effort. In both instances, the inequalities in question are rooted in ownership and control over productive resources.

The crucial difference between exploitation and nonexploitative oppression is that in an exploitative relation, the exploiters *need* the exploited, the exploiters depend upon the effort of the exploited. In the case of nonexploitative oppression, the oppressors would be happy if the oppressed simply disappeared. . . . Genocide is thus always a potential option for nonexploitative oppression. It is not an option in a situation of exploitation because exploiters require the labour of the exploited for their material well-being. The contrast between South Africa and North America in their treatment of indigenous peoples reflects this difference poignantly: in North America, where the indigenous people were oppressed (by virtue of being coercively displaced from the land) but not exploited, genocide was the basic policy of social control in the face of resistance; in South Africa, where the European settler population heavily depended upon African labour for its own prosperity, this was not an option.

This dependency of the exploiter on the exploited gives the exploited a certain form of power, since human beings always retain at least some minimal control over their own expenditure of effort. Purely repressive control is costly and often fails to generate the required levels of diligence and effort on the part of the exploited except under very special circumstances.

As a result, there is generally systematic pressure on exploiters to elicit in one way or another some degree of consent from the exploited, at least in the sense of gaining some level of minimal cooperation from them. Ironically perhaps, exploitation is thus a constraining force on the practices of the exploiter.

In these terms, an "underclass" can be defined as a category of social agents who are economically oppressed but not stably exploited within capitalist production. People in the contemporary American underclass are oppressed because they are denied access to various kinds of productive resources, including the necessary means to acquire skills and good jobs. But they are not consistently exploited. They are thus largely expendable from the point of view of capitalist rationality, and as a result repression is the central mode of social control directed towards them. Their potential power against their oppressors – their capacity to force concessions of various sorts – comes from their capacity to disrupt consumption, especially through crime and other forms of violence, not their capacity to disrupt production through their control over labour.

Class alliances and multiclass movements

One of the main objectives in elaborating these refinements in the concept of class structure is to facilitate the analysis of class formations and class politics. One crucial dimension of class formation is the problem of class alliances. Class alliances are situations in which people from different class locations come together to engage in collective action against a common class enemy by reaching, in one way or another, some kind of compromise on the differences in their class interests. A class alliance is thus to be contrasted with what can be termed a "multiclass movement" in which the actors agree to ignore class differences in order to form a solidaristic movement for some political objective. National liberation movements, for example, frequently place class differences among their supporters on a back burner in the name of "national unity". No real attempt is made to forge a class compromise between bourgeois, middle-class, working-class and peasant participants in the struggle. They are united in their opposition to a colonial power, but their unity is not grounded in any significant attempts at reconciling their conflicting class interests.

This contrast between multiclass movements and class alliances is, of course, somewhat stylized. Many situations involve variable mixes between these two ideal types. Nevertheless, the analytical distinction is important politically and theoretically. In many situations, multiclass movements are easier to form than class alliances, but equally, they frequently founder by virtue of the unresolved class tensions within them. Class alliances, on the other hand, may be harder to forge, but once forged may be more durable since conflicts of interest have been compromised rather than ignored.

The various complexities in the analysis of class structure we have been discussing can help to illuminate specific problems in the formation of class alliances. Consider the problem of alliances involving the middle class with either the capitalist class or the working class. People in the middle class and the working class are both exploited by capitalists; they are both employees dependent upon the labour market for their livelihoods. They thus share some common class interests vis-à-vis capital which constitute a basis for a class alliance. On the other hand, as skill and organization exploiters, the wages of middle-class employees contain a rent component of surplus which they are interested in protecting. Particularly when this component is large, people in the middle class have the capacity to capitalize their surplus and thus link their class interests directly to those of capitalists. These conflicting forces mean that within class struggles the middle class will be pulled between class formations involving alliances with workers or with capitalists. There are historical moments when the middle class seems to ally strongly with the bourgeoisie, as in Chile with the overthrow of the Allende regime, and other circumstances in which segments of the middle class forge fairly durable alliances with workers, as in Sweden in the heyday of Social-Democratic rule. An important task of class analysis is to sort out the conditions under which one or the other of these patterns of alliance occurs.

The underclass poses quite different problems for the analysis of class alliances. It might seem natural that the underclass and the working class would tend to form class alliances, but there are many obstacles to this occurring. In its effort to protect the jobs of workers and increase their wages, the labour movement often creates barriers within labour markets which act to the disadvantage of people in the underclass. In many historical cases, the underclass has been a source of scab labour in strikes and in other ways been manipulated by capitalists against workers. Thus, while both workers and the underclass share an interest in the state providing job training, regulating capital and increasing employment opportunities, in many contexts they see each other on opposing sides. Again, one of the tasks of class analysis is to understand the conditions which make solidaristic movements combining the working class and the underclass feasible. . . .

chapter 53

From Redistribution to Recognition?

Nancy Fraser

The "struggle for recognition" is fast becoming the paradigmatic form of political conflict in the late twentieth century. Demands for "recognition of difference" fuel struggles of groups mobilized under the banners of nationality, ethnicity, "race," gender, and sexuality. In these "postsocialist" conflicts, group identity supplants class interest as the chief medium of political mobilization. Cultural domination supplants exploitation as the fundamental injustice. And cultural recognition displaces socioeconomic redistribution as the remedy for injustice and the goal of political struggle.

This is not, of course, the whole story. Struggles for recognition occur in a world of exacerbated material inequality – in income and property ownership; in access to paid work, education, health care, and leisure time; but also, more starkly, in caloric intake and exposure to environmental toxicity, and hence in life expectancy and rates of morbidity and mortality. Material inequality is on the rise in most of the world's countries – in the United States and in China, in Sweden and in India, in Russia and in Brazil. It is also increasing globally, most dramatically across the line that divides North from South.

How, then, should we view the eclipse of a socialist imaginary centered on terms such as "interest," "exploitation," and "redistribution"? And what should we make of the rise of a new political imaginary centered on notions of "identity," "difference," "cultural domination," and "recognition"? Does this shift represent a lapse into "false consciousness"? Or does it, rather, redress the culture-blindness of a materialist paradigm rightfully discredited by the collapse of Soviet communism?

Neither of those two stances is adequate, in my view. Both are too whole-sale and unnuanced. Instead of simply endorsing or rejecting all of identity politics *simpliciter*, we should see ourselves as presented with a new intellectual and practical task: that of developing a *critical* theory of

recognition, one that identifies and defends only those versions of the
cultural politics of difference that can be coherently combined with the
social politics of equality. . . .

In formulating this project, I assume that justice today requires *both* redistribution *and* recognition. . . .

. . . I propose to distinguish two broadly conceived, analytically distinct
understandings of injustice. The first is socioeconomic injustice, which is
rooted in the political-economic structure of society. Examples include
exploitation (having the fruits of one's labor appropriated for the benefit
of others); economic marginalization (being confined to undesirable or
poorly paid work or being denied access to income-generating labor altogether), and deprivation (being denied an adequate material standard of
living). . . .

The second understanding of injustice is cultural or symbolic. Here
injustice is rooted in social patterns of representation, interpretation, and
communication. Examples include cultural domination (being subjected to
patterns of interpretation and communication that are associated with
another culture and are alien and/or hostile to one's own); nonrecogni-
tion (being rendered invisible by means of the authoritative representa-
tional, communicative, and interpretative practices of one's culture); and
disrespect (being routinely maligned or disparaged in stereotypic public
cultural representations and/or in everyday life interactions). . . .

Despite the differences between them, both socioeconomic injustice and
cultural injustice are pervasive in contemporary societies. Both are rooted
in processes and practices that systematically disadvantage some groups
of people vis-à-vis others. Both, consequently, should be remedied.

Of course, this distinction between economic injustice and cultural
injustice is analytical. In practice, the two are intertwined. Even the
most material economic institutions have a constitutive, irreducible cultural dimension; they are shot through with significations and norms.
Conversely, even the most discursive cultural practices have a constitutive, irreducible political-economic dimension; they are underpinned by
material supports. . . .

. . . The remedy for economic injustice is political-economic restructuring of some sort. This might involve redistributing income, reorganizing
the division of labor, subjecting investment to democratic decision making,
or transforming other basic economic structures. Although these various
remedies differ importantly from one another, I shall henceforth refer to
the whole group of them by the generic term "redistribution." The remedy
for cultural injustice, in contrast, is some sort of cultural or symbolic change.
This could involve upwardly revaluing disrespected identities and the
cultural products of maligned groups. It could also involve recognizing
and positively valorizing cultural diversity. More radically still, it could
involve the wholesale transformation of societal patterns of representation,

interpretation, and communication in ways that would change *everybody's* sense of self. Although these remedies differ importantly from one another, I shall henceforth refer to the whole group of them by the generic term "recognition." . . .

. . . [T]he politics of recognition and the politics of redistribution often appear to have mutually contradictory aims. Whereas the first tends to promote group differentiation, the second tends to undermine it. Thus, the two kinds of claim stand in tension with each other; they can interfere with, or even work against, each other. . . .

Imagine a conceptual spectrum of different kinds of social collectivities. At one extreme are modes of collectivity that fit the redistribution model of justice. At the other extreme are modes of collectivity that fit the recognition model. In between are cases that prove difficult because they fit both models of justice simultaneously.

Consider, first, the redistribution end of the spectrum. At this end let us posit an ideal-typical mode of collectivity whose existence is rooted wholly in the political economy. It will be differentiated as a collectivity, in other words, by virtue of the economic structure, as opposed to the cultural order, of society. Thus, any structural injustices its members suffer will be traceable ultimately to the political economy. The root of the injustice, as well as its core, will be socioeconomic maldistribution, and any attendant cultural injustices will derive ultimately from that economic root. At bottom, therefore, the remedy required to redress the injustice will be political-economic redistribution, as opposed to cultural recognition.

In the real world, to be sure, political economy and culture are mutually intertwined, as are injustices of distribution and recognition. Thus, we may question whether there exist any pure collectivities of this sort. For heuristic purposes, however, it is useful to examine their properties. To do so, let us consider a familiar example that can be interpreted as approximating the ideal type: the Marxian conception of the exploited class, understood in an orthodox way. . . .

In the conception assumed here, class is a mode of social differentiation that is rooted in the political-economic structure of society. A class exists as a collectivity only by virtue of its position in that structure and of its relation to other classes. Thus, the Marxian working class is the body of persons in a capitalist society who must sell their labor power under arrangements that authorize the capitalist class to appropriate surplus productivity for its private benefit. The injustice of these arrangements, moreover, is quintessentially a matter of distribution. In the capitalist scheme of social reproduction, the proletariat receives an unjustly large share of the burdens and an unjustly small share of the rewards. To be sure, its members also suffer serious cultural injustices, the "hidden (and not so hidden) injuries of class." But far from being rooted directly in an autonomously unjust cultural structure, these derive from the political economy, as ideologies of class inferiority proliferate to justify exploitation. The remedy for the injustice, consequently, is redistribution, not recognition. Overcoming class exploitation requires restructuring the political economy so as to alter the class distribution of social burdens and social benefits. In the Marxian conception, such restructuring takes the radical form of abolishing the class structure as such. The task of the proletariat, therefore, is not simply to cut itself a better deal but "to abolish itself as a class." The last thing it needs is recognition of its difference. On the contrary, the only way to remedy the injustice is to put the proletariat out of business as a group.

Now consider the other end of the conceptual spectrum. At this end we may posit an ideal-typical mode of collectivity that fits the recognition model of justice. A collectivity of this type is rooted wholly in culture, as opposed to in political economy. It is differentiated as a collectivity by virtue of the reigning social patterns of interpretation and evaluation, not by virtue of the division of labor. Thus, any structural injustices its members suffer will be traceable ultimately to the cultural-valuational structure. The root of the injustice, as well as its core, will be cultural misrecognition, while any attendant economic injustices will derive ultimately from that cultural root. At bottom, therefore, the remedy required to redress the injustice will be cultural recognition, as opposed to political-economic redistribution.

Once again, we may question whether there exist any pure collectivities of this sort, but it is useful to examine their properties for heuristic purposes. An example that can be interpreted as approximating the ideal type is the conception of a despised sexuality, understood in a specific way. Let us consider this conception, while leaving aside the question of whether this view of sexuality fits the actual historical homosexual collectivities that are struggling for justice in the real world.

Sexuality in this conception is a mode of social differentiation whose roots do not lie in the political economy because homosexuals are distributed throughout the entire class structure of capitalist society, occupy no distinctive position in the division of labor, and do not constitute an exploited class. Rather, their mode of collectivity is that of a despised sexuality, rooted in the cultural-valuational structure of society. From this perspective, the injustice they suffer is quintessentially a matter of recognition. Gays and lesbians suffer from heterosexism: the authoritative construction of norms that privilege heterosexuality. Along with this goes homophobia: the cultural devaluation of homosexuality. Their sexuality thus disparaged, homosexuals are subject to shaming, harassment, discrimination, and violence, while being denied legal rights and equal protections – all fundamentally denials of recognition. To be sure, gays and lesbians also suffer serious economic injustices; they can be summarily dismissed from paid work and are denied family-based social-welfare benefits. But far from being rooted directly in the economic structure, these derive instead from an unjust cultural-valuational structure. The remedy for the injustice, consequently, is recognition, not redistribution. Overcoming homophobia and heterosexism requires changing the cultural valuations (as well as their legal and practical expressions) that privilege heterosexuality, deny equal respect to gays and lesbians, and refuse to recognize homosexuality as a legitimate way of being sexual. It is to revalue a despised sexuality, to accord positive recognition to gay and lesbian sexual specificity.

Matters are thus fairly straightforward at the two extremes of our conceptual spectrum. When we deal with collectivities that approach the ideal type of the exploited working class, we face distributive injustices requiring redistributive remedies. When we deal with collectivities that approach the ideal type of the despised sexuality, in contrast, we face injustices of misrecognition requiring remedies of recognition. In the first case, the logic of the remedy is to put the group out of business as a group. In the second case, on the contrary, it is to valorize the group's "groupness" by recognizing its specificity.

Matters become murkier, however, once we move away from these extremes. When we consider collectivities located in the middle of the conceptual spectrum, we encounter hybrid modes that combine features of the exploited class with features of the despised sexuality. These collectivities are "bivalent." They are differentiated as collectivities by virtue of *both* the political-economic structure *and* the cultural-valuational structure of society. . . .

Both gender and "race" are paradigmatic bivalent collectivities. Although each has peculiarities not shared by the other, both encompass political-economic dimensions and cultural-valuational dimensions. Gender and "race," therefore, implicate both redistribution and recognition.

Gender, for example, has political-economic dimensions because it is a basic structuring principle of the political economy. On the one hand, gender structures the fundamental division between paid "productive" labor and unpaid "reproductive" and domestic labor, assigning women primary responsibility for the latter. On the other hand, gender also structures the division within paid labor between higher-paid, male-dominated, manufacturing and professional occupations and lower-paid, female-dominated "pink-collar" and domestic service occupations. The result is a political-economic structure that generates gender-specific modes of exploitation, marginalization, and deprivation. This structure constitutes gender as a political-economic differentiation endowed with certain classlike characteristics. When viewed under this aspect, gender injustice appears as a species of distributive injustice that cries out for redistributive redress. Much like class, gender justice requires transforming the political economy so as to eliminate its gender structuring. Eliminating gender-specific exploitation, marginalization, and deprivation requires abolishing the gender division of labor – both the gendered division between paid and unpaid labor and the gender division within paid labor. The logic of the remedy is akin to the logic with respect to class: it is to put gender out of business as such. If gender were nothing but a political-economic differentiation, in sum, justice would require its abolition.

That, however, is only half the story. In fact, gender is not only a political-economic differentiation but a cultural-valuational differentiation as well. As such, it also encompasses elements that are more like sexuality than class and that bring it squarely within the problematic of recognition. Certainly, a major feature of gender injustice is androcentrism: the authoritative construction of norms that privilege traits associated with masculinity. Along with this goes cultural sexism: the pervasive devaluation and disparagement of things coded as "feminine," paradigmatically – but not only – women. This devaluation is expressed in a range of harms suffered by women, including sexual assault, sexual exploitation, and pervasive domestic violence; trivializing, objectifying, and demeaning stereotypical depictions in the media; harassment and disparagement in all spheres of everyday life; subjection to androcentric norms in relation to which women appear lesser or deviant and that work to disadvantage them, even in the absence of any intention to discriminate; attitudinal discrimination; exclusion or marginalization in public spheres and deliberative bodies; and denial of full legal rights and equal protections. These harms are injustices of recognition. They are relatively independent of political economy and are not merely "superstructural." Thus, they cannot be remedied by political-economic redistribution alone but require additional independent remedies of recognition. Overcoming androcentrism and sexism requires changing the cultural valuations (as well as their legal and practical expressions) that privilege masculinity and deny equal respect to women. . . .

Gender, in sum, is a bivalent mode of collectivity. It contains a political-economic face that brings it within the ambit of redistribution. Yet it also contains a cultural-valuational face that brings it simultaneously within the ambit of recognition. Of course, the two faces are not neatly separated from each other. Rather, they intertwine to reinforce each other dialectically because sexist and androcentric cultural norms are institutionalized in the state and the economy, and women's economic disadvantage restricts women's "voice," impeding equal participation in the making of culture, in public spheres and in everyday life. The result is a vicious circle of cultural and economic subordination. Redressing gender injustice, therefore, requires changing both political economy and culture. . . .

. . . "Race," like gender, is a bivalent mode of collectivity. On the one hand, it resembles class in being a structural principle of political economy. In this aspect, "race" structures the capitalist division of labor. It structures the division within paid work between low-paid, low-status, menial, dirty, and domestic occupations held disproportionately by people of color, and higher-paid, higher-status, white-collar, professional, technical, and managerial occupations held disproportionately by "whites." Today's racial division of paid labor is part of the historic legacy of colonialism and slavery, which elaborated racial categorization to justify brutal new forms of appropriation and exploitation, effectively constituting "blacks" as a political-economic caste. Currently, moreover, "race" also structures access to official labor markets, constituting large segments of the population of color as a "superfluous," degraded subproletariat or underclass, unworthy even of exploitation and excluded from the productive system altogether. The result is a political-economic structure that generates "race"-specific modes of exploitation, marginalization, and deprivation. This structure constitutes "race" as a political-economic differentiation endowed with certain classlike characteristics. When viewed under this aspect, racial injustice appears as a species of distributive injustice that cries out for redistributive redress. Much like class, racial justice requires transforming the political economy so as to eliminate its racialization. Eliminating "race"-specific exploitation, marginalization, and deprivation requires abolishing the racial division of labor – both the racial division between exploitable and superfluous labor and the racial division within paid labor. The logic of the remedy is like the logic with respect to class: it is to put "race" out of business as such. If "race" were nothing but a political-economic differentiation, in sum, justice would require its abolition.

Yet "race," like gender, is not only political-economic. It also has cultural-valuational dimensions, which bring it into the universe of recognition. Thus, "race" too encompasses elements that are more like sexuality than class. A major aspect of racism is Eurocentrism: the authoritative construction of norms that privilege traits associated with "whiteness." Along with this goes cultural racism: the pervasive devaluation and disparagement of things coded as "black," "brown," and "yellow," paradigmatically – but not only – people of color. This depreciation is expressed in a range of harms suffered by people of color, including demeaning stereotypical depictions in the media. . . . [V]iolence, harassment, and "dissing" in all spheres of everyday life; subjection to Eurocentric norms in relation to which people of color appear lesser or deviant and that work to disadvantage them, even in the absence of any intention to discriminate; attitudinal discrimination; exclusion from and/or marginalization in public spheres and deliberative bodies; and denial of full legal rights and equal protections. As in the case of gender, these harms are injustices of recognition. Thus, the logic of their remedy, too, is to accord positive recognition to devalued group specificity.

"Race," too, therefore, is a bivalent mode of collectivity with both a political-economic face and a cultural-valuational face. Its two faces intertwine to reinforce each other dialectically, moreover, because racist and Eurocentric cultural norms are institutionalized in the state and the economy, and the economic disadvantage suffered by people of color restricts their "voice." Redressing racial injustice, therefore, requires changing both political economy and culture. . . .

Bibliography

Unless otherwise indicated, references to works by Marx and/or Engels are to *Karl Marx, Frederick Engels, Collected Works*, 48 vols., published by Lawrence and Wishart, London, from 1975 on.

WRITINGS OF KARL MARX

1837: Letter from Marx to his Father: in Trier. In *Collected Works*, vol. 1, pp. 10–21.

1842: Proceedings of the Sixth Rhine Province Assembly. In *Collected Works*, vol. 1, pp. 224–63.

1843a: *Contribution to the Critique of Hegel's Philosophy of Law*. In *Collected Works*, vol. 3, pp. 3–129.

1843b: Justification of the Correspondent from Mosel. In *Collected Works*, vol. 1, pp. 332–58.

1843c: Letters from the *Deutsche-Französische Jahrbücher*. In *Collected Works*, vol. 3, pp. 133–45.

1843d: *On the Jewish Question*. In *Collected Works*, vol. 3, pp. 146–74.

1844: *Economic and Philosophical Manuscripts of 1844*. In *Collected Works*, vol. 3, pp. 229–346.

1845: Theses on Feuerbach. In *Collected Works*, vol. 5, pp. 3–5.

1847: *The Poverty of Philosophy*. In *Collected Works*, vol. 6, pp. 105–212.

1850: *The Class Struggles in France: 1848–1850*. In *Collected Works*, vol. 10, pp. 43–145.

1852a: *The Eighteenth Brumaire of Louis Bonaparte*. In *Collected Works*, vol. 11, pp. 99–197.

1852b: Political Consequences of the Commercial Excitement. In *Collected Works*, vol. 11, pp. 364–8.

1852c: Political Parties and Prospects. In *Collected Works*, vol. 11, pp. 369–72.

1857–8a: *Outlines of the Critique of Political Economy [First Installment]*. In *Collected Works*, vol. 28, pp. 3–561.

1857–8b: *Outlines of the Critique of Political Economy [Second Installment]*. In *Collected Works*, vol. 29, pp. 3–255.

1859a: *A Contribution to the Critique of Political Economy*. In *Collected Works*, vol. 29, pp. 257–417.

1859b: *The Original Text of the Second and the Beginning of the Third Chapter of A Contribution to the Critique of Political Economy*. In *Collected Works*, vol. 29, pp. 430–507.

1865: *Value, Price, and Profit*. In *Collected Works*, vol. 20, pp. 101–49.
1867a: *Capital: A Critique of Political Economy*. Volume I: *The Process of Capitalist Production*, ed. Frederick Engels. In *Collected Works*, vol. 35, pp. 43–807.
1867b: Preface to the First German Edition [*Capital V. 1*]. In *Collected Works*, vol. 35, pp. 7–11.
1868: Letter from Marx to Engels: in Manchester. In *Collected Works*, vol. 43, pp. 20–5.
1871: *The Civil War in France: Address of the General Council of the International Working Men's Association*. In *Collected Works*, vol. 22, pp. 311–59.
1873: Afterword to the Second German Edition [*Capital V. 1*]. In *Collected Works*, vol. 35, pp. 12–20.
1875: *Critique of the Gotha Programme*. In *Collected Works*, vol. 24, pp. 75–99.
1881: Letter to Vera Zasulich. In *Collected Works*, vol. 24, pp. 370–1.
1885: *Capital: A Critique of Political Economy*. Volume II: *The Process of Circulation of Capital*, ed. Frederick Engels. In *Collected Works*, vol. 36, pp. 26–534.
1894: *Capital: A Critique of Political Economy*. Volume III: *The Process of Capitalist Production as a Whole*, ed. Frederick Engels. In *Collected Works*, vol. 37, pp. 25–912.
1905–10: *Theories of Surplus Value*, ed. Karl Kautsky. 3 vols. Repr. Moscow: Progress Publishers, 1963–71.

WRITINGS OF KARL MARX AND FREDERICK ENGELS

1845–6: *The German Ideology*. In *Collected Works*, vol. 5, pp. 19–608.
1848: *Manifesto of the Communist Party*. In *Collected Works*, vol. 6, pp. 477–519.
1850a: Address of the Central Authority to the League: March 1850. In *Collected Works*, vol. 10, pp. 277–87.
1850b: Address of the Central Authority to the League: June 1850. In *Collected Works*, vol. 10, pp. 371–7.
1872: Preface to the 1872 German Edition of the *Manifesto of the Communist Party*. In *Collected Works*, vol. 23, pp. 174–5.
1971: *Karl Marx and Friedrich Engels: Writings on the Paris Commune*, ed. Hal Draper. New York and London: Monthly Review Press.

WRITINGS OF FREDERICK ENGELS

1842: The Insolently Threatened yet Miraculously Rescued Bible or: The Triumph of Faith. In *Collected Works*, vol. 2, pp. 313–51.
1845: *The Condition of the Working Class in England*. In *Collected Works*, vol. 4, pp. 294–583.
1851–2: *Revolution and Counter-revolution in Germany*. In *Collected Works*, vol. 11, pp. 3–96.
1883: Karl Marx's Funeral. In *Collected Works*, vol. 24, pp. 467–71.
1885: Preface. In *Capital: A Critique of Political Economy*. Volume II: *The Process of Circulation of Capital*. In *Collected Works*, vol. 36, pp. 5–22.
1890a: Engels to Conrad Schmidt. Repr. in Karl Marx and Frederick Engels, *Basic Writings on Politics and Philosophy*, ed. Lewis S. Feuer, Garden City, NY: Anchor Books, 1959, pp. 395–7.
1890b: Engels to Joseph Bloch. Repr. in Karl Marx and Frederick Engels, *Basic Writings on Politics and Philosophy*, ed. Lewis S. Feuer, Garden City, NY: Anchor Books, 1959, pp. 397–400.

1892: *Socialism: Scientific and Utopian*. In *Collected Works*, vol. 24, pp. 281–325.

1894: The Effect of Turnover on the Rate of Profit. In *Capital: A Critique of Political Economy. Volume III: The Process of Capitalist Production as a Whole*, ed. Frederick Engels. In *Collected Works*, vol. 37, pp. 73–80.

WRITINGS OF OTHER AUTHORS

Antonio, Robert J. 2000: After Postmodernism: Reactionary Tribalism. *American Journal of Sociology*, 106, 40–87.

Antonio, Robert J. and Kellner, Douglas 1992a: Communication, Modernity, and Democracy in Habermas and Dewey. *Symbolic Interaction*, 15, 277–97.

Antonio, Robert J. and Kellner, Douglas 1992b: Metatheorizing Historical Rupture: Classical Theory and Modernity. In George Ritzer (ed.), *Metatheorizing*, Newbury Park, CA: Sage, pp. 88–106.

Aronson, Ronald 1995: *After Marxism*. New York and London: Guilford Press.

Berle, Adolf A. and Means, Gardiner C. 1932: *The Modern Corporation and Private Property*. Repr. New York: Harcourt, Brace & World, 1967.

Braverman, Harry 1974: *Labor and Monopoly Capital: The Degradation of Work in the Twentieth Century*. New York and London: Monthly Review Press.

Chandler, Alfred 1977: *The Visible Hand: The Managerial Revolution in American Business*. Cambridge, MA, and London: Harvard University Press.

Draper, Hal 1987: *The Dictatorship of the Proletariat: From Marx to Lenin*. New York and London: Monthly Review Press.

Friedman, Thomas L. 2000: *The Lexus and the Olive Tree*. New York: Anchor Books.

Fukuyama, Francis 1989: The End of History. *National Interest*, 16, 3–18.

Fukuyama, Francis 1992: *The End of History and the Last Man*. London and New York: Penguin Books.

Hegel, G. W. F. 1807: *The Phenomenology of Mind*. Repr. New York: Harper & Row, 1967.

McLellan, David 1973: *Karl Marx: His Life and Thought*. New York: Harper & Row.

Przeworski, Adam 1985: *Capitalism and Social Democracy*. Cambridge and New York: Cambridge University Press.

Seigel, Jerrold 1993: *Marx's Fate: The Shape of a Life*. University Park, PA: Pennsylvania State University Press.

Smith, Adam 1776: *An Inquiry into the Nature and Causes of the Wealth of Nations*. Repr. New York: Modern Library, 1937.

Weber, Max 1904–5: *The Protestant Ethic and the Spirit of Capitalism*. Repr. New York: Charles Scribner's Sons, 1958.

Index

accumulation, 269; of capital, 157–60; primitive, 79–81, 93; and surplus labor, 163–5
AFL-CIO, 363–4
Aghion, P., 269
agriculture, 155, 172–3
Alliance for Sustainable Jobs and the Environment, 354, 357
American Civil War, impact on British industry, 176
anarchists, 354

Bagdikian, B., 281
Baran, P., 177, 178
Bauer, Bruno, 4
Bell, D., 277
Berle, A. A., 38–9, 197
Berlin Doctors Club, 4
Blank, R., 301
bourgeoisie, 12–13, 27, 214, 270; as agents of modernization, 76–7; creation of, 86–7; destructive nature of, 76, 219–20; and development of powerful productive forces, 75; exploitation by, 90–1; failure of German, 13; power of, 92; recruited into proletariat, 222; revolt and counter-revolt, 229; and revolutionizing of production, 91–2; rise of, 76; wresting control from, 214
Braverman, H., 133
British East India Company, 176, 177; board of directors, 187; debts, 186; recipients of patronage, 187–8; stockholders of, 186–7
"British Incomes in India," 176
bureaucracy, 12, 215, 231

capital, accumulation of, 157–60; and application of science, 209; changes in, 88; concentration/centralization of, 87, 94, 154, 158–9; dominion of, 140–2; estate, 85; as exploitative, 201; general formula for, 127–9; global, 317; hypermobility of, 316; labor resistance to, 97–8; material composition of, 157; movement of, 88; naturally evolved, 83–4; organic composition of, 153; relationship to savings, 205; social, 204; and transformation of ownership, 204–5; transnational, 342; value composition of, 157
Capital (1867, 1883, 1894), 9, 11, 14, 27, 37, 39, 41, 54–5, 75–6, 77–8, 101–4, 195, 265
capitalism, and abolition of private industry, 205; ambivalence toward, 155; consumer, 216; corporate, 197; critique of, 10–15; crony, 348–9; cultural, 278–81; dangers of, 12; and decoupling of use values from living labor, 197; democratic, 336; and displacement of feudal system, 80–1; emergent, knowledge-based, 198; as exploitative, 71, 155; and fall in profit, 154; irrational, 196; Keynesian/Social Democratic, 177; knowledge-based, 274–5; labor time as superfluous, 198; labor, value and extraction, 26–32; managerial, 197; modernizing themes, 9–10; and money, 266; monopoly tendency, 268; mystified understanding of, 27; neoliberal, 47–9; opposition to, 5–6; origins of, 76; overcoming

398 *Index*